The Gospel in the Law

You are holding a reproduction of an original work that is in the public domain in the United States of America, and possibly other countries.You may freely copy and distribute this work as no entity (individual or corporate) has a copyright on the body of the work.This book may contain prior copyright references, and library stamps (as most of these works were scanned from library copies).These have been scanned and retained as part of the historical artifact.

This book may have occasional imperfections such as missing or blurred pages, poor pictures, errant marks, etc. that were either part of the original artifact, or were introduced by the scanning process. We believe this work is culturally important, and despite the imperfections, have elected to bring it back into print as part of our continuing commitment to the preservation of printed works worldwide. We appreciate your understanding of the imperfections in the preservation process, and hope you enjoy this valuable book.

THE

GOSPEL IN THE LAW.

THE
GOSPEL IN THE LAW.

THE

GOSPEL IN THE LAW;

A CRITICAL EXAMINATION OF THE CITATIONS
FROM THE OLD TESTAMENT IN THE NEW.

BY

CHARLES TAYLOR, M.A.,

FELLOW OF ST JOHN'S COLLEGE,
AND CURATE OF ST ANDREW'S THE GREAT, CAMBRIDGE.

CAMBRIDGE:
DEIGHTON, BELL, AND CO.,
LONDON: BELL AND DALDY.

1869.

PREFACE.

This work purports not to exhaust the deep subject of Citation from the Old Testament in the New, but to deal, in a manner more or less intelligible to the general reader, with select citations of pronounced critical and theological interest.

I am sensible that not a few of the questions herein discussed are, and must remain, inconclusively dealt with, owing to their intrinsic difficulty: some of the earlier chapters in particular leave ample room for renewed investigation: while, of points discussed later, the Symbolism of Sacrifice has been dismissed with less of elaboration than I could have desired.

Of works on the Citations Mr Grinfield gives a list in his *Apology for the Septuagint*, pp. 142 sqq. Certain of the treatises there mentioned, and, in addition, those of Surenhusius, Gough, and Turpie have been consulted. I have made much use of Hengstenberg's *Christo-*

logy: more of Kidder's *Demonstration of the Messias*. I am further indebted to the labours of Poole (ed. 1669-76), Rosenmüller, Gesenius, Bengel, Alford, and Wordsworth: not to mention the *Concordances* of Tromm, Fürst, and Bruder; the *Grammar* of Winer; with various special commentaries and other works of less generality referred to in due place.

Lastly, my best thanks are due to my friends who have revised the proof sheets; and to the Reverend the Master of Jesus College for several valuable suggestions received from him while those sheets were passing through the press.

ST JOHN'S COLLEGE,
May 12, 1869.

CONTENTS.

CHAP.		PAGE
	INTRODUCTION	ix
I.	I WILL HAVE MERCY AND NOT SACRIFICE	1
II.	DAVID HIMSELF CALLETH HIM LORD	16
III.	THE PROPHECY OF IMMANUEL	28
IV.	LOCAL COINCIDENCES	49
V.	THE SUFFERING MESSIAH	74
VI.	THE SURE MERCIES OF DAVID	128
VII.	HE GAVE GIFTS UNTO MEN	167
VIII.	A BODY HAST THOU PREPARED ME	176
IX.	THE ALLEGORY OF HAGAR	187
X.	THE APOLOGY OF ST STEPHEN	207
XI.	THE IMPRECATIONS OF PSALM LXIX.	224
XII.	THE IMPRECATIONS OF PSALM CIX.	244
XIII.	CHRISTIAN AND JEWISH ETHICS	260
XIV.	THE SYMBOLISM OF SACRIFICE	280
XV.	THE LXX. AS A MEDIUM OF CITATION	306
XVI.	MISCELLANEA	324
	APPENDIX	341
	INDICES	348

ERRATA.

Page 53, *line* 24, *for* Matt. iv. 18, *read* Matt. ii. 18.
„ 139, „ 12, „ *Michtab*, „ *Michtam*.
„ 186, Note C [iii.], *for* the κενοδοξία ἀνθρώπων, *read* idols.

TO THE REVEREND

PETER HAMNETT MASON

THIS THE KAYE PRIZE ESSAY FOR 1867 *IS DEDICATED.*

INTRODUCTION.

Πᾶς γραμματεὺς μαθητευθεὶς εἰς τὴν βασιλείαν τῶν οὐρανῶν ὅμοιός ἐστιν ἀνθρώπῳ οἰκοδεσπότῃ ὅστις ἐκβάλλει ἐκ τοῦ θησαυροῦ αὐτοῦ καινὰ καὶ παλαιά.

S. MATT. xiii. 52.

THE ministers of the New Covenant have approved themselves as good stewards of the great Householder by bringing forth out of His treasure things new and old. Sometimes the new supplements the old, and answers to the needs of a fuller growth. Sometimes the newest is identically the oldest, and supersedes that which by dint of use had come to be regarded as the old, while yet 'from the beginning it was not so.' And still, to the scribe instructed unto the kingdom of heaven, the old is ever new, and the new old; for the old lives in the new, as the new is rooted in the old; and old with new successively reveal one Truth, as the shifting seasons measure a world's cycle about its sun. The formal connection of new and old is not indeed peculiar to the Christian economy; for 'all nations who have ancient writings have endeavoured to read in them the riddle of the past.' But with the sacred writers this connection is not, as in the case of heathen authors, merely external; for 'the Old Testament looks forward to the New, as the New Testament looks backward to the Old;' and the New sees itself the more truly mirrored in the Old, as the Old, gazing ever fixedly on the New, is 'changed into the same image from glory to glory.'

Introduction.

I. *Preliminary Remarks.*

1. The relations of the new to the old are various; and the analysis of but few citations from the Old Testament in the New, clearly shews the great difficulty of harmonizing the citations and their originals in accordance with any of the preconceived theories which have been, from time to time, hazarded. What has been well said on another subject, Inspiration[1], has its application to this:—'In the outset let it be said that we heartily concur with the majority of our opponents in rejecting all theories of Inspiration, and in sweeping aside all those distinctions and definitions which, in only too many cases, have been merely called forth by emergencies, and drawn up for no other purpose than to meet real or supposed difficulties. The remark probably is just, that most of the current explanations err more especially in attempting to define what, though real, is incapable of being defined in an exact manner.' And again:—'It seems pretty generally agreed among thoughtful men at present, that definite Theories of Inspiration are doubtful and dangerous[2].' Definite theories of citation have proved scarcely less fruitful in controversies, and have tended to multiply the difficulties which they were devised to obviate. Nor, on the other hand, could any solid results be expected to accrue from *a priori* theories, which might not, at least as safely, be attained by a patient and unpretentious following of the inductive method. Let the passages cited be first scrutinized in the light of their original contexts, and without reference to the fact of their citation: let the true meaning of the citation be elicited, so far as may be, without reference to the original: and then, from a comparison or contrast of the separate results, as much, assuredly, may be gathered as from any theory on the mutual relations of the New and the Old: for so far as the

---

[1] *Aids to Faith*, Essay IX.   [2] *Ibid.*, Essay VII.

theory is sound, it must be borne out by the detailed investigation; and then, inasmuch as the same results might have been obtained independently, the antecedent theory is declared superfluous. But more often it is found partial, and applicable to few cases only; and thus, so far as it is acquiesced in, it bars the progress of enquiry, and forms a nucleus for accumulations which turn aside the natural current of healthful thought.

2. It is soon found upon examination that, as the formal correspondence of the citations with their originals varies from literal identity to ambiguous allusion, so their inner relation may be that of prophecy and fulfilment, of type and antitype; or it may consist in adaptations which are calculated to render the new more acceptable or more intelligible, as presented in the garb and semblance of the old. Between these extremes, all shades of variation in the mode and purport of citation are admissible. And herein lies the difficulty of the present investigation: this it is which renders a full discussion of all the citations which occur, or can be recognized, so lengthy and voluminous as to be well nigh impracticable. The plan then which will be adopted is to discuss more or less fully a select number of citations, each involving critical or theological questions of peculiar moment, and each suited to become a centre around which others of like nature, but involving less special difficulty, may be grouped. For the details of the plan, it is unnecessary to do more than refer the reader to the *Table of Contents*, and to the various *Indices;* and thus much being premised we proceed at once to the enquiry, commencing with a brief notice of the Formulæ of Citation.

II. *Formulæ of Citation.*

The formulæ of citation are of various degrees of definiteness, and their variety exhibits itself in a twofold way; for a reference to the Old Testament may or may not carry with it a seeming declaration of authorship; and, independently of this, there is the difficulty of determining whether the words cited are adduced by way of illustration, or as evidence of a predictive purpose. The former of these difficulties is noticed on pp. 132 sqq.: the latter calls for some remark, as having occasioned much controversy, and still remaining undetermined.

There is an appearance of definiteness in such formulæ as ἵνα πληρωθῇ, τότε ἐπληρώθη, and the like, which is not always easy to reconcile with the phenomena of individual citations; for the events to which Old Testament passages are applied in the New would seem ofttimes not to have been contemplated when the passages were written; and if so, the reference to such events would scarcely be direct and primary. Some accordingly have regarded the primary and historical allusion as typical of greater issues in the future, or have interpreted the disputed formulæ as implying that a prophecy, though fulfilled by contemporary events or in the immediate future, may yet have waited for its *completion* or perfect fulfilment till the Messianic time. Some again have allowed that the requirements of such formulæ as τότε ἐπληρώθη may be satisfied by accommodations of prophecy, while yet claiming for ἵνα πληρωθῇ a definite predictiveness. Others regard the ἵνα as frequently ecbatic or final, rather than causal; and Schleusner observes, 'tironum causa,' that the two classes of formulæ are alike ambiguous, and to be interpreted, in each case, by the context. Dean Alford so far agrees with this view as to hold, that 'we must not draw any fanciful distinction between τότε ἐπληρώθη and ἵνα πληρωθῇ, but rather seek our explanation in the acknowledged system of prophetical interpretation among the Jews, still extant in their Rabbinical books, and now sanctioned to us by New Testament usage; at the same time remembering, for our caution, how little even now we understand of the full bearing of prophetic and typical words and acts.' The particular passage[1], in connection with which these remarks occur, is said to be, 'apparently an accommodation of the prophecy in Jer. xxxi. 15, which was originally written of the Babylonish captivity... None of the expressions of this prophecy must be closely and literally pressed.' And yet with regard to the meaning of ἵνα no ambiguity is admitted. 'It is impossible to interpret ἵνα in any other sense than *in order that*... And of course these remarks apply to every passage where ἵνα or ὅπως πληρωθῇ are used. Such a construction can have but one meaning. If such meaning involve us in difficulty regarding the prophecy itself, far better leave such difficulty, in so doubtful a matter as the interpretation of prophecy, unsolved, than create one in so simple a matter as the rendering of a phrase whose meaning no indifferent person could doubt[2].'

The distinctions between the various New Testament formulæ are especially insisted upon by Surenhusius, who compares them with those employed by Rabbinic writers. 'But' writes Dr Owen[3] 'when we find the very same quotations, expressed in the same words, and brought to prove the very same points, are introduced by different *formulas* in the Gospels, we can pay but little regard to such an opinion. It seems to be the chief, if not the sole, intent of these *formulas*, to apprise the reader that the words annexed are either taken from, or have some reference to, the books of the Old Testament. And the variations observable in them may sometimes arise from the nature of the subjects, and sometimes from the cast or turn of the discourse; though more frequently, if I mistake not, to the Modes of speaking currently used at those times, and to the imitation of former writers. For the historical books of the Old Testament abound in forms similar to

---

[1] Matt. ii. 17.   [2] Alford, on Matt. i. 22.
[3] *Modes of Quotation*, Sect. II.

those which occur in the Gospels, and all subservient to the same ends.'

Without assuming beforehand that the above view is correct, we should at least contemplate the possibility of its being so. In other words, it is well to enter upon an analysis of the citations, not indeed with the assumption that the introductory expressions are indefinite, but with a disposition to allow that they may be, and to give due weight to any arguments from special contexts which may seem to bear upon the point. But it may be remarked in passing that, if formulæ like τότε ἐπληρώθη are to be tested by the Rabbinic standard, they do not of necessity imply predictive purpose, but might even be retrospective, as the subjoined remark of Rashi well illustrates. Referring to builders of the tower of Babel, and to their fear of being 'scattered abroad upon the face of the whole earth,' this commentator affirms, that *in them was fulfilled* what Solomon said (Prov. x. 24). 'The fear of the wicked, it shall come upon him[1].'

But the chief difficulty lies in such formulæ as ἵνα πληρωθῇ, which frequently introduces what may be styled provisionally a circumstantial agreement. It denotes sometimes the fulfilment of a definite prophecy in the same sense as that in which it was consciously uttered by the Prophet. Or it may introduce a result which would be recognized as the sole exhaustive fulfilment of a prophetic utterance, while the Prophet's mind may be conceived of as having contemplated what was in effect a partial accomplishment. But there are other cases in which some would see no more than an external coincidence, while yet the same formula of citation is used; and hence the question, How is this indiscriminate application of such formulæ to be accounted for?

There is indeed one principle on which ἵνα may have the

[1] נתקיים עליהם הוא שאמר שלמה
מגורת רשע היא תבואנו   This is given by Le Clerc in connection with the Greek quotations of Note C, p. 72.

causal sense, while ἵνα πληρωθῇ yet remains indefinite; the principle viz. that there is no room for chance in the Divine economy, but that all events are foreseen, and accommodated to the general plan. Thus the *final* and the *causal* are merged into one, by the assumption that, in Revelation as in nature, every *result* implies *design*. 'Known unto God are all His works from the beginning of the world' (Acts xv. 18). And if it be granted that, of any two series the whole and each particular were predetermined and foreknown, it would follow that all contingent coincidences are included in the general plan. On this broad principle then a formula may be said to argue design while yet it by no means follows that the design was intended to be exhibited—at least in such a way that the human mind should argue *a priori* to the coincidence. The fact would still remain that the phenomena are diverse, and demand classification at the hand of the observer before any more specific theories on the relations of Prophecy to fulfilment can be safely formed. We might still have to distinguish between fulfilments which are of evidential or argumentative value, and those coincidences which stand in an imperfectly understood relation to a recondite plan.

III. *On traditional Exegesis.*

It is not to be assumed arbitrarily, that what to the modern critic appears to be no more than illustrative was devoid of argumentative importance to an ancient Jew; but allowance should rather be made for differences as regards precision of ratiocinative *expression*, corresponding to differences of development in successive stages of language. 'It were mere dogmatism' urges Dr Lightfoot[1] 'to set up the intellectual standard of our own age or country as an infallible rule...Analogy, allegory, metaphor—by what boundaries are these separated the one from the other? What is true or false, correct or incorrect, as an analogy or an allegory? What argu-

[1] *Galatians*, Ed. 2, p. 197.

mentative force must be assigned to either? We should at least be prepared with an answer to these questions before we venture to sit in judgment on any individual case.'

But, whether or no any absolute standard could be discovered for apportioning to the several methods their exact 'argumentative force,' it is at any rate inconsistent to judge by one standard a system which tacitly claims to be judged by another. The true meaning of a document may be said to be a joint function of the meanings conveyed thereby to its author on the one hand, and to his hearers or readers on the other; and hence arises the importance of traditionary interpretations, so far as they exhibit approximations to the modes of thought current when the document to be interpreted was written. An analogy may be drawn from language. To interpret an ancient document, it is necessary to become acquainted with the language in which it was written, and to follow implicitly its laws and idioms, however arbitrary and illogical they may seem to minds which have been trained in another school. And as each language has its laws and idioms, there may be, so to say, laws and idioms no less various of thought itself. Such laws it would be needful, as in the former case, to determine and follow implicitly, despite their possible semblance of arbitrariness; and this principle, be it remarked, is peculiarly applicable to the case of Messianic interpretations, which will next be considered.

IV. *Messianic Interpretations of the Old Testament.*

The views of modern Jewish commentators are more or less influenced by polemical bias against Christianity, and their trustworthiness is thus proportionately diminished. But their ante-Christian interpretations are of special value as expository of views actually held, even if in some cases they should seem to have been illogically evolved. The so-called Christian interpretations of the Old Testament are in many

Introduction. xvii

cases adopted from ancient Jewish theology, and have come at length to be regarded as non-Judaic, only because Judaism has abandoned the position which it once held with respect to them. Rashi's oft-quoted saying on the Messianic interpretation of the second Psalm should be here adverted to. The antiquity of such an application is granted; yet *to refute the heretics*, or Christians, it is well (urges he) to interpret it literally of David[1]. But to view the matter generally, and apart from the consideration of special passages, there is the phenomenon in ancient Rabbinism of a widespread Messianic hope, derived professedly from the sacred writings, and entwined inextricably with the nation's political and religious life. And unless this phenomenon be taken into account, we can expect to arrive at none but a very meagre and partial understanding of the sacred writings wherein these Messianic anticipations centered.

Not a few of the partial and inadequate interpretations of Holy Scripture, which are accepted as the results of the highest criticism, are due in a measure to the refusal to treat the Bible like any other book: they arise in fact from the undue pressing of *a priori* theories, and an indisposition to allow due weight to the circumstances and modes of thought of those *by* and *for* whom its several parts were in the first instance composed. If the Messianic hope is altogether repudiated, as a natural consequence the Messianic element becomes imperceptible. But, on the other hand, if an all-pervading Messianic hope existed, it could not fail to suggest itself at every turn to those who lived under its influence; and that, through the medium of words, symbols, and imagery, which in default of such anticipations might have conveyed a simply naturalistic meaning. And, as to a child or uneducated per-

---

[1] רבּיתינו דרשו את הענין על מלך המשיח ולפי משמעו ולתשובת המינים נכון לפותרו על דוד. The clause italicized (in the text) has been expunged in some later editions. [See Phillips *in loc.*] In the copy which I have before me the word המינים is crossed out.

son no more than a description of natural scenery may be apparent in an allegorical writing, where to one who lives in a higher sphere of thought a higher meaning is seen not only to exist but to have been designed; so it is at any rate conceivable that to an ancient Jew, breathing an atmosphere of Messianic ideas, higher and 'non-natural' interpretations might be continually presenting themselves—interpretations albeit of which a later and unhistorical criticism could take no cognizance. Moreover, it would be difficult to limit the application of this principle; nor were it fairly matter of surprise if each lesser stream should flow down to the main current of national thought.

In interpreting the writings say of a Greek dramatist, we should be prepared to admit the possibility of a new light being thrown by some freshly-discovered tradition upon a word or phrase which had occasioned no grammatical difficulty, and of which the full meaning had been supposed known: whereas in fact the *allusion*, and with it the secondary and yet principal meaning of the word or phrase, may have lain buried in oblivion, to be exhumed only upon the revival of the tradition, which gives the peculiar combination of circumstances and the state of feeling to which allusion is made. Nor would it be difficult to find sayings and turns of expression now in vogue which exercise a real influence in the present, but would lose at once their chief and indirect meaning, if their traditional explanation were forgotten; while yet perhaps remaining grammatically intelligible, and appearing to convey no more than their surface meaning. Let a like principle be applied to the Old Testament Scriptures, and it would be granted, that even if such and such utterances should seem exactly correspondent to, and fulfilled in, contemporary events, they may yet have conveyed to the existing generation a further Messianic reference. If moreover it should appear, on the same principle, that the secondary reference may have been more or less directly contemplated by the Prophet from whose mouth the utterance proceeded; can we rightly affirm that the barely grammatical rendering is alone true and sufficient? Would it not be more rational to allow for the potential existence in the past of some *idiom of thought* which is unrecognized by a later criticism? Such considerations oppose themselves to negative *a priori* theories, and make it seem more reasonable that an interpreter should first make some attempt to enter into the spirit of the traditional exegesis, rather than at once cast aside its results without duly appreciating the methods by which they were attained. And be it added, that the idiosyncrasy of ancient Judaism was unique and unprecedented; its theology in great measure self-interpreting: its hopes for the future of unexampled strength, and unlike those of any other nation which the world has seen. Their sacred writings were the nucleus of their hopes: these and those act and react on one another: and in some cases where their interpretations of Holy Scripture are especially forced, the very grotesqueness of the interpretation may testify to the strength of the antecedent conviction, whereof the origin remains to be accounted for.

Thus much on the importance of the older Jewish traditions, on which however it is not the aim of the present work to enlarge. The medium of citation will next be considered. Are the citations drawn always or in general from the Septuagint Version, with or without an invariable reservation in favour of the original? Or are they drawn at times from the Hebrew, and at times independently from the Greek?

V. *On Citation from the Septuagint.*

1. It is soon found that the citations are for the most part no exact transcripts from the LXX., with which however their language has the greatest affinity; neither are they independent literal renderings of the Hebrew in all cases in which the LXX. fails to represent the meaning of the original.

It is the discovery of no late age, but has been explicitly stated by Christian Hebraists of old, that the Apostles refer in general to the purport of the passages adduced, rather than to the separate words of the original, or to any authorized and accepted version of it. Thus St Jerome: 'Et hoc in omnibus Scripturis sanctis observandum est, Apostolos et Apostolicos viros, in ponendis testimoniis de Veteri Testamento, non verba considerare, sed sensum, nec eadem sermonum calcare vestigia dummodo a sententiis non recedant.' In exceptional cases, it is true, that slight verbal discrepancies may give rise to disproportionate variations in the sense; but for the most part, it might be anticipated—and the comparison of extant versions will bear out the surmise—that a oneness of general meaning is consistent with a palpable variety of detail. 'The nature and teaching of prophecy may be collected from any tolerable version: and therefore the Apostles, guided from above, did not perplex the Gentiles by discussing the differences between the LXX. and the Hebrew text, but wisely used and sanctioned the use of that Greek Version, which they found providentially prepared[1].' The neglect or insufficient appreciation of the phenomena which the above quotations recognize, goes hand in hand with a trifling and unsound exegesis whereby the weightiest matters are postponed to a formal agreement in minutiæ. There is in fact a more or less clearly defined tendency sometimes observable, to regard that as the most complete harmony, wherein the maximum number of separate words are forced this way or that into an outward correspondence, while the spirit of the original may be altogether missed. But the wide divergence from Hebrew and Septuagint alike which is found in no few of the New Testament citations from the Old, is in itself (may we not affirm?) the source of no insuperable difficulty; for such divergence (as has been well remarked) is no

---

[1] *Aids to Faith*, Essay III.

sure sign of unfamiliarity, but is consistent with the fullest comprehension of the writings quoted. A writer drawing illustrations from works in a strange and unfamiliar language would be the more careful to transcribe with accuracy, in proportion to his consciousness of liability to err and misrepresent; and thus his very exactness might argue the insecurity or limitation of his knowledge, by shewing the necessity that he is under of taking heed to his goings at every step. The like may be said of writings which are not indeed in a strange language, but are more or less imperfectly understood. And conversely the verbal inexactness of a citation, or the bold abruptness of an adaptation, may be due to the just licence of a minute and comprehensive knowledge. The least direct allusion testifies to the firmest grasp and appreciation of a subject; and a writer must have made a predecessor's thoughts his own, before he can subtly interweave the old with the new, combining harmoniously in one texture their diverse and distinct lines of thought and argument. The casual mention of a name may imply an acquaintance with the history of a period: a single word may be the embodiment of a thought which ages have toiled in vain to define and comprehend. Inexactness of citation would seem then to carry with it no sure proof of unfamiliarity with the documents or the subject matter alluded to, but might in some cases even point to a directly opposite conclusion.

2. But it may be asked further, to what extent the LXX. is authorized and approved by its frequent use as a medium of citation from the Hebrew Scriptures: and to this it may be answered that, so long as the question is one of grammar and philology alone, there would seem to be no reason for the assumption that the LXX. rendering of a passage is to be pronounced accurate on the ground of its having been adopted by Apostles or Evangelists. Much less are we compelled to think the general exactness of the LXX. Version guaranteed by the frequent occurrence of Septuagintal citations. Further

remarks on the LXX. will be found in Chapter XV. Meanwhile we proceed to notice some points which affect the purity and preservation of the Hebrew text.

VI. *On the Preservation of the Hebrew Text.*

The absolute purity of the Masoretic text is not asserted even by so stout a champion of the *Hebraica Veritas* as the author of the *Anticritica*—the younger Buxtorf. Nor is perfection claimed by the Masora itself, as is shewn by the appearance in our Hebrew Bibles of various readings; though in most cases, it is true, the variations are of slight magnitude, not to say infinitesimal. But there is evidence that the text has been guarded with a singular scrupulosity, the extent whereof may perhaps be gathered from the minute directions to the copyist which are found in the notes of the Masora. Not only the verses of the several books, but the very letters would seem to have been counted[1]. Some traces of this numbering of the letters still remain. Thus the elongated *Vau* of Lev. xi. 42 is characterized in a note as the middle letter of the Pentateuch; and it is further remarked in the Talmud, that the suspended *Ayin* of Ps. lxxx. 14 is the medial letter of the Book of Psalms. More than this, there is extant a metrical composition, attributed to Saadiah[2], which gives the number of times that each letter of the Hebrew alphabet occurs in the Bible.

Particular letters again are written larger or smaller than the average; while some are suspended (as already exemplified), and others inverted, or marked mysteriously with dots: nor does the Masora omit to chronicle these and other the most minute peculiarities. What was originally intended by these typographical eccentricities does not now appear; for although there are diverse floating traditions upon the various

---

[1] Buxtorf quotes from *Qiddushin*, l. 30 a derivation of the name *Sopherim* from this numbering of the letters.

לפיכך נקראו ראשונים סופרים שהיו
סופרים כל אותיות שבתורה:

[2] Buxtorf, *Tiberias*, Cap. XVIII.

points, these might well have been invented to solve the mystery. What (we might ask) is the meaning of the small *He* in Gen. ii. 4: 'These are the generations of the heavens and the earth *when they were created*'? What again of the diminutive *Yod* in Deut. xxxii. 18: 'Of the Rock that begat thee thou art unmindful'? The one signifies that all created things must wane and perish; or, perhaps, that they must be *dissolved*, seeing that the letter ה is discontinuous. The other signifies, 'ut vix exigua illius Rupis memoria in populo extaret;' and further points to the 'decem tribuum defectio,' *ten* being the numerical value of the letter *Yod!* But others have conjectured that these peculiarities are connected with the numeration of the letters; a view which is in a measure borne out by two facts above mentioned, that an elongated letter marks the middle of the Pentateuch, and a suspended letter the middle of the Psalms.

From the above it might be conjectured, that the Hebrew text was likely to enjoy a comparative immunity from accidental corruption after the Masoretic recension, and that its chief presumed blemishes must have been contracted at some earlier period. But it may be urged with much plausibility that accidental errors were unlikely to insinuate themselves during the Christian era, and before the great recension, which would seem to have been a product of the activity of the time preceding. It has been argued in the first place that the Masoretic precautions were of high antiquity, and not devised for the occasion; and as evidence of this Buxtorf refers to the context of the passage above cited from *Qiddushîn*, where the middle letter, word, and verse of the Pentateuch, together with the middle verse and letter of the Psalms, are mentioned; these precautions being declared ancient in comparison with the Talmud itself by the terms in which scribes who used them are referred to[1].

[1] They are called ראשונים. See *Tiberias*, p. 44.

xxiv *Introduction.*

These facts have been thought by some to make the risk of accidental corruption very remote; but it should be added, that at the period now in question the attitude of Rabbinism was signally controversial, as against Christianity, and that this would naturally tend to an increase of vigilance, which would still further remove the probability of accidental deterioration in the text of the Hebrew Scriptures. On the other hand, there are some considerations which militate against the hypothesis that changes were introduced wilfully, with controversial aim.

(1.) The arguments of Christians were drawn mostly from the Septuagint, which would seem to render a change in the Hebrew text, so to say, unnecessary for the purpose of refutation. (2.) The great care bestowed upon the text was the sign of a real though often misapplied reverence for the very letters of Holy Scripture—a reverence which affords a strong argument against the hypothesis of wilful corruption. 'There is not in the Law a single letter whereon great mountains depend not;' and 'if thou subtract or add a letter, thou art found to destroy the whole world.' But (3), the singularity of the methods by which the scribe was trained to evolve unsuspected meanings from the sacred page, is perhaps the most striking evidence of the stability of the text itself: and more than this, the probability that alterations would be made deliberately, is inversely proportional (might we not say?) to the facility wherewith any desired or conceivable meaning could be extracted from the text as it stood. Some of these methods we proceed to notice.—

VII. *On some Cabbalistic Interpretations.*

1. What more pregnant with idle fancies, while yet testifying to an anxious custody of the literal text, than the principle of numerical equivalence? Each letter in Hebrew, as in Greek, represents a number; every word, viewed as the sum of its constituent letters, has a numerical value: and for

Introduction.

any word may be substituted one of equal value[1]. Thus the *one* language of Gen. xi. 1 becomes the *sacred*[2] tongue. On the same principle we may read, not: 'Rebekah *his wife* conceived' (Gen. xxv. 21), but 'Rebekah conceived *fire and stubble*,' i.e. *Jacob and Esau;* for is it not said that 'the house of Jacob shall be a *fire*...and the house of Esau for *stubble*' (Obad. 18)? The words 'till *Shiloh come*' (Gen. xlix. 10) refer, still on this principle, to the *Messiah*.

Two other methods of substitution, which will next be considered, have been thought to occur in the writings of Isaiah and Jeremiah respectively.

2. According to one of these methods, the letters of the alphabet, taken in their natural order, are divided into two sets of eleven, and any letter out of one set may be interchanged with that which holds a corresponding place in other. Thus *Aleph*, the first letter of the alphabet may be interchanged with *Lamed*, which begins its latter half: *Beth*, the second letter of the alphabet, with *Mem*, which follows *Lamed*: and so with the remaining letters taken in order. This method, which is styled *albam* (a word containing the four letters specified, and thus representing the principle on which the interchange proceeds), is thought to have been used in Is. vii. 6, as a cipher-writing; the name Tabeal becoming Remaliah[3], if treated by this method.

3. By another species of substitution, *athbash*, Babylon is thought to be disguised under the form Sheshach (Jer. xxv. 26; li. 41). This method is of the same nature as the preceding; the difference being, that the letters in the two halves of the alphabet are numbered in opposite directions, viz. from the extremities to the centre. Thus the central letters, *Caph* and *Lamed*, are interchangeable: the first letter, *Aleph*, may

---

[1] Compare the cipher-writing of Rev. xiii. 18.

[2] Buxtorf, *Lex. Talm.*, p. 447, states this case inaccurately. He writes: רמליהו.

' שפה אחת valet 794. Totidem לשׁן הקדשׁ.' But אחת = 409 = הקדשׁ.

[3] רמלא, not the Biblical form רמליהו.

xxvi   *Introduction.*

be interchanged with the last, *Tau ;* the second, *Beth,* with the last but one, *Shin ;* and so on, as the name *athbash* is designed to intimate.   But whether this method of cipher-writing was or was not used by Jeremiah, there is a palpable extravagance in the following application of it. In Ex. vi. 3, God thus speaks to Moses: 'And I appeared unto Abraham, unto Isaac, and unto Jacob, by the name of God *Almighty,* but by my name *JEHOVAH* was I not known unto them;' the truth of which statement is mystically represented by the circumstance, that if the word formed by combining the last letters of the names Abraham, Isaac, and Jacob, be transformed by the process *athbash,* there results the name, *Almighty*[1], by which God revealed Himself to the three patriarchs.

4. Sometimes again a single word is resolved into several, each of its letters being taken to stand for an abbreviation of a word. And very often a new meaning is imported into a verse or phrase by a change of pointing; which is not however to be viewed as an alteration of the text, but as a way of extracting from it a collateral meaning, over and above that which is its acknowledged primary meaning. Such changes are perpetually occurring. Does the Scripture say, 'The *lambs* are for thy clothing'?—Read not *lambs* but *secrets;* and the meaning will be, that the mysteries of the universe should be for thy clothing, *i.e.* for thyself alone, and not to be discussed before many people[2]. And again, to him who joins heartily in the response *Amen* the gates of Paradise are open. 'Open the gates' writes Isaiah 'that the righteous nation which keepeth *the truth* [read *Amens*] may enter in' (Is. xxvi. 2). Such examples might be multiplied indefinitely; but the preceding are enough to illustrate the Jewish Doctor's versatility in extracting desired meanings from the sacred page,

---

[1] בקם *i.e.* becomes שדי. Buxtorf, *Lex. Talm.*
[2] Bernard's *Maimonides*, p. 93.

and to diminish the plausibility of the hypothesis which has been hazarded, that the Hebrew Bible has undergone considerable changes at the hands of perplexed and daring controversialists.

VIII. *Further Remarks on the Preservation of the Hebrew Text.*

Thus far we have considered the probability of a deterioration in the text since the commencement of the Christian Era. But yet another question presents itself, viz. What was its previous condition? What was the state of its preservation at the coming of CHRIST?

It may be suggested in reply, that our LORD does not charge the Jews with any lack of care as regards the letter of Holy Writ, but credits them, on the contrary, with an excessive zeal in all the externals and minutiæ of religious duty. They had not openly neglected the lively oracles, but had overlaid them with their traditions. One expression from amongst many deserves special notice. 'Think not that I am come to destroy the law or the prophets: I am not come to destroy but to fulfil. For verily I say unto you, Till heaven and earth pass, *one jot or one tittle* shall in no wise pass from the law, till all be fulfilled' (Matt. v. 18). 'And it is easier for heaven and earth to pass, than one *tittle* of the law to fail' (Luke xvi. 17). The *jot* or *yod* is the smallest letter of the Hebrew alphabet, and the expression *tittle* alludes to the almost infinitesimal variations which distinguish certain of its consonants from others. The meaning intended to be conveyed is indeed a spiritual one; but its expression is comparable with extant Rabbinic sayings[1] whereby the need of accuracy in transcription is inculcated upon the scribe. And thus our Lord would seem to testify to the scrupulosity with which the text was then preserved, and to reassure such as doubted

---

[1] See p. xxiv.; and Lightfoot on Matt. v. 18.

of His purpose, by expressions which carry the thoughts at once to the form of the original Hebrew. To that text then lay the ultimate appeal: nor is it unreasonable to infer from our Lord's expressions, (1) that the Jews of that age were zealous custodians of the letter; and (2) that the text at that time was not replete with gross inaccuracies. The same truth which He inculcates might have been expressed had the Hebrew text been corrupt and the scribes indifferent; but it may at least be doubted whether the form actually used would have been chosen to express it. But however this may be, it appears that the Hebrew Scriptures have been guarded with an altogether unprecedented care, which must be taken into account when the accuracy of its readings is called in question. We now proceed to consider certain methods and principles applicable to the interpretation of the Old Testament.

IX. *On some Principles of Interpretation.*

Passages of the Old Testament are sometimes applied in the New with an apparent disregard of their original contexts; and although the citations which exhibit this phenomenon present many special and peculiar features, there are certain general principles of application, which must not be left unnoticed. Words of the Old Testament, which were spoken originally with a special reference, may be found not unfrequently applied in the New, with no very obvious traces of an allusion to the circumstances with which they were in the first instance conjoined. And not only so, but they seem to be credited with a true argumentative force in contexts the most diverse from those in which they originally stood. Argument and instruction for the future is found, where, at first sight, no more than a simply historical reference was discernible: the buried past is resuscitated: and words that were spoken of and to the men of one age are said to find their fulfilment in the history of another.

1. Under this head may be classed the whole scheme of prelusive 'types' (1 Cor. x. 11)—to retain a word which, from quasi-technical usage, has lost no little of its primitive vitality, and associates itself spontaneously, in some minds, with the idea of fanciful misapplication. And, in close connection with the preceding, may be mentioned the method of higher and spiritual applications, which, though natural enough with those who use it rightly, is shunned by many for its supposed taint of mysticism. In accordance with this method, a precept for guidance in common matters is claimed as an exponent of the highest mysteries—a process which, with unskilful handling, may lead doubtless to extravagances of exegesis, but which, if judiciously applied, will seem arbitrary and unsound only when the true relations of the higher and the lower are overlooked.

2. The propriety of citation without reference to the original context is sufficiently obvious in certain cases; when for example the words cited contain a statement of a general principle, which is applied indeed to special circumstances, or exemplified therein, but in no wise restricted to that or any one occasion. An example of this is found in the Gospel narrative of our Lord's temptation:

'And when the tempter came to Him, he said, If Thou be the Son of God, command that these stones be made bread. But He answered and said, It is written, *Man shall not live by bread alone, but by every word that proceedeth out of the mouth of God* (Deut. viii. 3). Then the devil taketh Him up into the holy city, and setteth Him on a pinnacle of the temple, and saith unto Him, If Thou be the Son of God, cast thyself down: for it is written, *He shall give His angels charge concerning Thee: and in their hands they shall bear Thee up, lest at any time Thou dash Thy foot against a stone* (Ps. xci. 11, 12). Jesus said unto him, It is written again, *Thou shalt not tempt the Lord thy God* (Deut. vi. 16). Again the devil taketh Him up into an exceeding high mountain, and sheweth Him all the kingdoms of the world, and the glory of them; and saith unto Him, All these things will I give Thee, if Thou wilt fall down and worship me. Then saith Jesus unto him, Get thee hence, Satan: for it is written, *Thou shalt worship the Lord thy God, and Him only shalt thou serve* (Deut. vi. 13). Then the devil leaveth Him, and, behold, angels came and ministered unto Him' (Matt. iv. 3—11; Luke iv. 3—13).

(*a*) The first of the above citations is an extract from a passage in which allusion is made to the forty years in the wilderness, the circumstances whereof were calculated to generate a spiritual frame of mind in the Israelites, and to wean them from overmuch reliance upon the things of sense. 'And He humbled thee, and suffered thee to hunger, and fed thee with manna, which thou knewest not, neither did thy fathers know: that He might make thee know that *man doth not live by bread only, but by every word that proceedeth out of the mouth of the* LORD *doth man live*' (Deut. viii. 3). The isolation of this general principle from its special context is too obviously natural to need more than a passing notice.

(*b*) The citation from Ps. xci. describes in general terms God's care for the ideal Righteous One; and over against it our Lord sets another citation from the book of Deuteronomy, detached, like the former, from its original reference; or rather, as it would be more correct to say, He *applies* the words there spoken (plurally) to an individual case. In the original it is said: 'Ye shall not tempt the LORD your God, *as ye tempted Him in Massah*' (Deut. vi. 16). This application likewise occasions no difficulty, for it is sufficiently obvious that the principle enounced, being general, will bear isolation from any special context in which it may occur. In the originals we find special exemplifications of general principles, and the attendant circumstances exhibit concretely, or are 'types' of, abstract truth. 'All these things happened unto them for examples: and they are written for our admonition, upon whom the ends of the world are come' (1 Cor. x. 11). (*c*) The citation from Deut. vi. 13 calls for notice only in respect of a slight verbal alteration (*worship* taking the place of *fear* or *reverence*), which is adopted as more closely correspondent to the form of the temptation, to 'fall down and *worship* me.'

3. The conversion of history into prophecy commends itself very readily to the thinking mind; for, if from an actual occurrence a law or principle can be gathered, it is needful only to assume the stability of the law or principle, in order to predict the same or like results when an analogous combination recurs. Thus, the inspired writers argue, not seldom, from a circumstance to a principle, and thence to a recurrence, seeing that with God 'is no variableness, neither shadow of turning' (James i. 17).

4. As general results are thus gathered from special facts, so they may be gathered likewise from special precepts. Thus St Paul does not hesitate to generalize particular provisions of the Mosaic system, which might have been supposed to stop short at their special primary applications: and more than this, the higher application is put forward as axiomatic, with those at least who are well versed in Holy Scripture and its interpretation. To take for instance what has been denounced as a perverse misapplication, St Paul writing to Timothy quotes from Deut. xxv. 4: 'Thou shalt not muzzle the ox that treadeth out the corn' (1 Tim. v. 18); and in this precept sees a Divine authority for his injunction: 'Let the elders that rule well be counted worthy of double honour' (1 Tim. v. 17). The same precept is quoted elsewhere, and with an explanation which, though brief, is enough to justify the whole system of such higher applications. 'Who goeth a warfare at any time at his own charges? who planteth a vineyard, and eateth not of the fruit thereof? or who feedeth a flock, and eateth not of the milk of the flock? Say I these things as a man? or saith not the law the same also? For it

is written in the law of Moses, *Thou shalt not muzzle the mouth of the ox that treadeth out the corn* (Deut. xxv. 4). Doth God take care for oxen? Or saith He it altogether for our sakes? For our sakes, no doubt, this is written: that he that ploweth should plow in hope; and that he that thresheth in hope should be partaker of his hope. If we have sown unto you spiritual things, is it a great thing if we shall reap your carnal things?' (1 Cor. ix. 7—11). It is sufficiently obvious that a single provision, like that in question, may evince the general tenour of the legislation, and serve as a 'type' of something which transcends itself, or be spiritually applied as by St Paul; nor that, without the sanction of Him who forearms His disciples against their coming trial, with a 'Fear ye not, therefore, ye are of more value than many sparrows' (Matt. x. 31; Luke xii. 7).

5. The method of spiritualization is analogous to that of teaching by Proverbs, which, though they may be propounded with limitations, are intended for guidance in all cases to which they can be applied. Nor is it necessary that sayings which differ from such proverbs in having been originally conjoined with an actual, and not merely conceivable, contingency, should, unlike the proverbs, be restricted rigorously, each to its special case. The precept quoted (*supra*) by St Paul serves to illustrate this remark, seeing that it is, in a manner, converse to the proverbial saying, that 'A righteous man regardeth the life of his beast' (Prov. xii. 10). The Precept, providing for external matters, manifests the benignity of the Legislator: the Proverb, presupposing a benignity of temperament, describes the form of its manifestation under special circumstances. This inversion is of course incidental, and not essential to the comparison between precept and proverb which it is adduced to illustrate. The main point to be observed is, that the Proverb sets forth a general principle by means of a particular manifestation, while an analogous special Precept serves for the groundwork of a like generality.

6. The spiritualization of history is analogous to the method of instruction by Parables, which are quasi-historical illustrations of principles. A significant historical narrative might be used as the groundwork of a parable: nor again would the generality of a parable be diminished by the supposition, which the uneducated sometimes make, that its externals are historical. From a narrative of facts, rightly interpreted, an underlying principle may be gathered: while, on the other hand, the parable undertakes to set forth the working of a principle by a special combination of facts and circumstances. The parable is commonly said—nor that wrongly—to be in a special manner the exponent of a *spiritual* truth; but we have preferred the more general term *principle* advisedly, seeing that it is the main characteristic of parables to compare spiritual things with natural, and to shew that one and the same principle is applicable to the twofold scheme of Nature and Grace. Parables are in fact arguments from analogy, and presuppose one Author and one *principle* in things natural and things spiritual.

The form of the Parable must be, as above assumed, quasi-historical; *i.e.* the circumstances and events described must be such as might exist or have happened, although it is not necessary that they should actually have occurred. Thus *e.g.* with the Parables of the Sower, the Ten Virgins, the Good Samaritan. But the expression quasi-*historical* must be taken in a broad sense, as relating not merely to the actions of men, but as including other and lower manifestations of natural laws. The growth of the Mustard-seed, and the working of the Leaven must not be omitted; nor can the animal creation be rightly passed by in the definition of a Parable. The 'proverb' quoted in 2 Pet. ii. 22, is implicitly a Parable; and Solomon's allusion to the ant (Prov. vi. 6) contains the two elements of a Parable, seeing that it is true to nature, and is the groundwork of a spiritual lesson. Perhaps then the PARABLE might be defined as *a natural illustration of a principle*, with special reference in all cases to the highest application of that principle; or, if it be desired to *express* rather than to *imply* this main characteristic, we might modify the above form and say, that

A PARABLE *is a natural illustration of a spiritual truth.*

7. In the cases which have been considered, the link between the lower and the higher is a common principle— in type and parable; in precept or history, and their spiritualized or mystical applications. One more principle of interpretation should not be left unnoticed. While the heathen poet dealt more especially with fiction, or looked back upon an imaginary golden age, the Prophet set his ideal in the future, and trusted to see his highest aspirations realized in the MESSIAH and Messianic times. Borrowing his imagery from the world around, he delineates, progressively with the vicissitudes of national life, the ideal SAVIOUR of the race; and this conception, once grasped, could not fail to permeate and leaven the national thought, to an extent which could never be duly estimated by the mind into which the conception has not been infused. Once in existence, it must gather into itself all lesser thoughts, and lend a higher meaning to ceremonial and to life itself. Its influence is felt when common things are described in words that transcend the occasion: it is found a stumblingblock to the purely negative or naturalistic expositor: it has fostered in other schools the theory of a discontinuous 'Double Sense.' But how, humanly speaking, were spiritual ideas to be expressed, unless concretely, and with the aid of natural types? How indeed does common language express mental processes, if not by metaphors and typifications, which assume an abstract form only when their origin has been forgotten? And, again, if formal anachronism was to be avoided, how could prophecy but be embodied in the surroundings of the present? Thus the seen and the unseen are blended harmoniously into one; and the present becomes the germ which developes without let or pause into

the infinity of the future; or the base and groundwork on which the higher thought is reared.

Thus much as regards general principles. We have next to address ourselves to the task of examining critically the several Citations from the Old Testament in the New; and in doing this, we shall attempt to insulate each passage considered, with intent to determine the primary meaning of the Old and of the New, each without reference to the other. Sometimes indeed the original or the citation may involve an ambiguity which makes it necessary to view one of them in the light of the other, rather than to determine the meaning of each separately. But it more frequently happens that the separate conclusions are obtained with less difficulty, and that the most complex task is that of harmonizing the two conclusions. This the present work does not profess to do invariably; nor is it involved in the conditions of our 'Critical Examination.' And thus, difficulties may sometimes be developed, and left unsurmounted: a received theory may be discredited: a common solution disturbed, and no conclusion surely established in its stead. But the development of objections is the first step towards their removal, and nothing is less conducive to the lasting settlement of a controversy than a too ready acquiescence in wavering theories. If then the investigation on which we now enter should threaten, in this or that detail, to disturb received conclusions, such an issue is neither to be wondered at, nor yet too hastily to be deprecated; for do not reason and experience proclaim with consentient voice, that perturbations for a time inexplicable may be found at length to harmonize with the laws which they seemed to defy; thus serving to develop our true but unmatured conceptions of truth, and guiding to the discovery of new worlds of thought?

τελος νομου χριστος
πληρωμα νομου η αγαπη

τί γάρ ἐστιν ὁ νόμος; εὐαγγέλιον προκατηγγελμένον.
τί δὲ τὸ εὐαγγέλιον; νόμος πεπληρωμένος.

    Novum Testamentum in Vetere latet :
    Vetus Testamentum in Novo patet.

CHAPTER I.

I will have mercy, and not sacrifice.

Matt. ix. 13; xii. 7; Hos. vi. 6.

THE words ἔλεος θέλω καὶ οὐ θυσίαν are susceptible of two interpretations. In the one the mercy spoken of is divine; in the other human. The meaning may be either that God delights in the exercise of mercy, and 'willeth not the death of a sinner, but rather that he may turn from his wickedness and live;' or, that He delights to see in men a charitable consideration for their brethren's trials and infirmities, and that such a disposition is pleasing in His sight rather than the strictest conformity with outer law. It may indeed be said that the general principle which underlies the statement admits no less the second application than the first; but a closer investigation is desirable, for the words do not only link together the old dispensation and the new and express the inner meaning of all divine legislation, but have been applied by our Lord Himself to a special controversy which the lapse of eighteen centuries has failed to deprive of either interest or importance.

I. The saying is first quoted in Matt. ix. 13.

'And it came to pass, as Jesus sat at meat in the house, behold, many publicans and sinners came and sat down with Him and His disciples.

'And when the Pharisees saw it, they said unto His disciples, Why eateth your Master with publicans and sinners?

'But when Jesus heard that, He said unto them, They that be whole need not a physician, but they that are sick.

'But go ye and learn what that meaneth, I will have mercy, and not sacrifice: for I am not come to call the righteous, but sinners to repentance.'

The 'mercy' here spoken of, if human, must be the mercy of the publicans and sinners, or the mercy of the Pharisees, or lastly that of Christ regarded as subject to the law and exemplifying its complete fulfilment.

It cannot be the first, for it is obviously foreign to the Saviour's purpose to describe those 'publicans and sinners' as other than truly sinners that have need to be called to the way of righteousness. He does not say 'these publicans, though failing in outward observance, are yet your equals or superiors in mercy, that weightier matter of the law.' He does not credit them with moral piety as a ground of acceptance despite their ritual deficiency, but implies that because they are sinners He calls them to repentance.

It cannot be the mercy of the Pharisees, unless, as seems improbable, the words are designed merely to silence the objectors, and have no bearing on the mutual relations of the sinners and their Guest. He does not say: 'If you had understood the service wherein God delights the most, you would have sought to please Him by meekness and by mercy; by charitable judgment rather than by sharp censure of your brethren:'—for the words, thus meant, would contain a dismissal of the Pharisees with a reproof of their ignorance and self-righteousness, but would contribute nothing to the answer of the all-important question 'Why eateth your Master with publicans and sinners?'

Against the third view, that the mercy is that whereby Christ in His humanity fulfils the Law, it may be urged that He is set forth in the context as an independent worker rather than as subject to ordinances. He is the great Physician, whose function, voluntarily chosen, is one of mercy. Sinners are those with whom He would associate. Their very sickness constitutes their claim.

The interpretation which makes the mercy spoken of divine seems most appropriate. The Pharisees are surprised that one claiming to be an exponent of the divine will should thus mingle with the outcasts of society, rather than leave them to the contempt and ruin which seemed most consonant with the purpose of the law. It was thought that the evil consequences which flow from the breaking of God's law must in themselves be well pleasing to the Lawgiver, and it had not occurred to the objectors that such consequences might be remedial. In the answer, mercy is fitly contrasted with sacrifice, and it is declared that God delights in 'showing mercy[1] and pity,' rather than in the exaction of pain and suffering, which are merely retributive. This then explains why the divine Healer should have risked, as it seemed, the defilement of evil companionship, and set before Him as His worthiest aim the calling of sinners to repentance.

Two remarks may be added in confirmation of the above. The first arises from a consideration of the context. The question 'Why eateth your Master with publicans and sinners?' being disposed of, 'then came to Him the disciples of John, saying, Why do we and the Pharisees fast oft, but thy disciples fast not?' or in the phraseology of St Luke (v. 33), 'but thine eat and drink.' The sequence is a natural one, on the supposition that the answer to the first question has direct reference to the divine purpose in the recovery of the lost. Why eat with publicans and sinners? Because 'I will have mercy.' But why eat at all? Why elect a social life in contradistinction to the asceticism of John? This second difficulty has respect to outward observances, and would have been in a measure anticipated by the commonly received solution of the first. If, however, the first answer has no direct bearing on the like outward observ-

---

[1] Stier contends for this application of ἔλεος, but dwells upon a different aspect of θυσία. God delights to show mercy: to give grace rather than to receive oblations. For other usages of *sacrifice* compare Ps. li. 17; Is. xxxiv. 6. 'The sacrifices of God are a broken spirit.' 'The Lord hath a sacrifice in Bozrah, and a great slaughter in the land of Idumea.'

ances, then the second question follows as a natural supplement to the first.

Lastly, there is a significant omission of the Greek article, which has been dwelt upon by Stier, but is unrepresented in the Authorized Version. Not *saints but sinners* would be more exact than our English rendering, I came not to call '*the* righteous but sinners' to repentance. The article before δικαίους would imply that there were some to whom the term righteous was applicable or applied. The article before ἁμαρτωλούς would imply that there were some to whom the term sinners was inapplicable. Its omission seems at variance with that 'ironica concessio' which our Lord's answer has been thought to convey.

By SS. Mark and Luke the citation is omitted. 'They that are whole need not a physician; but they that are sick. I came not to call *the* righteous but sinners to repentance' (Mark ii. 17; Luke v. 31, 32). There is first a statement of a well-known proverb, and next a spiritual application. It is the sick that have need of a physician: therefore to call sinners is the purpose of my coming. St Matthew records the answer more at length. The sick have need: it is the divine will that mercy should be shown those who need: and this explains why the divine Healer should be found with those whose souls are sick with sin.

II. The citation recurs in Matt. xii. 7, in answer to the charge that the disciples did that which it was not lawful to do upon the Sabbath day, when they 'were an hungred, and began to pluck the ears of corn, and to eat.' It is shown by the example of David, that such apparent illegalities were not invariably condemned by those self-same Pharisees, and further it is proved by words of Scripture that the disciples were guiltless and the Pharisees ignorant of the law.

'Have ye not read what David did, when he was an hungred, and they that were with him;

'How he entered into the house of God, and did eat the shewbread, which was not lawful for him to eat, neither for them which were with him, but only for the priests?

'But if ye had known what this meaneth, I will have mercy, and not sacrifice, ye would not have condemned the guiltless.'

'If with all their searching into the Scripture, all their busy scrutiny of its letter, they had ever so entered into the spirit of that law whereof they professed to be the jealous guardians and faithful interpreters, as to understand that Scripture, they would not have blamed them in whom no true blame can be found[1].'

The interpretation which makes the mercy spoken of that charitableness whereby the Pharisees should have sought to please God—'rather than in the way of sharp and severe censure of their brethren'—but ill accords with the implication that the disciples were absolutely guiltless. A second interpretation, which attributes the mercy to the disciples, has indeed a direct bearing upon the legality of their conduct, the real point at issue:—'If you had truly understood what God asks of men, what service of theirs pleases Him best, you would have understood that my disciples were offering that, who in true love and pity for perishing souls had so laboured and toiled as to go without their necessary food, being thus obliged to satisfy the cravings of a present hunger; you would have owned that their loving transgression was better than many a man's cold and heartless clinging to the letter of the commandment[1].' But to this it may be objected that it gives undue prominence to the disciples' previous conduct, and thus mars the applicability of the historical parallel, wherein David's act is viewed by the light not of his previous conduct but of his present need. 'Have ye never read what David did, when he had need, and was an hungred, he, and they that were with him?' (Mark ii. 25).

It remains to regard the mercy as God's mercy; an application which seems to satisfy the general requirements of the passage, and well suits the immediate context of the citation.

[1] Trench, *On the Miracles.*

'But if ye had known what this meaneth, I will have mercy, and not sacrifice, ye would not have condemned the guiltless.

'For the Son of Man is Lord even of the Sabbath day:'

Where the last verse is a conclusion from the saying, quoted only by St Mark,—

'The Sabbath was made for man, not man for the Sabbath' (ii. 27).

That the Sabbath should thus be for man, not man for the Sabbath, is a single exemplification of the truth that God wills mercy and not sacrifice:—that man's well-being is the purpose of God's law. He delights not to exact the penalty of non-fulfilment, nor to accept as meritorious the bearing of arbitrarily imposed burdens. But His delight is to show mercy, and He requires obedience as a means no less than a condition of the subject's well-being. If then it should seem that a fulfilment of Divine law is at variance with man's highest good, we may rest assured either that the seeming evil is not real, or that we have misinterpreted the law and wrongly judged that such and such sacrifices are required. A conclusion here specially applied, but universal in its bearing, which cuts at the root of all blind self-sacrifice, and shows that God's laws are not mere aimless and arbitrary enactments, even though to beings of a finite capacity they should so appear.

A clause peculiar to St Matthew has yet to be considered.

'Or have ye not read in the law, how that on the Sabbath days the priests in the temple profane the Sabbath, and are blameless?

'But I say unto you, That in this place is one greater than the temple' (xii. 5, 6).

These verses seem to comprise in themselves an argument altogether distinct from that which is founded upon the example of David, and unconnected with the principle enunciated in the following verse :—

'I will have mercy and not sacrifice.'

If the priests engaged in the temple service may profane the Sabbath and be blameless, how much more these disciples 'in their appointed following of Him who is greater than the Temple, the true Temple of God on earth, the Son of Man.' The whole passage thus presents an example of that introverted parallelism so congenial to the Hebrew style; the sixth and seventh verses corresponding respectively to the fifth and fourth. Allusion is first made (v. 4) to the act of David, and next (v. 5) to the priests in their public ministrations. The sixth verse follows as a sequel to that immediately preceding, and the seventh enunciates a general principle having a special application to the example recorded in the fourth. 'But if ye had realized that God's laws are made in mercy and not arbitrarily, and in particular that the Sabbath was designed to be not a burden, but a benefit, ye would not thus have condemned the guiltless.'

The disciples were doubly right. As David's act was justified by his absolute need, without reference to any service in which he was engaged, so the disciples were right in acting as they did, because 'they had need and were an hungred,' and that without reference to the service of Christ wherein they were engaged. And secondly, as the priests were authorized and required to disregard the general law of the Sabbath so far as might be necessary for the temple service, the disciples in like manner were justified by the exigencies of Christ's service, independently of any wants incidental to themselves.

The exception in favour of the temple service might have been viewed as an exaltation of ritual requirements above the general law of the Sabbath; and this is in a manner confirmatory of the opinion that no direct contrast between the ritual and the spiritual, between 'Charity and Churchgoing[1],' is intended.

It may be added that the argument as above expounded, far from being apologetic or deprecatory, contains an uncompromising assertion of the disciples' innocence, and may therefore be the more fitly coordinated with such arguments on the same topic, elsewhere recorded, as

'My Father worketh hitherto, and I work.'

'I must work the works of Him that sent me while it is day.'

'Is it lawful to do good on the Sabbath day or to do evil? to save life or to destroy?'

III. The original context of the saying, 'I desire mercy, and not sacrifice,' will next engage attention.

The words, 'Come and let us return....,' which in the Authorized Version commence the sixth chapter of Hosea, are best read, as by the LXX, in close connexion with the last words of the fifth.

'For I will be unto Ephraim as a lion, and as a young lion to the house of Judah: I, even I, will tear and go away; I will take away, and none shall rescue him.

'I will go and return to my place, till they acknowledge their offence, and seek my face: in their affliction they will seek me early, *saying;* (v. 14, 15)

'Come and let us return unto the Lord: for He hath torn, and He will heal us; He hath smitten, and He will bind us up.

'After two days will He revive us: in the third day He will raise us up, and we shall live in His sight.

'Then shall we know, if we follow on to know the Lord: His going forth is prepared as the morning; and He shall

---

[1] Pusey on Hosea vi. 5.

I will have mercy, and not sacrifice.

come unto us as the rain, as the latter and former rain unto the earth' (vi. 1—3).

Where God is represented—under the figure of a lion carrying off prey to his den—as having decreed the punishment of His people till such time as, in their affliction, they should reason one with another;

'Come and let us return unto the Lord: for He hath torn, and He will heal us; He hath smitten, and He will bind us up.'

As the passage which follows is of considerable difficulty, it may be well first to state the received interpretation, and next to consider whether another be not in some ways preferable.

The third verse precedes the address:

'O Ephraim, what shall I do unto thee? O Judah, what shall I do unto thee? for your goodness[1] is as a morning cloud, and as the early dew it goeth away.

'Therefore have I hewed them by the prophets; I have slain them by the words of my mouth: and thy judgments are as the light that goeth forth.

'For I desired mercy, and not sacrifice; and the knowledge of God more than burnt-offerings.'

The 'mercy' spoken of is that essential piety[2] which God prefers to outward worship. The unstedfastness of Ephraim and Judah was the sole cause of the evil that had come upon them. And seeing that they were not unwarned, but all kinds of severe discipline had been tried in vain, the justice of God's judgments would be clear as the light of day. 'Thy judgments, *O my people*, shall be as the light that goeth forth:' or, with the reading of the LXX, 'My judgment[3] shall go forth as the light.'

---

[1] חֶסֶד, or mercy, is here taken in the secondary sense of moral goodness.

[2] 'Uti et Chaldæus expressit: *nam iis qui pietatem exercent magis delector quam sacrificiis.*'

[3] משפטי כאור for משפטיך אור There is a reading σου. See Holmes and Parsons' edition of the Septuagint.

Exception is taken to the received reading on account of its sudden trans-

The following is an alternative rendering, which will afterwards be considered in detail.

God has been represented as awaiting the time when in their affliction Ephraim and Judah should seek Him early[1], with the full confidence of finding Him. 'His going forth is certain as the dawn's[1]; and He shall come unto us as the rain, as the latter and former rain unto the earth.' But while sure as the dawn, their opportunity would soon pass away.

'O Ephraim, what shall I do for thee[2]? O Judah, what shall I do for thee? for *your mercy*[3] (or proffered grace) is as the morning cloud, and as the dew that early goeth away.

'Therefore have I smitten the prophets[4]; I have slain them by the words of my mouth; that thy impending judgments might be manifest, *might go forth*[5] light.

'For I desire mercy (towards thee), and not sacrifice; and the knowledge of God more than burnt offerings.' (vi. 4—6.)

That the saying 'I desire mercy' may indicate God's gracious disposition towards men rather than his requirements from them, is shown by the recurrence of the combination in Micah vii. 18, where the context clearly defines the meaning.

'Who is a God like unto Thee, that pardoneth iniquity, and passeth by the transgression of the remnant of his heritage? He retaineth not His anger for ever, because He delighteth in mercy[6].'

The mercy then which God declares by Hosea that He desires, may be that which He would bestow upon His people. And again '*your* mercy' (vi. 4) may be the mercy of which you are the objects, in strict accordance with the analogies

'They that observe lying vanities forsake *their own* mercy.' Jonah ii. 9.

---

itions in person and number. 'Your goodness is as a morning cloud. Therefore I have hewed them by the prophets. Thy judgments are as the light that goeth forth.'

[1] See Note 1, p. 13.

[2] See Note 2, p. 13.
[3] See Note 3, p. 13.
[4] See Note 4, p. 13.
[5] See Note 5, p. 15.
[6] כִּי חָפֵץ חֶסֶד הוּא, ὅτι θελητὴς ἐλέους ἐστίν.

I will have mercy, and not sacrifice.

'For as ye in times past have not believed God, yet have now obtained mercy through their unbelief:

'Even so have these also now not believed, that through *your* mercy they also may obtain mercy.' Rom. xi. 30, 31.

The disputed passage would thus signify that every means had been tried to warn Ephraim and Judah of their danger, and so turn them from their evil ways ere yet their day of grace had passed. 'Therefore did I smite the prophets; I slew them by the words of my mouth; I spared them not, but sacrificed them for thy warning, that thy impending judgments might be as clear as day. All this because I desired mercy and not sacrifice; because I sought to recall thee to the knowledge of God rather than exact the full penalty and expiation of thy sins.'

This smiting of the prophets may be interpreted in diverse ways.

The word of the Lord[1] is 'like a hammer that breaketh the rock in pieces' (Jer. xxiii. 29), and the smiting may be that of lying prophets for encouraging a false security; or secondly, such a smiting of truthful prophets as when 'the Spirit of the Lord began to smite' Samson, or when Daniel 'was grieved in his spirit in the midst of his body, and the visions of his head troubled him.' Or again, the divine commission may have proved indirectly the destruction of the prophets, by exposing them to the fury of the people whose sins they denounced; as for example, when 'the Spirit of God came upon Zechariah...and they conspired against him, and stoned him with stones.' 2 Chron. xxiv. 20, 21.

The last interpretation develops a striking parallelism between Hos. vi. 4—6, and the Saviour's lament over Jerusalem:

'Wherefore, behold I send unto you prophets, and wise men, and scribes: and some of them ye shall kill and crucify; and some of them ye shall scourge in your synagogues, and persecute them from city to city.

[1] Compare Heb. iv. 12.

'That upon you may come all the righteous blood shed upon the earth, from the blood of righteous Abel unto the blood of Zacharias[1] son of Barachias, whom ye slew between the temple and the altar.

'O Jerusalem, Jerusalem, thou that killest the prophets, and stonest them which are sent unto thee, how often would I have gathered thy children together, even as a hen gathereth her chickens under her wings, and ye would not!' Matt. xxiii. 34, 35, 37.

The knowledge of God, viewed not as a qualification required of man, but as a blessing bestowed upon him from without, is well suited to stand in parallelism with the mercy which God desires to bestow. 'This is life eternal, that they may know Thee the only true God' (Joh. xvii. 3). And 'it is elsewhere promised as a great privilege of Christ's kingdom that then they should *all know the Lord;* and as a great blessing that He would *give them an heart to know Him*[2].'

The same 'mercy' and 'knowledge' serve in an earlier chapter of Hosea for complementary expressions of God's grace[3]; 'And I will betroth thee unto me for ever; yea, I will betroth thee unto me in righteousness, and in judgment, and in *loving-kindness*, and in mercies.

'I will even betroth thee unto me in faithfulness: and thou shalt *know* the Lord.' (ii. 19, 20.)

The dew moreover (vi. 4) most fitly represents that divine grace, which had already been compared with 'the latter and former rain,' and is now likened, for transitoriness, 'to the early dew that goeth away.' The first comparison is tacitly approved, but the emphasis is on the supplementary consideration of evanescence. I will indeed be as the dew to Israel (xiv. 5); as the early dew that goeth away. The same figure is used in xiii. 3, of the destruction of idolaters; 'Therefore shall they be as the morning cloud, and as the early dew that passeth away:' and if a similarity of application, here and in vi. 4, be

---

[1] See Note 6, p. 15.   [2] Pococke on Hosea vi. 3.
[3] Stier on Matt. ix. 15—17. See also Note 7, p. 15.

presupposed, an argument, not indeed to be pressed, arises, for understanding the 'mercy,' in the latter passage, of transitory *opportunities*. 'So as that they were passive, not active, therein, and that mercy from God to them was by their fault hindered, and removed, and made ineffectual, as a morning cloud or dew dispelled or dried up by the sun endureth not.'

The three passages which predicate God's preference of mercy to sacrifice having now been considered separately, it has been seen that there are reasons for concluding that in each case the mercy is that which He would show to man, not that which He requires from man. There is, however, no necessity for concluding *a priori* that if this be the true interpretation in one case it must be so in the remaining two: for if God wills mercy absolutely, He will both act mercifully and regard with favour such human mercy as is the reflection of His own attribute. From either of these applications, through the intervention of the general principle, might well have been deduced the other.

NOTES ON CHAPTER I.

[1] 'In that last verse of the fifth chapter God saith, In their affliction יְשַׁחֲרֻנְנִי, *they will seek me early*, or, *in the morning;* and here they say His coming forth to them shall be prepared בְּשַׁחַר, *as the morning*, which well allude one to the other. They shall seek for Him as they that seek or desire the coming of the morning, and He will come to them as the morning, as certainly and as readily as the morning.' (Pococke.)

[2] לְךָ *to* thee for thy good, as in Is. v. 4, 'What could have been done more *to* my vineyard (לְכַרְמִי)?'

[3] Stier notes a parallelism between *your* mercy and *thy* judgments, both of the possessive affixes being taken objectively.

[4] This construction of חָצַבְתִּי with the following בְּ had occurred

as worthy of *consideration*, and been applied as in text, before the writer had discovered that there was authority for adopting it. The LXX read in like manner, ἀπεθέρισα τοὺς προφήτας ὑμῶν.

Pococke commends the exposition that to smite and slay by the prophets was to denounce judgment and destruction by them as messengers: 'yet because there are others backed with great authority both by Jews and Christians, it may not be inconvenient to give some account thereof; and that is of such who either taking no other notice of the preposition בְּ than as serving only to the construction of the verb without signifying anything, render it, *I have hewed the prophets and slain them by the words of my mouth;* or else so as to denote *in* or *among*, i. e. *some of* or *among* the prophets (קְצָת הַנְּבִיאִים, Aben Ezra); and so look not on the people but on the prophets as those whom he saith he had hewed; and those, either the true prophets, as some will (Kimchi), *viz.* to signifie that he had put them to much trouble and labour in sending them to call upon them again and again, and that he had by so incessantly imploying them even worn them out to death, yea, more than so, might be said really to have slain them, according to the known examples of Zachariah and Uriah, with others. Such may he be said to have slain by the words of his mouth, because they died for those words: or else, secondly, the false prophets, as others will, that so the meaning should be that it might not be to them for a pretence in their evil doings, that therefore he had cut off from among them those false guides, whom, saith Aben Ezra, because they had lied, and spake the words of their own mouth, God saith that he slew with the words of his mouth, if so be the Israelites would be converted, and not be any more seduced by such.'

The preposition בְּ may be used after verbs of striking, to denote the object or thing struck. The niphal of חָצַב is thus construed in Job xix. 24, Would that my words בַּצּוּר יֵחָצְבוּן, *might be graven into the rock;* and אִישׁ חֹצֵב בָּהָר (2 Chron. ii. 1) should perhaps be rendered quarrymen, literally, *hewers into* the mountain.

With few exceptions חָצַב is followed by a simple accusative, and means to *form by hewing* rather than to smite destructively. The latter meaning may perhaps be appropriated to חָצַב construed with בְּ.

If the smiting be *by* the prophets, it may still be by way of warning, and the interpretation of חֶסֶד (vi. 6) as God's mercy may be retained.

⁵ וּמִשְׁפָּטַי אוֹר יֵצֵא. The verb agrees with the singular 'light' by attraction. Another rendering is possible. 'All means have been tried to warn thee, *seeing that thy judgments shall go forth light:*' where the impending judgments are compared with the full, enduring day, in contradistinction to the grace which being neglected was so soon to be lost; 'seeing that your mercy is as the morning cloud, and as the early dew that goeth away.'

⁶ Dean Alford, commenting on the parallel passage in Luke xi. 49—51 (Διὰ τοῦτο καὶ ἡ σοφία τοῦ Θεοῦ εἶπεν......ἐκζητηθήσεται ἀπὸ τῆς γενεᾶς ταύτης) remarks that 'the whole saying is a reference to 2 Chron. xxiv. 18—22. The words in our text are not indeed a *citation*, but an amplification of ver. 19 there—a paraphrase of them,—giving the true sense of what the wisdom of God intended by them.' The word ἐκζητηθήσεται refers to the יִדְרֹשׁ of the original: 'The Lord look upon it and *require* it.' The LXX have, less exactly, κρινάτω.

The same commentator would thus account for the occurrence of υἱοῦ Βαραχίου in St Matthew's Gospel. It 'does not occur in Luke xi. 51, and perhaps was not uttered by the Lord Himself, but may have been inserted by mistake, as *Zacharias the prophet* was son of Barachiah. See Zech. i. 1.'

⁷ The declaration ἔλεος θέλω...καὶ ἐπίγνωσιν Θεοῦ may be paraphrased in St Paul's words πάντας ἀνθρώπους θέλει σωθῆναι καὶ εἰς ἐπίγνωσιν ἀληθείας ἐλθεῖν. 1 Tim. ii. 4.

In His application of θυσία our Lord has been supposed to have regard to the ultimate significance of sacrificial offerings. Compare the use of *baptism*. Luke xii. 50.

CHAPTER II.

David himself calleth Him Lord.

Matt. xxii. 44; Mark xii. 36; Luke xx. 42; Ps. cx. 1.

THERE is a passage of Ezekiel which may be applied to remove the indefiniteness still clinging to some portions of the hundred and tenth Psalm; and less directly, to indicate the substratum of its imagery in the clause which has given occasion for perhaps the greatest divergence in critical exegesis and application, 'The dew of thy birth is of the womb of the morning.'

But first what is meant by that *rod of thy power* which the Lord should send out of Sion; and by the concluding verse, 'He shall drink of the brook by the way: therefore shall he lift up his head?'

The phrase 'rod of thy power' assumes at once that definiteness which at first it seems to lack, if the royal object of Jehovah's care be conceived of as a vine that *sends out* its boughs unto the sea and its branches unto the river; or as a stately tree planted by the water-side, whose leaf shall not wither, and 'whatsoever he doeth it shall prosper.' (Ps. lxxx. 11; i. 3.)

This *rod of power*[1] is then primarily a strong healthy shoot, but not to the exclusion of the meaning sceptre; for in

---

[1] An attempt should be made to preserve the double reference. Perhaps some such rendering as the subjoined might express it: 'The Lord make the sceptre of thy might to branch forth from Zion.'

David himself calleth Him Lord.

Hebrew a word or phrase may be used not merely to convey its own proper and most obvious meaning, but at the same time more or less plainly to give intimation of a second. In the present case this idiom is well illustrated by the subjoined passage from Ezekiel, wherein the same phrase[1] is used expressly with this double meaning;

'Thy mother is like a vine planted by the waters: she was fruitful and full of branches by reason of many waters.

'And she had *strong rods* for the sceptres of them that bare rule, and her stature was exalted among the thick branches, and she appeared in height with the multitude of her branches.

'But she was plucked up in fury: her strong rods were broken and withered; the fire consumed them.

'And now she is planted in the wilderness, in a dry and thirsty ground.

'And fire is gone out of a rod of her branches, which hath devoured her fruit, so that she hath no strong rod to be a sceptre to rule' (xix. 10—14).

As this vine was fruitful and full of branches, and her stature was exalted, by reason of many waters; so the tree in the Psalm was to be developed by an exuberance of moisture; it should drink of the brook by the way, and so flourish, and lift up its head on high[2].

The same image suggests an interpretation of the difficult third verse:

עַמְּךָ נְדָבֹת בְּיוֹם חֵילֶךָ ׃
בְּהַדְרֵי קֹדֶשׁ מֵרֶחֶם מִשְׁחָר
לְךָ טַל יַלְדֻתֶךָ

The royal priest is depicted as on the day of the marshal-

---

[1] מַטֵּה עֹז, strong rod, lit. rod of power.

[2] רֹאשׁ may be the top of *anything*, e.g. of the tower of Babel (Gen. xi. 4).

[3] 'In the day of thy power:' i.e. of the mustering of thy *forces.* חֵילֶךָ, is in parallelism with יַלְדֻתֶךָ, thy youth (an abstract noun to be understood concretely).

ling of his host. His people are a free rain¹ that comes copious and unbidden. 'In saintly glories' his youth around outshine the dew that glistens upon the herbage in the rising sun. He himself, the tree, is besprinkled with them as with the rain and dewdrops, which are, here and elsewhere, emblematic of lasting freshness and prosperity. Thus: 'My root was spread out by the waters, and the dew lay all night upon my branch. My glory was fresh in me, and my bow was renewed in my hand.' (Job xxix. 19, 20.)

The whole Psalm consists of a divine effatum alternating with utterances which are appropriated by the sacred writer. It is the latter who dwells expressly on the vision of slaughter; while to suppose that Jehovah again breaks silence in the last verse seems to add to the sublimity of the peaceful conclusion².

I. That Davidic authorship is claimed for the Psalm is allowed to be among the first and most natural inferences from our Lord's argumentative citation of its first verse. Is the balance of testimony in favour of this conclusion, or does it drive us to reconsider the justice of our inference?

The Psalm may well have been written from amid the glory and prosperity of David's reign, and there is a lack of internal evidence for a later date. Its age is limited in the other direction by a local allusion, from which it has even been inferred, and with some probability, that the occupation of Zion was still fresh in the memory of the writer. Thus much being granted, it would remain to consider whether the Psalm could have been spoken of David, and whether David could have spoken it. He could not have answered truly to the aspirations of the psalmist, whose praises if ascribed to

---

¹ נרבת parallel with טל. Compare נשם נדבות, Ps. lxviii. 10; בהתנדב עם, Jud. v. 2. See Mendelssohn's rendering, quoted by Phillips.

There is doubtless an allusion to their multiplicity as well as to the splendour of their array. Another comparison of a host to dew is supplied by Hushai's advice to Absalom, viz. 'that with his forces he should light upon David like the dew, and so surprise and overwhelm him.' 1 Sam. xvii. 12.

² See Note A, p. 26.

him would have been not merely hyperbolical in degree, but strange in kind; for there is force in the objection that priesthood, not to say eternal priesthood, could not have been predicated of David, while but slight evidence has been adduced for an opposite conclusion. He is said indeed to have offered burnt-offerings and peace-offerings on the procession of the ark to the tabernacle (2 Sam. vi. 13, 17), but in no other sense it would seem than did *all the congregation of Israel* that were assembled unto king Solomon before the ark (1 Kings viii. 5, 62—64). Such expressions do not necessarily exclude the ministrations of the regular priesthood, no more in fact, than Solomon's own building of the temple (ver. 19) was to exclude the intervention of artificers. Saul sinned in taking upon himself a priestly function, and on David devolved *the same office* as on his predecessor. 'And Saul said, Because I saw that thou camest not within the time appointed, I forced myself therefore, and offered a burnt-offering. And Samuel said to Saul, Thou hast done foolishly: thou hast not kept the commandment of the Lord thy God, which he commanded thee: for now would the Lord have established thy kingdom upon Israel for ever. But now thy kingdom shall not continue: the Lord hath sought him a man after his own heart, and the Lord hath commanded him to be captain over his people, because thou hast not kept that which the Lord commanded thee' (1 Sam. xiii. 11—13).

Whilst the king might not usurp this most characteristic of sacerdotal functions, it seems unnatural that there should be attributed to him another and a higher priestly office. If so the Psalm can contain no mere address to David personally[1]. But can he, on the other hand, be conceived of as appropriating the utterances of the Psalm?

As a first, and that no extravagant postulate, it would have to be laid down, that David must be admitted to have embraced a more or less clear Messianic hope; having its starting point in the trust that his house would continue for ever before the Lord: 'For thou, O Lord God, hast spoken it:

[1] See Note B, p. 26.

and with thy blessing let the house of thy servant be blessed for ever' (2 Sam. vii. 29), and finding a loftier expression in his obscure 'last words,' which reflect so truly the unique imagery of the Psalm.

The *last words* (2 Sam. xxiii. 1—7) and the Psalm are oracular declarations[1], the latter of Jehovah, the former 'of David the son of Jesse, the man who was raised up on high, the anointed of the God of Jacob, the sweet psalmist of Israel.' Both alike refer their origin to the supreme source: 'The Lord said;' 'The Spirit of the Lord spake by me, and His word was on my tongue.' Both enounce an immutable decree; 'He hath made with me an everlasting covenant, ordered in all things and sure;' 'The Lord hath sworn and will not repent, Thou art a priest for ever, after the order of Melchizedek.' The God of Israel had promised him a righteous Ruler, the Rock of Israel had spoken. Like morning's light should He, the Sun, arise; nay in greater splendour than raindrops glistering at sunrise on the grass[2]; more glorious than the dew from the womb of dawn[3].

Thus far we may not unnaturally think of David as the author of the Psalm. Nor would it be hard to account conjecturally for its most distinctive feature still remaining—the allusion viz. to Melchizedek.

Some have thought, for example, that in the bringing up of the ark to the tabernacle which he had prepared for it on Mount Zion, we must look 'for the secret impulse of David's song;' and that when he offered burnt-offerings and peace-offerings and blessed the people in the name of the Lord, he 'thus, though but in a passing and temporary manner, prefigured in his own person the union of the kingly and priestly offices.' The solemnities of such a time may have revived the august traditions of the site, and 'thus have helped David to understand how the true Ruler, Priest as well as King, should be Priest not after the ancient and venerable

---

[1] נְאֻם. [2] מֵרֶחֶם מִשְׁחָר. Ps. cx. 3. Supply טַל before רֶחֶם.
[3] מִנֹּגַהּ מִמָּטָר דֶּשֶׁא מֵאָרֶץ. 2 Sam. xxiii. 4.

order of Aaron, but after the order still more ancient and venerable of Melchizedek.' If however David 'offered' not in person but mediately, can he be said to have prefigured any joint discharge of regal and sacerdotal functions? In contrast with his own disabilities, rather than by way of comparison, he may have described the transcendant dignity of One to come.

II. David's twofold relation to the Messiah involves a difficulty which Christ thus propounds to his already baffled assailants.

'What think ye of Christ? whose Son is He? They say unto him, The Son of David. He saith unto them, How then doth David in Spirit call Him Lord, saying, The Lord said unto my Lord, Sit thou on my right hand, till I make thine enemies thy footstool? If David then call Him Lord, how is He his Son?' (Matt. xxii. 42—45.)

The very natural inference that our Lord here introduces David as the actual speaker is not indeed invalidated by the hypothetical form of St Matthew's statement, but neither is it established by the *prima facie* directness of the parallel passages in SS. Mark and Luke (xii. 36, 37; xx. 41—44). If then the Davidic authorship be not directly affirmed, the implied sanction claimed for any theory on such a point must be evolved from the exigencies of the argument.

That King David in the Psalm addresses the Christ as Lord must have been granted by Christ's adversaries as undeniable; for how else could their silence be interpreted? But it has been doubted whether Christ himself does more than argue on the received hypothesis, and thus dismiss them with a more embarrassing dilemma than their utmost ingenuity had contrived for Him. We may deny, with Neander, that it would consist with the dignity of Christ to put questions with no higher aim than this; but that such an aim might well find place is made clear by a conspicuous example: 'And Jesus answered and said unto them, I also will ask you one thing, which if ye tell me, I in like manner will tell you by what authority I do these things. The baptism of John, whence was it? from heaven or of men? And they reasoned with themselves, saying, If we shall say, From heaven; he will say unto us, Why did ye not then believe him? But if we shall say, Of men; we fear the people; for all hold John as a prophet. And they answered Jesus, and said, We cannot tell. And he said unto them, Neither tell I you by what authority I do these things' (Matt. xxi. 24—27).

With the question about John's baptism He was thus pleased to silence His opponents; and with like intent the question of the Messiah's lordship may have been propounded. Had His sole purpose been to silence gainsayers, our Lord's authority could not be claimed for the Davidic authorship. *They* even might be supposed to have harboured doubts upon the point which they were unwilling to discuss before the multitude. The last-mentioned hypothesis is made incredible by external testimony; but the exact nature of their difficulty is obscured by its very magnitude, which precluded all attempts to grapple with and overcome it: for 'no man was able to answer him a word, neither durst any man from that day forth ask him any more questions.'

The view that the authorship of the Psalm is left undetermined, although Christ looked far beyond the captious criticism of the moment, is a view that finds an advocate in the above-named commentator:

'Even though it be proved that David was not the author of the Psalm quoted, Christ's argument is not invalidated thereby. Its principal point is precisely that of the Psalm; the idea of the theocratic King, King and Priest at once, the one founded upon the other, raised up to God, and looking with calm assurance for the end of the conflict with His foes, and the triumphant establishment of His kingdom. This idea could never be realized in any *man;* it was a prophecy of Christ, and in Him it was fulfilled. This idea went forth necessarily from the spirit of the old dispensation and from the organic connexion of events in the old theocracy; it was the blossom of a history and a religion that were, in their very essence, prophetical. In this regard it is matter of no moment whether David uttered the Psalm or not. History and interpretation perhaps may show that he did not. But whether it was a conscious prediction of the royal poet, or whether some other, in poetic but holy inspiration, seized upon this idea, the natural blossom and off-shoot of Judaism, and assigned it to an earthly monarch, although in its true sense it could never take shape and form in such a one—still it was *the* idea by which the Spirit, of which the inspired seer, whoever he may have been, was but the organ, pointed to Jesus. The only difference is that between conscious and unconscious prophecy. And if Christ really named David as the author of the Psalm, we are not reduced to the alternative of detracting from His infallibility and unconditional truthfulness, or else of admitting that David really wrote it. The question of the authorship was immaterial to His purpose; it was no part of His Divine calling to enter into such investigations; His teachings and His revelations lay in a very different sphere.'

Such is the opinion of Neander, who holds that the ascription to David is without significance: that Christ used the common title of the Psalm as 'the one to which His hearers were accustomed.' But if the Messiah's true dignity be deduced in the Gospel from His relation of superiority to David, it is far from obvious that the allusions to King David may be classed with things indifferent. Moreover, it is not certain that our Lord's aim is 'precisely that of the Psalm:' to present viz. as a portraiture of the Messiah what 'could never be realized in any man.'

Some thought one-sidedly of the Christ as 'the Son of David.' Others looked for such a predominance of the supernatural as was incompatible with the conditions of humanity; and against the latter it may have been no less his purpose to assert his claim to Messiahship, which they were indisposed to grant: 'We know this man whence he is: but when Christ cometh no man knoweth whence he is.' (Joh. vii. 27.)

It seems best to conclude that He purposed simultaneously to embarrass His opponents and to combine the current half-views of Christ in one harmonious whole. In so doing He goes beyond the scope of the Psalm, and assumes on other grounds that the Christ is David's Son. To perplex His opponents it was enough to assume, without sanctioning, their premises; but for His other purpose the authorship would seem to be a matter of no slight importance. Christ was David's Lord, and therefore higher than the highest of human kind. And, again, how can Christ be David's Lord and yet his Son? The argument would fail unless Christ be proved thus superior to *David*, and for the direct proof of His superiority it is essential that the words cited should have been used by David[1].

III. A Messianic reference is assumed in Heb. i. 13, where the Psalm is quoted as containing a direct address of Jehovah to Christ, and thus establishing His precedence of the angelic hierarchy: 'But to which of the angels said He at any time, Sit on my right hand, until I make thine enemies thy footstool? Are they not all ministering spirits, sent forth to minister for them who shall be heirs of salvation?' The same original has lent its form to the declaration in 1 Cor. xv. 25, that 'Christ must reign till He hath put all enemies under His feet,' although it is another Scripture (Psalm viii. 6) that is referred to for a direct authorization of the statement. In Heb. x. 12, 13, the finality of Christ's sacrifice is gathered from His undisturbed session at the right hand of God: 'But this man, after he had offered one sacrifice for sins, for ever sat down on the right hand of God. From henceforth expecting till His enemies be made His footstool.' In Acts ii. 34, 35, St Peter cites the first verse of this Psalm at length, and makes the argument depend upon David's express admission that the Messiah's exaltation is superior to his own. 'For David is not ascended into the heavens: but he saith himself, The Lord said unto my Lord, Sit thou on my right

[1] See Note C, p. 26.

hand, until I make thy foes thy footstool.' St Peter stamps the Psalm as a prophetic utterance of David. Such is the reader's first impression; and it increases the difficulty of explaining it away to note as a characteristic of St Peter's method, that he presents to the Jews his hearers, 'rather the facts than the doctrines of the new dispensation; and insists not so much on the miraculous nature of those facts, as on their agreement with what he elsewhere calls the *more sure word of prophecy*' (2 Pet. i. 19); for in proportion to the logical effectiveness of an illustration is the strictness with which the words that introduce it are to be interpreted.

The fourth verse is quoted in Heb. vii. 21—28, where the superiority of Christ's priesthood to the Levitical is argued from the greater solemnity of His inauguration: 'For those priests were made without an oath; but this with an oath by him that said unto him, The Lord sware and will not repent, Thou art a priest for ever after the order of Melchisedec;' and again from the unchangeableness of His office, for 'this man, because he continueth ever, hath an unchangeable priesthood....For the law maketh men high priests which have infirmity: but the word of the oath, which was since the law, maketh the Son, who is consecrated for evermore.' Christ's superseding of the Aaronic order was in harmony with the divine purpose; for that order was but appointed for a time, and as 'no man taketh this honour unto himself, but he that is called of God, as was Aaron. So also Christ glorified not himself to be made an high priest;' but He who in the hundred and tenth Psalm thus addresses Him[1], 'Thou art a priest for ever after the order of Melchisedec.' (Heb. v. 5, 6.)

The meeting of Abraham and Melchizedek (Gen. xiv. 17—20) is referred to at the commencement of Heb. vii., and from the transactions of the occasion the typical preeminence of the latter is deduced. He blessed Abraham: to him Abraham, and Levi by implication, gave tithes of all: He was King of righteousness and King of peace: without

[1] See Note D, p. 27.

father, without mother, without descent, having neither beginning of days, nor end of life; but, made like unto the Son of God, he abideth a priest continually.

On the significance of his being without genealogy (ἀγενεαλόγητος), it may be remarked, that a certain mysteriousness is here claimed for Christ, the lack of which is declared, in a passage already quoted, to be fatal to His claims to the Messiahship. That 'when Christ cometh no man knoweth whence he is,' was one element in a popular conception of His advent; but whether the writer here originates a corroborative inference or stamps with his approval a familiar argument, is a question which we must still leave undetermined.

NOTES ON CHAPTER II.

A. Other renderings leave the king toiling wearily after his enemies; 'and in order to keep up his strength till he had fully accomplished his purpose, he quenches his thirst from the brook, as occasion may require.' (Phillips.)

Compare the description cited from Grotius by Rosenmüller:

... qui dum hostes persequitur, non quærit diversoria ut vino se refoveat, sed aqua contentus est, quam obiter et raptim sumit ex quovis, quem reperit, non fluvio tantum, sed et torrente.

B. David might be addressed as priest *representatively*, if the Psalm were mediately Messianic. Compare Bishop Horsley's note on Psalm xvi. 'The whole is uttered *in the character of the High-priest*. But with what propriety could David speak in that character, otherwise than prophetically; in the hope of that priesthood which was to come into his family, in the person of his descendant?'

C. David might thus have used the words even if they had been addressed in the first instance to himself. Nor would there be anything unnatural in such a transference, if the Psalm be supposed to have been composed with a Messianic reference, and to have borrowed its form only from the circumstances of David.

To complete the cycle of hypothesis it may be added, in the words of Bishop Horsley, that of the Psalms 'the far greater part are a sort of dramatic ode, consisting of dialogues between persons sustaining certain characters;' and that the hundred and tenth Psalm may be a composition of some unknown inspired writer, who attributes the Psalm in general to David, in the same way that the Psalm attributes certain declarations to Jehovah. David's relation of inferiority to the Messiah is thus portrayed, and the argument in the Gospel may be supposed to assume that the words of the citation were by the Holy Spirit thus *put into the mouth of David*.

Interpretations which stop short with David or any temporal sovereign are excluded by considerations advanced in the text. The simplest solution is afforded by that interpretation which makes the words strictly David's. For the general question of Messianic reference, see *Introduction*.

D. An intervening reference to the second Psalm has been omitted: 'So also Christ glorified not himself to be made an Highpriest; but he that said unto Him, *Thou art my Son, to-day have I begotten thee.* As he saith also in another place, Thou art a Priest for ever after the order of Melchisedec.' Compare the subjoined extract from Dean Alford's commentary :—

'It must be carefully observed that the writer does not adduce this text (Ps. ii. 7) as containing a direct proof of Christ's divine appointment to the High priesthood: that follows in the next verse: nor again does it merely assert without any close connexion that the same divine Person appointed Him High-priest, who said to Him, *Thou art my Son:* but it asserts that such divine appointment was wrapped up and already involved in that eternal generation to the Sonship which was declared in these words.'

CHAPTER III.

The Prophecy of Immanuel.

Isaiah vii. 14; Matth. i. 23.

IT is a perplexing task to assign the exact relation of the prophecy of Immanuel to contemporary history; for that history has to be constructed from scattered notices wherein points of resemblance are so intermixed with points of difference, that commentators have not yet agreed whether to appropriate some of the most closely corresponding portions of the narrative to consecutive or to simultaneous events. We may, with some, regard the narrative of 2 Chron. xxviii. 5 as identical in its subject matter with the record of the second book of Kings (ch. xvi.): or we may see pictured to us in the latter a combined action of Rezin king of Syria, and Pekah son of Remaliah king of Israel; and in the former, distinct and independent inroads of the Israelite and Syrian monarchs. Perhaps the fact that either history claims to be supplemented by the other (2 Kings xvi. 19; 2 Chr. xxviii. 26), and the brief allusion (2 Kings xv. 37) to a commencement of Judah's troubles in the preceding reign, may suffice to establish at least a slight presumption that something more than one solitary onslaught may have taken place in the reign of Ahaz. But amid the overwhelming difficulties that beset the exact apportionment of times and seasons, it may be possible and sufficient to grasp somewhat of the circumstantial appropriateness of the prophecy, though we abandon the hope of assigning accurately the temporal order of events.

The youthful king was one that 'walked in the ways of the kings of Israel, and made also molten images for Baalim. Moreover he burnt incense in the valley of the son of Hinnom, and burnt his children in the fire. He sacrificed also and burnt incense in the high places, and on the hills, and under every green tree. Wherefore the Lord his God delivered him into the hand of the king of Syria. And he was also delivered into the hand of the king of Israel, who smote him with a great slaughter' (2 Chron. xxviii. 1—5). A knowledge of the way in which king and people bore themselves beneath the calamities that had come upon them, will be regarded as no unnecessary prelude to the right understanding of Isaiah's words: if at least it be assumed that each prophetic announcement was adapted to the circumstances of those to whom it was delivered.

The prophet, speaking as it seems of the collective Holy Land, records (ix. 13) that the people turned not to Him that smote them, neither would they seek the Lord of hosts; and he looks forward to the time when 'the remnant of Israel, and such as are escaped of the house of Jacob,' should 'no more again stay upon him that smote them' (only as an instrument), but should 'stay upon the Lord, the Holy One of Israel, in truth' (x. 20). The history, which had declared the troubles of Ahaz to be a retribution for his evil practices, states also that 'in the time of his distress did he trespass yet more against the Lord. For he sacrificed unto the gods of Damascus which smote him: and he said, Because the gods of the kings of Syria help them, therefore will I sacrifice to them, that they may help me' (2 Chron. xxviii. 22, 23). It can scarcely be imagined that Ahaz was first drawn to worship the Syrian idols (2 Kings xvi. 10) when they had been found powerless to protect 'the riches of Damascus.' It is more probable that, before obtaining assistance from Tiglath-pileser, he had striven to make his peace with them, and so by their help to escape the evils that he feared. He

run with thorns and briers, and used for hunting grounds. The choicest vineyards—on 'all hills that are cleared with the mattock, that no fear of briers and thorns should thither come'—shall be 'a place for the sending forth of oxen, and for the treading of lesser cattle' (vii. 17—25).

III. The difficulties that beset the interpretation of the expression *the land* (ver. 16) will in great part vanish if regard be had to the logical sequence of the clauses. Immanuel, it is said, shall be fed in his infancy with butter and with honey, *because* 'the land' shall be left desolate, and so yield butter and honey in abundance. Butter and honey shall he eat; *for* the land shall be desolate. 'The land' must therefore be that of Immanuel, for otherwise its devastation could scarcely be thus described in connection with the infant's fare.

It might at first be thought that this land of Immanuel is defined by the parallelism in viii. 8 to be the land of Judah: but this inference is not very obviously necessary. The arrangement may express a climax. He shall *pass through* Judah; he shall overflow and *go over;* till the stretching out of his wings shall fill the full breadth of the collective Israel, 'Thy land, O Immanuel.' And even if the two clauses be strictly parallel, rather than in a manner consecutive, it still does not follow that Immanuel's land is to be restricted to Judah proper. This *Judah* may, on the contrary, represent the whole land of '*Israel,*' of which it forms a part; and it is, in any case, as well suited to stand in parallelism with the collective Israel, as is the last clause of viii. 14, '...for a gin and for a snare to *the inhabitants of Jerusalem;*' to stand as it does in parallelism with the more broadly expressed declaration which precedes, 'And he shall be for a sanctuary; but for a stone of stumbling and for a rock of offence to *both the houses of Israel.*'

As the answer of Ahaz was fair-seeming, so was it with the prophecy. A land 'flowing with milk and honey' was the 'glory of all lands' (Ezek. xx. 6). The image was not one that would suggest in the first instance desolation. But the birth of the infant whose name should be called 'Wonderful, Counseller, the mighty God, the everlasting Father, the Prince of Peace,' was most strangely to be the signal for the depopulation of his realm. Milk and honey were to be the produce of its ruined villages. And though, late in time, a remnant should return (x. 21), and the throne of David be set up for ever (ix. 7), yet the distant restitution could give no comfort to the unbelieving king. Some indeed, dwelling on prospective laudations of the land of promise, as a land which flowed spontaneously with milk and honey, have imagined that in ver. 22 one ray of light shoots suddenly across the dark picture. But a return in aftertime to its natural condition involves a devastation of the land.

We are accustomed, it may be added, to regard Israel and Judah as rival states: but with prophets and apostles, and sometimes even with historians, the 'Israel of God' (Gal. vi. 16) is a sacred name that unites the scattered and divided family. Isaiah speaks of Israel as a whole, including within itself two factions. The names of Ephraim, Zebulun, Naphtali, are cast aside, and he speaks, as we have seen, of One that shall be 'a stone of stumbling and a rock of offence to *both the houses of Israel*' (viii. 14). Such language has its counterpart in 2 Chron. xxviii. 19, where it is written, 'For the Lord brought Judah low because of Ahaz king of *Israel*, for he made Judah naked, and transgressed sore against the Lord.' The prophet predicts (vii. 16) a common ruin; and foresees a common restoration of the tribes. 'Ephraim shall not envy Judah, and Judah shall not vex Ephraim;' but one Branch from the worn out stem shall shelter all; and 'shall stand for an ensign of the people; and His rest shall be glorious' (xi. 10, 13).

IV. *Is the prophecy of Immanuel Messianic?*

The prophecy itself describes certain events that are to take place in connexion with Immanuel's birth, and growth

---

[1] *Lacte et melle vesci*, Jes. vii. 15, 22: de his qui terram habitant ab hostibus vastatam, agri frugibus carentes.—Gesen. *Thesaur.* 486 a.

to years of discretion. His nature and office, except so far as they are symbolized by the name itself, are to be gathered from other passages wherein mention is made of Him.

To pass by for a time the descriptive titles of ix. 6, we may gather something of His transcendant dignity from the general terms in which the restoration is described.

As the former season humbled[1] Zebulun *to the ground;* and Naphtali *to the ground;* so the after time hath glorified[2] them. That whole sea-lying tract, once humbled, is made glorious. The power of the great deliverer is felt far and wide: 'Beyond Jordan, in Galilee of the nations. The people that walked in darkness have seen a great light; they that dwell in the land of the shadow of death, upon them hath the light shined.' Thou hast multiplied the nation, whose[3] joy Thou hadst minished: they have waxed joyous as with men's joy in harvest; as they rejoice when they divide the spoil. 'For thou hast broken the yoke of his burden, and the staff of his shoulder, the rod of his oppressor, as in the day of Midian.' All the military gear[4] and blood-reeking garments shall be food for flames. 'For unto us a child is born, unto us a son is given: and the government shall be upon His shoulder: and His name shall be called, *wonderful Counsellor, mighty God, Father of eternity, Prince of peace.* Of the increase of His government and peace there shall be no end, upon the throne of David, and upon His kingdom, to order it, and to establish it with judgement and with justice, from henceforth even for ever. The zeal of the Lord of hosts will perform this.' (ix. 1—7).

The titles of ver. 6 demand special notice. The parallelism suggests the propriety of connecting the words *wonderful* and *Counsellor,* as the LXX. have done. The words would mean literally, *marvel of a counsellor.* The collocation is borne out by an expression in xxviii. 29: 'This also cometh

---

[1] Lit. *made light,* i. e. *despicable.* Not 'lightly afflicted.'
[2] Lit. *made weighty.* Not 'did more grievously afflict.' See 2 Cor. iv. 17.
[3] See note E, p. 48.
[4] LXX. πᾶσαν στολήν.

The Prophecy of Immanuel.

from the LORD of hosts, which *is wonderful in counsel*[1], and excellent in working.' Others, as Delitzsch, prefer to regard the two words in question as separate titles: *Mystery, Counsellor.* Even as the angel, when asked by Manoah, 'What is thy name,' replied 'Why askest thou thus after my name, seeing it is Secret?' (Jud. xiii. 18)—indicating thereby His divine nature; a nature incomprehensible to mortal man—'so here the God-given Ruler is also *Secret*, a phenomenon lying altogether beyond human conception or natural occurrence. Not only is this or that wonderful in Him; but Himself is throughout a wonder—$\pi\alpha\rho\alpha\delta o\xi\alpha\sigma\mu\acute{o}s$, as Symmachus renders it.'

Of the remaining titles, the first is defined by its recurrence in x. 21. 'The remnant shall return, even the remnant of Jacob, unto *the mighty God.*' The second, *Father of eternity*, in any case declares eternity to be an attribute of Immanuel; and it has been compared with such expressions as 'Father of all mercies.' Some stop short at this meaning, and make the phrase equivalent to, *possessor of eternity*. Others, as Luther, expound it of One 'Who at all times feeds His kingdom and church, in whom there is a fatherly love[2] without end.' *The latter view*, adds Hengstenberg, *is to be preferred unconditionally*. The last title declares the great aim of His mission; announcing Him as *Prince* and independent Giver of the divine gift, peace[3] (Ps. xxix. 11; cxlvii. 14).

IV. The ascription of royalty to Immanuel would, of itself, justify the rejection of all non-Messianic interpretations that have been propounded; with one exception, which we proceed to consider.

It is demonstrable *by clear proofs*[4], writes Kimchi, that Immanuel is not *Hezekiah.*

---

[1] הפליא עצה.

[2] And he shall be a father to the inhabitants of Jerusalem, and to the house of Judah.—Is. xxii. 21.

[3] Hengstenberg, *Christology*, I. 84, would make Shiloh mean (etymologically) this same *Peaceful One.*

[4] בראיות ברורות. *Sepher Shorashim*, under the root עלם. Kimchi thinks that Immanuel may be some other son of Ahaz. But why was Hezekiah to be *superseded?*

To pass over the improbability of Isaiah's alluding to the queen as *the almah*[1], it is to be noted that the prophecy is expressed in terms which exclude a reference to the past. The birth of Immanuel was still in the future. Whether in the immediate, or in the far distant (though prophetically present) future, is a point on which interpreters might differ; but the terms of the prophecy exclude the past; and exclude therefore the identification of Immanuel with Hezekiah, who was already born. For 'that these words were spoken whilst Ahaz was king, is evident from the text, and owned by the Jews. Now Ahaz reigned but sixteen years; and Hezekias, his son and successor, was twenty-and-five years old when he began to reign; and therefore must be born several years before Ahaz was king, and consequently before these words were spoken[2].' We must therefore reject the application to Hezekiah, which is the best supported of all the non-Messianic applications.

VI. The state of the argument is then as follows.

1. In favour of the exclusively Messianic interpretation, we have the titles and general terms by which Immanuel is described; for these are such as would be extravagant and non-natural, if applied to any other than the Messiah. This view is confirmed, directly, by a strong current of tradition; and still more by the admissions of those who, while contending for other interpretations, are constrained to find room for a further Messianic reference. Some hold that no Messiah is still to be expected, because Israel *has already enjoyed Him in the days of Hezekiah*. 'He himself, it was said,' believed the prophecy to refer to him, and 'with the expectation of immortality thus engendered, took no care to marry or secure the succession till startled by his alarming illness[3].' Such a belief involves two distinct propositions; as a learned writer

---

[1] The propriety of the LXX rendering ἡ παρθένος will be discussed in the Appendix.

[2] Kidder's *Demonstration of the Messias*, II. 313.

[3] Stanley, *Lectures on the Jewish Church*, II. 462.

has well remarked. For the first ; viz. that Isaiah's prophecy was delivered *with a distinct Messianic reference;* we might claim the authority of Hillel, and if it should so chance, of Hezekiah himself: but whether the prophecy was fulfilled in Hezekiah is a point which would still remain to be decided. 'It is a known saying of Hillel, recorded in *Sanhedrin* c. Chelek, that *There is no Messias to the Israelites, because they have already enjoyed Him in the days of Hezekiah.* Divers of the later Rabbins endeavour to mollify these words of Hillel by their several expositions, but in vain. And R. Joseph understood him better, who thought he took away all expectations of a Messias, and therefore fairly prayed for him, *Condonet Dominus hoc R. Hillel.* Howsoever, it appears that from two principles, whereof one was false, he gathered that false conclusion. For first, he thought those words in Isaiah were spoken of the Messias: which proposition was true. Secondly, he conceived that those words were spoken of Hezekiah, and fulfilled in him, which proposition was false. From hence he inferred that the Israelites were not to expect a Messias after Hezekiah: which conclusion was also false[1].'

2. Against the Messianic interpretation, there is one argument that has been urged with much plausibility. There is indeed no *specific* solution in contemporary history on which non-Messianic interpreters are agreed; but it is argued that Isaiah's words point to a fulfilment in the immediate future, and could not therefore have been spoken of the Messiah. Isaiah does indeed declare that in the early years of Immanuel, a great, and that an immediate inroad of the Assyrian power should desolate the land. The invasion was to take place before the child should 'know to refuse the evil and choose the good.' Does it follow that Immanuel is not the Christ?

VII. If it be part of the scheme of Divine Providence—and here history speaks plainly—that Christian people should have looked prematurely for the accomplishment of their

[1] Pearson *On the Creed.* Art. III. Note 17.

Lord's prophecies about "the end of all things;" there is little difficulty in conjecturing that a like uncertainty may have been permitted to prevail in the minds of Jews to whom Isaiah spoke. The hope of a deliverer would be none the less comforting, though his Epiphany might seem nearer than it was. As with the people, so with the prophet. It is needless to assume that every prophet of the former dispensation must have been gifted with a degree of prescience for which apostles longed in vain. The question: 'When shall these things be?' (Matt. xxiv. 3), does but elicit the assurance, that 'of that day and hour knoweth no man, no not the angels of heaven, but my Father only' (ver. 36). And even after the Resurrection it was not for men "to know the times or the seasons, which the Father hath put in His own power" (Acts i. 7.) Their part was to 'Watch,' and to 'be ready.' 'In an hour when ye think not, the Son of man cometh.' They were to maintain an uncalculating expectancy; and their consequent frame of mind was not unfavourable to those premature anticipations, into which, as some think, they were actually led. If this be the case, it is hard to avoid the conclusion that a like uncertainty in the matter of times and seasons may have found place with the chief of Messianic prophets: and thus the way is prepared for such an application of the prophecy in question, as at once satisfies the strict requirements of grammatical sequence, and gives their full natural force to those remarkable descriptive epithets, which it has been found by those who have attempted it, no easy task to explain away.

Isaiah, it might be conjectured, now contemplates as imminent the fulfilment of the ancient prophecy of Shiloh (Gen. xlix. 10). The time was at hand when the sceptre should depart from Judah; ere long to be recovered by the great Restorer, who should unite the scattered "peoples" beneath His sway. With no thought of comforting the impious Ahaz (who is regarded in prophetic vision as superseded), Isaiah dwells, in his hearing, on the prelusive calamities; and assures him that the inroad of Rezin and

Pekah is but a beginning of sorrows. Soon will that land be wholly desolate[1], of whose two kings he is afraid.

For himself, the prophet hopes to see that *Salvation of the Lord*, which his own name symbolized. Nor is he the only prophet that was disappointed in that his hope.

'Verily I say unto you,' are the words of Christ Himself to His disciples, "that many prophets and righteous men have desired to see those things which ye see, and have not seen them; and to hear those things which ye hear, and have not heard them.' Matt. xiii. 17.

In words spoken afterwards, not addressed to Ahaz, the prophet describes the ultimate deliverance of the people of God, which evangelists have claimed as fulfilled in Jesus.

We conclude that Isaiah prophesied of Christ, as 'God with us;' and that the New Testament writers apply his prophecy as directly Messianic. It may suffice to notice some of their most conspicuous citations.

St Matthew, having described the Annunciation, thus continues: 'Now all this was done, that it might be fulfilled which was spoken of the Lord by the prophet, saying, Behold, the virgin shall be with child, and shall bring forth a son, and they shall call his name Emmanuel, which being interpreted is, God with us.' Matt. i. 22, 23; Is. vii. 14; viii. 8. The words ὁ θεὸς μετ' αὐτῶν (Rev. xxi. 3), refer, it may be, to the same passages. The child to be born 'shall be great, and shall be called the Son of the Highest: and the Lord God shall give unto him the throne of his father David: and he shall reign over the house of Jacob for ever: and of his kingdom there shall be no end,' Luke i. 32, 33; Is. ix. 7. The Baptist, by preparing the way of his coming Lord, was 'to give light to them that sit in darkness and in the shadow of death' (Luke i. 79; Is. ix. 2). A citation by St Matthew (iv. 15, 16) of the same verse, in connexion with the preceding, will be noticed in the following chapter. The proverbial

---

[1] For this absolute use of עָזַב, compare תֵּעָזֵב אֶרֶץ Job xviii. 4. For its meaning see also Is. vi. 12; xvii. 2.

question; 'Why seek ye the living among the dead?' (Luke xxiv. 5), corresponds to the words of Isaiah, which the Authorized Version thus renders: 'Should not a people seek unto their God? for the living to the dead?' Is. viii. 19. The *stone of stumbling* (Is. viii. 14, 15) is referred to by our Lord: and again by SS. Paul and Peter. 'Whosoever shall fall on this stone shall be broken: but on whomsoever it shall fall, it will grind him to powder.' Matt. xxi. 44. Luke xx. 18. 'For they stumbled at that stone; as it is written, Behold I lay in Sion a stumbling-stone and rock of offence.' Rom. ix. 32, 33. Cp. Is. xxviii. 16. 'And a stone of stumbling and a rock of offence, even to them which stumble at the Word.' 1 Pet. ii. 8.

VIII. The prophecy above considered has been a central point and nucleus of controversy from the commencement of the Christian era.

Dr Nicoll has observed, in a sermon on Is. ix. 6, that, 'These words contain a most remarkable prophecy relating to the nativity, divine nature, and general description of Christ; as must appear incontrovertibly certain to every unprejudiced mind. But there are few passages of the Old Testament, which have been more (either designedly or otherwise) perverted, and more differently interpreted in ancient and modern times. Indeed, the manner in which we find it explained may invariably be regarded as a criterion, by which we may know whether the expositor was, or was not, a Christian; or at least what sentiments he entertained concerning the nature of Christ.'

There is much truth in this statement. But, on the other hand, when every allowance has been made for the controversial element of the investigation, it must be confessed that there have remained two real difficulties, already alluded to; one on each side of the question. It is easy to see that the non-Messianic interpreter has been forced into non-natural explanations, in his attempt to explain away the exalted description of the nature and functions of Immanuel. It is no less easy to detect the inherent weakness of attempts that have been made to sever the prediction of His birth from the immediate context. The real closeness of its connexion with that context best appears from some of the expedients which have been devised to meet the difficulty.

One solution, adopted by Vitringa and many others, is that the prophet does but measure the time present[1] by the anticipated stages of Christ's life on earth. On this it may justly be remarked, that an opponent might declare the view to be non-natural and *ab extra*, without thereby standing convicted of any unfairness arising from polemical bias.

A second explanation, set forth below, I venture to characterize as artificial.

"On Isaiah vii. 14, we are told that in the primary but lower sense, the sign was given to assure Ahaz...The *sign* given had, secondarily and mystically, a respect to the miraculous birth of Christ. I answer: In the first place, there appears to have been no sign given, if we except the prediction itself; and if the prediction alone was the sign or wonder (which I contend is the case), then the birth of the Messiah was its one and sole object; and on the faith of this the safety of Israel entirely depended...The fifteenth verse, I suppose, must refer to the child to be named Immanuel. 'Butter and honey,' it is said, 'he shall eat,' *on account of his knowing;* not, *that he may know*, &c. The Hebrew is לדעתו מאום, *for*, or *because of*(!), his knowing the refusal. That is: His character shall be such, that even when a child, He shall have knowledge sufficient to choose what is good for Himself, contrary to the character of all others, who are perfectly passive at this age..."

"Let us now come to ver. 16. Here we are told that, 'before the child shall know to refuse the evil, and to choose the good, the land shall be forsaken of both her kings.' I think it must be evident that the child Immanuel cannot be meant here; because we are assured (!), in the preceding

---

[1] *Ita mysterium tangit ut statim ad sua tempora redeat.* Poli *Synopsis*, III. 80 h.

verse, that he shall, even as a child, know to refuse the evil, and to choose the good: besides the fulfilment of the prediction respecting Him was too remote to admit of comparison with the fate of these kings. This last consideration has been felt and acknowledged by every writer, I believe, who has touched upon the subject. At the third verse preceding, we are informed, that Isaiah was to take his own son Shear-jashub, and to go and meet Ahaz on this occasion. If, then, the child just alluded to was not Immanuel; why may it not have been this son of the prophet? This view of the subject seems to be fully confirmed by similar phraseology used with respect to another son of Isaiah in viii. 4. Such language could not, after what has been said, properly apply to Immanuel, but will be suitable enough to Isaiah's son; and this will perhaps be sufficient to account for the circumstance of his having been taken to meet Ahaz. Besides, the events predicted respecting these kings must have taken place within the time thus limited."

IX. What was the characteristic feature of the 'sign' given to Ahaz? And what the significance of the article in the expression 'the virgin'?

These questions have been answered variously, yet without consequent disturbance of the general conclusions reached above. It may suffice therefore to dismiss them briefly.

1. Four kinds of *signs* are catalogued by Hengstenberg[1]: Sometimes the sign is 'a mere naked word' (Ex. xiii. 12). Sometimes the sign is an embodiment of a prediction, 'so that the word assumes, as it were, flesh and blood' (Is. viii. 18). Sometimes the sign is a fulfilment in the immediate future of some natural event, which could not, except supernaturally, be foreseen: and this furnishes the proof that in the distant future, that will be fulfilled which was foretold as impending. The fourth kind of sign consists in 'the immediate performance of a miraculous work going beyond the

---

[1] *Christology*, II. 39.

ordinary laws of nature' (Is. xxxviii. 7). 'In the passage before us,' adds Hengstenberg, 'no other sign can possibly be spoken of than one of the two last classes.' Rosenmüller, having propounded the same two alternatives, declares, with a '*dubium non potest esse*,' for the last.

Delitzsch draws his answer to the same question, 'What constituted the extraordinary character of the fact announced?' from the descriptive titles of ix. 6. 'Immanuel Himself was to be a *wonder*, or *wonderful*. HE would be God in corporeal self-manifestation, and therefore a *wonder*, as being a superhuman person. We should not venture to assert this if it went beyond the line of Old Testament revelation; but the prophet himself asserts it in ix. 6 (cf. x. 21): His words are as clear as possible; and we must not make them obscure to favour any preconceived notions as to the development of history. The incarnation of Deity was unquestionably a secret that was not clearly unveiled in the Old Testament; but the veil was not so thick but that some rays could pass through.' The '*virgin*,' observes the same writer, continued throughout 'an enigma, stimulating inquiry (1 Pet. i. 10—12), and waiting for a historical solution.'

2. 'The[1] virgin,' might grammatically refer to one present in person, and pointed out; or to one present only in prophetic vision. Or again, the expression might denote, 'the virgin' that had already formed the subject of prophetic announcements. Nor is this view refuted by the apparent uniqueness[2] of the prophecy in question; unless it be assumed that the sum total of Old Testament prophecy (unlike, e.g. some Epistles[3] of St Paul) has been handed down to us.

---

[1] Virgo *illa*: nam ח Articuli virginem certam, ὡρισμένην, audientibus notam indicat. The indefinite rendering is defended by a vague allusion to the 'generic use' of the article. ח might be *translated* 'a,' in the sense of *any;* not in the sense, *some one*. In Ps. lix. 6, 'grin like *a dog*,' means the same as the plural, 'like *dogs;*' and implies that what one would do, *any other* of the species would do.

[2] Compare the *now obscure* allusion: 'And now ye know what withholdeth, that he might be revealed in his time.'— 2 Thess. ii. 6.

[3] Compare Col. iv. 16.

NOTES ON CHAPTER III.

A. Dr Henderson thus defends the rendering, *shall be forsaken of.* "It (מִפְּנֵי) is also used after the verb עָזַב, Is. xvii. 9, and appears, in such connexion, to have no more force than מִן (Lev. xxvi. 43)." This view is not borne out by the same commentator's note on the passage of Isaiah to which he refers: "עָזְבוּ מִפְּנֵי forms a constructio prægnans, *which they left* (when they fled) *before the children of Israel.*" This implies the *presence* or approach of the children of Israel. *To be forsaken of* such and such persons, implies the *absence* or departure of such persons.

Grievous complications have resulted from the attempt to join עָזַב and מִפְּנֵי in Is. xvii. 9. It seems best to make the latter word refer back to יִהְיוּ, thus:

'In that day shall his strong cities be—
like the leavings of a thicket or a *tree top*, that men have left—
before the children of Israel.'

This rendering stands self-commended by its symmetry, and preserves the accentuation of the original. The same image is presented in the sixth verse: 'Yet gleaning grapes shall be left in it, as the shaking of an olive-tree, two or three berries in the top of the *uppermost bough.*'

B. Cappellus wishes to read 6 + 5, for 60 + 5. Buxtorf declares it unprecedented in Holy Scripture thus to express a number greater than ten; "duobus minoribus, addendis sc." (*Anticritica*, p. 946.) Perhaps the strangest emendation proposed is Vitringa's, שֵׁשׁ י' וְחָמֵשׁ, *six + 10 + five.* 'Denn wer in aller Welt schrieb wohl...eine Zahl halb mit Buchstaben, halb mit Ziffern; z. B. 6 zehn, vi decim?' (Gesenius.) Rosenmüller concludes: 'Habes conjecturas varias, quibus perlectis multo eris incertior quam fueras ante...Minime igitur mihi dubium, genuinum esse id in quo libri omnes consentiunt...'

Buxtorf gives authorities for two of the principal methods by which the full complement of 65 years may be obtained, viz. (i) by going back for a starting point, לְיוֹם שֶׁנִּגְזַר בִּימֵי עָמוֹס, *to the day*

Notes on Chapter III. 47

that was decreed in the days of Amos (Jarchi); and (ii) by reckoning onward to the deportation by Esarhaddon. For a defence of the second method see Delitzsch, I. 211.

C. The hiphil of אמן means 1. *to stand fast* (Job xxxix. 24); 2. *to believe*. The niphal has, corresponding to (1), the meaning *to be established;* and by a proportionate variation from (2), would come to mean, *to be confirmed in belief*, as in the text.

Perhaps it is best to arrange the clauses as follows: 'If ye will not believe, except ye be confirmed (by a sign), then spake the Lord again to Ahaz, saying, Ask thee a sign...' Compare Mark ii. 10, 11, 'But that ye may know that the Son of man hath power on earth to forgive sins, he saith to the sick of the palsy, I say unto thee, Arise.' See *Poli Synopsis*, III. 74 n.

D. For cases in which ל approximates to עד, see the Lexicons. With לדעתו, '*that* he may know,' compare Lev. xxiv. 12, 'And they put him in ward, *that* the mind of the Lord might be shewed them.' The ל in לפרש expresses the connection between the act described in the first clause, and the discovery of the mind of the Lord: but the essential connection is, that the one gave time for the other: hence the ל must express, more or less exactly, the duration of that time, '*till* the mind of the Lord should be shewed.' In לדעתו, the ל, in like manner, expresses duration, '*till* his knowing.' The eating of butter and honey does not directly contribute to the knowledge of good and evil; but the early years, during which the feeding on such fare continues, give time wherein that knowledge may spring up. Some such explanation of the ל is necessitated, independently, by the context, 'For before the child shall know...'

The most natural rendering of לדעתו, taken alone, is, *to the end that he may know*. If the words were separated from those which follow, they would *seem* to mean that the eating of butter (or curdled milk) and honey was to contribute in some direct way to the power of discernment between good and evil; and this suggests a figurative interpretation, in accordance with many comparisons, as Ps. xix. 10; Prov. xxiv. 13, 14; 1 Pet. ii. 2. Compare the Rabbinic usages of such texts as, 'Honey and milk are under thy tongue.' Cant. iv. 11. See Bernard's *Yad Hachazakah*, p. 93. Regard being had to the professedly enigmatic nature (viii. 16) of his prophecy, it seems far from improbable that Isaiah may have intended to hint at such a secondary application; and this would account for the occurrence of an expression which, apart from the context, is so misleading as לְדַעְתּוֹ.

E. הרבית הגוי לא הגדלת השמחה. From this reading of the text (ix. 3) the Authorized Version has been led to the contradictory rendering, 'Thou hast multiplied the nation, and not increased the joy: they joy before thee according to the joy in harvest, and as men rejoice when they divide the spoil.' A superficial simplification is introduced by the reading of the קרי; '*its* (לוֹ) joy Thou hast increased;' but this gives an unnatural position to the לוֹ.

The כתיב may be rendered literally, 'Thou hast multiplied the nation: Thou hadst not increased the joy:' and this would mean, in accordance with one of the very commonest of Hebrew idioms (the omission of the relative), 'Thou hast now multiplied the nation, whose joy Thou hadst formerly not-increased:' where לֹא *not*, attaches itself to the following word as an *inseparable* prefix. [For a striking example, compare x. 15, לֹא עֵץ, and see Lowth's note. The idiom has found its way into the Greek Testament, οὕτως οὐκ ἰσχύσατε, Matt. xxvi. 40, Were ye so unable to watch with me one hour?]

In Is. ix. 3, the LXX, though on the whole obscure, testifies to the accuracy of the reading לֹא הִגְדַּלְתָּ by its rendering ὃ κατήγαγες, where the ὃ is explanatory, and the κατήγαγες arises from a combination of the *negative* with the following *exaltedst*. The ellipsis thus supplied is not peculiar to the Hebrew language. In English we might write idiomatically, 'the nation Thou minishedst.'

A rendering which conveys an explicit *contrast* (ἐπλήθυνας τὸ ἔθνος ὃ οὐκ ἐμεγάλυνας, Symmachus) has strong claims to a place in the series of antitheses:

        Humiliation; glory .... ix. 1.
        Darkness; light................... 2.
        Independence; oppression ... 4.
        War; peace .... 5.

We conclude that the passage has no need of emendation. See, on the other side, Smith's *Dict. of Bible*, Art. *Septuagint*.

CHAPTER IV.

Local Coincidences.

Matth. ii. 6, 15, 18, 23; iv. 15.

ST Matthew records as correspondent to prophetic announcements five circumstances in the history of the Saviour's life. 1. The birth in Bethlehem. 2. The murder of the Innocents. 3. The settlement in Capernaum. 4. The sojourn in Egypt. 5. The return to Nazareth. The nature of the correspondence has to be sought in detail; each case presenting its peculiar difficulties: and the above arrangement has been chosen to facilitate the inquiry; the third case leading naturally to the more complex fourth and fifth. The last in order involve a two-fold difficulty in prophetic reference and in fulfilment. In what sense does Hos. xi. 1 apply to Christ; and how does the sojourn in Egypt bring about an accomplishment of the prophecy? Whence is it gathered that Christ was to be a 'Nazarene'; and how are the prophecies on that point fulfilled by His residence in Nazareth? The third case presents as the sole subject for inquiry, the nature of the correspondence between Christ's dwelling 'in Capernaum, which is upon the sea-coast, in the borders of Zabulon and Nephthalim:' and the prophecy, supposed Messianic, of Is. ix. 1, 2.

I. *Bethlehem Ephratah.* Mic. v. 2; Matt. ii. 6.

The connection between the prophecy of Immanuel and those in Mic. v. is so plain and so generally admitted that a detailed examination of the latter may be dispensed with.

If the former be Messianic, as has been concluded, so too are the latter. Isaiah speaks of 'the virgin' of the house of Judah as the mother of the Messiah: Micah localizes the conception, and assigns to Bethlehem Ephratah[1] the distinction which contrasts so strongly with its own intrinsic power and dignity: 'But thou, Bethlehem Ephratah, little one to be among the thousands of Judah, from thee shall come forth for me, to be ruler in Israel, one whose procession is from of old, from everlasting.'

Micah, like Isaiah, had denounced the iniquities of the people, and proclaimed the judgments that awaited them. The words of the two prophets have points of coincidence, and it has been supposed that the phraseology of a passage wherein Micah deals so roughly with the false confidence and security that had arisen, was formed upon Isaiah's prophecy of *God with us*. 'The heads thereof judge for reward, and the priests thereof teach for hire, and the prophets thereof divine for money: yet will they lean upon the Lord and say, *Is not the Lord among us?* none evil can come upon us.' Mic. iii. 11.

However this may be, Isaiah prophesies of the great Deliverer, and as it were in the same breath, of the Assyrian flood that should desolate the land. The same invasion is present to Micah's gaze, while he looks forward to the coming 'Ruler, whose goings forth are from of old, from everlasting.' From the lowly Ephratah must He come. That village, too insignificant to be represented among the magnates of its tribe, should give birth to no merely local ruler, but One who should bear sway in the collective Israel. 'This man,' adds the prophet, 'shall be *Peace*, when the Assyrian shall come into our land: and when he shall tread in our palaces.' (Mic. v. 5.) This same, an apostle declares to be 'our *Peace*,' (Eph. ii. 14,) who fulfils the prophetic utterance, and works out the predicted deliverance, abstracted from the local imagery by which it had been veiled.

---

[1] 'And Rachel died, and was buried in the way to Ephrath, which is Bethlehem.' Gen. xxxv. 19.

The promise made to Bethlehem Ephratah is the same, now set forth with greater concentration and definiteness, as that by which the preeminence was first assigned to Judah among the tribes.

Few passages have been more disputed than the prophecy of Shiloh (Gen. xlix. 10); and it is now, as of old, extremely difficult to assign with accuracy the true etymological meaning of its leading word. But all difficulties notwithstanding, one thing is clear, viz. that to Judah the sceptre is assigned[1]. To him a marked preeminence is given, which is not to cease till a certain *coming;* and 'to him shall the submission of peoples be.' The dominion of Judah is spoken of as even then commencing; and this remark is of the last importance in its bearing upon King David's words:

'Howbeit the Lord God of Israel chose me before all the house of my father to be king over Israel for ever; for He hath chosen Judah to be the ruler, and of the house of Judah the house of my father; and among the sons of my father He liked me to make me king over all Israel.' (1 Chron. xxviii. 4.)

This selection of Judah does not date from the actual appointment of David, but seems clearly to refer to a former time; and to what time, it may be asked, but to that of the expiring patriarch?

All doubt on the point is apparently removed by 1 Chron. v. 2, where this preeminence is distinctly referred back to the paternal blessing; and it is moreover pointed out as something in itself remarkable that while Joseph succeeded to the forfeited primogeniture of Reuben, it was for Judah that the princedom was reserved. This point is well brought out by the Authorized Version.

'For Judah prevailed above his brethren, and of him came the chief ruler; *but*[2] the birthright was Joseph's.'

---

[1] On the ambiguous word מחקק in the same verse see note A p. 72.

[2] Micah's צעיר להיות may signify: 'Thou little one, *minor natu,* (that

These quotations alone bridge over the ages which had elapsed since the days of Jacob; and thenceforward the Messianic prerogative of the tribe of Judah is dwelt upon with more and more distinctness. The name of David is used to designate the coming ruler long after David's self had ceased to rule; and when prophets speak of restoration and return to power, it is the throne of *David* which is to be set up; it is the 'sure mercies of *David*' that can never fail. The Apocalypse conjoins the prophecies and aspirations of centuries when it speaks in one verse (v. 5) of 'the root of David,' and of the 'Lion of the tribe of Judah.' (Gen. xlix. 9.)

We conclude then that the Jews of old looked to the tribe of Judah, and afterwards more specifically to the house of David, for the Messiah. The prophet Micah apostrophises Bethlehem as His birthplace; and there is evidence in the Gospels that the prophecy was thus interpreted.

In answer to Herod, the theologians refer to Mic. v. 2, as an *a priori* ground for believing Bethlehem to be the destined birthplace of the Christ:

'Now when Jesus was born in Bethlehem of Judea in the days of Herod the King, behold, there came wise men from the east to Jerusalem, saying, Where is he that is born King of the Jews? for we have seen his star in the east, and are come to worship him. When Herod the King had heard these things, he was troubled, and all Jerusalem with him. And when he had gathered all the chief priests and scribes of the people together, he demanded of them where Christ should be born. And they said to him, In Bethlehem of Judea; for thus it is written by the prophet, And thou, Bethlehem, in the land of Juda, art not the least among the princes of Juda; for out of thee shall come a Governor, that shall rule my people Israel,' (ii. 1—6).

Here is no question of accommodation: no room for

---

art) to be....' For this common use of צָעִיר see Gen. xxv. 23; xliii. 33. 'The elder shall serve the *younger*.' 'The *youngest* according to his youth.' Compare Ps. lxviii. 27, '*Little* Benjamin their ruler.'

doubt in explaining the connection between the Scripture, and that which is put forward as its accomplishment. Nor is there anything recondite in the prophecy or its application. It is the popular acceptation[1] (ver. 4) of a plain prophecy which Matthew records. The original declares that Bethlehem, despite its *littleness*, shall give birth to the ruler, not of a tribe, but of all Israel. The citation proclaims Bethlehem 'not the least,' for the reason that 'out of thee shall come'[2] that Ruler; and it thereby implies that but for this it would be indeed 'the least.' The LXX. agreeing with our Hebrew text, reads: 'among the *thousands*[3].' The citation has 'among the *princes* (ἡγεμόσιν).' The one depicts Bethlehem as too small for a place among the principalities of the land: the other, as unworthy to send forth a ruler who should stand in the congregation of its princes. The discrepancy may be accounted for by the change of a single vowel point[4]; or again the word ἡγεμόσιν may have arisen from an instinctive assimilation to the Greek word for *a Governor* which follows. The latter explanation resembles that given by Dr Hengstenberg, who sees an argument for the non-Aramaic origin of St Matthew's Gospel, in this correspondence of ἡγεμόσιν with ἡγούμενος. The former method of reconciliation is more commonly thought satisfactory.

II. *Rachel weeping for her children.*
Jer. xxxi. 15; Matt. iv. 18.

The prophet Jeremiah, in describing 'the time of Jacob's trouble' (xxx. 7), and his subsequent restoration, makes use, once and again, of a poetical *prosopopœia*. 'This is a figure

---

[1] 'Hath not the scripture said, That Christ cometh of the seed of David, and out of the town of Bethlehem, where David was?' Joh. vii. 42.
[2] Some have thought that the '*Judæa profecti*' of Suetonius and Tacitus is to be referred to the LXX. ἐκ σοῦ γάρ ἐξελεύσεται.

[3] אלף is translated *family*, in Judg. vi. 15. Compare 1 Sam. x. 19, 'By your tribes, and by your *thousands*.'
[4] אֱלָפַי for אַלְפֵי. Is. lx. 22 might be referred to in support of the Hebrew text: 'A little one shall become a thousand, and a *small one* a strong nation.'

very common to all authors, to bring in a person speaking; and there is no man in his wits quarrels with them for it.' St Matthew selects one instance out of the many, and represents Rachel, who was buried in the vicinity, as bewailing the victims of Herod's massacre, in words first applied by the prophet to the Babylonish captivity. 'Then was fulfilled that which was spoken by Jeremy the prophet, saying, In Rama was there a voice heard, lamentation and weeping, and great mourning, Rachel weeping for her children, and would not be comforted, because they are not.' Matt. ii. 17, 18.

This might be thought a sufficient account of the matter; but objections have been raised, partaking in some cases of the nature of refinements, which it may be well to notice. It is urged that Rachel, as not being the mother of Judah (Gen. xxix. 35), could not rightly be said to weep for Bethlehemites as her children: Leah ought to have been introduced, not Rachel. The appropriateness of the allusion may be vindicated on general grounds; but the mode of *citation* has first to be considered. Can the evangelist be said, in this particular, to have distorted or misapplied the words of Jeremiah? The prophet, it has been remarked above, has been speaking in general terms of the captivity, and has already made use, on more than one occasion, of *prosopopœia*. Jacob is personified in xxx. 10, 11; Zion in xxx. 12—17. So too are Israel, the virgin of Israel, and Ephraim, in the following chapter, that viz. from which the citation is drawn.

It would scarcely occur to the reader of Jer. xxxi. to restrict Rachel's solicitude (ver. 15) to those who were actual descendants of her own sons, as opposed to Leah's; or in fact to make her mourning and her comfort (ver. 17) one whit less general than such as is described both before and after. The place Ramah is mentioned subsequently[1] in connection with a general gathering of prisoners from the surrounding

---

[1] 'The word that came to Jeremiah from the Lord, after that Nebuzar-adan the captain of the guard had let him go from Ramah, when he had taken him being bound in chains among all that were carried away captive of Jerusalem and Judah, which were carried away captive unto Babylon.' Jer. xl. 1.

districts. This (to say nothing of the prophet's personal share therein) gives a clue by which we might account for the mention of the great mourning in Jer. xxxi. 15 ; and at the same time excludes any such artificial hypothesis as that Rachel was but weeping for her own personal descendants. The allusion is mainly local; and in such a passage, to descend to further particulars would be repugnant to the spirit of the Hebrew style. More than this, it would seem that in the immediate context of the citation the family of Jacob is thought of as at one, and that Rachel weeps for all[1] as for her children. It may be assumed at any rate, until the contrary is proved, that the promise of restoration includes the tribe of *Judah:* 'there is hope in thine end, saith the Lord, that *thy children* shall come again to their own border' (xxxi. 17): and if Jeremiah includes Judah in his expression, '*thy children,*' his words suffer no distortion by being applied, as in the Gospel, to the infants of Bethlehem.

On the general propriety of the allusion little needs be said. Rachel is a fit type of maternal fondness: 'Give me children, or else I die' (Gen. xxx. 1). Her burial place was in the neighbourhood[2] of Bethlehem, the central point of Herod's outrage. The hearing of the voice in Ramah, supposed beyond the immediate precincts of the massacre, would import the loudness of the lamentation, as in Is. x. 30 : ' Lift up thy voice, O daughter of Gallim : cause it to be heard unto[3] Laish, O poor Anathoth.' But Ramah may have fallen within the limits of Herod's edict, which was not confined to Bethlehem itself : for 'Herod, when he saw that he was mocked of the wise men, was exceeding wroth, and sent forth,

---

[1] Jacob's words to Joseph, 'Shall I and *thy mother* and thy brethren indeed come to bow down ourselves to thee to the earth?' (Gen. xxxvii. 10) were spoken when Joseph's own mother was dead.

[2] 'Rachel died...when there was yet but a little way (כברת ארץ) to come to Ephrath : and I buried her there in the way of Ephrath ; the same is Bethlehem.' Gen. xlviii. 7 ; xxxv. 19. Rachel's sepulchre is mentioned in 1 Sam. x. 2, and it is inferred that it was near to Ramah, since, on the way thence to Gibeah, ' primum occurrit sepulchrum Rachelæ, deinde terebinthus Thabor, tum Gibea.' *Rosenmüller. Poole.*

[3] Or ' Hearken, O Laish' (*Delitzsch*): which implies a hearing 'unto Laish.'

and slew all the children that were in Bethlehem, and *in all the coasts thereof*, from two years old and under, according to the time which he had diligently inquired of the wise men' (Matt. ii. 16). 'The slaughter of the Innocents,' concludes Bishop Kidder[1], 'was not restrained to the town of Bethlehem, but extended to all the coasts and confines thereof: and then the voice might well be heard in Ramah; and Rachel (from whom the tribe of Benjamin sprang) might be truly said to weep for her own children in the closest and strictest sense.'

III. *The land of Zabulon and the land of Nephthalim.*
Is. ix. 1; Matt. iv. 15.

Our Lord's settlement in Capernaum is thus described: 'Now when Jesus had heard that John was cast into prison, He departed into Galilee: and leaving Nazareth, He came and dwelt in Capernaum, which is upon the sea-coast, in the borders of Zabulon and Nephthalim: that it might be fulfilled which was spoken by Esaias the prophet, saying, The land of Zabulon, and the land of Nephthalim, by the way of the sea, beyond Jordan, Galilee of the Gentiles; the people that sat in darkness saw a great light; and to them which sat in the region and shadow of death light is sprung up.' Matt. iv. 12—16.

1. The fifteenth verse presents a grammatical difficulty, which does not however affect the application and general understanding of the prophecy. How is the accusative, *way[2] of the sea* (breaking in as it does upon a series of nominatives or vocatives), to be explained or accounted for? 'It is difficult to maintain, with Meyer, that εἶδε in ver. 16 is the governing verb:' and to render accordingly, 'The land of Zebulun and the land of Naphthali (saw) the way of the sea[3]

---

[1] *Demonstr. of the Messias*, II. 211.

[2] The words, 'by the way of the sea,' as above quoted, correspond to the simple accusative ὁδὸν θαλάσσης.

[3] The tract in question being made visible by the light of Christ shining across from Capernaum (Alf. *in loc.*).

Local Coincidences. 57

on the other side of the Jordan. Galilee of the Gentiles, the people that sat in darkness, saw a great light[1].' It is difficult, argues the same grammarian, to render ὁδὸν in an absolute adverbial sense, as equivalent to *by the way:* 'for passages such as 1 Sam. vi. 9[2], Numb. xxi. 33, Ex. xiii. 17, are no authority for an accusative without government by a verb, in an address containing vocatives.' Whether or no this be thought conclusive against an interpretation which makes ὁδὸν obliquely indicative of the prophet's point of view, as he looks 'seaward beyond Jordan,' it may be worth while to suggest that the citation *may* be, of set purpose, fragmentary, and incapable of exact rendering as a whole, without reference to the original context from which it is taken. The former verse might then be regarded as a catalogue of names to which the Evangelist designs to call attention: in the latter, with retrospective reference to the districts mentioned, he declares that they, 'the people that sat in darkness, saw great light.' The citation, we might conjecture, is discontinuous, while the ring of the *familiar version* is retained. The verses in question are, for all the purposes of citation, an exact counterpart of the original. They express plainly, whatever be their grammatical arrangement, that a region once lying in darkness had been illumined by the light of Christ; and the region that lay in darkness is that described in ver. 15.

2. The chief point to be considered is the nature of the correspondence between the prophecy and that which is here set forth as its fulfilment. The answer to this question might throw some additional light upon the formula of citation, *that it might be fulfilled*[3]; and thus prepare the way for the better understanding of those more difficult citations to which it is

---

[1] Winer, *Grammar of New Test. Diction*, XXXII. § 6.

[2] ὁδὸν ὁρίων αὐτῆς πορεύσεται. Corresponding to ὁδὸν θαλάσσης (Is. ix. 1), the LXX. read καὶ οἱ λοιποὶ οἱ τὴν παραλίαν. They may, possibly, have anticipated a governing verb from the following πορευόμενος (seeing that ὁδὸν πορεύεσθαι is an ordinary expression and παραλίαν corresponds to דרך, or ὁδόν). St Matthew however changes πορευόμενος into καθημένος, and thus renders such an explanation inapplicable. See also Note B. p. 72.

[3] See Note C. p. 72.

prefixed: 'Out of Egypt have I called my son;' 'He shall be called a Nazarene.' Matt. ii. 15, 23.

It has been assumed that the passage cited had an original Messianic reference, and must consequently have received a definite fulfilment when Christ took up his abode in Capernaum. But was that fulfilment a final and exhaustive one?

This question has been answered in the affirmative by many commentators, who explain ἵνα πληρωθῇ as here signifying: 'That the prophecy which, as far as the mournful part of it is concerned, was in some degree verified in the abduction by Tiglath Pileser (2 Kings xv. 29), and by the religious debasement of those cities, might now have its *full* and *final* accomplishment in the light of the Gospel of Redemption, diffused by the preaching of Christ and His Apostles who were Galileans, in that land *first*, which was *first* overshadowed by the darkness of captivity.'

But Isaiah seems to contemplate Immanuel as making His power felt far and wide from *Zion*, rather than as resident in the district named. More than this, he depicts His light as truly *seen*, rather than as shining forth unheeded upon the spiritually blind: nor can he be thought to have contemplated a merely passing illumination, which should fade, and leave the darkness thicker than before. 'Woe unto thee, Chorazin! woe unto thee, Bethsaida! for if the mighty works which were done in you had been done in Tyre and Sidon, they would have repented long ago in sackcloth and ashes. But I say unto you, It shall be more tolerable for Tyre and Sidon at the day of judgment, than for you. And thou, Capernaum, which art exalted unto heaven, shalt be brought down to hell: for if the mighty works which have been done in thee had been done in Sodom, it would have remained until this day. But I say unto you, That it shall be more tolerable for the land of Sodom in the day of judgment than for thee.' (Matt. xi. 21—24.)

More might be added to the same effect: but the above will suffice to indicate that Christ's residence in Capernaum *may* have been adduced, not as the full and final accomplishment[1] of the prophetic announcement, but as a partial though distinct realization, which *symbolized the fulfilment of the whole prophecy in* HIM.

IV. *The flight into Egypt.* Matt. ii. 15; Hos. xi. 1.

St Matthew thus describes the flight from Herod's massacre: 'And when they were departed, behold, the angel of the Lord appeareth to Joseph in a dream, saying, Arise, and take the young child and his mother, and flee into Egypt, and be thou there until I bring thee word: for Herod will seek the young child to destroy him. When he arose, he took the young child and his mother by night, and departed into Egypt: and was there until the death of Herod: that it might be fulfilled which was spoken of the Lord by the prophet, saying, Out of Egypt have I called my son.'

This citation suggests two subjects for discussion: viz. (i) the applicability of the prophecy to Christ; and (ii) its fulfilment in Him. The first involves no difficulty which is peculiar to the case before us; and may therefore be dismissed for the present, with few words. The Messianic ideal of the prophets borrowed its expression from the vicissitudes of the national life. The attributes of Jehovah were displayed by His dealings toward the chosen people: but His gracious purposes were, so to say, frustrated by their unfaithfulness. Those purposes could not ultimately fail, but must of necessity be realized; and He in whom they would be realized was the Messiah. To Him one side of the nation's history was applicable; not the nation's own shortcomings, but whatever was expressive of Jehovah's unchanging purpose toward them. Their sacrificing to Baalim, and their burning incense to graven images (Hos. xi. 2), might be things of the past; but every expression of God's love must find a realiza-

---

[1] This suggestion may be expressed interrogatively: would the prophecy have remained *ipso facto* unfulfilled, if Christ had not thus resided in the district named?

tion, and that in God's true Son (Hos. xi. 1). Hence arose such comparisons between the externals of Christ's life and the history of the nation as that which has now to be inquired into. But we could not, it may be premised, have arrived by *a priori* reasoning at the nature of the correspondence, in such a way as to anticipate the circumstances of Christ's life by way of necessary inference from the life of the nation. This is well expressed by Dr Wordsworth, in his note on Matt. ii. 15.

'This was spoken, in the first instance, of the ancient Church of God delivered by Him from Egypt in its infancy. The Holy Spirit applies it to Christ; and He thus teaches us:—

'To regard Christ as One with His Church in all ages of her history. In the persecution of the literal Egypt, He teaches us to see a persecution of Christ. In all their affliction He was afflicted, and the Angel of His presence saved them (Is. lxiii. 9). He was with them in the Exodus, and led them through the Red Sea: they drank of that Spiritual Rock that followed them, and that Rock was Christ (1 Cor. x. 4—9). They were in Him, and He in them.

'To regard what is said by the Holy Spirit concerning the literal Israel as God's Son, as having a prelusive reference to what is declared in the Gospel concerning the only begotten Son of God; and to see under the guidance of the Holy Spirit speaking in the Gospel, its $\pi\lambda\acute{\eta}\rho\omega\sigma\iota\nu$, or *accomplishment*, in Christ.

'Thus, in His dealings with His own prophecies, the Holy Spirit opens to us new lights as to their meaning, lights which we could never have hoped to receive.'

There are two classes of interpretation here to be considered:

1. The words of St Matthew, above quoted, are commonly supposed to indicate that Christ went down into Egypt, in order that by a subsequent exodus He might give occasion for the fulfilment of the prophetic utterance, 'Out of Egypt have I called my Son.' The analogy of the two

calls, as thus limited to the times of exodus, is seemingly a slight one. The bringing up of Israel out of Egypt was a signal deliverance from oppression there endured; Christ, on the contrary, escaped Herod's massacre by this descent into Egypt and sojourn there. Egypt was to Him a refuge; to them a house of bondage (Ex. xx. 1). The journey of Moses (Ex. iv. 20) bears a certain resemblance to that of Joseph, 'and the young child and his mother:' but the latter was undertaken in fear of Herod, and the former when all danger had passed away. The command to leave Egypt, in the one case, has an obvious verbal correspondence with the command to return into Egypt in the other. To Moses it was said, 'Go, return into Egypt; *for all the men are dead which sought thy life*' (Ex. iv. 19). The command to Joseph was, 'Go into the land of Israel: *for they are dead which sought the young child's life.*' In all this there is more almost of contrast than of agreement; the solitary coincidence being, that as Israel was brought up out of Egypt, so the infant Jesus, though under very different circumstances, was brought up out of Egypt. These contrarieties would, however, testify to the historic truth of the account; for it is incredible that an analogy so precarious should have formed the basis of the narrative.

2. Dr Lee, who rejects the above rendering, writes[1] as follows:

"It is said that the child was in Egypt until the death of Herod. It is added, 'that it might be fulfilled which was spoken of the Lord by the prophet, saying, Out of Egypt have I called my son.' Thus the passage stands in our version; but I ask, How can this apply to the context? It is only said here that Christ remained so long in Egypt that it might be fulfilled, &c.; and then the prophecy is cited. It is not said that He left Egypt, and so the prediction was fulfilled: the account of His leaving Egypt is not entered upon till we come to the twentieth verse; and then we hear

---

[1] *Serm. and Diss.* p. 278.

nothing of this prophecy. I prefer taking it therefore in the sense in which I have translated the passage from Hosea: *Since* or *from* (*the times of*) *Egypt, I have named* (Israel) *my son.*"

To this second method of interpretation Bengel *e.g.* has not hesitated to give in his adherence. It is required, argues this commentator, by the parallelism; and the expression '*call*' is inapplicable to what is invariably described as a *leading*, or *bringing* out from Egypt. Several points in the original context have to be considered.

The first clause of Hos. xi. 1, describes God's love of the infant nation Israel; the second clause speaks of that 'call from Egypt,' the meaning of which remains to be determined. The above argument from the parallelism assumes that as the first clause speaks of Israel as *a child*, so the second, by its expression, 'from Egypt,' must denote a reckoning onward from the nation's infancy. The parallelism may be illustrated from the writings of the same prophet:

'And I will give her her vineyard from thence, and the valley of Achor for a door of hope: and she shall sing there as in the days of her youth, and as in the day when she came up out of the land of Egypt.' (Hos. ii. 15.)

Whatever may be the precise value of this argument from the parallelism, it may be noted that, *from the Egypt-time*, is an admissible interpretation of the words, '*from Egypt*,' as is shewn by Hos. xii. 9; xiii. 4: 'And I that am the Lord thy God *from the land of Egypt* will yet make thee to dwell in tabernacles, as in the days of the solemn feast.' 'Yet I am the Lord thy God *from the land of Egypt*, and thou shalt know no God but me: for there is no Saviour beside me.' Where 'the expression, *from the land of Egypt*, may not be restrained only to the act of bringing them out[1] of Egypt, but comprehend both his preservation of them there and his bringing them out thence, and all other great benefits by which, from that time of declaring them to be his people,

---

[1] See Pococke on the passages cited; where the LXX., agreeing with the Targum, insert ἀνήγαγον.

Local Coincidences. 63

he approved himself to be *their God*, a God to them in a more peculiar manner than to other nations...' 'The Lord and God of them and of all was he from the beginning, but their Lord by more particular interest, *from the land of Egypt, in framing them wherein into a people to himself*, and bringing them out thence with mighty signs and wonders, and protecting them thenceforward, he shewed such evident tokens of his power and favour, as neither before nor to any other people.'

Several authorities agree in the rendering, 'I named.' Thus, 'the author of the MS. Arab. translation, *from Egypt have I named him my son;* according to which way Kimchi also gives this meaning: *Out of Egypt I began to call him my son.* They seem to follow the Chaldee, which hath *out of Egypt I called them sons.*' Israel there began to exist as the chosen *nation*, and was there first named 'my son': 'Thus saith the Lord, Israel is my son, even my first-born' (Ex. iv. 22). In all this, however, the rendering of the phrase, *from Egypt*, is most important. The clause might be rendered, without great variation in the sense: *from the Egypt-time I called to* (*i.e.* summoned or invited) *my son.* This gives perhaps the simplest construction, and agrees best with the apparent meaning of the context, which will next be briefly noticed.

In the second verse of Hos. xi. the word *call* recurs, and there in the sense, *invite:* 'As they called them, so they went from them:' which many interpret of an unheeded call by God's prophets to His worship. Others interpret it of invitations to idolatry, as seems most in accordance with the marked contrast in the next verse: *Whereas I*[1], *even I, had taught Israel to go.* The preceding verses may be rendered:

'When Israel was a child, then I loved him; and from the Egypt-time I called my son.

'They called them, so they went from before them: to[2] sacrifice to Baalim, to burn incense to graven images.'

---

[1] ואנכי תרגלתי. Le Clerc's rendering shews the emphasis: 'Sed vocarunt Israelitas alii, et propter hos sic abierunt...Ego docui Ephraimum ire, cepit eum Moses in brachia sua.'

[2] Fut. *lit.* 'that they might.'

God's lifelong care is contrasted with their unfaithfulness, and His love with their ingratitude; till it is declared at length (ver. 5) that they 'shall not return to the land of Egypt (*i.e.* to the good times of old[1]), but the Assyrian shall be his king, because they refused to return.' The name Egypt was associated with the spring-time of national existence, with Jacob's blessing of the nascent tribes, with their election to divine sonship *in* that land, before the exodus.

This interpretation, which makes the *call* precede the exodus, seems to simplify St Matthew's application of the prophecy:

'When he arose, he took the young child and his mother by night, and departed into Egypt. And was there until the death of Herod: that it might be fulfilled which was spoken of the Lord by the prophet, From the Egypt-time[2] called I my son' (ii. 14, 15).

Subjoined are extracts from the Arabic Gospel of the Infancy, to which Dr Lee thus refers. 'In the apocryphal gospel of our Saviour's infancy, I find this text cited, not with reference to Christ's egress from Egypt, but to his being preserved there from the cruelty of Herod. It will not be too much, therefore, to suppose that, in the early times of the church, this view of the text may have generally prevailed.'

This Gospel sets forth Christ as miraculously designated God's Son, and there, *in Egypt*, so acknowledged. It then adds, 'Here was fulfilled the prophecy which saith, From Egypt have I called my son.' Israel was called 'My son, my first-born,' (Ex. iv. 22) in Egypt and thenceforward. Christ was acknowledged as God's son *in* and *from* that land. The extracts are taken from Mr Cowper's translation of the *Apocryphal Gospels*, pp. 178—180.

---

[1] Compare Hos. ii. 15, already cited.

[2] To illustrate this rendering of the Greek, compare ἐκ κοιλίας μητρός, Matt. xix. 12; ἐκ νεότητος, Acts xxvi. 43; and the corresponding classical usages.

'Here the Greek says *out of*, viewing the time specified not as a *point* from which something is reckoned, but, by a more vivid conception, as an expanse *out of* which something is diffused.' Winer.

On the arrival of 'Joseph and lady Mary,' the people inquire of a certain idol, 'What is this agitation and commotion which hath arisen in our land?' The idol replies: 'There cometh hither a God in secret, who truly is a God, neither is any God beside Him worthy of worship, because He is truly the Son of God. And the same hour that idol fell, and at its fall all the inhabitants of Egypt and others ran together.' In the next chapter (the eleventh) a demoniac child of the ministering priest describes his cure by contact with the swaddling clothes of the Lord Christ. 'Having taken one of them I placed it on my head, and the demons left me and fled away.' And his father, greatly rejoicing because of him, said, 'My son, it may be that this child is the Son of the living God who created heaven and earth; for when he came to us, the idol was broken, and all the gods fell, and perished through the might of his magnificence.'

The twelfth chapter opens with the statement that the prophecy in question was *then and there* fulfilled: it then describes the consternation of Joseph and Mary, and their preparation for departure.

'Here was fulfilled the prophecy which saith, Out of Egypt have I called my son. But Joseph and Mary, when they heard that the idol had fallen and perished, feared and trembled. Then they said, When we were in the land of Israel Herod thought to slay Jesus, and therefore he slew all the children of Bethlehem and its borders; and there is no doubt but the Egyptians, as soon as they hear that this idol is broken, will burn us with fire.'

The most noteworthy point in connection with the sojourn in Egypt is here taken to be the acknowledgment of Christ's divinity consequent upon the fall of the Egyptian idols in His presence. The same view, it may be added, is set forth in the gospel of pseudo-Matthew, where the prophecy of Hosea is not quoted. 'If this were not the God of our gods, our gods would by no means have fallen on their faces before him, neither would they lie prostrate in his sight; wherefore they silently avow him to be their Lord... Then all the people of that city believed in the Lord God through Jesus Christ.' The departure from Egypt is very cursorily alluded to: 'Not much time after, an angel said to Joseph, Return to the land of Judah, for they are dead who sought the child's life. And it came to pass that after the return, &c.'

Whichever of the renderings considered in this section be adopted; whether, *from Egypt I named my Son*, or (as seems more consonant with the Hebrew) *from Egypt I called to* (*i.e.* invited) *my Son*, the reference would be, not to a single act in history, like the bringing up of Israel out of Egypt, but to the continued display of that divine favour which was first shewn to Israel as a nation in the land of Egypt[1]. The prophet describes God's lifelong care for the chosen nation, and in so doing he employs expressions which are in themselves symbolical, and which therefore, in their literal sense, have no necessary application to the Messiah. In this case too, as above, it may be questioned whether the prophetic utterance would have failed of its realization in Christ, if He had escaped Herod's massacre by a flight to any other than the literal[2] Egypt. It would seem rather that the realization would have been as complete, even though its literal expression may have been different; and that St Matthew does but adduce the external coincidence as *symbolizing the fulfilment in Christ of what Hosea had expressed symbolically.*

V. *He shall be called a Nazarene.* Matt. ii. 23; Is. xi. 1.

Of the various explanations that have been given of this citation, the form *Nazoræus* seems to exclude that which assumes a derivation from *Nazir* (or Nazarite), for this would necessitate the vocalization *Naziræus*. Of other interpretations there are two, running up into one, which seem to satisfy the requirements of the case. The one is that Christ should be despised, or obscure, as an inhabitant of Nazareth: 'Can there any good thing come out of Nazareth?' (Joh. i. 47). The other that the reference is to Isaiah's prophecy of

---

[1] See Note D, p. 73.   [2] Rev. xi. 8.

the *Netser*, or *Branch* (xi. 1); or rather to the whole class of prophecies which represent the Messiah, not indeed by the word *Netser* (which is used of Him once only), but by some synonymous expression. There is one antecedent objection to this solution, on which Bengel *e.g.* has very reasonably laid great stress, viz. that a Z in the Greek points *invariably* to such a spelling in the Hebrew as would exclude the derivation from *Netser*. There are exceptions, far from numerous, to the rule here laid down: but one exception will suffice to remove the objection, and, not indeed to afford any presumption that the proposed derivation is the true one, but to prepare the way for other considerations which would seem to point to that conclusion. An example is presented by the LXX. form of *Uz*[1] (Gen. x. 23); and to this may be added, from extraneous sources, Ζωφασημίν[2].

In favour of the derivation *Netser* are the spellings of the Arabic and Syriac versions, and still more, the names by which Christ and His followers were designated in later Jewish writings. There is apparently no sufficient reason for doubting that the contemptuous expression, 'the sect of the Nazarenes' (Acts xxiv. 5), corresponds to those later contumelious expressions derived from *Netser;* a word used indeed of the Messiah in Is. xi. 1, but occurring too in Is. xiv. 19, in a sense well suited to its application as a title of contempt: 'But thou art cast out of thy grave like an abominable *branch*.' In the name of the city Nazareth, it would seem that the termination *eth* is non-essential. In the oft-quoted passage of David de Pomis, we find *Netser* given as the name of the town: 'A Nazarene is one born in the town Netser, of Galilee, distant three days' journey from Jerusalem.' And 'even at the time of Eusebius (*Hist.* I. 7) and of Jerome, the place was called *Nazara*.' The latter identifies Nazareth with the still existing Nazara, a village of Galilee, near Mount Tabor, and fifteen miles to the east of Legio. In *Epist.* xvii.

---

[1] Οὖζ, for עוץ. Fürst. *sub lit.* ץ. μίν, צוּפִי שׁמִים. Sanchun, p. 10, Orell.'
[2] 'Perraro Z adhibent, ut Ζωφασή- (Gesen. *Thesaur.* 1143 b).

ad Marcellum, he alludes expressly to the derivation from *Netser:* 'Let us go to Nazareth, and according to a right interpretation of that name we shall see there the *flower* of Galilee[1].' This view of the primitive form of the word explains, as Dr Hengstenberg further remarks, the non-occurrence of the letter *T* in the adjectival forms *Nazoræus*, *Nazarenus;* where *Nazaretæus* might have been expected if the form Nazareth involved the *th* as other than an excrescence.

Buxtorf in his Talmudic Lexicon, mentions first of all, under the title *Ben-netser*, a notorious freebooter called the 'chief of robbers[2].' The name recurs, as descriptive of the 'regnum impium,' in a comment upon Dan. vii. 8: 'I considered the horns, and, behold, there came up among them another little horn, before whom there were three of the first horns plucked up by the roots; and behold, in this horn were eyes like the eyes of a man, and a mouth speaking great things.' And Isaac Abarbanel further declares this same Ben-netser to be Jesus the Nazarene (Notsri). To this Buxtorf adds the saying from *Aruch*, 'Netser is the accursed Nazarene.' Jerome writes of the Jews that, 'three times a day they anathematized Christians in their synagogues under this name of Nazarenes;' and it may be added that even a verb to Nazarize[3] (*Christianus fieri*) was in vogue amongst them. Having then a strong external presumption that St Matthew's *Nazaræus* includes a reference to the *Netser* of Is. xi. 1, we proceed in the next place to consider what, with the Evangelist, was the probable significance of the allusion.

'Out of the stumps of Jesse,' writes Dr. Delitzsch on the passage alluded to, 'i. e. out of the remnant of the chosen royal family, which has sunk down to the insignificance of the house from which it sprang, there comes forth a twig which promises to supply the place of the trunk and crown; and down below, in the roots covered with earth, and only

---

[1] See Hengstenberg, *Christol.* II. 108. The neighbourhood is said to have been *virgultis consita*, which favours the above derivation.

[2] ראש לסטים, lit. *caput latronum*.

[3] נתנצר or התנצר.

rising a little above it, there shows itself a *netser*, i. e. a fresh, green shoot.' The prophecy is thus pregnant with a meaning which is altogether missed in some allusions to the passage, which seem to indicate that the name *Branch* is a sort of casual appellation of the Messiah, e. g. 'There may be an allusion to *Netser* (a branch), by which name our Lord is called in Is. xi. 1, and from which word it appears that the name Nazareth is probably derived.' The true significance is brought out still more emphatically in Is. liii. 1, 2: 'What manner of man[1] is this on whom the arm of the Lord hath been revealed? For he grew up like a sucker or small sideshoot from a root or stump, left for dead in barren ground: he had no form nor comeliness; and when we saw him, there was no beauty that we should desire him.' By the word Netser are symbolized those characteristics of the Messiah which are here prophetically set forth. He was to be 'despised and rejected of men; a man of sorrows, and acquainted with grief.' Christ answered to this description in all those circumstances of his life which contrasted with the popular anticipations of 'King Messiah.' The obscurity of Nazareth forced itself on so ready an adherent as Nathanael (John i. 47); from it the title on the cross borrowed an epigrammatic significance (John xix. 19); it entered into an opprobrious designation of Christ's followers, adopted by Tertullus (Acts xxiv. 5); and was applied by Jews in aftertime, in a way that has already been dwelt upon at sufficient length.

Our Lord, it may be concluded, is set forth by St. Matthew in the passage before us, as realizing a conspicuous series of prophetic announcements, not by dwelling in a city connected etymologically[2] with a word once met with in those prophecies, but by all those circumstances in his earthly life that were naturally attendant upon, and suggested by, His residence in Nazareth. His dwelling in Nazareth, and being

---

[1] See next Chapter.

[2] Compare *e.g.* 'נזר est *regii capitis insigne:* et נזרת, Hillero interprete, est oppidum quo vertex montis *coronatur.* Itaque *Nazareni* cognomen Germanice exprimi posset: *Zu Cronberg hat der Gekrönte gewohnet.* Vid. Psalm cxxxii. 18.'

named therefrom is adduced as *symbolizing the fulfilment of that whole class of prophecies in* HIM.

The formula of citation[1] which introduces the prophetic reference considered above, has been more or less refined upon as a means of solving the difficulties which the passage presents. Lost and *unwritten*[2] prophecies have been referred to. Others have inferred from the use of the plural 'by the prophets,' that there is a merely general reference to the import of those prophetic descriptions wherein Christ is set forth as lowly and despised, and that no more definite solution is to be sought. This laxer view is not, indeed, excluded by the formula of citation, but all things considered, is untenable as it stands: it requires, in fact, to be modified as above, by supposing a reference to a particular expression (Is. xi. 1), itself symbolical, and set forth, not as an actual name by which the Messiah was to be called, but as representing his circumstances and condition. The fulfilment does not consist in merely 'being called,' but in *being* all that the name implied: such in fact is the common Biblical usage of the word 'to call.' It has been urged against the interpretation above adopted, that in the far more precise prophecies of the branch, in Zech. iii. 8; vi. 12; Jer. xxiii. 5; xxxiii. 15; Is. iv. 2, the word *Tsemach* is used. The objection thus stated involves a misconception of the prophecy of the *Netser*, that frail, feeble shoot, whose increase was to transcend anticipation; and confounds it with other prophecies which describe the aftergrowth without explicit reference to its small beginning. The objection however may be re-stated, and in its revised form requires an answer. The word Netser, it might be urged, is not used in Is. liii. 2, where the Messiah's lowliness is brought out by a like similitude. This is doubtless an argument against the notion that the 'prophets' cited told of Christ as one who should be a Nazarene *by name;* but it is of no force as against the view explained above, viz. that the prophecies

---

[1] τὸ ῥηθὲν διὰ τῶν προφητῶν. See Matt. i. 23: ii. 15, 18; iv. 15.

[2] 'Non ait Matthæus *scriptum est*, sed *dictum est*.'

in question described him, without reference to name or place[1], as he should truly be. St Matthew singles out *retrospectively*, one typical example which contains a reference to the name, itself typical of Nazarene; and this actual correspondence is adduced as itself typifying the fulfilment of a whole class of Messianic predictions in JESUS of Nazareth. If Christ had not resided in Nazareth, or been *called* a Nazarene, it could scarcely have been affirmed that the collection of prophecies of which Isaiah's prophecy of the Netser is viewed as a nucleus, had lacked their accomplishment; no more, in fact, than such failure could now be argued from the non-appearance of any title of our Lord derived from the word *choter*, which stands in parallelism with *netser*.

The Evangelist's reference, above considered, was doubtless plain to his contemporaries, however difficult it may be for a later generation to fix its meaning. The prophecy of the *netser* was familiar to the populace, as descriptive of the Messiah, but it does not follow that its significance was generally accepted; for it is notorious that some passages wherein the unostentatious demeanour of the coming King is most clearly portrayed, were glossed over and explained away in the received Chaldee versions of Holy Writ. The Jews would at once grant the true Messiah to be the antitype of the *Netser*, but might yet regard the title as inapplicable in its Messianic significance to the lowly *Nazarene*. There is however an example of our Lord's recognition as at once the *Nazarene* and the Messiah, which seems to favor the hypothesis of an allusion to Isaiah's prophecy, 'There shall come forth a rod *out of the stem of Jesse*, and a Branch (*Netser*) shall grow out of his roots:' the same collocation of ideas is perhaps discernible in the following passage: 'And they came to Jericho: and as he went out of Jericho with his disciples and a great number of people, blind Bartimeus, the son of

---

[1] One writer, anxious to discover a local reference, observes that Zebulon (Is. ix. 1), which contains Nazareth, is derived from בזל, κατῴκησεν. 'Ibi ergo habes, sed occulte et prophetice, ὅτι Ναζωραῖος κληθήσεται, h.e. Hebræorum more erit.'

Timeus, sat by the highway begging. And when he heard that it was Jesus *of Nazareth*, he began to cry out, and say, Jesus, *thou son of David*, have mercy on me. And many charged him that he should hold his peace: but he cried the more a great deal, Thou son of David, have mercy on me.' (Mark x. 46—48; Luke xviii. 35—39).

NOTES ON CHAPTER IV.

A. מחקק (Gen. xlix. 10) has been variously rendered, *lawgiver* and *ruler's staff*. The latter rendering is illustrated by Ps. lx. 7, 8; cviii. 9: Ephraim is my helmet; Judah my *sceptre;* Moab is my washpot; over Edom will I cast out my shoe. The former by Is. xxxiii. 22: 'For the Lord is our judge, the Lord is our *lawgiver*, the Lord is our king; he will save us.' But it matters little whether Judah, conceived of as living in the person of a descendant, be described as in possession of the ruler's staff; or whether it be declared explicitly that his descendant shall bear rule, until a certain *terminus ad quem*.

B. It has been suggested that the accusative ὁδόν (Matt. iv. 15) might be governed by a verb (which would be either *humbled*, or *glorified*) understood from the original Hebrew. But why is not '*land*' also in the accusative, as in the original? There are traces indeed of a reading γῆν, but it ill agrees with the general run of the LXX. rendering. Others seem to have supplied κατοικοῦντες. See *Holmes and Parsons*.

C. It may be here noted that we are not confined, even by classical usage, to what may be called the strict interpretation of τότε ἐπληρώθη, ἵνα πληρωθῇ, and the like. This is well illustrated by the subjoined passages quoted by Le Clerc, in his note on Matt. ii. 14:

(i). Διογενὴς ὁ Σινωπεὺς συνεχῶς ἐπέλεγεν ὑπὲρ ἑαυτοῦ, ὅτι τὰς ἐκ τῆς τραγῳδίας ἀρὰς αὐτὸς ἐκπληροῖ καὶ ὑπομένει, εἶναι γὰρ πλανῆς, ἄοικος, κ.τ.λ. Ælianus, Lib. III. c. 29.

Notes on Chapter IV.

Diogenes Sinopensis perpetuo dicebat de se, exsecrationes tragœdiæ *se explere* et ferre, esse enim erronem, sine domo, &c.

(ii). Simili ratione Olympiodorus, in vita Platonis, ei aptat versum Homeri :

κειμένου αὐτοῦ, μέλιτται προσελθοῦσαι πεπληρώκασιν αὐτοῦ τὸ στόμα κηρίων μέλιτος, ἵνα ἀληθὲς περὶ αὐτοῦ γένηται·
τοῦ καὶ ἀπὸ γλώσσης μέλιτος γλυκίων ῥέεν αὐδή.

Cum jaceret, apes accedentes impleverunt os ejus favis mellis,' *ut verum de eo fieret* illud Homeri : 'Cujus a lingua vox dulcior melle fluebat.'

D. In Ezek. xxiii. 8, this phrase ἐξ Αἰγύπτου refers to what had been begun ἐν Αἰγύπτῳ (ver. 3), and continued thenceforward : καὶ τὴν πορνείαν αὐτῆς ἐξ Αἰγύπτου οὐκ ἐγκατέλιπεν. In Hos. xi. 1, the LXX. read ἐξ Αἰγύπτου μετεκάλεσα τὰ τέκνα αὐτοῦ. 'But this seems so inconvenient, that a noted learned man (Vossius) as great a defender of the LXX. as any, not flying to a various reading, as if they read לבניו, as Cappell supposeth, saith, sane LXX. interpretes sic vertisse stultum est existimare, *that it is a foolish thing to think that the seventy Interpreters did so render*...Yet a long while hath this gone for the real version of the LXX. in this place. So Eusebius took it to be, and saith that Aquila reading it in the singular, τὸν υἱόν μου, did it δουλεύσας τῷ Ἑβραικῷ, addicting *himself to the Hebrew.* St Jerome also looked on it as so, while he hence takes an argument to shew that St Matthew cited this place, juxta Hebraicam veritatem, *according to the Hebrew truth*, and not according to the LXX.' There is an opinion, mentioned by Eusebius, and held chiefly by defenders of the LXX. reading, that St Matthew's reference is to Num. xxiv. 8, or elsewhere, instead of to Hosea. This opinion has been taken up by Vossius, who gives a caution, ne quis somniet ex Os. xi. 1 verba esse deprompta.

The Arabic follows the LXX. The Syriac has, *from Egypt I called him my son.* Symmachus, ὅτι παῖς Ἰσραὴλ καὶ ἠγαπημένος, ἐξ Αἰγύπτου κέκληται υἱός μου. In Matt. ii. 15, Wiclif has, *fro egipt I haue clepid my sone.* Other old English translations agree, word for word, with the Authorized Version. Compare, further: ἐκ κοιλίας μητρός μου ἐκάλεσε τὸ ὄνομά μου (Is. xlix. 1). St Paul may allude to Hos. xi. 1, 3, in Acts xiii. 17, 18 : He *reared* them (Is. i. 2) in Egypt; He *nursed* them in the wilderness.

CHAPTER V.

The suffering Messiah.

Is. lii. 13—15 ; liii.

GREAT as is the contention about the meaning and application of this prophecy, it may be laid down as generally admitted that a doctrine of vicarious satisfaction is contained therein, and that it must have formed the groundwork of apostolic teaching on the sacrificial death of Christ. Allusions to the passage and appropriations of its phraseology are frequent, while from the majority of its verses direct citations have been borrowed. There are more or less direct citations from lii. 15 ; liii. 1, 4, 5, 7—9, 11, 12, some needing only to be pointed out, while others, as presenting peculiar difficulties, invite a more detailed inquiry. But before proceeding to consider the citations, it may be well to attempt by a retranslation of the passage to elucidate some points which in the Authorized Version are obscure ; and in this retranslation it seems best to retain for the most part the familiar phraseology, even though it should appear that in some few cases another phrase might have been chosen with advantage, or another word have recommended itself as a more striking and exact representation of the original. It may be premised that some details which have no very obvious bearing on the question of citation have been passed by without discussion.

lii. 13. Lo, my servant shall deal prudently,
    He shall rise, and be extolled, and be very high.

The suffering Messiah.

14. Even as many were astonished at thee;
   So marred was his[1] visage more than any man,
   And his form more than the sons of men.
15. So shall he agast[2] many nations;
   Kings shall shut their mouth at him:
   When they see the like whereto had not been told them;
   And ponder the like whereto they had not heard[3].

liii. 1. Who had[4] believed the tidings told us,
   And for what manner of man[5] hath the arm of the LORD been displayed.
2. For he sent up as it were a shoot before him,
   As a stock[6] sendeth from parched ground,
   With no form thereto nor any beauty.
   And when we saw him, there was no sightliness that we should desire him.
3. He was despised and forsaken of men;
   A man of sorrows and acquainted with ills:
   And we hid as it were our faces from him;
   He was despised, and we esteemed him not.

---

[1] 'They marvelled, *saying*, How marred was his visage...' Thus the change to the third person is accounted for. The prophet *takes up* the direct form of address in ver. 15. [p. 122.]

[2] Or thus: 'So shall he make...to stand agaz'd.' The active verb *agast* (=*set a gaze*) is used by Chaucer, Spenser, &c. The Hebrew is יַזֶּה, which is here taken as fut. hiphil from הָזָה (Is. lvi. 10); *yahzeh* becoming *yazzeh*, just as *mah-seh* becomes *masseh* (Ex. iv. 2). See Note A, p. 124.

[3] Some see an allusion to this verse in 1 Cor. ii. 9 (but see Is. lxiv. 3). This view is in a manner confirmed by St Paul's words in ver. 8: 'Which none of *the princes of this world* knew...'

[4] This chapter (ver. 1—10) has been supposed to express the thoughts of the kings and nations as they stand 'aghast in speechless trance.' The past, '*had believed*,' may be conditional, as in Lam. iv. 12, 'The kings of the earth, and all the inhabitants of the world, *would not have believed* that the adversary and the enemy should have entered into the gates of Jerusalem.' Compare Hab. i. 5; Acts xiii. 41, 'which ye will not believe, though it be told you.'

[5] עַל מִי, 'who would have thought that for such an one...? What was he that for him...?' So in Amos vii. 2, 5: מִי יָקוּם יַעֲקֹב, 'What *is* Jacob that he should arise?'

[6] The *root* or stump did not spring up *en masse* from the ground, but sent out a small sucker or side shoot, *before* or in front. A *netser* grew 'out of his roots.' Is. xi. 1. See Rev. v. 5.

4. Surely himself took up our ills,
   And bare the burden of our sorrows:
   And we did esteem him
   Plagued, smitten of God, and afflicted.
5. Yet was he pierced for our transgressions,
   He was bruised for our iniquities:
   The chastisement of our peace was upon him;
   And with his stripes we are healed.
6. All we like sheep had gone astray;
   We had turned every one to his own way;
   And the LORD made to meet on him
   The iniquity of us all.
7. It[1] was exacted, and he was evil entreated,
   Yet he opened not[2] his mouth:
   As a lamb is led to the slaughter,
   And as a ewe before her shearers is dumb,
   So he opened not his mouth.
8. He was taken from prison and from judgment:
   (And of his generation who could tell?
   For it was cut off from the land of the living)
   For the transgression of my people that were plagued[3]:
9. And they appointed him a grave with wrongdoers;
   But with a rich man was his tomb[4]:
   Because he had done no violence,
   Neither was guile found in his mouth.
10. For the LORD purposed when he sorely bruised him:
    That if his soul would make an offering for sin,

---

[1] Viz. our *iniquity*, or its penalty. The Heb. *nagas* is applied to the exaction of debts. Lowth's rendering is: 'It was exacted, and he was made answerable.'

[2] Or: 'yet *would he not open.*'

[3] The plague spot of divine displeasure was on them, whereas we had thought *Him* plagued (ver. 4). For the construction, cp. Job iii. 15: 'Or with princes *that had gold,*' lit. *gold to them.*

The LXX. add a ה, thus נגע למות, ἤχθη εἰς θάνατον.

[4] 'It (viz. his honourable burial) was the beginning of the glorification which commenced with His death.' This first note of just requital leads up to the declaration in ver. 10, that suffering had been set before Him as the gate of glory. The LORD'S purpose, from first to last, was the conditional glorification of his Servant. See note B, p. 126.

The suffering Messiah.

He should see a seed prolong its days.
And the purpose of the LORD shall prosper in his hand.
11. Of the travail of his soul he foreseeth that he shall be satisfied[1],
By his knowledge that[2] he my servant, being righteous, shall make many righteous[3];
And their burden of iniquities himself will bear.
12. Therefore will I divide him a portion with the great[4],
And he shall divide the spoil with the strong;
Because that he poured out his soul unto death,
And was numbered with transgressors.
Yet himself took up the sin of many,
And He shall make intercession[5] for the transgressors.

The passage opens with the Divine sentence that the servant of the Lord shall deal prudently or prosperously and shall attain to the highest degree of exaltation that can be expressed or conceived. He shall be exalted (to borrow an expression from the old Messianic interpreters) 'above Abraham, and above Moses, and above the ministering angels.' The horror with which multitudes regarded, or rather shrunk from the sight of a form and visage so marred as scarcely to seem human, shall be surpassed only by the blank astonishment of kings and peoples at the glorious end of His self-sacrifice. They shall stand agazed, and dumbly ponder on the like whereunto had not before been seen or heard. Who *could* have believed such tidings? Who would have

---

[1] Since from the travail of his soul he is enabled to foresee a satisfaction, (by the consciousness that his undeserved sufferings shall redound to the justification of the many) he takes up the burden, and the purpose prospers. Heb. xii. 2.

[2] 'By his knowledge that'—There is a stop on this word in the Hebrew; the 'knowledge' referring equally to the *remainder of the clause*, and not specially to any portion of it. So the stop at 'him' (ver. 4) marks the *mutual coherence* of the following clause.

[3] Rom. iii. 26: δίκαιον καὶ δικαιοῦν-τα. Rom. v. 18, 19.

[4] Or: 'I will apportion him the many' (LXX. κληρονομήσει πολλούς). See Ps. ii. 8. '*Therefore*' means: *and so, for the* following *reason*, viz. 'because'.

[5] *Fut.* Having taken their sin upon him, he has obtained the right to intercede on their behalf. Heb. vii. 25. Cp. Heb. iv. 25.

thought that on the behalf of such an one the arm of JEHOVAH would have been displayed? seeing that in His first estate He was frail, and unsightly, and unpromising, like a side-shoot from a stump that had been left for dead in a thirsty soil. He was a man of pains and ills; we shrunk from the very sight of Him; He was despised and we esteemed Him not. But while we thought Him divinely plagued, His ills and pains were in truth what He had *taken up* from us, and was bearing as His own burden. We were *scattered* every one to his own way, and the Lord caused our multiplex iniquities to *clash together* upon Him. Satisfaction for others' sins was required of Him, yet He murmured not. He was dragged from confinement and the judgement-seat, for the transgression of 'my people,' on whom in truth lay the curse, and whose was of right the punishment. No trace of His generation remained upon the earth: none knew whence He came, or whither He went. He is like one that has been immured in a dungeon for long years till his antecedents are clean forgotten, and the circumstances that bring him then at length before the notice of the world, and draw the eyes, and soon the hearts, of all men unto Him, are His hasty condemnation and violent death. Not till after they had appointed Him a common grave with a heap of malefactors do they discover something of His true worth; and then they relent, and consign Him at last to a rich man's private burial mound. Here begins the glorification which the LORD had purposed from the beginning; and which *He* had as constantly foreseen from amid His sufferings. Because He suffered wrongfully, and poured forth His life in behalf of many, I will grant Him 'the many' for His inheritance, and the uttermost parts of the earth for His possession. He died once for their sins, and so shall ever live to make intercession for them.

I. *On the Messianic interpretation.* The application of the prophecy to the Messiah seems to have been accepted by the Jews of old without hesitation, and to have been abandoned subsequently with controversial aim.

The threefold exaltation: 'He shall rise, and be extolled, and be very high:' was applied, as we have seen, in its several gradations, to King Messiah. It describes, according to Kimchi, who avoids the Messianic interpretation, the greatest exaltation that can be expressed or conceived. The bearing of others' sins and diseases was also attributed to the Messiah; the only restriction being that He was viewed, at least by some, as solely or especially the deliverer of *Israel*. It has been well remarked by Gesenius, that to the Jew, with his notions of sacrifice and substitution, there was but one obvious and natural interpretation of those portions of the prophecy which told of one bearing the sins of others, and making expiation by His death. The Messianic interpretation was and in fact *must* have been, the oldest and the plainest to Jewish minds; and such considerations are of weight, as is elsewhere remarked, independently of the results to which any of the more modern methods of interpretation might seem to lead.

The frequent direct and indirect citations of the prophecy by Apostles and Evangelists, which will be considered in the sequel, show clearly the importance which they attached to it as a portraiture of the suffering Messiah. There is a distinct reference to Is. liii. 12, in the words of our Lord Himself: 'For I say unto you, that this that is written must yet be accomplished in me, And He was reckoned among the transgressors' (Luke xxii. 37); and it is not improbable that the intimation, 'how it is written of the Son of Man, that He must suffer many things, and *be set at nought*[1] (Mark ix. 12), had a principal reference to the prophecy in question. The allusion may have been thus definite, or it may, on the contrary, have been entirely general; but it assumes in any case, by its very brevity and indirectness, that the ancient Scriptures spoke more or less plainly and intelligibly of a suffering Messiah; for it is no merely didactic and explanatory statement, but appeals unmistakeably to an existing belief, and

---

[1] ἐξουδενωθῇ. Hengstenberg notices that in Is. liii. 3, Symmachus and Theodotion render נִבְזֶה by ἐξουδενωμένος.

would seem to imply that the prophecies alluded to were explained in accordance with Christ's words by 'the scribes' that had been mentioned in ver. 11. The correspondence between the historical Christ and his prophetic portraiture is so exact that it leaves nothing to be desired. A writer after the event could have produced no more graphic delineation of his life and person. 'Indeed the prophetic picture of the sufferings of Jesus of Nazareth is so lifelike, that when it has been for the first time brought before Jews ignorant of the passage, they have affirmed that the chapter has been inserted in the Christian editions of the Hebrew Bible[1].' On the other hand, such alternative applications as have been proposed cannot but be allowed to have fallen short of the description, which is thus made extravagant and untrue: there is, in fact, no attempt to appropriate the prophecy to any definite individual other than Jesus of Nazareth, which is sufficiently successful to call for notice. The theory that the description is borrowed from an older account of some individual martyr, besides standing solely on its merits, does not go to the root of the matter, or determine in what sense the prophet used the words and phrases which, according to this hypothesis, he had borrowed, as apt embodiments of his ideas, from some ancient source[2]. Nor again is there good reason for the assertion that the Messianic interpretation was an afterthought, and that it was natural for a later age, but not so for the prophet and his contemporaries, to discern in his description the lineaments of Christ[3].

There is another interpretation which explains the expression, '*my servant*[4],' as designating the prophetic order taken collectively; an interpretation which has little to recommend it, and which Rosenmüller, *e. g.* one of its former advocates, has rejected, for a more plausible but still incomplete inter-

[1] Aids to Faith, *Essay* III.
[2] Da er seine Gedanken nicht besser als durch solche *älterer* Worte ausgedrucken wusste...(*Ewald*). It may be added that Ewald regards Is. xl.—lxvi. as for the most part the composition of a later hand than Isaiah's.
[3] Der Glaube der Spätern hier den geschichtlichen Messias zu finden lag gewiss sehr nahe,.... (*Ewald*).
[4] The Messiah is called '*my servant* the branch,' in Zech. iii. 8 (Fürst).

pretation. This last demands consideration: the whole people are thought to be referred to under the collective title *servant*, and the prophet is supposed to describe their sufferings (in terms unprecedented) as an expiation for the sins of others. It needs scarcely be pointed out that on this supposition a far from literal interpretation must be adopted. The description must in fact be taken as ideal even to Jewish minds, and *a fortiori* to the kings of the nations who are depicted as astounded at their discovery then made, that the humiliation of the Jews had an expiatory virtue for their oppressors. But the difficulty of supposing the whole Jewish people to be alluded to has been felt by many interpreters, and accordingly a modification of this last view has been proposed. Since the reference cannot be to all, some would have it that the more pious Jews alone are designated[1]. This last eclectic theory may be dismissed with the remark, that it serves as a protest against the preceding application to the collective people. The requisite discrimination it would be especially unnatural to ascribe to the kings that wonder as they behold; nor is the criticism of Rosenmüller to be overlooked, that it is difficult to conceive of a part of the nation as suffering vicariously for the rest when one and all were involved in a common calamity.

The application to the collective people has some arguments in its favour which, though inconclusive, deserve consideration, and may contribute in a measure to the required solution. It is not remarkable that the modern Jews, attracted on the one hand by the national instinct, and repelled on the other by the polemical bias against Christianity, should have acquiesced in the conclusion that the expiatory value of Israel's sufferings and the future glorification of the race are here described. It must not however be denied that, prejudice apart, the arguments for this application are of some force, though not convincing.

The passage in question follows closely upon the summons: 'Loose thyself from the bands of thy neck, O captive daugh-

[1] So Paulus: 'non totum populum Hebræum sed meliorem duntaxat ejus partem intelligi existimat.'

ter of Zion. Break forth into joy, sing together, ye waste places of Jerusalem: for the Lord hath comforted his people, he hath redeemed Jerusalem. The Lord hath made bare his holy arm in the eyes of all the nations, and all the ends of the earth shall see the salvation of our God. Depart: touch no unclean thing. The Lord will go before you; and the God of Israel will be your rereward.' (Is. lii. 2—12).

The prophecy in question intervenes, and in immediate sequence the enlarged hopes and functions of the Jewish Church are set forth. It is henceforth to be a Church of the Gentiles. 'Enlarge the place of thy tent...For thy Maker is thine husband; and thy Redeemer the Holy One of Israel. The God of *the whole earth* shall he be called.' (liv. 2, 5).

From the form as well as from the general tenour of the context it might seem at first sight that the intervening passage now under consideration is descriptive of the collective chosen people; for not only are their sufferings and their restoration described before and after, but they are spoken of in the collective singular as the 'captive daughter of Zion,' and again, as 'a woman forsaken and grieved in spirit, and a wife of youth' for a moment forsaken, but now comforted with the assurance: 'with great increase will I gather thee.' All this however is very unlike the definite and sustained personality of the *servant of the* LORD, which is brought out the more clearly by comparison and contrast, and by the recurrent interchange of singular and plural, in relation to other personages there dramatically represented. He, the despised and forsaken one, becomes the marvel of great kings and nations, He alone bears the sins of multitudes that had wandered, each upon his several way. His generation was cut off and he suffered, one for all. He was numbered with criminals, but buried at length in a rich man's private tomb. He was upborne in suffering by the consciousness that his individual self-renunciation would issue in the restoration of the many. Throughout the passage, it may be asserted, there are as clear marks of sustained individualism as there could be if one only person were certainly described; whereas of the context, both before and after, nothing that at all approaches to this can be affirmed; but, on the contrary, the 'woman forsaken,' and 'the captive daughter,' are professedly representative of God's people and the holy city. The abrupt change to a pure singular in the intermediate passage is in itself striking, and needs to be accounted for: the more so that not only is a change of form adopted, but the individual, or what is presented individually, is very different in essential character from the city or collective people addressed before and after. It is nowhere intimated that the sufferings of the captive daughter of Zion were voluntarily undergone, or that they were endued with any power of expiation for the sin of others. At first Zion is afflicted: then restored. They had sold themselves for nought; they were redeemed without money (lii. 3), not by their own act or instrumentality, nor yet for any merit of their own. Zion restored is the purely passive recipient of the Redeemer's gift. Such contrasts must not lightly be passed over. Such distinctions remain to be accounted for, and they seem assuredly to militate against the more modern applications of the intermediate verses, or at any rate against the finality of such applications.

Like phraseology to that of Is. liii. 2 is indeed used elsewhere of the Jewish people, as *e. g.*, in a previous chapter of Isaiah: 'The vineyard of the Lord of Hosts is the house of Israel and the men of Judah his *pleasant plant*' (v. 7): and the immediate context is in a measure favourable to this acceptation. But the main conception of the passage has assuredly not been realized historically by any event in the national life; nor can it be said that any actually existent disposition of heathens towards Judaism is described in those verses, which some of the greatest commentators have referred not to the prophet, speaking in his own person, but to the Gentile kings, 'the princes of the world.' The description then must either depict something to be accomplished in the future (*i. e.* it must be *prophetic*), or it must embody an ideal which corresponds to no reality past, present, or to come. On the latter supposition it would be erroneous not in degree only but in kind. It would err, that is to say, not merely by predicting for Zion a more glorious future than was to be her heritage, but by attributing to her sufferings a propitiatory value, and to herself a perfect sinlessness at variance with fact and with the apparent tendency of other declarations of this same prophet.

As it is much disputed whether the fifty-third chapter contains the reflections of the heathen potentates or of the prophet himself, it may be well to notice some particulars tending to obviate objections to the former view, which has up to this point been presupposed. One of the chief objections arises from the expression '*my people*' in verse 8, which it is assumed must designate 'the covenant people, for whose benefit the atonement and substitution of the servant of God were, in the first instance, intended (Matt. i. 21); yea, were to a certain degree, exclusively intended, inasmuch as the believing Gentiles were received into it as adopted children[1].' But, in the first place, this same word *people* is in itself as applicable to heathens as to Jews; thus, 'Thou hast made us as the offscouring and refuse in the midst of the *peoples*' (Lam. iii. 45); and, secondly, the expression '*my people*' would come quite naturally from the mouths of the several Gentile kings. Nor is the term so obviously inappropriate even from Dr Hengstenberg's point of view, as above set forth. Whether indirectly or directly, the affliction of the servant of God was to bring peace, as Rashi remarks upon the passage, *to all the world;* and the Gentiles who are supposed to be expressing their astonishment, and acknowledging their criminality, may very naturally be regarded as converted and received within the pale of the 'covenant people.' They that were *lo-ammi*, not my people, had now become my people, *ammi*[2]. There are besides some considerations which directly favour the appropriation of Is. liii. 1—10 to the Gen-

---

[1] Hengstenberg, *Christology*, II. 292. The text referred to, 'He shall save *his* people from their sins,' seems scarcely to favour the narrower application of '*my people*.' Also, God is *not* speaking.

[2] The *former* view, viz. that one of the Gentile kings uses the expression 'my people' in its ordinary sense, is the view adopted in the text. Gen. xli. 40; Ex. ix. 27; 1 Kings xxii. 4.

tile kings. The most obvious interpretation of those passages which describe the servant of God as bearing the sins of others, seems to point to the conclusion that the whole punishment fell upon Him, while the guilty escaped the merited infliction. If this be so, then by an extension of Rosenmüller's argument against Paulus, we are led to reject the view that the suffering was endured vicariously for the redemption of *Israel;* for it cannot be denied that the chosen people suffered in their own persons, and are described by the prophets as reduced to the last extremity. 'We have transgressed and have rebelled: thou hast not pardoned. Thou hast covered with anger, and persecuted us: thou hast slain, thou hast not pitied. Fear and a snare is come upon us, desolation and destruction. Mine eye runneth down with rivers of water for the destruction of the daughter of my people.' (Lam. iii. 42—48.) 'Awake, awake, stand up, O Jerusalem, which hast drunk at the hand of the Lord the cup of his fury: thou hast drunken the dregs of the cup of trembling, and wrung them out. There is none to guide her among all the sons whom she hath brought forth; neither is there any that taketh her by the hand of all the sons that she hath brought up.' (Is. li. 17, 18.) Zion cannot then be said to have escaped punishment; nor were her sufferings other than the fit penalty of her own proper sins. What then is the relation of the servant of the Lord to the covenant people?

The Messiah, it would seem, is represented as the last relic of the chosen people; the one sprout that springs from the worn-out stem. His generation is cut off from the land of the living (Is. liii. 8); just as, in a verse above quoted, it is said of Zion that 'there is none to guide her among all the sons whom she hath brought forth.' As in a former chapter the individual Shear-jashub symbolises the *remnant* that *shall return*, so in the passage before us the remnant that returns from the captivity forms conversely the starting-point for the ideal conception of that solitary and mysterious Personage who makes atonement by his death for the whole world's transgressions. The world sins; he only suffers. He is slain by lawless hands; and the nations are drawn unto Him by the attraction of His death. Two representations above alluded to are thus avoided: viz. (i) that the chosen people escaped all sufferings; and (ii) that their actual sufferings were voluntary and undeserved. It remains only to consider whether there is anything unnatural in the supposition that the Gentile kings are here dramatically represented as contemplating and reflecting upon the sufferings and glorification of the servant of God. It may suffice to remark, in answer to any objection hence arising, that such dramatic representations are to be found in the Lamentations of Jeremiah. The desolated Zion is there depicted as crying to the outer world: 'Is it nothing to you, all ye that pass by? behold, and see if there be any sorrow like unto my sorrow, which is done unto me, wherewith the Lord hath afflicted me in the day of his fierce anger' (i. 12). The world treats her with derision: 'All that pass by clap their hands at thee; they hiss and wag their head at the daughter of Jerusalem, saying, Is this the city that men call The perfection of beauty, The joy of the whole earth? All thine enemies have opened their mouth against thee: they hiss and gnash the teeth: they say, We have swallowed her up: certainly this is the day that we looked for; we have found, we have seen it.' (ii. 15, 16). And again, in a verse already quoted, the astonishment of the whole world at her humiliation is described. (iii. 12).

II. *On the popular conception of the Messiah.*

There is an appearance of vacillation in the Chaldee paraphrase of this prophecy; some portions of it being referred to the Messiah, and others *to the nation*. This peculiarity of the version affords a ready answer to one objection against the Messianic interpretation. It is urged that the Christ is invariably depicted as a king or warrior[1]; and it is further assumed

---

[1] On the later fiction of 'a double Messias,' of a *son of Joseph* to suffer, and a *son of David* to reign, see Pearson *on the Creed*, Arts. II, IV, VII; Buxtorf. *Lex. Chald.*, root משח, and *s. v.* ארמילוס, root ארם.

that if predictions of a suffering Messiah really existed, the popular expectations at the time of Christ's appearance must have been very different from what they are admitted to have been. But the national bias would suffice to explain the prevalence of the actually existent notion, more especially if chief prominence was given even in Holy Scripture to the view which would in any case have commended itself most strongly to the populace. In the Targum above alluded to the sufferings of the Messiah are glossed over or more directly perverted. The descriptions of His sufferings are accommodated to their antecedent conceptions of Him as a subjugator of the heathen world; and that, 'haud raro contra planum et apertum verborum sensum.' If in their Authorized Version the notion of a suffering Messiah was thus suppressed, it was surely no more than natural that it should have gained but slight hold on the popular imagination. Nor is it difficult to account for the prevalence of such anticipations as in those times were uppermost in the Jewish mind. The triumph of Messiah was, so to say, an *elementary* conception. His sufferings were the teaching of a more advanced age. The result, His glory, was first proclaimed; and afterwards His career of suffering, the means whereby His glorification was to be achieved.

Nor again is it unnatural that even in later times the glories of Messiah should take precedence of His sufferings; that the former should be dwelt on ofttimes alone; the latter rarely, and then only in connexion with the former[1]. The apparent confusion in the Chaldee paraphrase is, as it would seem, in approximation to the clear and consistent rendering which assumes that the conception is ideal, but that the basis of the conception is the *national development*. This ideal, like others, was to be realized in the Messiah, to whom the prophet points. The humiliation complements but does not contradict the exaltation; and CHRIST is then more minutely

---

[1] This does not necessarily involve the assumption that the particular stage of such development is conceived of by the prophet as past or present: it may still be future.

portrayed when the temporary rejection of His people is in view.

III. *Recognized citations.*

The distinct references to this prophecy are numerous and range over the greater portion of the fifty-third chapter, besides including a citation from the last verse of the fifty-second. If the Messianic purport of the whole be first established, these direct citations occasion for the most part but slight difficulty: but besides the distinct and readily discoverable allusions, it is no more than a natural assumption that there must exist many latent and informal coincidences, which would yield at length to a careful scrutiny, and might when discovered give a clew to the argument and train of thought in some obscure and doubtful passages. Such a clew seems to be given in the vexed passage Phil. ii. 5—11, which will be considered in the sequel; but it is proposed first to discuss the chief recognized citations. In the subjoined list the numbers prefixed mark the verses of the original to which allusion is made, beginning from the last verse of the fifty-second chapter.

15. As it is written, To whom he was not spoken of, they shall see; and they that have not heard shall understand. (Rom. xv. 21).

1. That the saying of Esaias the prophet might be fulfilled, which he spake, Lord, who hath believed our report? and to whom hath the arm of the Lord been revealed? (Joh. xii. 38).

1. But they have not all obeyed the gospel. For Esaias saith, Lord, who hath believed our report? (Rom. x. 16).

4. That it might be fulfilled which was spoken by Esaias the prophet, saying, Himself took our infirmities, and bare our sicknesses. (Matt. viii. 17).

5, 6. By whose stripes ye were healed. For ye were as sheep going astray. (1 Pet. ii. 24, 25).

7, 8. The place of the scripture which he read was this, He was led as a sheep to the slaughter; and like a lamb

The suffering Messiah.

dumb before his shearer, so opened he not his mouth: In his humiliation his judgment was taken away: and who shall declare his generation? for his life is taken from the earth. (Acts viii. 32, 33).

9. Who did no sin, neither was guile found in his mouth. (1 Pet. ii. 22. Cp. Rev. xiv. 5).

11. Who his own self bare our sins in his own body on the tree, that we, being dead to sins, should live unto righteousness. (1 Pet. ii. 24).

12. And the scripture was fulfilled, which saith, And he was numbered with the transgressors. (Mark xv. 28).

12. For I say unto you, that this that is written must yet be accomplished in me, And he was reckoned among the transgressors. (Luke xxii. 37).

12. So Christ was once offered to bear the sins of many. (Heb. ix. 28. Cp. Joh. i. 29; 1 Pet. ii. 24; 1 Joh. iii. 5).

12. Who was delivered for our offences. (Rom. iv. 25. Cp. Matt. xvii. 22.)

Remarks on the foregoing citations.

15. St Paul here follows the LXX.: 'They to whom it was not announced concerning him shall see:' where the words, 'concerning *him*' (i. e. *my servant*, Is. lii. 13), are explanatory, and do not occur in the Hebrew. The original describes prospectively the astonishment of Gentile kings and nations, when they shall have seen what (*or*, such a thing as) had not been told them...;' the unheard-of marvel being the exaltation of the servant of the LORD, whose first estate gave no promise of so glorious an end. But the original certainly admits of the turn which has been given to it by the LXX.; 'when they to whom it had not been announced shall have seen.' These two renderings are ultimately coincident in meaning, and either might, without material change, be substituted for the other. St Paul has been asserting the independence of his Gospel labours: 'Yea, so have I strived to preach the gospel, not where Christ was named, lest I should build

upon another man's foundation: but as it is written, To whom he was not spoken of, they shall see: and they that have not heard shall understand.' He had made it his endeavour so to distribute his labours that he might tell of Christ to such as had never heard of Him; and this is precisely the same as saying that he had striven to make his announcement come freshly to his hearers, *sc.* by preaching to nations that had not named the name of Christ before.

1. The Evangelist and the Apostle agree in following the LXX., who prefix Κύριε, and this seems to confirm the *prima facie* impression that the question cited is put into the mouth of Esaias, and not merely referred to as occurring in the writings of that prophet. In the foregoing translation from the original it has been assumed, on the contrary, that converted heathens are represented as the speakers. This however involves no *essential* contrariety; for in the one case the prophet would be the actual speaker, and in the other would be representing mediately his own views and impressions. There are two points remaining to be considered, viz. the meaning of ἀκοή, for which the Authorized Version has *report*; and the propriety of the conditional rendering from the Hebrew, 'Who would, or could, have given credence?'

The word ἀκοή occurs in St Paul's citation, and is repeated in his inference from the citation; although its recurrence is not apparent to the English reader. The Authorized Version is as follows: 'But they have not all obeyed the gospel. For Esaias saith, Lord, who hath believed our *report?* So then faith cometh by *hearing*, and hearing by the word of God.' The corresponding word in the Hebrew may be roughly rendered *hearsay:* it means, not *report* or *preaching*, but something *heard*. In the last verse of Is. lii. the nations are represented as considering such a thing as they had never before been told of, and as reflecting thereupon: 'Who could have believed our *herynge*[1]' (liii. 1). The Greek ἀκοή represents, both in etymology and usage, the Hebrew word which it

---

[1] For Isaye seith, lord who bileued to our herynge. *Wiclif.*

replaces, and in its most natural acceptation is equivalent to the 'word of hearing,' or *word heard*[1]. Is this meaning necessary or admissible in St Paul's citation? 'The sense in the inference from the citation,' argues Tholuck, 'must be the same as in the citation itself[2]:' and the ordinary meaning seems most appropriate in the inference, for faith comes not immediately from *preaching*, but from the *hearing* and appropriation of the preaching. To adopt the rendering *preaching* or *report*, throughout the passage, gives rise, moreover, to the singular inconsequence: 'But they have not all obeyed the gospel. For Esaias saith, Lord, who hath believed our *report?* So then faith cometh by *report*.' A conclusion which would have followed more naturally upon the affirmation that *all had obeyed*. If however ἀκοή in the citation denotes what the Prophet, and those to whom it had been revealed, had 'heard of the Lord of hosts' (Is. xxi. 10), and in consequence believed, while others had not believed, because they had not heard; a logical connexion between the two verses, Rom. x. 16, 17, becomes at once apparent. 'Who believed the hearing that we heard?' Only we who heard. 'So then faith cometh not but by hearing.' *They* did not and in truth *could* not believe; 'for how shall they believe in him of whom they have not heard?' (ver. 14). This agrees, in all that concerns the Apostle's purpose in adducing it, with the original Hebrew as it has been rendered on p. 75. Whether Isaiah or the Gentiles speak the words, St Paul's argument for the necessity of preachers is the same. The Gentiles, we have assumed, are represented in the original as exclaiming; 'Who could have believed[3] (*sc.* had it not been revealed to him from without) the great mystery which we, having heard and seen,

---

[1] λόγος ἀκοῆς (Heb. iv. 12; 1 Thess. ii. 13). So Hengstenberg.

[2] Tholuck is here arguing *against* the meaning adopted in the text. See Alford, *in loc.*

[3] They say, 'who could have believed the report that we have heard?' as St Paul's quotation of the passage (Rom. x. 16) requires the sense to be, when he says, 'But they have not all believed the Gospel, for Esaias saith, who could have believed what we have heard?' (Mason and Bernard, *Heb. Gram.* II. 314). But their incapacity to believe is rather implied than expressed by τίς ἐπίστευσεν; 1 Cor. i. 21.

at length believe? St Paul represents them as not having believed, or been in a position to believe, antecedently to that *hearing* which cometh 'by the word of God.' But had they not heard at all? In a certain sense they had, though not effectually. 'Yes verily, their[1] sound went into all the earth, and their words unto the end of the world' (ver. 18).

St John cites Is. liii. 1, as fulfilled in the Jews, who, 'though he had done so many miracles before them, yet believed not on him: That the saying of Esaias the prophet might be fulfilled which he spake, Lord, who hath believed our *herynge?* and to whom hath the arm of the Lord been revealed?...These things said Esaias, when he saw his glory, and spake of him.' (Joh. xii, 38, 41). The writer had truly *heard*, and to him the Lord's mighty working had been revealed. Not so with all to whom the arm of the Lord had been displayed externally. Their disbelief is taken as implying their *inability* to believe, which is accounted for in the words of the same prophet[2]. For this reason could they not believe, 'because that Esaias said again, he hath blinded their eyes, and hardened their heart; that they should not see with their eyes, nor understand with their heart, and be converted, and I should heal them.' (Is. xi. 10). The Evangelist and the Prophet alike lay stress upon a revealing of the mystery as a pre-requisite for faith in what the world could not imagine for itself. Before believing they must hear, and the arm of the Lord must be revealed to them, even as to Esaias and his fellows. Not at the outward ears must the message stop; but it must penetrate, and be appropriated, and impress itself by a Divine power upon the inner sense.

4. The Evangelist renders and applies the Hebrew literally. The two Hebrew words rendered *took*, and *bare*, import respectively his *taking up* (*sc.* from others to himself) and his *bearing as a burden* the pains[3] and ills thus taken up. The

---

[1] This citation of Ps. xix. 4 describes the testimony of the material universe to the glory of God.

[2] 'Sequitur amplius, non poterant credere.' *Bengel*.

[3] The word *pain* is perhaps the best rendering of מַכְאוֹב, although the familiar 'sorrows' has been retained in the

Hebrew implies the continued burdensomeness of these 'infirmities;' the servant of the Lord was bowed down beneath the weight, from which others had been relieved by the transference of their sicknesses to Him. In the Gospel the chief stress is laid upon the removal of literal diseases by Christ, and except so far as *sympathy* with the afflicted is implied, there is no reference to the oppressiveness of His burden; no intimation that it fell with its full force upon Him. He is represented rather as one able to bear, without sensible depression, the infirmities which were found too heavy for the powers of frail humanity. He was preeminently the strong One who 'pleased not himself,' but vouchsafed 'to bear the infirmities[1] of the weak.' (Rom. xv. 1—3). The original more plainly implies, and the LXX. expresses[2], that he was *afflicted* on behalf of others.

5, 6. The words, 'by whose stripes *we* were healed,' stand, in the Hebrew, in parallelism with the statement: 'the chastisement of our *peace* was upon him.' The word 'peace' might also be rendered *soundness*[3]; and the meaning would thus correspond more exactly with the succeeding clause, viz. that cited by St Peter. As 'the blueness of a wound cleanseth away evil' (Prov. xx. 30); so 'the stripes and weals that were inflicted upon Him have made us sound and well.' In a word which follows the citation: 'ye were as sheep going astray; but are now returned unto the Shepherd and *Bishop*[4] of your souls;' there may be, as it has been suggested, a passing reference to Ezek. xxxiv. 11, 'Behold I, even I, will both search my sheep, and *seek*[5] them *out*.'

7, 8. This citation has given rise to great diversity of interpretation, and none of the current renderings can be said to recommend itself as convincing, or to have been accepted by general agreement as other than provisional. The Greek

---

translation on p. 76. The words ἀσθενείας and νόσους aptly correspond to the original expressions.

[1] τὰ ἀσθενήματα βαστάζειν.
[2] περὶ ἡμῶν ὀδυνᾶται.

[3] '*Venustissimum* ὀξύμωρον,' exclaims Vitringa here. He means the same as Jerome when he says: *suo vulnere vulnera nostra curantur* (Delitzsch).

[4] ἐπίσκοπον. [5] ἐπισκέψομαι.

words are in themselves difficult, and perhaps, it may be found, misleading; for they suggest, as most obvious, what are far from satisfactory renderings of at least one clause. The rendering of the Hebrew is no less disputed; and both the original and the citation being thus unsettled, various attempts have been made to force each into accordance with some more or less arbitrary interpretation of the other. An independent investigation will suggest as admissible and appropriate, a rendering which had been presented *in paraphrase*, by some of our own older translators, but has been, as it would seem, owing to the form in which it was presented, now for a long time set aside, neglected and forgotten. In this rendering, it should be premised, there is no attempt to make it appear that the special verses cited are, throughout, exactly correspondent to the particular words or verses in the Hebrew for which they stand; but while no approach is made towards harmonizing in the literal and grammatical sense, it will be found in the end that we have set before us in the passage considered, what is in all other than merely critical respects a most apt citation, and an appropriate *text* for a discourse upon the passage from which it is taken. But before entering upon this direct examination, it may be well to state some of the principal explanations as now accepted of the clauses wherein lie the chief difficulties and stumbling-blocks: 'In his humiliation his judgement was taken away: and who shall declare his generation? for his life is taken from the earth[1]?'

(i) Bengel and others understand this *taking away of judgement* as equivalent to *justification*. This view is drawn out by Dr. Wordsworth as follows: *In his humiliation, &c.*, represents the Hebrew, 'He was taken from oppression and judgement;' and it seems the LXX. means to say that *by his humiliation his condemnation was taken away*, i.e. *He was justified:* and thus the words are a paraphrase of the original, and mean that, 'He was made perfect, through (as well as from) sufferings,'

---

[1] ἐν τῇ ταπεινώσει αὐτοῦ ἡ κρίσις διηγήσεται; ὅτι αἴρεται ἀπὸ τῆς γῆς ἡ ζωὴ αὐτοῦ ἤρθη, τὴν δὲ γενεὰν αὐτοῦ τίς αὐτοῦ.

The suffering Messiah.

and was exalted not only *from* His humiliation, but *because* 'He humbled Himself and became obedient unto death.' (Phil. ii. 8; Heb. ii. 10).

Who shall declare His duration? i.e. although He is cut off as man, yet He is the eternal God. He is ἀγενεαλόγητος ὡς Θεός.

Because His life is cut off from earth (Dan. ix. 26), He endures for ever in heaven; that is, He as God-man is exalted for ever by His temporary humiliation on earth.

(ii) Another explanation corresponding to Lowth's rendering of Is. liii. 8:—'By an oppressive judgement (*lit.* oppression and judgement) He was taken off:'—is thus alluded to by Mr Humphry in his note on Acts viii. 23:

The following explanation of this difficult verse is, with some shades of difference, generally adopted by commentators; 'In His humiliation, when He was arraigned by the Jews, He was unjustly dealt with; the true judgement of Him was taken away. And who shall describe the wickedness of the generation which treated Him thus? For His life is taken away by them from the face of the earth.'

In each of the above interpretations there is an assimilation of the Greek to what are in fact unsatisfactory renderings of the original Hebrew. But it is perhaps needless to seek for an exact agreement between the particular verses cited from the Greek and the corresponding verses in the Hebrew. Such assimilation would seem almost to be declared unnecessary by the terms in which the citation is introduced. What we have presented is professedly an extract or summary, and it would suffice to show that it well represents the general tenour of the passage from which it has been taken. Philip is commanded by the angel of the Lord to 'go toward the south unto the way that goeth down from Jerusalem unto Gaza, which is desert. And he arose and went: and, behold, a man of Ethiopia, an eunuch of great authority under Candace queen of the Ethiopians, who had the charge of all her treasure, and had come to Jerusalem for to worship, was returning, and, sitting in his chariot, read Esaias the prophet.

96 *The suffering Messiah.*

Then the Spirit said unto Philip, Go near, and join thyself to this chariot. And Philip ran thither to him, and heard him read the prophet Esaias, and said, Understandest thou what thou readest?...The *place*[1] of the Scripture which he read was this, He was led as a sheep to the slaughter[2], &c.' (Acts viii. 26 —33). This word 'place' may be equivalent to our *paragraph* or *section;* or it may denote only the *general contents*[2] of the passage read. 'And the eunuch answered Philip and said, I pray thee, of whom speaketh the prophet this? of himself, or of some other man? Then Philip opened his mouth, and began at the same Scripture[4], and preached unto him Jesus.' No comment on the passage is subjoined, and nothing more specific is implied about it, than that it was applicable to JESUS, and formed a suitable text for a discourse upon His life and death. The literal rendering, 'In His humiliation His *judgement* was taken away,' represents effectually the ambiguity of the Greek. The word *judgement* suggests naturally, but not necessarily, a *judicial* sentence; and so too does its Greek equivalent. But either word might be applied to a mere estimate or opinion, that is passed unauthoritatively upon any person or thing. There is a passage in the LXX. version of the second book of Kings which affords a peculiarly apt illustration of the meaning that seems most appropriate in the passage before us. 'What *manner of man* was he which came up to meet you, and told you these words?' where the literal rendering would be: 'What is the judgement[5] (i.e. the true *estimate, character*, and *status*) of the man?' This meaning of 'judgement' leads to a clear and appropriate rendering of the clause in question: viz. 'in (or *by*) humiliation, the true estimate[6] of Him was taken away:'

---

[1] περιοχή.
[2] "May not this be a kind of summary or heading of the passage meant? Such a manner of introducing a passage is found in Classical Greek." In Rabbinic Hebrew, it is *usual* to quote fragmentarily, and to presuppose in the reader a familiarity with the passage alluded to.
[3] The *tenoure*. Tyndale, Cranmer.
[4] 'Commoda ratio doctrinæ, ordiri a textu oblato, et reliqua quæ dicenda sunt, subnectere.' *Bengel.*
[5] τίς ἡ κρίσις τοῦ ἀνδρός; 2 Kings ii. 7.
[6] κρίσις is here abstract. In 1 Kings i. 7, it may be said to be taken con-

and this is found upon examination to be coincident with the rendering of Tyndale and Cranmer[1]: 'Because of His humbleness He was not esteemed.' The clause would thus depart very widely from the particular words of which the Greek is professedly a rendering, but would aptly correspond to a main feature in the prophetic picture of the Messiah, who was despised and rejected, 'and we esteemed Him not,' but judged Him according to appearance, not with rightful judgment (Joh. vii. 24).

The remaining clauses may be rendered, in accordance with patristic exegesis: 'And who shall declare His generation[2]? seeing that His life is upraised from earth;' where the present αἴρεται denotes not the single act of removal from the earth, but (solely or supplementarily) a chronic state of exaltation above it, which contrasts with the 'humiliation' of the former clause. The whole verse would thus describe the mystery and greatness of His being, which were wrongly deemed of through His humiliation. The clause: 'who shall declare His generation?' may have given rise to the prevalent opinion, expressed in Joh. vii. 27, that 'when Christ cometh, no man knoweth whence He is.' The Hebrew, as we have rendered it, represents His generation as cut off from the earth, so that no trace could be found of the stock from which He sprung. The Greek amounts to a sublimation of the original, and expresses, what the prophet may have intended to shadow forth in such guise as his general treatment of the subject admitted. The representation in this particular would be necessarily imperfect and inadequate, in its

---

cretely of the man's true worth, which is the *thing estimated*. It may be remarked that the word *character* has this same double use.

[1] Wiclif's rendering is: 'in mekenesse his dome was *taken up*,' or *accepted* by him.

[2] Delitzsch observes that the LXX. τὴν γενεὰν κ.τ.λ. 'can only mean, so far as the usage of the language is concerned: *Who can declare the number of his generation?*' i.e. of his spiritual *posterity*. But this is not required by the usage of γενεά. See Ps. xlviii. 20, γενεᾶς πατέρων αὐτοῦ. The word may mean *stock*, or, abstractly, *lineage*. Perhaps it here signifies, more diffusively, the whole nature of his life and being. It would thus very properly stand in parallelism with '*life*,' as does the same Hebrew word דוֹר in Is. xxxvii. 12: 'Mine *age* is departed, &c.'

literal acceptation; in like manner with the succeeding declaration: 'He shall see a seed prolong its days.' The latter must be spiritualized, and so the former; and this former when spiritualized takes not unnaturally such a turn as the patristic commentators, above alluded to, have given it. The admissibility of this interpretation may be regarded from another point of view. In Heb. vii. 3, the mysteriousness of Christ's origin is regarded as symbolized by the absence of any recorded genealogy of Melchisedec. The *same* writer might be conceived of as drawing a like inference from Isaiah's words: 'who could declare His generation, for it was cut off from the land of the living?' And if so, there is little difficulty in conceiving that such a view may have been present to the *Prophet's* mind, and may be developed legitimately from his words.

Other explanations of γενεά[1].

(*a*) In the original Hebrew, the word 'generation' stands in parallelism with the common word for 'life,' just as in the hymn of Hezekiah, referred to in the notes; where the meaning *contemporaries* is not obviously appropriate, for it seems harsh, in that context, to speak of the king's 'generation' as removed from him, rather than of the king himself as taken from their midst. More than this, it is probable, as lexicographers remark, that this word for *generation* means, firstly, *a period*[2], and only secondarily, the generation of men living at that period; but, whatever may be the *order* of significations, the word is clearly used in numerous passages for a period, and measure of time. (*b*) Or it might signify (as some think) in the first instance, not *age* but *dwelling-place:* thus Ps. xlix. 20 has been interpreted: 'he shall go to his fathers' *dwelling-place,*' the grave. The meaning, *fleshly* '*tabernacle,*' is appropriate in the hymn of Hezekiah, and would lead, if adopted in Is. liii. 8, to the same meaning, *manner of life*[3], which commentators, in this or that way, have arrived at, as

---

[1] But see, especially, § (i), p. 123. βίωσις. The classical βίος includes both.
[2] דוֹר might mean *ætas*, and hence, [3] See note D, p. 127.

best suited to the passage. This meaning is applied by Bishop Lowth, *in loc.*:—It is said that, before any one was punished for a capital crime, proclamation was made before the prisoner by the public cryer in these words: quicunque noverit aliquid de ejus innocentia, veniat et doceat de eo. And our Saviour seems to refer to such a custom, and to claim the benefit of it, by His answer to the High Priest, when he asked Him of His disciples and of His doctrine: 'I spake openly to the world; I ever taught in the synagogue and in the temple, whither the Jews always resort; and in secret have I said nothing. Why askest thou me? ask them which heard me, what I have said unto them: behold, they know what I have said' (Joh. xviii. 20, 21). St Paul likewise, in similar circumstances, standing before the judgment seat of Festus, seems to complain of the same unjust treatment; that no one was called, or would appear to vindicate his character. 'My *manner of life* from my youth, which was at the first among my own nation at Jerusalem, know all the Jews: which knew me from the beginning, if they would testify; that after the straitest sect of our religion I lived a Pharisee.' (Acts xxvi. 4, 5).—Such a meaning of 'generation' may be adopted, perhaps even more appropriately, if this commentator's rendering be not accepted as a whole, but modified in one particular. 'His manner of life who *would* declare?' is Lowth's rendering: *i.e.* who would come forward *i.e.* to declare His innocence, to which it was actually in his power to testify? But the *potential* rendering, 'who *could* declare?' is at least equally admissible, and, brings out moreover the same meaning from the original that has been assigned, independently, to the corresponding clauses in Acts viii. 33:—He was dragged from confinement and the bar; and who could describe or imagine the whole tenour of His being: *cut off* as he was, in the dungeon, from communion with the living world? 'They have cut off my life in the dungeon, and cast a stone upon me. Waters flowed over my head; then I said, *I am cut off.*' (Lam. iii. 53, 54).

9. This word 'sin' corresponds to *violence* in the original,

and to *lawlessness* in the LXX. In the second clause the LXX. read *guile*, in the accusative, thus making it depend on the verb *did*. The true construction seems to be: 'neither guile in his mouth;' where the copula has to be supplied. St Peter supplies it in the form εὑρέθη, *was found*, which has been adopted in the translation on p. 76.

11. Besides the verbal coincidence, 'bare our sins,' there is apparently a paraphrastic agreement between the conclusion of the verse from St Peter, and a clause of Is. liii. 11. 'My righteous servant shall *make many righteous*, for he shall bear their iniquities.' 'He bare our sins, that we should live unto righteousness.'

12. Our Lord's citation in Luke xxii. 37 gives an example of *a priori* application, and thus approves most emphatically the Messianic interpretation of the prophecy. In Heb. ix. 28, the statement that 'Christ was once offered to bear the sins of many,' is supplemented by the declaration that 'unto them that look for Him shall He appear the second time without sin unto salvation;' which agrees with the true rendering of the last clause in the Hebrew: 'and He *shall* make intercession for the transgressors.' The LXX. conclude less accurately with: 'He *was* delivered for their offences.' This form of words has been adopted by St Paul, who does not however stop short at their conclusion, but adds that He 'was raised again for our justification.'

IV. There is a difficult passage in the Epistle to the Philippians, which seems to have been formed upon the concluding verse of the fifty-third chapter of Isaiah. The Authorized Version, which is considered open to objection, runs as follows: 'Let this mind be in you, which was also in Christ Jesus: Who, being in the form of God, *thought it not robbery to be equal with God: But made Himself of no reputation*[1], and took upon Him the form of a servant, and was made in the likeness of men: And being found in fashion as a man, He humbled Himself, and became obedient unto death, even the

---

[1] οὐχ ἁρπαγμὸν ἡγήσατο τὸ εἶναι ἴσα Θεῷ, ἀλλὰ ἑαυτὸν ἐκένωσεν, κ.τ.λ.

death of the cross.' (Phil. ii. 5—8). The meaning of the English, which perhaps the majority of commentators now reject as inappropriate, is that, though conscious of His divine dignity, and feeling equality with God to be His of right, He yet 'made Himself of no reputation,' and condescended to assume the servile form of man. The explanation by which the above is commonly replaced, is, that He did not treat His equality with God as a piece of plunder, or a thing to be clutched greedily and guarded jealously, but divested Himself of the glories and prerogatives of Deity by taking to Himself the form of man. The main obstacle[1] to the acceptance of some such rendering as this latter is the palpable impropriety of likening Christ's equality with God, *more or less directly*, to a spoil or thing external. Attempts have indeed been made to prove that this Greek word *plunder* frequently signifies nothing further than a thing to *set store by*, the idea of plunder and robbery having passed out of sight; but it would seem that the examples adduced to prove this are not quite convincing, and fail at their best to do more than remove the idea of acquisition one step into the background. If a *spoil* does come to mean a thing to be held to pertinaciously, it is only because it is still regarded as a thing external, not inherent, and which *because of its externality* may escape one's grasp, if it be not guarded jealously. A way of meeting this difficulty will be suggested in the sequel: meanwhile, the verses following will be considered.

'*He made Himself of no reputation*,' is a paraphrase of the Greek words, *He emptied Himself*, which is explained as meaning that, *He divested Himself* of the external attributes of Deity, and 'stripped Himself of the insignia of majesty.' 'The emphatic position of ἑαυτόν' continues Dr Lightfoot, 'points to the humiliation of our Lord as *voluntary*[2], self-

---

[1] The concrete use of ἁρπαγμός 'presents greater difficulty' from a *scholar's* point of view : but, all things considered, the most telling objection seems to be the theological one. Mr Wratislaw observes (*in loc.*) 'so too δόσις has constantly the meaning of δόμα,' and compares ἀσπασμός to which (conversely) ἀσπασμα is frequently equivalent.

[2] This (without αὐτόs) seems destructive of the emphasis on ἐκένωσεν.

imposed.' There is however another explanation of the words: 'Himself He *emptied:*' admissible alike in English, Greek, and Hebrew, viz.; *He poured out*[1] *His soul or self*[2]: and that, as it is added in ver. 8, *unto death.* Here then it would seem that we have a reference to Is. liii. 12, where it is written that, 'He hath poured out His soul unto death.' The citation is presented in two parts, and the Apostle, in a running comment, fills in the several steps whereby the lowest depth of degradation has been reached. He poured out His divine Self, by taking the servile form of man, and keeping His divinity in abeyance. He further humbled His human self by obedience, to the extent of death, and that death the death of the cross. In the expression 'servant' there is a phraseological coincidence with Is. lii. 12, *My servant* shall deal prudently. Christ, from his pre-existence as coequal God, assumes the servant-form of man. He becomes, *i. e., God's* servant, by becoming man; and then, as above described, He further bowed Himself to the most degrading of deaths. 'Therefore,' declares JEHOVAH by the prophet, 'will I divide Him a portion; because He hath poured out His soul unto death.' (Is. liii. 12). 'Wherefore,' adds the Apostle, 'God also hath highly exalted him, and given Him a name which is above every name.'

It remains to ask by what train of thought the Apostle may be supposed to have arrived at the comparison or contrast in ver. 6; 'He deemed it not ravin[3] to be as God.' With these concluding words has been well compared the '*Ye shall be as*[4] *God(s)*' of Gen. iii. 5. St Paul once and again contrasts the characteristics of the first and the second Adam, 'As in

---

Besides, mere spontaneity is expressed sufficiently in the preceding clause.

[1] אל תער נפשי (Ps. cxli. 8); where Aquila has, μὴ ἐκκενώσῃς. Symmachus and Theodotion, μὴ ἀποκενώσῃς. Compare the classical, ἐκκενοῦν θυμὸν εἰς σχεδίαν γέροντος, and εἰς με κένωσον πᾶν βέλος (*Lidd. and Scott*).

[2] In Ps. cv. 18, the Hebrew words: 'his soul (i. e. *person* or *self*) entered into iron:' are rendered in the Bible version: '*He* was laid in irons.' The Prayer Book inverts the construction and renders: 'The iron entered into his soul.'

[3] He demed not raueyn, that him silf were euene to god. *Wiclif.*

[4] The particle of comparison, כ, is here rendered ὡς (LXX), but in many other places ἵνα.

Adam all die, even so in Christ shall all be made alive.' 'The first man Adam was made a living soul; the last Adam was made a quickening spirit.' 'The first man is of the earth, earthy; the second man is the Lord from heaven.' (1 Cor. xv. 22, 45, 47). In the passage before us, as some think, there may be an explicit contrast between the mind of Adam and the mind which was in Christ Jesus, who stands out in marked contrast with the natural man, and reverses alike his actions and their consequences. If the negative particle be taken as not merely excluding a supposition, but as *reversing*[1] it, and implying its direct opposite; so that the 'thought *not* ...*but* made,' of ver. 6, 7, would mean: 'so far was he from thinking...that he made;' there results an explanation which accounts for the origin of the comparison with 'ravin,' and at the same time obviates the difficulty which would arise from comparing, more or less remotely, to a thing external, what in the immediate context has been declared to be inherent in Christ. At the same time, to recognize this word *ravin* as describing a thing external, brings out very effectually what seems the true significance of the emphatic ἑαυτόν, His very Self: so far was He from clutching at equality with God as a thing external, that He renounced His inmost SELF, and kept in abeyance his inherent equality with God. He did not as did Adam, who deemed it ravin to be equal with God; but emptied out His divine Self, and took the servant-form of man. And so He shall rise and be extolled and be very high. He shall be seated far above all principality, and power, and might and dominion, and every name that is named, not only in this world, but also in that which is to come. Every knee shall bow to do Him homage; every tongue shall confess that He is LORD. Angels and men are

---

[1] Is. x. 15 may be again referred to for a typical example of this *reversing* power of the negative. 'Shall the axe boast itself against him that heweth therewith? shall the saw magnify itself against him that brandisheth it? as if the rod brandished them that wield it; as if the staff wielded the *no-wood*:' i.e. *man*, who, so far from being dead matter like itself, is 'of a quite different and superior nature.'

given over to His dominion, and become His portion. 'He inherits multitudes, and divides *the mighty for*[1] *a spoil.*'

This the LXX. may intend to express. But independently of the Greek, many think that the balance of argument is for a like rendering of the Hebrew: 'I will give Him a portion in[2] the many; and He shall apportion for Himself the[3] mighty (*or* the numerous).' The word here rendered *many* is so rendered by the Authorized Version in lii. 14, 15; liii. 11, 12; and has been replaced by *great* in the first clause of the twelfth verse, merely to avoid a rendering which would be palpably inappropriate; for to share the spoil along with many others, argues the comparative smallness of the individual share. It is more in accordance with the general tenour of the passage to represent Him as at length exalted far above all rivalry, and moreover there is a marked retributive propriety in His *possessing* the multitudes for whom He suffered. Such, we conclude, *must* be the meaning of the Hebrew, if *rabbim* in the first clause of ver. 12 means the same as both before and after. The righteous One, foreseeing that He should justify the *many* (ver. 11), resolves to take upon Himself the burden of their sins: He bears the sin of *many* (ver. 12): and JEHOVAH bestows upon Him the *many* for His portion.

If this be the true interpretation of liii. 12, the representations of our Lord as, strictly speaking, a *Redeemer*, are traced at once to their source. A further examination of the LXX. rendering shews that they probably intended to express this more explicitly than had been supposed above. Their words should perhaps be rendered: 'Therefore shall He[4] (that

---

[1] τῶν ἰσχυρῶν...σκῦλα, a spoil consisting of the mighty (Is. liii. 12). So Jud. v. 30, σκῦλα βαμμάτων.

[2] As *in* a territory.

[3] The parallelism favours this rendering; the *article* before 'many' corresponding to את, taken as the mark of the objective case.

[4] διὰ τοῦτο αὐτὸς κληρονομήσει πολλούς, καὶ τῶν ἰσχυρῶν μεριεῖ σκῦλα, ἀνθ' ὧν παρεδόθη εἰς θάνατον ἡ ψυχὴ αὐτοῦ, κ.τ.λ. Comp. ἀντὶ τοῦ θανάτου αὐτοῦ (ver. 9). αὐτὸς refers back to αὐτὸς ἀνοίσει, and strongly marks the consequential connection of the two verses.

bare the sins of many) inherit *many*, and divide the spoil of the mighty, *for whom His life was given up* to death...' Our Lord declares that 'the Son of Man came not to be ministered unto, but to minister[1], and *to give His life a ransom for many*[2]' (Matt. xx. 28; Mark x. 45); where the last clause expresses the same idea as the LXX., and exhibits, too, the same form of words, with the addition of the epexegetical λύτρον, or *price of redemption*. St Peter appeals to the elect as knowing that they 'were not *redeemed* with corruptible things, as silver and gold[3], But with the precious blood of Christ, as of a *lamb*[4] without blemish, and without spot' (1 Pet. ii. 18, 19). And St John expresses the same more at length, in other words: 'And when he had taken the book, the four beasts and four and twenty elders fell down before the *Lamb*, And they sung a new song, saying, Thou art worthy to take the book, and to open the seals thereof: for thou wast slain, and hast redeemed[5] us to God by thy blood out of every kindred, and tongue, and nation' (Rev. v. 8, 9).

V. *The Lamb of God.* Joh. i. 29, 36.

1. The form of the above expression, and the manner in which it is introduced by the Baptist, combine to prove that the appeal is to some pre-existent and definite conception, the origin of which would naturally be sought for in Holy Writ. The title must refer—as Dean Alford justly remarks—to some known and particular lamb. It is inconceivable that the expression should, in a testimony so precise and formal as that of the Baptist, be nothing but an hyperbole, and that, *one wholly unprecedented*, and to his hearers *unintelligible*. Christ is designated as at once the Lamb of God, and the taker away of the sin of the world[6]; and this double title[7]

---

[1] εὖ δουλεύοντα πολλοῖς (Is. liii. 11).
[2] δοῦναι τὴν ψυχὴν αὐτοῦ λύτρον ἀντὶ πολλῶν. See 1 Tim. ii. 6.
[3] οὐ μετὰ λύτρων οὐδὲ μετὰ δώρων (Is. xlv. 14).
[4] Is. liii. 7.   [5] ἐξηγόρασας.
[6] 'Agnus Dei primum a mundo in se recepit, deinde a seipso devolvit peccati sarcinam.' *Bengel.*
[7] Bengel's view of the construction is the following: 'Chrysost. *Dicit Johannes, ἀμνὸν καὶ ὅτι αἴρει κ.τ.λ.*' Vulg. '*Ecce agnus Dei, ecce qui tollit* etc. Uterque illud ὁ ἀμνός, ὁ αἴρων, non per con-

points to Isaiah's prophecy of One who Himself bears the sins of others, and is likened in ver. 7 to a lamb led to the slaughter. Some see a mere reference to the paschal lamb, to which St Paul compares our Lord in 1 Cor. v. 7: 'Christ our passover is sacrificed for us.' Such a reference is by no means to be excluded, but rather to be held in conjunction with the former[1]: indeed it is by the whole scheme of sacrificial typology that the special reference would itself be instinctively interpreted by the Baptist's hearers. That system would naturally present itself to the Jewish reader of Is. liii., and at once open to him a meaning which a mind untrained by the sacrificial system would have passed over. The prophecy is a gem set in the sacrificial framework; the main pinnacle to which the whole structure converges. The system was contrived with such regard to minute details, and those details were adhered to with so religious a scrupulosity, that it is at least more natural to regard them as having, than as not having, some designed meaning and significance. It is unnecessary to suppose that those details, standing alone, would have been understood as clearly prophetic types of the Messiah; but it may be affirmed that they entered largely into the prophetic ideal of Is. liii., and that this ideal with its after realization in Christ, threw a flood of light on what before had been perceived but dimly, and deepened by its intense illumination the shadows of the past. There are clear indications in the Old Testament that such external acts as the offering of slaughtered animals, were without efficacy in themselves; their typical import was apprehended; their true spiritual significance had been gathered up and set forth, in this fifty-third chapter of Isaiah, many ages before the coming of the just ONE, whom Evangelists announce as the final Antitype.

2. St John, in his Apocalyptic vision, 'beheld, and lo, in the midst of the throne and of the four beasts, and in the midst of the elders, *stood a Lamb*[2] *as it had been slain.*' And

---

structionem substantivi et adjectivi, sed per appositionem accepit.'

[1] 'Atque ipsum pascha tum prope erat' (Joh. ii. 13). *Bengel.*

[2] ἀρνίον ἑστηκὸς ὡς ἐσφαγμένον (Rev. v. 6). The LXX has, ὡς πρόβατον ἐπὶ

The suffering Messiah.

in his account of the crucifixion he quotes, as fulfilled in Christ, what was ordained in the law of Moses about the paschal lamb: 'When they came to Jesus, and saw that he was dead already, they brake not his legs. These things were done that the scripture might be fulfilled, A bone of Him shall not be broken.' (Joh. xix. 33, 36.) It is doubted whether the Evangelist refers to Ex. xii. 46: *Ye shall not break a bone thereof:* or to Ps. xxxiv. 20: Many are the afflictions of the righteous: but the Lord delivereth him out of them all. He keepeth all his bones: *not one of them is broken*. There is too 'another place which speaks of the same point, viz. Numb. ix. 12: *and a bone they shall not break in it*.' But the language of the Psalm would itself, no doubt, have been formed upon the familiar phraseology of the Law; and, accordingly, we may adopt the view expressed by Bengel, 'Psalmus Mosen, Johannes Psalmum, nec non Mosen respicit.' A passing allusion, from whatever chapter and verse taken, would at once bring before a Jewish reader the details of the familiar paschal solemnities: one word, with its sudden flash, would light up all around.

VI. *The good Shepherd.* Joh. x. 11—19.

The appropriation by our Lord of this title shepherd might be regarded as a gathering up of many prophetic utterances, with a particular[1] reference to Is. liii. The strength of the evidence for this connection lies in the uniqueness of the reiterated expression, '*lay down*[2] *my life*.' 'I am the good shepherd: the good shepherd *giveth his life*[2] for the sheep. But he that is an hireling, and not the shepherd, whose own the sheep are not, seeth the wolf coming, and leaveth the sheep, and fleeth: and the wolf catcheth them and scattereth the sheep. The hireling fleeth, because he is an hireling, and

σφαγὴν ἤχθη (Is. liii. 7), and in the *following* clause has ἀμνός for 'ewe.'

[1] '*Pastor bonus*) ille de quo prædictum est per prophetas...*Ponit*) Hoc quinquies dicitur, summa vi. Hoc summo omnia reliqua beneficia pastoralia præsupponuntur, includuntur, inferuntur [*Esai.* liii. 10, 6].'

[2] τὴν ψυχὴν αὐτοῦ τίθησιν. Comp. παρατίθεμαι (Luke xxiii. 46): and τέθηκας, used of temporary deposition, Luke xix. 21.

careth not for the sheep. I am the good shepherd, and know my sheep, *and* am known of mine; as the Father knoweth me, *and*[1] I know the Father: and *I lay down my life* for the sheep. And *other sheep I have, which are not of this fold:* them also I must bring, and they shall hear my voice; and there shall be one fold, and one shepherd. Therefore doth my Father love me, because *I lay down my life*, that *I might take it again.* No man taketh it from me, but *I lay it down* myself. I have power *to lay it down*, and I have power to take it again. This commandment have I received of my Father.' 'The expression, *to put one's soul for some one*,' writes Dr Hengstenberg, 'does not, independently and by itself, occur any where else in the New Testament; in John xiii. 37, 38, Peter takes the word out of the mouth of the Saviour, and in 1 Joh. iii. 16, it is used in reference to these declarations of our Lord. The expression is nowhere met with in profane writers, nor in the Hellenistic *usus loquendi.* In the discourses of our Lord, no less than in Is. liii. 10, the expression is used of His sacrificial death.' These considerations might be thought sufficient to establish the allusion to the prophecy; but it may be added that the sheep are there represented as actually scattered (Is. liii. 6; Joh. x. 8, 12); and that the laying down of his life by the servant of the Lord, is one act only in a *set purpose*[2], which lacks completion till the life is taken up again. (Is. liii. 10; Joh. x. 17.) 'This commandment have I received from my Father.' This, 'the LORD purposed when He sorely bruised him.'

Mr Robertson thus depicts the risks incidental to the shepherd-life: 'Beneath the burning skies and the clear starry nights of Palestine there grows up between the shepherd and his flock an union of attachment and tenderness. It is the country where at any moment sheep are liable to be swept away by some mountain-torrent, or carried off by hill robbers,

---

[1] 'There is a reciprocal affection between the Shepherd and the sheep. There is a reciprocal affection between the Father and the Son; and the one is the parallel of the other.' (Robertson, *Sermon on Joh.* x. 14, 15.)

[2] With βουλή (Acts ii. 23; iv. 27) compare חפץ, βούλεται (Is. liii. 10). For ἅγιον παῖδα (iv. 27), see the following ver. of Isaiah.

or torn by wolves. At any moment their protector may have to save them by personal hazard. The shepherd-king tells us how, in defence of his father's flock, he slew a lion and a bear: and Jacob reminds Laban how, when he watched Laban's sheep in the day, the drought consumed. Every hour of the shepherd's life is risk. Sometimes for the sake of an armful of grass in the parched summer days, he must climb precipices almost perpendicular, and stand on a narrow ledge of rock, where the wild goat will scarcely venture. Pitiless showers, driving snows, long hours of thirst—all this he must endure, if the flock is to be kept at all.' This shews something of the significance of our Lord's $\psi v \chi \grave{\eta} v \ \tau i \theta \eta \mu \iota$. He risks or stakes His life for the sheep, not without a clear prescience of the issue; and thus, in other words, he casts away or deposits that life to save the sheep. If the passage of St John above cited be taken as explanatory of the passage in Isaiah, we may trace the prophet's form of expression (ver. 6, 8) to its source. We were like lost sheep: He, the shepherd, was made responsible for our wanton strayings: He took to Himself the consequences of our iniquities, that He might be able to say, 'Of them which Thou gavest me have I lost none.'

The cardinal passage to which the New Testament constantly refers in connection with redemption by Christ's death, is on all sides allowed to be this fifty-third chapter of Isaiah. If then in references to the subject generally (and still more, where a reference to the actual passage is discernible) we note a reiterated expression of any doctrine about the extent of the efficacy of that death: it is only natural to ask whether that doctrine reflects any new light upon the prophecy itself, or favours this or that of the conflicting views upheld by commentators. Now our Lord refers in His discourse upon the good shepherd, to His *other sheep*, 'which are not of this fold.' The Baptist again, referring to the same cardinal passage of Isaiah, speaks of JESUS as taking away the sins of the *world*. The Evangelist marks with strong emphasis this universality of the redemption. 'And one of them, named Caiaphas, being the high priest that same year, said unto them, Ye know nothing at all, nor consider that it is expedient for us that one man should die for the people, and that the whole nation perish not. And this spake he not of himself: but being high priest that year, he prophesied that Jesus should die for that nation; and not for that nation only, but that also He should gather together in one *the children of God that were scattered abroad.*' (Joh. xi. 49—52.) Such passages fall in with the view adopted in the text, that Is. liii. 1—10 contains the reflections of the Gentile world.

VII. *The twenty-second Psalm.*

This Psalm has been compared with the passage from Isaiah above discussed, and is regarded, from various points of view, as distinctly applicable to the Messiah. Some have supposed a primary reference to David (to whom it is inscribed), with a mystical appropriation to Christ; others have held that it is simply and solely Messianic. On the other hand non-Messianic interpretations have been built upon the hypothesis of a personal reference, (*e. g.* to David or to Hezekiah), and again of a reference by personification to the exiled Jewish nation. 'I may however mention,' writes Dr Phillips, 'that there is this one great objection to either David or Hezekiah being made the subject, viz. the utter impossibility to find events in the life of one or the other to correspond with the statements which are here recorded. There is not indeed one expression throughout the Psalm which would lead the student to the history of David or Hezekiah, for the purpose of searching out the agreement of statement with event.' Against the application to the collective Israel, the clearly marked individuality of the Psalm is very reasonably adduced: 'The mother[1] of the sufferer is mentioned; a tongue, jaws, hands and feet, bones, and garments, are ascribed to him; nay, in ver. 7, he is distinguished from the ungodly, and in ver. 23, from his brethren.' And further, 'it must be noticed that there is nothing from which we can conclude that the sufferings of the individual were a punishment for his sin;

---

[1] Ps. xxii. 11 illustrates Hos. xi. 1, 3.

his innocence, although not expressly asserted, may yet be inferred. Whereas the sufferings of the Jewish people were always regarded as merited; they have been usually considered as the consequences of their abandoning God, and adopting a heathenish idolatry.' This however does not necessarily exclude a reference *of some kind* to the captivity and its circumstances, the existence of which is rendered probable both from a direct view of the Psalm taken separately, and from its phraseological and other coincidences with Psalms wherein the circumstances of the captivity are commonly supposed to be alluded to. The hundred and second Psalm is very generally referred to that occasion, and to this the twenty-second is in many respects similar, as also to the disputed sixty-ninth, on which more hereafter. The following is a transcript of Dr Phillips' preface to Ps. cii. 'The title of this Psalm is either, a prayer *of,* or a prayer *for,* the afflicted. In the latter case, this portion of Scripture may be regarded as a form of prayer adapted for the use of a Church or an individual when oppressed by heavy affliction. From several passages, it appears that the Psalmist prays either for himself, or *as representing in his own person the people of Israel* who were at that time in captivity, but who were by certain circumstances induced to expect a speedy return to their country, and the restoration of the temple in Zion.' To the same effect, Mr Perowne: 'This Psalm must have been written by one of the exiles in Babylon, probably towards the close of the captivity, when the hope of a return seemed no longer doubtful. In mournful strains he describes his bitter lot. His very heart was smitten within him, as the grass is withered in the hot eye of the sun. His enemies turned his misery into a proverb; his life was drawing to a close under the heavy wrath of God.' Then comes the prospect of deliverance; of the rebuilding of Zion; and the conversion of the kingdoms to serve the Lord.

This much being premised with regard to the reference of Ps. cii., we proceed to indicate its general and particular agreement with Ps. xxii. and lxix.

The suffering Messiah.

In each case an individual, reduced to the last extremity, cries to God for aid. He is parched and blasted by his fiery trial: 'my strength is dried up like a potsherd' (xxii. 15); 'my throat is dried' (lxix. 3); 'my bones are burned as an hearth. My heart is smitten and withered like grass' (cii. 3, 4). He is a *reproach* of men (xxii. 6; lxix. 20; cii. 8) and is grieved especially by the taunt that JEHOVAH is not indeed the Salvation of His people (xxii. 8; lxix. 6). The LORD at length is glorified in heaven and earth, when it is seen that 'He hath *not despised* nor abhorred the affliction of the afflicted' (xxii. 24); 'for the Lord heareth the poor, and *despiseth not* his prisoners' (lxix. 33). 'He will regard the prayer of the destitute, and *not despise* their prayer' (cii. 17). The allusion to the captivity[1] seems clearly marked in Ps. lxix and cii., while the general result is described by similar expressions in all three of the psalms considered. 'All the ends of world shall remember and turn unto the Lord: and all the kindreds of the nations shall worship before Thee. A *seed* shall serve Him; it shall be accounted to the Lord for a generation' (xxii. 27, 30). 'Let heaven and earth praise Him, the seas and every thing that moveth therein. For God will save Zion, and build the cities of Judah: that they may dwell there, and have it in possession. The *seed* also of his servants shall inherit it: and they that love His name shall dwell therein' (lxix. 36). 'So the heathen shall fear the name of the Lord, and all the kings of the earth his glory. When the Lord shall build up Zion....The children of thy servants shall continue, and their *seed* shall be established before thee' (cii. 28). This conclusion[2], common to the three Psalms, seems to point to the speaker as no merely ordinary individual —'an exile in the hands of the heathen, in extreme peril, and

---

[1] It is not argued that the three Psalms refer to the same time, but only that there is a general similarity in their structure. The indefinite term 'afflicted' (xxii. 24) is quite appropriate to 'prisoners.' It stands in the heading of Ps. cii., which refers to 'the groaning of the *prisoner*,' in ver. 20.

[2] Add to this the form of address in ver. 4: '*our* fathers trusted, &c.', which falls in with the suggestion in the text. See Ps. xxxix. 12.

condemned to death,' who shews 'how a worshipper of Jehovah could at such a time win his way to hope from the depths of despair'—but as a *typical* Sufferer, whose deliverance is the turning point in the world's destiny and the sign for the converting of the nations from scorners (ver. 8) to worshippers. The allusions to different stages of captivity in the general Psalms by no means proves that those Psalms were actually written contemporaneously with the circumstances described, and with a merely historical reference to them; but only that the circumstances of those times lent an imagery for the expression of certain feelings and conditions, which *we still retain* as suited for the representation of spiritual ideas. There is something more than a conventional propriety in such an expression as being *tied and bound by the chain of our sins;* nor is there any very obvious reason for the assertion, that the like expressions when they occur in a Psalm are necessarily literal, and that it was left for a later age to discover their true spiritual application. If such applications now present themselves as natural to the devotional reader, it is allowable to conjecture that the like may have been the case with the older Jews (who used the same Psalms devotionally[1]); and it is very far from incredible that they may have been *actually composed* with a meaning which some interpreters would now call non-natural. If the speaker in the Psalm be a typical sufferer, the Psalm might naturally be appropriated by individual worshippers—as Psalms still are—and yet point, κατ' ἐξοχήν, to an individual MESSIAH as its perfect antitype. The probability of a Psalm's having been so used, and of its having conveyed a Messianic reference to the ancient Jews, must be tested, obviously, by such indications as may be gathered (from whatever source) of their scriptural exegesis and modes of thought. Such indications are afforded by the New Testament applications, which, to take the lowest ground, express the thoughts of the individual writers, and more than this, *were intended to be* (and doubtless were)

---

[1] The heading of Ps. cii. may be roughly rendered, *Penitential Psalm.*

understood by their contemporaries, to whom they were addressed by way of illustration or of argument.

VIII. *Ps. xxii. compared with Is. liii.*
Assuming that the Psalm is, in some one of the senses proposed by commentators, to be applied to the Messiah, we remark that it portrays him less minutely than does the Prophet, or rather that it is an essentially partial representation, which shews forth one side only of the sufferer's condition. It tells simply of *suffering* and *restoration*, without implying that the suffering was voluntarily undergone, or that it contributed by way of merit to the wellbeing of the nations. In Isaiah, on the contrary, the Servant of the LORD deliberately takes up the sin of others, and by so doing frees them from their burden. Here, the Gentiles are convinced of Jehovah's power and faithfulness by the delivery of His worshippers, and so they turn and serve Him. Here again the restored sufferer praises the LORD in the great congregation; while there all conduces, as the LORD had purposed, to the glory and exaltation of His servant. The Psalmist tells of hope to God's chosen One from the abyss of despair, and of a world's conversion at the sight of His deliverance: the Prophet describes Him as the world's Redeemer, and tells of a glory and dominion that He purchases by the outpouring of His Soul.

IX. *Narrative of the Crucifixion.*
In Ps. xxii, as in the sixty-ninth, we have presented to us the picture of a typical sufferer, and in the circumstances of Christ's crucifixion the Gospel history shews a literal correspondence of *word* and *deed* with the description in the Psalms. 'And when they were come unto a place called Golgotha, that is to say, a place of a skull, *They gave him vinegar to drink mingled with gall* (Ps. lxix. 21): and when he had tasted thereof, he would not drink. And they crucified him, and parted his garments, casting lots: that it might be fulfilled which was spoken by the prophet, *They parted my*

The suffering Messiah.

garments among them, and upon my vesture did they cast lots (Ps. xxii. 18). And sitting down they watched him there; and set up over his head his accusation written, THIS IS JESUS THE KING OF THE JEWS[1]. Then were two thieves crucified with him, one on the right hand, and another on the left. And they that passed by[2] *reviled*[3] *him, wagging their heads* (Ps. xxii. 7), and saying, Thou that destroyest the temple, and buildest it in three days, save[4] thyself. If thou be the Son of God, come down from the cross. Likewise also the chief priests mocking him, with the scribes and elders said, He saved others; himself he cannot save. If he be the King of Israel, let him now come down from the cross, and we will believe him. *He trusted in God; let him deliver now, if he will have him* (Ps. xxii. 8): for he said, I am the Son of God. The thieves also, which were crucified with him, cast the same in his teeth. Now from the sixth hour there was darkness over all the land unto the ninth hour. And about the ninth hour Jesus cried with a loud voice, saying, '*Eli, Eli, lama sabachthani*[5]' (Ps. xxii. 1), that is to say, *My God, my God, why hast thou forsaken me?*' 'Some of them that stood there, when they heard that, said, This man calleth for Elias. And straightway one of them ran, and took a spunge, and filled it with vinegar, and put it on a reed, and gave him to drink. The rest said, Let be, let us see whether Elias will come to save him' (Matt. xxvii. 33—49). 'And when Jesus had cried with a loud voice, he said, Father, *into thy hands I commend my spirit* (Ps. xxxi. 5): and having said thus he gave up the ghost' (Luke xxiii. 46).

St John also describes the offering of this same potion, but with the variation of a word; and describes it moreover as necessary for the complete fulfilment of the scripture. 'After this, Jesus knowing that all things were now accomplished[6],

---

[1] JESUS is thus marked out by *heathens* as a representative personage. So in the Psalm, as had been concluded independently, the sufferer is to the heathen view a representative of Israel.

[2] 'And the people stood *beholding*' (Luke xxiii. 35, and LXX).

[3] μυκτηρίζω (Mark and LXX).

[4] σωσάτω (Luke and LXX).

[5] אלי אלי ממול מה שבקתני, is the Targumic version of the clause.

[6] τετέλεσται.

"that the scripture might be fulfilled[1]," saith, I thirst. Now there was set a vessel full of vinegar: and they filled a spunge with vinegar, and put it upon *hyssop*, and put it to his mouth. When Jesus therefore had received the vinegar, he said, It is finished: and he bowed his head, and gave up the ghost' (Joh. xix. 30). The allusion is, apparently to Ps. lxix. 21; 'They gave me also gall for my meat; and in my thirst they gave me vinegar to drink:' and the formula of citation would seem to testify emphatically to a Messianic reference in the Psalm. The precise nature of that reference is left undetermined by the citation, and is to be gathered, as is elsewhere remarked, from a study of those ancient Jewish modes of thought, to which the words and imagery of the Jewish Scriptures appealed. The hypothesis of a *typical* representation which would adapt a Psalm for individual[2] devotions, and at the same time convey to those who used it the notion of a perfect individual Antitype, fulfilling literally what was expressed symbolically, is not *prima facie* at variance with the affirmation that though 'all things (in themselves necessary) were *completed*,' it was further requisite to *complete* the series of external agreements between the words of Scripture and the circumstances of Christ.

X. *The 'vinegar mingled with gall.'*

It is remarkable that, while the second potion mentioned by SS. Matthew and Mark corresponds to the *one* mentioned by St John, yet the first, as described by St Matthew, presents the closest verbal resemblance to what is spoken of in Ps. lxix. 21. St Matthew's description *suggests* the propriety of a modified rendering in the Psalm; and St Mark's variation has given rise to a subjoined conjecture of Dr Nicoll which well deserves attention.

1. St Matthew speaks of 'vinegar *mingled with* gall;' the

---

[1] τελειωθῇ.
[2] The form of some Psalms which treat of national events, while the speaker is clearly an individual, may be accounted for by supposing them to have been written expressly for congregational use.

Psalm, in separate hemistichs, of 'gall *for meat*,' and 'vinegar *to drink*.' The question which presents itself is whether the hemistichs should not rather be taken as referring alike to the potion, and as thus connecting the ὄξος and the χολή— in like manner with the Evangelist's account. The Hebrew 'gall' presents no objection, but on the contrary, the evidence is rather in favour of its use as a decoction: 'The Lord our God hath put us to silence, and given us *water of gall* to drink' (Jer. viii. 14). The word with which it is joined in the Psalm, is of greater difficulty. It does not occur again[1], but its meaning has been conjectured from a few passages to be *solid food*. It is allowable however to conjecture that it means generally *a ration*[2], without exclusive reference to solids or to liquids; or even that it may have referred *originally* to liquids, and may have come at length to be applied generally, like the common expression for a banquet, *mishteh* (Gen. xix. 3). The verse in question might then be explained to mean (with strict adherence to the tenses of the original), that they put 'gall' into my allowance, when they were on the point of giving me my ration of 'vinegar' to quench my thirst. The anesthetic potion customarily administered to the condemned is treated of in the standard commentaries. It was supplied, as Lightfoot notes[3], by the 'daughters of Jerusalem,' and was refused by the Saviour because (in the words of Bengel) *sensus plane imperturbatos volebat retinere ad mortem usque*. Some arguments will be adduced in a later section, for the stupefying qualities of the 'gall,' as mentioned in the *Psalm*. With regard to the second potion, it may be observed that there are two ways of reconciling the three accounts. It is usual to conform St John's account to that of SS. Matthew and Mark, by taking *hyssop* to mean a *rod* which chanced to be of hyssop. If however it be thought more natural to

---

[1] But see Lam. iv. 10 (LXX).

[2] ברות, *a portion*, might be referred to ברה, *to select*. In 2 Sam. iii. 35, the rendering, 'All the people came to cause David to *partake of* bread,' is, seemingly, as appropriate as '*eat*.' See 2 Sam. xiii. 6, 10, &c. Symmachus has, τροφήν.

[3] So *Poole*: 'Sanctæ mulieres vinum myrrhatum Christo pararunt more gentis.'

The suffering Messiah.

explain St John's account as meaning that some hyssop was placed *in* or *round*[1] the sponge, we might then bring St Matthew's account into conformity with it by the simple expedient of rendering κάλαμος, *reed-plant*[2], and understanding it, not of an instrument wherewith the saturated sponge was presented[3], but of some drug or aromatic substance, which was sprinkled or infused before the 'vinegar' was offered.

2. The late Professor Nicoll has proposed[4] to reconcile the two descriptions of the first potion, by referring both accounts to an Aramaic original, wherein the variation *myrrh* for *gall*, might have arisen from the corruption of a single letter[5]. The same writer makes suggestions for harmonising other varying accounts; beginning with the accounts of our Lord's baptism, which it is proposed to reconcile as follows. "St Matthew thus describes the baptism of Christ: 'And Jesus, when He was baptized, *went up* straightway out of the water: and lo, the heavens were opened upon him' (iii. 16). St Mark has nearly the same words: 'And straightway *coming up* out of the water, He saw the heavens opened' (i. 10); where both of them make use of the same words, *to go or come up*. But St Luke, in relating the same circumstance, expresses himself somewhat differently: 'Jesus also being baptized, and *praying*, the heaven was opened' (iii. 21). Instead of saying that Jesus *went up* out of the water, he says that He was *praying*. This little difference may be accounted for, by supposing that St Luke read in the document the word denoting *prayer*, which differs from that denoting to *go up* by a single letter, which is very similar to its corresponding one, and might easily be taken for it[6]. In the same passages SS. Matthew and Mark represent the Spirit of God descending upon Him 'as a dove,' where St Luke has 'in a bodily shape like a

---

[1] ὑσσωπίτης οἶνος, *wine prepared with hyssop* (Lidd. and Scott, *Lex.*). Περιθείς, like περιβάλλειν, circumdare, &c., admits either construction.

[2] νάρδος καὶ κρόκος, κάλαμος καὶ κινάμωμον. Cant. iv. 14.

[3] Luke xxiii. 36.

[4] *Sermons*, p. 124.

[5] מורא for מרא (usually written מרירא). The word for *hyssop* is מרוא.

[6] One reading may have been, *on his praying* (צלה); the other, *on his going up* (עלה).

dove.' The reason of this difference might be easily explained by supposing that SS. Matthew and Mark used the word denoting similitude in a pleonastic sense[1], (like a particle of similitude) while St Luke gave to it its strongest signification."

XI. *The Serpent of brass.* Numb. xxi. 9; Joh. iii. 14.

There are two matters in relation to the brazen serpent, which it will be best to consider separately. First, what was its probable significance, to those who looked to it for healing, and before any typical reference to Christ had been pointed out? And, secondly, in what way was His crucifixion antitypical to the elevation of the serpent?

1. To a people saturated with the principle of religious symbolism the lifting up of the serpent could scarcely fail to suggest the *existence of* some esoteric meaning, which may or may not have been grasped more definitely than such general conviction would of necessity imply. The following is the account of the transaction: 'And the people spake against God, and against Moses....And the LORD sent fiery serpents among the people, and they bit the people; and much people of Israel died. Therefore the people came to Moses and said, We have sinned, for we have spoken against the LORD, and against thee; pray unto the LORD, that He take away the serpents from us. And Moses prayed for the people. And the LORD said unto Moses, Make thee a fiery serpent, and set it on a pole: and it shall come to pass, that every one that is bitten, when he looketh upon it *shall live*. And Moses made a serpent of brass, and put it upon a pole. and it came to pass, that if a serpent had bitten any man, when he beheld the serpent of brass, he lived' (Numb. xxi. 5—9). There are some reflections upon the narrative in the *Wisdom of Solomon* (xvi. 5—7): 'For when the horrible fierceness of

---

[1] Compare: 'דמות, *a likeness, a thing like;* Is. xl. 18, *what likeness will ye compare with him?* Usually concrete, *an image,* &c. An adverb: *like as,* instar. Is. xiii. 4.' (Fürst, *Lex.*) So כנו, *sicut similitudo, quasi* (Buxtorf, *Lex. Chal.*).

beasts came upon these, and they perished with the stings of crooked serpents, thy wrath endured not for ever: but they were troubled for a small season, that they might be admonished, having a sign of salvation, to put them in remembrance of the commandment of the law. For he that turned himself toward it was not saved by the thing that he saw, but by thee that art the Saviour of all.' 'Certain it is that the Jews do allow that this brazen serpent was a figure of something else, and that it had a spiritual sense and meaning. And when Justin Martyr, in his dialogue with Trypho the Jew, insisted upon this as a type of the death of Christ, and appealed to the company what reason (excluding that) could be given of this matter; one of them confessed that he was in the right, and that himself had enquired for a reason from the Jewish Masters, but could meet with none[1].' That it had a meaning, all allow: what the meaning was some do their best to explain, others deprecate the attempt as impious: '*challâ! challâ!* the thing was done by God's command, and it is not for us to inquire into the why and wherefore of the serpent form.' So writes R. Aben Ezra; and lest his warning should be disregarded, he puzzles the too curious inquirer with some further questions:—"Where is the wood that will sweeten bad water when honey cannot? What is the meaning of *laying a lump of figs upon the boil*, when it is not in the nature of them to remove it? But the truth is: 'Such knowledge is too wonderful and excellent for me: I cannot attain unto it." Another commentator (Rashi) writes: 'And our authorities have said, *Can a serpent kill or make alive?* Nay, but when Israel looked upward, and humbled their heart to their Father which is in heaven, they were healed, and if they refused, they perished.' All this is testimony to the *existence* of a meaning which has still to be sought. Here a noted allegorist comes to the inquirer's aid, and *leads up to* a plausible interpretation. 'Philo the Jew does in several places mention the difference between the *serpent of Eve*, and the *serpent of Moses*, or this brazen serpent of which I am now

---

[1] Kidder, *Demonstr. Messias*, I. 211.

speaking¹. He makes one directly opposite to the other; and that which deceived Eve to be a symbol of voluptuousness, and in token thereof doomed to *goe upon his belly* (Gen. iii. 14): but this of Moses to be a symbol of fortitude and temperance. That was the destroyer of mankind, this the saviour of the Israelites: *every one that sees it* (the brazen serpent) *shall live. Very true: For if the mind bitten with* Eve's *Serpent*, which *is voluptuousness, can spiritually discern the beauty of temperance:* i.e. *The Serpent of* Moses, *and through it, God himself, he shall live. Onely let him see and consider.*' That the serpent should carry back the thoughts of a Jew to the serpent of Eve, seems natural, not to say unavoidable; but that the serpent of Moses should have been thought to represent directly something *good* would be least of all likely when the plague was a plague of serpents. The way to salvation was by a bruising of the serpent's head (Gen. iii. 15); and Moses, by affixing the serpent to the flagstaff, seems to have symbolised *the impalement and extermination of the* BODY OF SIN.

2. Our Lord's *lifting up* is thus compared by Him to the lifting up of the serpent: 'As Moses lifted up the serpent in the wilderness, even so must the Son of man be lifted up: that whosoever believeth in Him should not perish, but have eternal *life*' (Joh. iii. 14, 15). Where it is not affirmed that the serpent was a direct representation of Christ, but in reverse order, the lifting up of Christ is assimilated to the elevation of the serpent. The type is not formed upon the model of Christ, but Christ is assimilated thereunto. 'Christ hath redeemed us from the curse of the law, being made a *curse* for us: for it is written, Cursed is every one that hangeth on a tree²' (Gal. iii. 13). 'He hath made Him to be *sin* for us, who knew no sin; that we might be made the righteousness of God in Him' (2 Cor. v. 21). In the familiar sacrificial system the victim 'is regarded as bearing the sins of those for whom atonement is made. The curse is transferred

[1] Kidder, *Demonstr. Messias*, I. 211. metu sic loqui, nisi apostolus præiret?'
[2] 'Quis auderet sine blasphemiæ *Bengel.*

from them to it. It becomes in a certain sense, the IMPERSONATION of the sin and of the curse[1].'

Additional remarks.

1. The transition to the third person, in lii. 14, has been explained briefly as arising from a sudden (*idiomatic*) change in the speaker's point of view. We are expecting: 'so marred was *thy* visage:' but the prophet throws himself into the beholder's point of view, and writes: *so marred was* 'his' *visage*. This commingling of direct and indirect narrations is quite in accordance with Hebrew usage. A striking example occurs in Ps. xi. 1: 'How say ye to my soul, Flee as a bird to your mountain?' Where the Psalmist, in the middle of a quotation, comes back suddenly to his own point of view, and instead of sustaining the *quotation*, 'Flee as a bird to our mountain,' he writes, 'Flee as a bird to' your 'mountain.' In Is. lii. 14, 15, the prophet thus passes from the second person to the third (which he then retains):

Even as many marvelled because of thee,
That so marred was 'his' visage more than any man:
So shall he agast, &c.

2. *His rest shall be glorious* (Is. xi. 10). 'Abravenel brings these words as a proof that what is said (Is. liii. 9), *He made His grave with the wicked*, cannot belong to the Messiah, because it is said that His rest shall be glorious[2]. The vulgar Latin renders these words, *erit sepulchrum ejus gloriosum*. And we find the Greek interpreters elsewhere render the word *rest* in this sense. Thus, *he shall enter into peace, they shall rest in their beds*...is by the Greek rendered, *his burial shall be in peace*.' The objector here takes for granted that the earlier chapter of Isaiah is Messianic. If this be so, it is difficult, as Stier well observes, to avoid the conclusion, that Is. liii. (which so strikingly reproduces the prophecy of the *Netser*) must itself be Messianic.

---

[1] See Lightfoot on *Gal.* iii. 13. In Hebrew, *sin-offering* actually means *sin*.

[2] Kidder, *Demonstr. Messias*, I. 261.

3. *Who shall declare His generation?*

(i) One of the meanings above suggested is, Who could describe Him, *sc.* by defining the stock from which He sprang? There is a common usage of *generation*, which entirely justifies some such explanation. 'It is also taken[1] for men of like quality and disposition, though neither of one place nor age. Ps. xiv. 5. God is in the *generation* of the righteous' (Prov. xxx. 11—14; Matt. iii. 7; Acts ii. 40; 1 Pet. ii. 9). In Ps. xxiv. 3, the question is asked, 'Who shall ascend into the hill of the LORD? or who shall stand in His holy place?' Then follows a *description* of one duly qualified, and, in immediate sequence; 'This (*talis*) is the generation of them that seek thee.' To know the stock whence such and such a man has sprung, is thus used, by an easy transition, of knowing *the class to which he belongs*. To know his γενεά, is to know his CHARACTERISTICS. Hence, for the meaning of Acts viii.: 'In His humiliation He was lightly esteemed, but who could adequately describe Him?'

(ii) Another explanation (γενεά=βίωσις[2]) has been proposed, which leads to a like general result. If γενεά can mean, the *class* to which so and so belongs, it may be naturally transferred to his general surroundings, or to the *affairs* with which he is conversant. In Luke xvi. 8, the meaning is that the children of this world are wiser *in respect of their own* (worldly) *matters*[3] than are the children of light in theirs. It is perhaps best to render: 'in dealings with their own *class*[4],' and to explain γενεά as in the foregoing paragraph: but very slight variation would result from rendering γενεά by *affairs*. Such a meaning is appropriate (if not required)

---

[1] Cruden, *Concordance.* This meaning is applied by Mr Perowne to Matt. xxiv. 34; 'where ἡ γενεὰ αὕτη means, *this race, with all its moral characteristics;* not *the people now alive.*'

[2] In Chaldee דור means *habitare:* also, *disponere,* which bears out Lowth's rendering, *manner of life.*

[3] εἰς τὴν γενεὰν τὴν ἑαυτῶν, which

Theophylact explains, ἐν τῷ βίῳ τούτῳ, Weisse (correctly), '*Im Verkehr mit ihrem Gleichen;*' Neander (too vaguely), '*Von ihrem Standpunkte.*' (Trench, *Parables.*)

[4] 'An allusion, strangely often missed, to the debtors in the parable.' (Trench.)

in Gen. vi. 9, where it is said that Noah was 'perfect in his *generations*:' a phrase which from the parallelism (Noah *walked* with God) and from the contrast in ver. 8, must be ultimately equivalent to the more usual, 'perfect in his *ways.*'

4. *Further references to Psalms xxii.; xxxiv.; cii.*

'For which cause He is not ashamed to call them brethren, saying, I will declare thy name unto my brethren, in the midst of the church will I sing praise unto thee' (Heb. ii. 11, 12; Ps. xxii. 22). 'For thine is the kingdom' (Matt. vi. 13; Ps. xxii. 28). 'My soul doth magnify the Lord, and my spirit hath rejoiced in God my Saviour' (Luke i. 46, 47; Ps. xxxiv. 3; Is. lxi. 10). 'If so be ye have tasted that the LORD is gracious' (1 Pet. ii. 3; Ps. xxxiv. 8). 'Follow peace with all men.' 'For he that will love life, and see good days, let him refrain his tongue from evil, and his lips that they speak no guile: let him eschew evil, and do good; let him seek peace and ensue it. For the eyes of the LORD are over the righteous, and His ears are open unto their prayers; but the face of the LORD is against them that do evil' (Heb. xii. 14; 1 Pet. iii. 10—12; Ps. xxxiv. 12—16). 'And thou, LORD, in the beginning hast laid the foundation of the earth, and the heavens are the works of thine hands: they shall perish, but thou remainest; and they all shall wax old as doth a garment; and as a vesture shalt thou fold them up, and they shall be changed; but thou art the same, and thy years shall not fail' (Heb. i. 10—12; Ps. cii. 25—27; Heb. xiii. 8). Ps. lxix. will be considered in another section.

NOTES ON CHAPTER V.

A. In Richardson's *Engl. Dict.* the following lines are quoted from Chaucer, Surrey, Spenser, Milton, Gray, respectively:

That me *agasteth* in my dream.

Notes on Chapter V. 125

The silence selfe of night *agast* my sprite.

Neither of idle shews nor of false charmes *aghast.*⎫
So sore him dread *agast.* ⎭

With shuddering horrour pale and eyes *aghast.*

Stout Glo'ster stood *aghast* in speechless trance.

Milton's use favours the derivation from *gaze*. Fuller uses the expression, *stood a gaze*. Shaks. *Henry VI., Part I.:*

All the whole army stood *agaz'd* on him.

יַזֶּה is commonly taken as fut. hiphil from נָזָה, *to sprinkle*. Against the rendering, 'he shall sprinkle,' there are two main objections: (i) its apparent incongruity; and (ii) the usage of the word, which means *to sprinkle* water, &c. *upon*...; never, *to sprinkle... with*. The Targum, adopting the former of these constructions, renders, by יְבַדֵּר, 'he shall *scatter*' (*sc.* like drops of water) the persons spoken of. The rendering of the text harmonises with the LXX, θαυμάσονται, which the majority of commentators now seek to arrive at by different devices. The strength of the conviction that some such rendering is required, is best shewn by the various conjectures to which it has led: e. g. 1. *sic mirabuntur*, &c. o', 'Non male, nam *mirari* est veluti aspergi fulgore alicujus.' 2. *Persperget stupore*. 3. He shall make them jump (the rendering now commonly received). 4. To sprinkle, is used for to surprise and astonish, as people are that have much water thrown upon them. And this sense is followed by the LXX. 'This is ingenious,' adds Lowth, 'but rather too refined. Dr Durell conjectures that the true reading may be יֶחֱזוּ, *they shall regard*, which comes near to the θαυμάσονται of the LXX, who seem to give the best sense of any to the place.' Hereupon follows a suggestive citation from Dr Jubb: "I find in my papers the same conjecture which Dr Durell made from θαυμάσονται in the LXX. And it may be added that חָזָה is used to express 'looking on any thing with admiration' (Ps. xi. 7; xvii. 15; xxvii. 4; lxiii. 2; Cant. vi. 13). It is particularly applied to 'looking on God' (Ex. xxiv. 11; Job xix. 26). G. Cuper, in *Observat*. Lib. ii. 1, though *aliud agens*, has some observations which shew how nearly ὁράω and θαυμάζω are allied, which (with the peculiar sense of the verb חָזָה above noted) add to the probability of θαυμάσονται being the version of יֶחֱזוּ in the text. Οἱ δέ νυ λαοὶ Πάντες ἐπ' αὐτὸν ὁρῶσι

(Hesiod.), i. e. cum veneratione quadam admirantur. Hinc ὁράω et θαυμάζω junxit Themistius *Or.* I.: εἶτα παύσονται οἱ ἄνθρωποι πρὸς σὲ μόνον ὁρῶντες, καὶ σὲ μόνον θαυμάζοντες. Theophrastus, in *Charact.* Cap. III.: Ἐνθυμῇ ὡς ἀποβλέπουσιν εἰς σε οἱ ἄνθρωποι. Hence the rendering of this verse seems to be, 'So many nations shall look on him with admiration,' &c." The conjecture in the text embodies the chief part of Dr Jubb's suggestion, but avoids any departure from the reading of the Hebrew. The word הזה is a *softened* form of חזה, and expresses, accordingly, a *refinement* of its meaning. The latter means simply *to regard;* the former, *to stare vacantly.* The participle הזים, in Is. lvi. 10 (the only other place where the root occurs), is variously rendered: ἐνυπνιαζόμενοι (LXX), φανταζόμενοι (Aquila), ὁραματισταί (Symmachus). These 'sleepy *starers,*' be it remarked, are both *blind* and *dumb;* just as the kings and nations (Is. liii. 15) stand '*aghast* in *speechless* trance.'

B. Rosenmüller urges that ישוחח cannot be construed with a simple accusative, and renders: 'Quod attinet ad coævos suos, quis meditatur: quando excisus esset,' &c. But Hengstenberg cites Ps. cxlv. 5, ודברי נפלאתיך אשיחה. If Rosenmüller's objection were valid, we might still render, 'As for his generation—who could tell, *or* form any conception' *sc.* of it? [Prepositions are often thus omitted when the verb follows its case.] The rendering adopted by Rosenmüller is harsh in respect of מי, who *of them?* and is not favoured by the use of the *future,* instead of either preterite or participle. The explanation, 'Who of them would have thought that he was cut off.. *for the transgression of my people,*' would require (by the law of emphasis) a different arrangement: 'Who would have thought that *for the transgression of my people,* &c.'

C. The first clause of ver. 8 (as on p. 76) implies that what 'they appointed' was not carried out. But it might perhaps signify no more than that they executed him as a criminal, without reference to any formal burial; in like manner as a person is said *ipso facto* to 'find his grave,' wherever he may chance to die. 'Lucem accipiet hic locus ex Nahum i. 14: *Domum ejus ponam sepulchrum tuum:* non quod ibi sepultus est Sennacherib, sed quod ibi occisus' (Poole, *Synops.* III. 519). The next clause speaks of an actual tomb, if the rendering in the text be the true one. Ewald *e. g.* considers that בְּמֹתָיו (as he would point it) *scheint nothwendig für Grabhügel zu stehen.* [See Is. xxii. 16.] There may be two

Notes on Chapter V.   127

pointings of this word, as of סָרִיִ֫ים Gen. xl. 7; Esth. ii. 21. Aben Ezra mentions the rendering *tomb* or *monument*, which is perhaps preferable; the *plural* being appropriate in describing a *complex* superstructure. See Poli *Synops*.

Some make עָשִׁיר parallel and nearly synonymous with רְשָׁעִים, arguing that the ideas of *riches* and *violence* are usually conjoined in scripture. But such connexion is fortuitous and non-essential. In Eccl. x. 20, עָשִׁיר is parallel to מֶ֫לֶךְ, and (it may be repeated) the speakers in the verse before us are taken to be heathen *kings*. *Rich* rather than *righteous* would be the prophetic designation of a heathen dignitary. Riches, again, naturally associate themselves with *honourable burial*. The rich man dies and *is buried* (Luke xvi. 22), Kings, and princes *that have gold*, build desolate places (mausoleums) for themselves (Job iii. 14, 15). It may be added, that the words for *rich man* and *wrong-doers* contain the same root-letters; and that *paronomasia* commonly implies *contrast* rather than mere parallelism. The change of number favours the rendering of the text.

D. There is little difficulty in connecting the meanings, *dwelling, manner of life*. Compare '*Conversor*. (1) To abide, live, dwell *somewhere*. (2) To live *somehow*, pass one's life.' So οἰκέω, which refers properly to dwelling (in the local sense), comes to be applied to the *manner* of living, and in this sense is susceptible of the modifications (οἶκον) εὖ, κακῶς (οἰκεῖν). In Hebrew, שָׁכֵן may be used in describing a *condition*, or a *quality*. Thus: '*lay* mine honour in the dust' (Ps. vii. 5); 'I wisdom *dwell with* prudence [κατεσκήνωσα βουλήν], and find out knowledge of witty inventions' (Prov. viii. 12). Compare the derived usage, πόρρω ἐσκήνωται [ἐσκήνηται] τοῦ θανάσιμος εἶναι (Plato, *Rep*.).

CHAPTER VI.

The sure Mercies of David.

Is. lv. 3; Acts xiii. 34.

THIS citation may be taken as the characteristic of two apostolic addresses[1], wherein the Resurrection of JESUS is described as consummating the 'sure mercies' of which David was, in some sense, the object. It is not indeed adduced by St Peter, but a cognate citation is common to the two addresses. St Paul continues (Acts xiii. 35): 'Wherefore he saith also in another psalm, Thou shalt not suffer thine *Holy One* to see corruption.' And St Peter (Acts ii. 25—28) quotes more at length from the same place: 'For David speaketh concerning him, I foresaw the Lord always before my face, for he is on my right hand, that I should not be moved. Therefore did my heart rejoice, and my tongue was glad; moreover also my flesh shall rest in hope: because thou wilt not leave my soul in hell, neither wilt thou suffer thine *Holy One* to see corruption. Thou hast made known to me the ways of life; thou shalt make me full of joy with thy countenance' (Ps. xvi. 8—11). The citation from David, equally with that from Isaiah, deals with 'mercies of David,' which are apostolically referred to JESUS: but, more than this, there is a verbal similarity (not apparent to the English reader) which links the two passages still more closely to one another. Isaiah speaks

---

[1] By SS. Peter and Paul respectively: Acts ii 14—40; xiii. 16—41.

The sure Mercies of David.

of the 'sure mercies of David¹:' David represents himself as 'Thy favoured one,' the recipient of God's mercies². These citations are a natural starting-point for various critical and theological discussions, to which it is proposed to give some attention in the present chapter.

(1) It is needful, as a preliminary, to inquire in what cases a reference in the New Testament to the Old is to be taken as (directly or indirectly) testifying to the authorship of the passage cited. Is David declared to be the author of a passage because it is introduced by some such formula as 'David saith'? If not, under what circumstances does the mention of a name amount to a declaration of authorship? (2) What is the internal evidence for the Davidic authorship of Ps. xvi.? This question leads up to a discussion of the vexed title *Michtam*, by which Ps. xvi. is designated, in common with five others (lvi.—lx.). (3) Supposing Ps. xvi. to have been written by David, and with a reference to Christ, what was the nature and extent of the writer's prophetic consciousness? (4) What is the relation between the so-called *primary* and *secondary* applications of the second Psalm (Acts xiii. 33) and of other passages to which a DOUBLE SENSE has been assigned?

I. *The Authorship of Passages cited.*

In his comment on Prov. xix. 5, R. Shalom ben Abraham has some reflections upon *Truth* and *Falsehood*:—If you observe the spelling of the word for *truth*³, you will find that it contains the first, middle and last letters of the alphabet, shewing that truth is the groundwork of all society: whereas the word for *falsehood*⁴ has its letters consecutive, to intimate that false witnesses cannot make their accounts mutually confirmatory, without first meeting together, and agreeing upon what they shall say. Faithful witnesses on the contrary, however widely scattered, simply make up their minds to

---

¹ חסדי ד, τὰ ὅσια Δ.   ³ אמת.
² חסידך, τὸν ὅσιόν σου.   ⁴ שקר.

speak the truth, and have no occasion to meet together and compare notes. And then again, observe the stability of the letters in *truth,* which, unlike those of *falsehood,* have a basis and pair-of-feet[1] to stand upon. 'And let not this thing seem trivial in thine eyes, for by the shapes of our letters great secrets are hinted at.'

The above serves to illustrate a tendency, which is not peculiar to Jews, but has shewn itself, in more insidious guise, in the works of Christian commentators: the tendency, viz. to see in Holy Scripture an authority for preconceived opinions, and instinctively to set forth those opinions as derived in the first instance from such passages as may be thought to give them countenance. The reflections cited are not, indeed, unlike what Bishop Butler has affirmed of the natural tendency of virtue, and of the consistence, and mutual harmony that would prevail in a community, if its members were one and all actuated by a single aim:—'Now, I say, virtue in a society has a like tendency to procure superiority and additional power: whether this power be considered as the means of security from opposite power, or of obtaining other advantages. And it has this tendency, by rendering public good an object and end to every member of the society; by putting every one upon consideration and diligence, recollection and self-government, both in order to see what is the most effectual method, and also in order to perform their proper part, for obtaining and preserving it; by uniting a society within itself, and so increasing its strength; and, which is particularly to be mentioned, uniting it by means of veracity and justice. For as these last are principal bonds of union, so benevolence or public spirit, undirected, unrestrained by them, is, nobody knows what[2].' But though R. Shalom's sentiments are irreproachable in themselves, they have an appearance of ludicrousness, springing from the form in which they are presented. They are not indeed inconsistent

---

[1] 'Apud Rabbinos, השקר אין לו *Lex. Chald.*) רגלים, *Mendacium non habet pedes,* i.e. inconstans et evanidum est.' (Buxtorf.

[2] *Analogy,* Part I. Ch. iii.

with any declaration of Holy Writ; they might, on the contrary, be abundantly confirmed by its explicit declarations: but they are assuredly not contained in the words or letters from which the commentator has striven to evolve them. While professing to educe the inner mysteries of the sacred text, he is unconsciously seeking to corroborate his preconceived and independent (though in this case true) conclusions.

But the preconceived opinions which the Bible has been quoted to corroborate, have not always been so sound as in the case alluded to; and, as a natural consequence, the increase of knowledge has shewn the incompatibility of such and such interpretations with observed facts. The appearance of antagonism between Scripture and Science, has given rise, first of all, to an attempted repression of the latter, and, in other quarters, to a repudiation of the authority of the former; but more mature reflection has led to a change of *interpretation*, and thus removed the first difficulty which beset the reconciliation of superficially antagonistic claims. A divine authority has been claimed for the old popular astronomy, which made our earth a fixed centre for the sun's diurnal course. It is difficult indeed to determine to what extent the view in question was preconceived, and to what extent generated or developed by the language of the Bible, as once interpreted: but it may be affirmed that, if the modern astronomy could be conceived of as having preceded the Biblical statements which seem to bear upon the subject, the literal interpretation of those statements would not easily have gained general acceptance.

The astronomical controversy, now matter of history, may serve as a type of others which have yet to be decided. It may excite surprise that some of the more poetical passages adduced to prove that the sun moves round the earth, should have been accepted as evidence in the case; and even in prosaic passages it is now seen that there is no necessity for regarding certain descriptions as other than phenomenal, and comparable with such as are still employed in chronicling the results of scientific observations. The sun is still said to *rise* and *set;* and a modern writer who employs a language thus phenomenal, is not supposed to stand thereby committed to a faulty science. The same measure is at length meted out to the Biblical language, and it comes rightly to be denied that Scripture purports to be a Revelation of Science, or was designed to forestall and anticipate any conclusion that might in due time be arrived at by human industry, unaided by supernatural enlightenment.

It might be assumed, as a sequel to the preceding, that Holy Scripture would leave other things discoverable, in philology as in science, to be discovered, in like manner, by human reason. Its language may seem at first sight to sanction such and such critical conclusions; but experience should suggest the misgiving that those conclusions may be preconceived and extra-Biblical, while their Scriptural sanction is apparent and not real. In any case, it is incumbent upon the theologian to gather light from whatever source, and either to confirm, or to prove the fallacy of, his *prima facie* impressions.

The particular question now to be considered is, in what case *a citation in the New Testament determines the authorship of the passage cited.* The first impression is, doubtless, that the mention of a name is decisive, and that if a citation is introduced by such a formula as 'David saith,' David is thereby declared to have been the writer of the passage in question. By a commentator who brings to the discussion of such a formula of citation the *antecedent* conviction that the Psalm referred to was written by David, the *prima facie* interpretation would naturally be accepted as final; nor would it, for the most part, present itself as a fit subject for enquiry, whether the inspired writer definitely intended to give countenance to such conviction, or indeed to affirm anything whatever with regard to the authorship of the passage cited. When however independent research has suggested doubts about the authorship of a Psalm alluded to in the New Testament as Davidic, it then at length comes to be doubted

The sure Mercies of David.

whether the *prima facie* meaning of the formula of citation[1] is the true one, or whether, as in modern phrase, the Psalm is styled one of '*the Psalms of David*,' for convenience of reference, and without critical intent. That such a practice is not repugnant to Jewish usage may be gathered from the following examples of their Biblical nomenclature.

Several books of the Old Testament are named by them after their opening word or the first distinctive word occurring. Thus, the five books of Moses are called, respectively, by the words italicized in their opening verses, as below. '*In the beginning* God created the heaven and the earth.' 'Now these are *the names of* the children of Israel, which came into Egypt.' '*And* the LORD *called* unto Moses.' 'And the LORD spake unto Moses *in the wilderness of* Sinai.' 'These be the *words* which Moses spake unto all Israel.' The book of Lamentations is called (*sc.* from its first word) '*How?*' Two other books are called by the name of an individual, although the former contains an account of the individual's death and burial (1 Sam. xxv. 1), and the remaining portion of it combines with the whole of the second book in the narration of subsequent events. These examples sufficiently evince a tendency, in the Jews, to name the scriptural books with a view to *convenience of reference*, and, this end being gained, to rest satisfied with a title more or less significant, but not exhaustively descriptive. The tendency thus manifested in the nomenclature of separate books, repeats itself in the general classification of Luke xxiv. 44: 'And He said unto them, These are the words which I spake unto you, while I was yet with you, that all things must be fulfilled, which were written in the *law of Moses*, and in *the prophets*, and in *the Psalms*, concerning me.' Where 'the Psalms' include the whole Hagiographa, and not only the *Psalms* properly so called.

---

[1] Aben Ezra, *e.g.* does not think the title *David-psalm* intended always to mark David as the actual author. If this be true of an *Inscription*, לדוד, it is easy to understand that an Apostle may have alluded to a Psalm, and that with every appearance of definiteness, as Davidic, without thereby intending to pronounce upon its authorship.

Remarks on special Formulæ of Citation.

In Heb. iv. 7, the expression, '*In David*,' might very naturally be taken as referring to what is called, in modern phrase, 'the Psalms of David,' but without any implied determination of the authorship of the passage: 'To-day if ye will hear his voice harden not your hearts.' Perhaps, again, St Paul's formula, 'David saith,' would be allowed by many to be itself a mere reference to the book of Psalms, leaving it still an open question whether the sixty-ninth Psalm was written by David. More difficulty, however, arises from St Peter's reference to this Psalm (in connexion with the hundred and ninth) in his address to the disciples before the election of Matthias. 'Men and brethren, this scripture must needs have been fulfilled, which the Holy Ghost *by the mouth of David*[1] spake before concerning Judas, which was guide to them that took Jesus' (Acts i. 16). But in ver. 20 he continues: 'For it is written *in the book of Psalms*, Let his habitation be desolate, and let no man dwell therein: and his bishopric let another take:' and he thus seems to interpret the preceding formula of citation as a simple reference to the book of Psalms. Whether or no this inference be thought a fair one, it may be doubted whether the phrase διὰ στόματος is so distinctly expressive of personality as appears at first sight; for the Hebrew language abounds in *pleonastic* prepositional usages, and the Greek words quoted may correspond to one of these; perhaps to an expression meaning *according to the mouth of*[2], which is used indiscriminately of persons and things. In later Hebrew, this phrase, in its merely prepositional sense, is so common that it is expressed by the initial letters of its two component words. Another expression meaning literally, *according to the mouth of this*[3], is used pleonastically in the sense, *accordingly;* and so often, that the phrase is written as one word and usually abbreviated.

---

[1] Cf. Acts iv. 25: 'Who *by the mouth of* thy servant David hast said, Why did the heathens rage, and the people imagine a vain thing?'
[2] עַל פִּי, abbreviated, עַ״פ.
[3] לְפִיכָך, abbreviated, לְפִי׳.

On the indirect determination of the Authorship of Citations.

If in any case it remains doubtful whether the authorship of a citation is unpronounced upon by way of direct affirmation, it has still to be enquired whether it is determined implicitly by the requirements of the argument. The latter cannot be affirmed (*a*) of St Peter's citation in Acts i. 16: 'This scripture must needs have been fulfilled, which the Holy Ghost by the mouth of David spake before.' Where the *fulfilment of inspired Scripture* is the sum and substance of the argument, and 'the mouth of David' is but the channel of the Holy Spirit's utterance. Nor again, (*b*) of the conclusion: 'There remaineth therefore a rest to the people of God;' which is led up to (Heb. iv. 9) by a series of scriptural quotations, adduced to prove the non-finality of Joshua's rest. 'For if Jesus had given them rest, then would he not afterward have spoken of another day' (ver. 8). Amongst the quotations is one from Ps. xcv. 7, 8, of which the characteristic word is σήμερον:—*Again* he limiteth a certain day, saying in David, 'To-day,' as is *aforesaid:* 'To-day if ye will hear his voice, harden not your hearts.' The argument is independent of the precise interval between the two occasions, and therefore, of the Davidic authorship. It would obviously not be weakened by extending the τοσοῦτον χρόνον, and setting its lower limit after the age of David. There seems in this case to be no obvious reason, deducible from the general argument, why the expression, 'in David,' should be taken as (necessarily) more definite than, 'in the book of Psalms.' Nor again (*c*) in the case of St Paul's citation from Ps. lxix.: 'And *David saith*, Let their table be made a snare, and a trap, and a stumblingblock, and a recompence unto them' (Rom. xi. 9), where the substitution of, '*It is written*,' for, 'David saith,' would leave the argument intact. (*d*) With the citation from Ps. xvi. by SS. Peter and Paul, the case is to all appearance different. St Peter, after quoting as from David: 'Thou wilt not leave my soul in hell, neither wilt thou suffer thine Holy One to see corruption' (Acts ii. 27); thus continues in ver. 29, 'Men and brethren, let me freely speak unto you of the patriarch David, that he is both dead and buried, and his sepulchre is with us unto this day. Therefore being a prophet, and knowing that God had sworn with an oath to him, that of the fruit of his loins, according to the flesh, he would raise up Christ to sit on his throne; He seeing this before spake of the resurrection of Christ, that his soul was not left in hell, neither his flesh did see corruption.' St Paul emphasises the same contrast in Acts xiii. 36, 37: 'For David, after he had served his own generation by the will of God, fell on sleep, and was laid unto his fathers, and saw corruption. But he, whom God raised again, saw no corruption.' The Davidic authorship seems here to be asserted; and accordingly we proceed to a consideration of the group of Psalms to which the sixteenth belongs.

II. *The Monumental Psalms.*

The sixteenth Psalm is bound up in one group with five others (lvi.—lx.) by the title *Michtam*, prefixed to one and all; a title which has given rise to much discussion, and to a variety of conjectures, for the most part unsatisfactory. The discussion of the title is one important element in an investigation of the authorship of the Psalms thereby designated; and upon this we accordingly enter, premising that the result will be a confirmation of the oldest traditions on the point, as embodied in the Targum and the LXX.

1. The LXX. rendering of Michtam is στηλογραφία, which agrees with the Chaldee, *sculptura recta*[1], and is represented in the Vulgate by *tituli inscriptio*. In his *Sepher Shorashim*, R. Kimchi gives the meaning *stamp* or *seal*, agreeably with the requirements of Jer. ii. 22: "For though thou wash thee with nitre, and take thee much soap, yet thine iniquity is marked before me." Vain are all attempts to wash it out, for it is *graven* as in the rock for ever (Job xix.

[1] גליפא תריצא.

24). Gesenius connects Michtam with the common word used of *writing*[1], which itself means primarily *incidere*, 'nam primitus litteræ lapidibus insculptæ sunt;' and this view seems plausible enough to be accepted, in default of evidence pointing to any well-defined antagonistic conclusion.

The root of Michtam occurs once only (*supra*) in the verb form, though several times as a noun, which has been rendered, *gold*. But is it clear that the various contexts in which the noun occurs *require* this rendering? Is it not even more appropriate to attach to it the idea of *shape*, or *workmanship*, rather than of *material;* and to render it, not *gold*, but *jewels*, or *jewelry?* which necessitates no departure from the abovementioned plausible hypothesis. The word occurs in Job xxviii. 16, 19, in connexion with gold and precious stones: 'It cannot be valued with the *gold* of Ophir, with the precious onyx, or the sapphire. The gold and the crystal cannot equal it: and the exchange of it shall not be for jewels of fine gold. No mention shall be made of coral, or of pearls; for the price of wisdom is above rubies. The topaz of Ethiopia shall not equal it, neither shall it be valued with pure *gold*.' In Is. xiii. 12, it is rendered, 'The *golden wedge* of Ophir.' In Lam. iv. 1, 2, the meanings *jewels*, and *jewellers' workmanship*, are not less appropriate than *gold*. 'How is the gold become dim! how is the most fine *gold* changed! the stones [gems] of the sanctuary are poured out in the top of every street. The precious sons of Zion, comparable to fine gold, how are they esteemed as earthen pitchers, the work of the hands of the potter!' In Cant. v. 10, 'the beloved' is likened to a banner towering above the host; he is set up like a banner, 'the chief among ten thousand[2].' His head is as the boss upon its summit; his locks are pendant, raven-black. In the Authorised Version, the meaning *gold* is, indeed, retained; 'His head is as most fine gold;' but the idea of *shape* is admissible, if not required. In Ps. xlv. 9, the queen-mother is said to be decked with '*gold*[3] of Ophir;' unless

[1] כתב.   [2] דגול מרבבה.   [3] כתם.

the phrase should be rendered *jewels*, or *workmanship* of Ophir, with reference to the texture and ornamentation of her robes. In ver. 13, the 'king's daughter' is arrayed, not in gold, but in '*wrought gold*[1].' With this may be compared Dan. x. 5, 'Then I lifted up mine eyes, and looked, and behold a certain man clothed in linen, whose loins were girded with *fine gold*[2] of Uphaz.' There are two other occurrences of the disputed word, viz. in Prov. xxv. 12, and Job xxxi. 24. Its meaning in these and the preceding instances, may be ambiguous; but if not strongly confirmatory of, is on the other hand, not definitely opposed to, the foregoing conclusion, that the root signifies, firstly, *to engrave*, and may even be organically connected with the word *to write*. *Michtam* may itself be practically equivalent to *Michtab*, the title of Hezekiah's hymn, 'The *writing* of Hezekiah, king of Judah, when he had been sick, and was recovered of his sickness' (Is. xxxviii. 9).

2. The present state of the controversy on the applicability of *Michtam*, this or that way interpreted, to the Psalms thereby designated, may be gathered from the following statement by Dr Phillips:—

"This word occurs in the title to Psalms xvi., lvi.—lx. There are some persons who consider it to be identical with *chethem, gold;* and hence they understand either that it was a name given to these Psalms on account of their peculiar excellence, or that they were engraven in letters of gold for some public purpose, perhaps to be hung up in the sanctuary, that the people might become more generally acquainted with the truths which they teach, or with the events to which they may refer, and may be designed to commemorate. For a similar purpose, the Lord's Prayer, the Creed, and the ten Commandments, are found on the walls of our churches. With respect to the first-mentioned reason for the distinction which was thus conferred on these Psalms, it has been asked in what does their particular excellence consist, on what

[1] משבצות זהב. [2] כתם.

account should they be regarded as subjects of greater interest than the others? If the term had been confined to the sixteenth, we might have replied, that this Psalm was eminently entitled to this distinguishing mark, because it communicates truths of vast interest and importance connected with the person and offices of the Messiah. But with respect to the other Psalms, we cannot assert that the instruction which they convey, valuable though it be, as indeed must all instruction which is derived from inspired Scripture, is yet of a higher order than that which is afforded by any other portion of the Songs of Zion. Mendelssohn, in his third preface to the Psalms, says that *Michtab* may be applied to any writing the object of which is to commemorate some event which happened either to the poet himself, or to one of his acquaintances; and in the titles to four out of the six Psalms above enumerated, the events which occasioned their composition are mentioned; thus to the fifty-ninth we have, *Michtam of David, when he fled from Saul in a cave.* He goes on to observe, that in the two, viz. the sixteenth and the fifty-ninth, which have no such headings, it is probable, owing to the long interval between the writing of these Psalms and of their titles, that the particular cause of their production was forgotten. But this explanation is certainly not sufficient; for in many of the titles to the other Psalms, as in that to the fifty-fourth, where Michtam does not occur, the event upon which it is founded is also stated at length. We are therefore disposed to concur with those who think Michtam is the same as Michtab..."

There are then two main currents of opinion, each carrying with it portions of truth, to be traced to their common source. According to one view, these Psalms are 'writings,' or commemorations of events which are for some reason or other to be specially kept in mind. According to the other, they are either 'jewel-Psalms,' so called from a peculiar (though undefined) intrinsic excellence; or such as, for this reason, are deemed worthy to be written in letters of *gold*, and exposed to public view. 'Sed non facile dicas,' urges

Gesenius, 'quibus virtutibus ista carmina præ reliquis eminent, neque ejus quem Harmerus respicit, moris ullum apud Hebræos vestigium est, ipsaque illa derivatio a nomine mere poëtico displicet.' From all this it appears that some characteristic mark or principle of classification is the great desideratum, without which it is impossible to determine accurately the relation of the Psalms in question to their title, however satisfactorily derived.

3. The title Michtam has been compared to that of Hezekiah's hymn; and this similarity of titles suggests a further comparison of the compositions themselves. Hezekiah had been restored to health after a dangerous illness, and wrote the hymn contained in Is. xxxviii. 10—20, as a thanksgiving for recovery. More than this, he provides for the lasting public commemoration of the great deliverance which he, the Lord's Anointed, had experienced[1]. 'The Lord was ready to save me: therefore we will sing my songs to the stringed instruments all the days of our life in the house of the Lord.' The hymn contains no thoughts more specially deserving to be remembered, than such as may be found in many a Psalm of thanksgiving; but it treats of a matter of public interest, a crisis in the king's life, a fit subject for public commemoration. For this reason it is formally placed on record, which accounts for its being described by the title Michtab, or 'writing.' May not the title Michtam be similarly accounted for? There is the same kind of difference between Michtam (as above interpreted), and Michtab, as between *inscriptio* and *scriptio*, or between στηλογραφία and γραφή. If Michtab denotes a Psalm preserved among the public records, not solely for its intrinsic excellence, but with reference to an event which it is designed to commemorate, may not the Michtams be Psalms thrown into the form of monumental inscriptions; public manifestoes, and declarations of principle; records of

---

[1] Compare the public mournings in honour of Josiah, 2 Chron. xxxv. 25: 'And Jeremiah lamented for Josiah: and all the singing-men and the singing-women spake of Josiah in their lamentations to this day, and made them an ordinance in Israel; and behold they are written in the lamentations.'

events of national interest and importance? If the Michtams were thus known and read of all men, it may be surmised that tradition would be the more likely to have preserved the true account of their origin and reference; or in other words, that their inscriptions would be the more to be relied upon.

Four of the six Michtams are referred to circumstances in David's life, while the remainder are assigned to no specific occasion. The inscriptions as rendered in the English Bible, are as follows:—

Ps. xvi. Michtam of David.

Ps. lvi. To the chief Musician upon Jonath-elem-rechokim, Michtam of David, when the Philistines took him in Gath.

Ps. lvii. To the chief Musician, Al-taschith, Michtam of David, when he fled from Saul in the cave.

Ps. lviii. To the chief Musician, Al-taschith, Michtam of David.

Ps. lix. To the chief Musician, Al-taschith, Michtam of David; when Saul sent, and they watched the house to kill him.

Ps. lx. To the chief Musician upon Shushan-eduth, Michtam of David, to teach; when he strove with Aram-naharaim and with Aram-zobah, when Joab returned, and smote of Edom in the valley of salt twelve thousand.

The fifty-eighth Psalm is referred by Mr Mason to the occasion of Absalom's rebellion, which completes the cycle of references, in Psalms lvi.—lx., to the most noteworthy crises in the life of David; while the sixteenth is a general acknowledgement of Jehovah's sole being and protecting care. David, according to this hypothesis, is addressing his subjects through the medium of these Monumental Psalms; and, be it remarked in conclusion, there are expressions in the Michtams which borrow a new significance from this supposition.

By 'sons of men' are designated the undistinguished masses with whom David expostulates for their rebellion. 'Do ye indeed speak righteousness, O congregation[1]? do ye

---

[1] 'Proinde de *hominibus e vulgo, &c.*' Gesen. *Thesaur.* s. v. אֻלֶם.

judge uprightly, O ye *sons of men*?' (Ps. lviii. 1). Again the Psalmist speaks in kingly phrase in Ps. lix. 11, 'Slay them not, lest *my people* forget.' But perhaps the most remarkable expression is one commonly passed over with no more than a grammatical discussion; 'the saints that are in the earth, and *the excellent, in whom is all my delight*' (Ps. xvi. 3). The royal Psalmist renders acknowledgement to JEHOVAH in the form of a proclamation to his subjects, and declares that none but worshippers of the LORD his God, shall be held in honour by him, or find favour in his sight.

III. *David the Prophet.*

The 'sure mercies of David,' which St Paul sees realized in Christ, are thus spoken of by Isaiah: ' Incline your ear, and come unto me: hear, and your soul shall live; and I will make an everlasting covenant with you, even the sure mercies of David. Behold, I have given him for a witness to the people, a *leader* and commander to the people' (Is. lv. 3, 4); where the 'Prince' to come is called by the name of David, as in other passages of Holy Writ. Thus: 'Therefore will I save my flock, and they shall be no more a prey; and I will judge between cattle and cattle. And I will set up one shepherd over them, and he shall feed them, even my servant David; he shall feed them, and he shall be their shepherd, And I the LORD will be their God, and my servant David a prince among them; I the LORD have spoken it' (Ezek. xxxiv. 22—24). 'And David my servant shall be king over them; and they all shall have one shepherd: they shall also walk in my judgements, and observe my statutes, and do them. And they shall dwell in the land that I have given unto Jacob my servant, wherein your fathers have dwelt; and they shall dwell therein, even they, and their children, and their children's children for ever: and my servant David shall be their prince for ever. Moreover I will make a covenant of peace with them; it shall be an everlasting covenant with them: and I will place them, and multiply them, and will set my sanctuary in the midst of them for evermore' (Ezek. xxxvii. 24—26). 'But they shall serve the LORD their God, and David their king, whom I will raise up unto them' (Jer. xxx. 9). 'For the children of Israel shall abide many days without a king, and without a prince, and without a sacrifice, and without an image, and without an ephod, and without teraphim: Afterward shall the children of Israel return and seek the LORD their God, and David their king; and shall fear the LORD and his goodness in the latter days' (Hos. iii. 4, 5).

Such passages testify to a deeply rooted conviction that a promise remained to be fulfilled to David long after David 'had served his own generation by the will of God, and was laid unto his fathers, and saw corruption.' In the following, the allusion is more direct to the *promise* by which those mercies were assured.

'For thy servant David's sake turn not away the face of thine anointed. The Lord hath sworn in truth unto David; he will not turn from it; of the fruit of thy body will I set upon thy throne. If thy children will keep my covenant and my testimony that I shall teach them, their children shall also sit upon thy throne for evermore. For the Lord hath chosen Zion; he hath desired it for his habitation. This is my rest for ever: here will I dwell; for I have desired it' (Ps. cxxxii. 10—14). 'I have made a covenant with my chosen, I have sworn unto David my servant. Thy seed will I establish for ever, and build up thy throne to all generations....Then thou spakest in vision to thy *holy one*, and saidst, I have laid help upon one that is mighty; I have exalted one chosen out of the people. I have found David my servant; with my holy oil have I anointed him...My faithfulness and my mercy shall be with him: and in my name shall his horn be exalted. I will set his hand also in the sea and his right hand in the rivers. He shall cry unto me, thou art my father, my God, and the rock of my salvation. Also I will make him my first-born, higher than the kings of the earth. My mercy will I keep for him for evermore, and my covenant shall stand fast with him. His seed also will I make to endure for ever, and his throne as the days of heaven...My covenant will I not break, nor alter the thing that is gone out of my lips. Once have I sworn by my holiness that I will not lie unto David' (Ps. lxxxix. 3, 4, 19, 20, 24—29, 34, 35).

The promise to which these later passages refer is found in 2 Sam. vii. 12—16; and in 1 Chron. xvii. 11—14; where it is given to David personally, through Nathan the prophet. It is therefore to be assumed that David had an anticipation of what Isaiah and others still looked forward to after David's death, as the '*mercies* of David.' With reference to the same promise, David is called (*supra*) in Ps. lxxxix. 19, '*thy holy one;*' an expression connected etymologically, as above remarked, with the '*mercies*' of the foregoing phrase. What David is called in this later Psalm, with reference to those mercies, he may without difficulty be supposed to style himself, in Ps. xvi. 10, with conscious anticipation of the same; and indeed, thus only can its natural meaning be given to, 'thy *holy one*[1],' which is a passive adjectival expression signifying, 'one in whom *mercies* are, or are to be, fulfilled.' The two expressions are brought into close proximity in 2 Chron. vi. 41, 42: 'Now therefore arise, O LORD God, into thy resting-place, thou and the ark of thy strength: let thy priests, O LORD God, be clothed with salvation, and let *thy saints* rejoice in goodness. O LORD God, turn not away the face of thine anointed: remember the *mercies of* David thy servant.' Where the *mercies of* David are, *favours* promised *to* him, and, 'thy *saints*' are, literally, 'thy *favoured ones;*' members of a favoured community which is summed up in its anointed king. Etymological reasons thus lead us to conjecture that there may be reference in Ps. xvi. 10, to the same 'mercies of David,' as in Is. lv. 3, and elsewhere.

But, more than this, it is far simpler to suppose the conscious object of eternal mercies actuated, in one of his loftiest utter-

[1] In Ps. xvi. 10, there is a reading חסידיך instead of the singular חסידך; but the latter is supported by the parallelism, the ancient versions, and a great preponderance of MS. authority. In Ps. lxxxix. 19 there is a like various reading.

ances, by a sense of the promised blessing than, denying all such prophetic reference, to confine his words and aspirations within the limits of his individual personality. It seems natural, even apart from the citations in the Acts, to suppose in Ps. xvi. some prophetic reference; but to define the reference is hard, not to say impossible.

The words from the Psalm call in detail for brief remark.

1. It is disputed whether the Hebrew word corresponding to διαφθοράν should not rather be rendered *pit* or grave; a meaning which seems appropriate in almost all of the passages where the word occurs, and which Gesenius *e.g.* applies in Ps. xvi. 10, and even in Job xvii. 14: 'I have said to corruption, Thou art my father: to the worm, Thou art my mother and sister.' It may be that διαφθορά is a derived meaning, springing from the primary signification *grave;* but it cannot be affirmed with certainty that even the Greek word is always to be taken strictly in the sense *corruption*. That sense is not required, *e.g.* in Prov. xxviii. 10: 'Whoso causeth the righteous to go astray in an evil way, he shall fall himself into his own *pit*[1];' or in Hos. xi. 5, and elsewhere. The internal evidence of the passage in question is conflicting, for, on the one hand, the parallelism with 'hell,' favours the rendering 'pit[1];' while on the other, the following expression, 'to see *life*,' favours the abstract rendering 'corruption.' It may be added that the close affinity between the two renderings constitutes one main obstacle to a decision between them.

2. The word *nephesh* is no less disputed. According to some, it is here used generally, in the sense *person* or self: according to others, it means *soul*, as opposed to *flesh*. Thus David is understood as saying: 'Thou wilt not leave my *soul* in *hell;* neither wilt thou suffer thine Holy One to see *corruption:*' where the first hemistich is referred to the *spirit*, and the second to the *flesh*. It could not be inferred from the tenth verse alone that such a contrast is intended, for the word *nephesh* has a wide range of meanings, and does not

[1] εἰς διαφθορὰν αὐτὸς ἐμπεσεῖται.

naturally oppose itself to that part of a man which is susceptible of 'corruption,' viz. the flesh. But in the preceding verse the contrast is apparent: 'Therefore my heart is glad, and my glory rejoiceth: my flesh *also* shall rest in hope.' By *glory*[1] is signified the soul, the highest and most glorious part of man's being; and the second hemistich is shewn to be supplementary to the first, not merely by the word *flesh* alone, but by the particle preceding it: '*yea* my flesh, my very flesh shall rest securely.' This distinction is dwelt upon by Rabbinic commentators, including Kimchi who explains, 'my glory rejoiceth,' as implying a confidence of the soul's being joined to its Maker, after separation from the body. The same commentator gives as the primary meaning of the next clause, that the flesh, while life lasts, shall find rest in the assurance that God will save it from all harm: and he adds, by way of *midrash*, that after death it was not subject to corruption[2].

3. It does not seem to be the *prima facie* meaning of the Hebrew[3] or of the Greek[4], that 'Thou wilt not leave my soul *in* hell,' &c.; but rather that 'Thou wilt not abandon my soul *to*[5] hell.' The same construction recurs in the following passages (quoted by Bengel): 'And thou shalt not glean thy vineyard, neither shalt thou gather every grape of thy vineyard: thou shalt leave them *for* the poor and stranger' (Lev. xix. 10). 'For He seeth that wise men die, likewise the fool and the brutish person perish, and leave their wealth *to* others' (Ps. xlix. 10). Where the things left *come*, in each case, freshly into possession. The corresponding Hebrew words in Ps. xvi., exactly rendered by St Peter, do not then express directly that God's Holy One, having been given over to death and the grave, should be delivered therefrom;

---

[1] 'Denique 'כבוד ם, *honor alic.* poët. dicitur de *animo, corde*, utpote nobiliore hominis parte. Gen. xlix. 6, &c.' Gesen. *Thesaur.* 655 *b*.

[2] ונדרש אחר מיתה מלמד שלא שלטה בו רימה ותולעה.

[3] לא תעזב נפשי לשאל

[4] οὐκ ἐγκαταλείψεις τὴν ψυχήν μου εἰς ᾅδου.

[5] Cf. Job xxxix. 14, 'She must entrust her eggs *to* the earth' (Bernard. *in loc.*). See ver. 11, where אל replaces ל.

but, more generally, that He should not in the ordinary sense of the words, be subjected to death's power. 'It was not possible that He should be holden of it' (Acts ii. 24). David, on the contrary, was holden of death; 'his sepulchre is with us to this day.' By St Paul, the phrase, 'to see corruption,' seems to be used in Acts xiii. 34, with the implication that Christ once εἶδε διαφθοράν, and was raised from the dead, 'no more to return to corruption.' In ver. 37 it is affirmed, that He did *not* (sc. like David) '*see corruption.*' 'For David, after he had served his own generation, by the will of God, fell asleep, and was laid unto his fathers, and saw corruption: but He whom God raised again, saw no corruption.' Christ, in one sense, 'saw corruption,' *ipso facto*, by taking *flesh and blood;* which, in Cor. xv. 50, stand in parallelism with φθορά. 'Now this I say, brethren, that flesh and blood cannot inherit the kingdom of God; neither doth corruption inherit incorruption.' He became subject indeed to death, as the common lot of flesh and blood; but, unlike David, whom death still holds, 'Christ being raised from the dead dieth no more; death hath no more dominion over Him. For in that He died, He died unto sin once; but in that He liveth, He liveth unto God' (Rom. vi. 9, 10).

Psalm xvi., how applied to Christ?

The applicability of David's words to Christ demands further consideration. It has been maintained above that the Psalmist may most naturally be supposed to speak prophetically, with a view to the future fulfilment of the 'sure mercies' promised to him; but, on the other hand, seeing that he speaks in the first person, and so primarily of himself, on what principle are his words to be applied to Christ?

From the usual rendering of Acts ii. 31, it would perhaps appear that David is represented as uttering his prophecy, in its full particularity, as applied by St Peter. 'He seeing this before spake of the resurrection of Christ, *that* his soul was not left in hell, neither his flesh did see corruption.' But the *seeing*, and the *being left*, are here spoken of in the past, whereas in the original, and in the direct citation (ver. 27), both verbs are in the future. Moreover, to render ὅτι *for* or *because*, instead of *that*, would accord with the usage of the same Apostle in the preceding chapter; where, speaking of Judas, he explains how he was brought within the range of the prophecy applied to him. 'The Holy Ghost by the mouth of David *spake before concerning Judas*....Let his habitation be desolate, and let no man dwell therein: and his bishopric let another take....*For* he was numbered with us, and had obtained part of this ministry' (Acts i. 16, 20, 17). Judas is shewn by the event to be included by the Psalmist; *for*[1], being numbered with us, he had obtained an ἔπαυλις and an ἐπισκοπή. With a like construction in Acts ii. 31, the Apostle's application of Ps. xvi. may be thus expounded: 'Men and brethren, it being competent to affirm as a plain fact, without risk of contradiction, that the patriarch David is dead, and has not in his own person corresponded to his utterances in the Psalm; it follows that he must have prophesied, *sc.* of Christ, *for* His soul was not left in hell, neither His flesh did see corruption. David's words could not fail. As regards himself they did fail, and therefore could not have been spoken of himself. They were fulfilled in Christ; and the event thus shews that they were spoken of Him.' According to this view of the argument, St Peter appeals to the event as the interpreter of prophecy; not assuming that before the event it could have been thus specifically understood, to his present hearers, or to the Prophet himself.

It may be concluded that David spoke indeed of himself, according to the natural interpretation of his words, and by the phrase, 'Thy favoured one,' intended to designate himself. This however he does, not limiting his utterances to his own natural life, but having regard to the organic oneness of his posterity with him[2]. His personal deliverances are viewed

---

[1] 'Ratio, sub qua Judas hic memoratur, quia habuerat *munus*.' Bengel.
[2] And as I may so say, Levi also, who receiveth tithes, payed tithes in Abraham. *Heb. vii.* 9.

typically as evidences of God's eternal purpose, which must somehow be fulfilled, but could not expend itself in him: and as an uninspired thinker is ofttimes conscious of aspirations, which are seen to be unfulfilled by such and such occurrences as successively present themselves, and are then only *understood* when the thing is found which truly answers to them; so David the Prophet expresses hopes not to be grasped specifically apart from the event, in words which contain obscurely, as in embryo, all that should in after time be of necessity evolved therefrom.

The preceding may appear to some to imply an improper limitation of the prophetic consciousness; but there is a passage in St John's Gospel, which goes further, and speaks of an altogether perfunctory and unconscious prophesying, or enunciation of the Divine purpose: 'And one of them, named Caiaphas, being the high-priest that same year, said unto them, Ye know nothing at all. Nor consider that it is expedient for us, that one man should die for the people, and that the whole nation perish not. And this spake he not of himself: but being high-priest that year, he prophesied that Jesus should die for that nation' (Joh. xi. 49—51). The difficult passage, 2 Pet. i. 20, 21, does not, according to some, define the limits of prophetic consciousness; but affirms only that the prophets were borne irresistibly upon the Spirit's blast, leaving it undetermined whether or no they were fully conscious of the direction of their course. It was given them what they should speak, and they may or may not have understood their words; but, its origin being divine, we have in prophecy a sure guide, 'whereunto ye do well that ye take heed, as unto a light that shineth in a dark place, until the day dawn, and the day-star arise in your hearts.'

IV. *The Double Sense of Prophecy.*

The tendency to despiritualize the interpretation of the Old Testament language has sprung very naturally from an antagonism to the manifest extravagances of mystical exegesis. To the historico-critical interpreter it seems, rightly or wrongly, that much of this extravagance owes its origin to a lack of acquaintance with Hebrew criticism, such as characterised portions of the theology of the early Christian Church: but that all was not traceable to this one source may be gathered from the coexistence of far greater extravagance in the systems of the Rabbinists, who aimed at evolving all science and philosophy, by this or that direct process, from the sacred page. With Jew, as with Christian, a superstitious regard for the very words and letters of Holy Writ, led by strangely tortuous ways to a practical disregard of the literal and historical sense. But it will be granted that a peculiar reverence for their Scriptures had ever existed in the Jew, and with it, must we not say, a proclivity to higher interpretations, rendered grotesque only in a later age by incongruous accretions? The same psalm which seems to contain merely poetical allusions to historical events, may suggest to the worshipper, with no less ease and naturalness, not allusions to past events, but eternal truths. The mystical may be to him *the most literal* sense of all[1]. If this be so, a further question at once suggests itself. How far back is the spiritual interpretation to be traced? Is it not conceivable that it may be found as old, in some cases, as the psalm itself?

One theory for the reconciliation of the literal and the spiritual interpretations is the theory of the *Double Sense;* which assumes that "Scripture prophecy is so formed in some of its predictions as to bear a sense directed to two objects; of which structure the predictions concerning the kingdom of David furnish a conspicuous example; and I should say an unquestionable one, if the whole principle of that interpretation had not been by some disputed and denied. But the principle has met with this ill acceptance, for no better reason, it should seem, than because it has been injudiciously applied, in cases where it has no proper place; or has been suspected, if not mistaken, in its constituent character, as to

---

[1] Lowth, *Is. lii.* 13.

what it really is. The double sense of prophecy, however, is of all things the most remote from fraud or equivocations, and has its ground of reason perfectly clear. For what is it? Not the convenient latitude of two unconnected senses, wide of each other, and giving room to a fallacious ambiguity; but the combination of two related, analogous, and harmonising, though disparate subjects, each clear and definite in itself; implying a two-fold truth in the prescience, and creating an aggravated difficulty, and thereby an accumulated proof, in the completion....So that the double sense of prophecy, in its true idea, is a check upon the pretences of vague and unappropriated prediction, rather than a door to admit them.

But this is not all. For if the prediction distribute its sense into two remote branches or systems of the divine economy; if it shew not only what is to take place in distant times, but describe also different modes of God's appointment, though holding a certain and intelligible resemblance to each other; such prediction becomes not only more convincing in the argument, but more instructive in the doctrine, because it expresses the correspondence of God's dispensations in their points of agreement, as well as His fore-knowledge[1]."

The above statement presupposes a two-fold futurity of application; but may be taken, with some latitude, as including the cases, to be considered below, wherein the so-called primary application is to past or contemporaneous events. Such a 'double sense' is that described by Dr Phillips in the subjoined extract, and persistently opposed throughout his commentary on the Psalms.

"It may be proper to offer a few remarks on what is called the double sense of Scripture, on account of its having been adopted by so many and such able divines of the present as well as of past times. To enunciate their theory in a few words, they propose to give to the language of prophecy two meanings; a primary or lower one, which is extracted

[1] Davison, *On Prophecy*.

from the words of the passage taken literally, and with reference to the temporary circumstances under which it was written; and afterwards a secondary one, which they believe the same words will afford, and which teaches some event or some truth connected with the Christian dispensation....But one grand objection to the theory in question is, that it admits all language to be so vague and ambiguous that persons engaged in interpreting it cannot possibly come to any settled conclusion. Another objection, equally strong, may be made to the practice in which the adherents to this theory indulge, *viz.* that of abandoning the primary sense in expressions which either from the loftiness of their language, or because they contain remarkable terms, seem exclusively to demand the secondary. Surely nothing can be more unsatisfactory than to apply, for instance, in the second Psalm, one verse to David or Solomon, and another to Christ. Such a system, which requires the student of prophecy to pass so abruptly from one personage to another, and back again, and this process to be gone through perhaps several times in the same composition, must be calculated to exercise a pernicious influence on his faith in the Word of God. Besides, the system obtains no authority from the New Testament: of all the quotations we find in it from the Old, there is not any which leads us to suppose that the sacred writer who made the quotation ever thought the passage he cited to have more meanings than one."

The objections to the *double sense* are, certainly, of great weight. Nor can the purely *historical* application be characterised as other than, in some cases, eminently unsatisfactory; for a Jew, with his depth of religious feeling, full of hopes for the future, and breathing an atmosphere of ceremonial symbolism, could scarcely fail to be transported far beyond the thought of this or that historic event by terms and expressions which if referring simply to that event would be the language of hyperbole. Hence a third theory, well deserving of consideration, viz. 'that the literal sense is to be regarded as a kind of vehicle' for the spiritual. This theory is advocated by Mr Mudge:—" As God is ever the same, and His doings uniform, His conduct towards mankind must exactly be proportioned to His conduct towards the Jewish nation. Let us therefore place God in common over them both, and there will be on the one side the Jewish nation; and on the other mankind: on one side national and temporary saviours, kings, prophets, &c.: on the other all this universal and eternal: on one side the Law, and every branch of it adapted to a favoured nation; on the other the everlasting Gospel suited to all mankind. It is impossible therefore that God can say anything to David, under the quality of king of the chosen nation, which He does not speak at the same time to Jesus Christ as king of all the elect, and that in a truer and nobler sense. If He says to one, for instance, 'Thou art my Son,' and 'Sit on my right hand till I make thy enemies thy footstool,' He says it to the other too; to each of them in a sense adapted to the nature of their respective kingdoms. Nor is this latter a bare accommodation of words, but the first and highest meaning of them, and which only, absolutely speaking, can be the true sense of God, the other being this sense confined to a particular circumstance; in other words, *an absolute truth made history and matter of fact.* This is a principle which shews that, far from denying the Christian application, I consider the literal and historical sense only as a kind of VEHICLE for it."

This theory may be exemplified by the later use of the name of *David* for Him in whom the 'mercies of David' were still to be realised, or, as Rabbinic commentators join with others in affirming, for the MESSIAH. Thus the name of David is used as the 'vehicle' of a higher sense: and as with his name, so with the circumstances of his life, which might with no less propriety be thus applied, as the vehicles of spiritual conceptions. A mode of expression has, in general, a proportion to the definiteness of the thought expressed, and hence this question connects itself with that of the limits of prophetic consciousness, above considered. In default of such definiteness of conception as was granted only in the retrospect, the prophets depict CHRIST as an ideal David, and in like manner idealize the circumstances of his temporal princedom, out of the sphere of history, into the Messianic future.

This relation between the *primary* sense of prophecy and the *secondary* may be illustrated by a reference to the analogy of language. As is the literal meaning of a word to its metaphorical usage, so may be the temporal imagery of a Psalm to its spiritual application; and in such cases, the discovery of the historical allusions is explanatory, not subversive, of the higher sense. It must be remembered that the Biblical writers, were, so to say, the framers of a spiritual language, which we still, in substance, retain, although some of its expressions may have lost no little of their *objectivity*. They represented by concrete types, what in the later stage of the *spiritual* language as of any other, is expressed abstractly. We speak *e.g.* of the '*service* of sin,' using an abstract term, where they would have inclined to a special type (perhaps the bondage in Egypt or the Babylonian captivity) as representing the same idea. We speak, broadly, of 'a *contest* with evil,' where they would have drawn in detail the picture of a battle, perhaps a specific battle with some living foe. So too they would naturally choose out some special circumstance as a vehicle for the description of this or that attribute of the Messiah; or would address their words directly to a present king, not personally, but as an official type, from which the thought glanced upward to the half-grasped antitypical idea. In their spiritual metaphors the constituent parts are clearly distinguishable; while our later usages seem at first sight to defy analysis, but yet involve what could only be expressed *completely* by such detailed pictorial representations as above described[1].

The Messianic application of Psalms ii., xlv.

That portions of these Psalms are applicable to Christ is

---

[1] Their modes of thought might be described as *pleonastic*, in great matters, as in small [*supra*].

not disputed; but whether each application is primary or by way of accommodation is contested by modern writers. The Messianic interpretation was favoured in each case by antiquity[1], and continued to hold its own even with the mediæval Rabbis. The merely historical interpretation does not commend itself as exhaustive to the modern reader, and must have been still less compatible with the Messianic aspirations of the ancient Jew.

1. The second Psalm is thought to have been written after the building of the temple, from the occurrence of the expression, 'my *holy* hill of Sion;' and a correspondence of its phraseology with that of 2 Sam. vii. 14, has been thought to mark Solomon as the king described. If the allusion be to any one temporal monarch, it is perhaps to Solomon; but this application is very precarious, however preferable to any other of the same class. Many commentators, accordingly, agree in the conclusion, that it 'probably applies to no particular king, but is a glorification of the theocratic kingdom in general, with poetic reference to the universal dominion promised to it.' Mr Perowne, who assumes that 'the poem was *occasioned* by some national event,' admits that 'we must not confine its application to that event, nor must we even suppose that the singer himself did not feel that his words went beyond their first occasion. He begins to speak of an earthly king, and his wars with the nations of the earth, but his words are too great to have all their meaning exhausted in David, or Solomon, or Ahaz, or any Jewish monarch. Or ever he is aware, the local and the temporal are swallowed up in the universal and the eternal...The picture is half ideal, half actual. It concerns itself with the present, but with that only so far as it is typical of greater things to come.' This

---

[1] Rosenmüller thus concludes, on Ps. ii.: 'Quare tutissimum erit, vetustiorum Hebræorum sententiam sequi, canere Psalmum magnum illum regem, המשיח, *Unctum* κατ' ἐξοχήν dictum, quem Hebræi sperabant, &c.;' and on Ps. xlv.: 'Verum optime omnia in hoc Psalmo inter se congruent, si antiquiorum Hebræorum sequuti sententiam... magni illius regis, Messiæ, virtutes et laudes... carmine hoc celebrari statuamus.'

is to grant, indirectly, the Messianic interpretation which Rosenmüller adopts explicitly. It seems unnecessary to suppose that the Psalmist, engaged in the same historical description, found his words outrun the occasion. May not the Messianic idea have *sought to express itself* through the medium of contemporary fact, and thus have produced a picture corresponding in outline to the present, but in richness of colouring to the more glorious future?

The forty-fifth Psalm may perhaps be similarly characterised. Mr Perowne, who describes it as 'evidently a Marriage-song composed for some day of royal espousals,' and thinks it 'more justly applicable to Solomon than to any other of the Jewish monarchs, so far as we are acquainted with their fortunes,' is not insensible to the difficulties which beset this application. 'Nor is it necessarily,' he continues, 'an objection to this view, that the monarch in the Psalm is spoken of as a warrior, whilst Solomon was peculiarly *a man of peace*. Something must be allowed to poetry. An extended dominion would naturally be associated with ideas of conquest. And, with the recollection of his father's exploits fresh in his mind, the Poet could not but regard warlike virtues as essential to the glory of the son. Besides Solomon himself does not seem to have been deficient in military spirit ... But a greater than Solomon is here. Evident as it is that much of the language of the Poem is only properly applicable to the circumstances of the royal nuptials which occasioned it, it is no less evident that much of it greatly transcends them;' as may well be explained on the above-mentioned hypothesis, that the circumstances therein described were used as exponents of an antecedent spiritual idea.

Dr Phillips again adopts the Messianic sense, to the exclusion of any definite so-called *primary* allusion. 'It must be mentioned that the testimony of these [Rabbinic] writers, as well as that of the Christian Fathers, and a great part of modern commentators, is not only in favour of Christ being the subject of the Psalm, but farther, of His being *exclusively* the subject. They give no countenance whatever to a primary interpretation with respect to Solomon, or any other king of the Israelitish nation ... In many of the grand leading characteristics such interpretation entirely fails; and hence I cannot but remark, that to introduce another person as the primary object of representation is fearfully weakening a prophecy of such magnitude and importance as the present; for it is throwing a vagueness over language which is in reality as strict and accurate as prophetic language can possibly be.'

But it may be questioned whether such primary allusion to particular events would of necessity be thus detrimental to the higher interpretation. The Hebrew Prophets ofttimes prophesied *by* typical actions, and may have prophesied, no less appropriately, *through* contemporary events. In any case, it is granted that their general conceptions of regal state &c. formed a vehicle for the Messianic idea; and that such conceptions were not *innate*, but had come to them in the course of natural experience (whether directly or by hearsay) from without. They were, then, ultimately referable to one or more of individual monarchs, and it is a question of not prime moment, whether the sacred writer, in his prophetic delineation of King MESSIAH, used some special type of royalty, or an abstraction gathered from successive types.

Is Psalm ii. 7 applied to the Resurrection?

The seventh verse of this Psalm is quoted by St Paul in Acts xiii. 33: 'as it is also written in the second psalm, Thou art my Son, this day have I begotten thee.' The reference is commonly supposed to be to the Resurrection, but this view is not without its opponents, who consider that the application is to the 'raising up' of JESUS, not from the dead, but in the sense of Deut. xviii. 15, 18, 19, quoted by St Peter in Acts iii. 22, 33: 'For Moses truly said unto the fathers, A prophet shall the LORD your God *raise up* unto you of your brethren, like unto me; him shall ye hear in all things whatsoever he shall say unto you:' and quoted by St Stephen in Acts vii. 37: 'This is that Moses, which said unto the children of Israel, A prophet shall the LORD your God raise up unto you of your brethren, like unto me; Him shall ye hear.' The latter view is adopted by Mr Humphry, who remarks on Acts xiii. 32, that ἀνίστημι, in the New Testament, 'only refers to the resurrection when ἐκ νεκρῶν is added, as at ver. 34, or the context in some other way defines that to be the sense[1]; as at ii. 24, *whom God hath raised up having loosed the pains of death.*' Dean Alford is of opinion that 'the meaning, *having raised him from the dead*, is absolutely required by the context: both because the word is repeated with ἐκ νεκρῶν (ver. 34), and because the Apostle's emphasis throughout the passage is on the Resurrection, as the final fulfilment of God's promises regarding JESUS ... Meyer well remarks that this meaning would hardly in our passage have been thought of or defended, had it not been that the subjoined citation from Ps. ii. had been thought necessarily to apply to our Lord's mission upon earth.'

1. The applicability of Ps. ii. 7, to the Resurrection would probably have occurred to few, apart from the supposed exigencies of St Paul's citation now to be considered. If this application be a true one, then the passage in the Acts will have thrown a new light upon the Psalm; but seeing that it has been powerfully controverted, it becomes necessary to examine the Apostolic address, with a view to determine, so far as may be, whether the disputed words are there so applied or not.

St Paul, responding to the request of the rulers of the synagogue, stands up to propound his word of exhortation to the people. "The God of this people Israel chose our fathers. With an high arm brought he them out of Egypt. And when he had destroyed seven nations in the land of Chanaan he divided their land to them by lot. He gave them judges, and the prophet Samuel, and king Saul, and David—'a man after mine own heart, which shall fulfil all my will.' Of this man's seed hath God according to his promise *raised* unto Israel a Saviour Jesus.

[1] But see Joh. vi. 39, 40; xi. 23, 24.

But they that dwell at Jerusalem, and their rulers, because they knew him not, nor yet the voices of the prophets which are read every sabbath-day, they have fulfilled them in condemning him. And though they found no cause of death in him, yet desired they Pilate that he should be slain. And when they had fulfilled all that was written of him, they took him down from the tree, and laid him in a sepulchre. But God *raised him from the dead*" (Acts xiii. 15—28). St Paul, having thus laid the historical foundations of his argument, now shews the fulfilment of ancient prophecies in JESUS. He is addressing himself, be it remarked, to *unbelievers*, and so does not begin by assuming a general belief in Christ, and pass on without prelude to the doctrine of His resurrection; but first affirms that in Him the promise had its end; He was the seed of David, and that Prophet which should come into the world. God fulfilled this promise by the raising up of JESUS; 'as it is also written in the second Psalm, Thou art my Son, this day have I begotten thee. *But* that he raised him *from the dead*, now no more to return to corruption, he said on this wise, I will give you the sure mercies of David. Wherefore he saith also in another psalm, Thou shalt not suffer thine Holy One to see corruption.' The occurrence of the adversative particle δέ indicates that the Apostle is about to introduce something in a manner contrasting with what had gone before; some detail (might we not anticipate?), some sequel to the general *raising*. This surmise is at once confirmed by the immediate occurrence of ἐκ νεκρῶν. Psalm ii. is applied to the *raising up* of the promised seed; 'but that he raised him *from the dead*, he said on this wise...' The same citation from Ps. ii. recurs in Heb. i. 5, in close connection with the bringing in of the Christ into this lower world. 'For unto which of the angels said he at any time, Thou art my Son, this day have I begotten thee? And again, I will be to him a Father, and he shall be to me a Son. And again, when he bringeth in the first-begotten *into the world*[1], he saith, And let all the angels of God worship him.' In Heb. v. 5, the

---

[1] εἰς τὴν οἰκουμένην.

verse in question is made the source of the collateral deduction, that 'Christ glorified not *himself* to be made an high priest; but he that said unto him, Thou art my Son, to-day have I begotten thee.'

2. The application of Ps. ii. 7 to the resurrection is advocated by Bishop Kidder[1]:—

'To this purpose belong those words, *Thou art my Son, this day have I begotten thee.* That that Psalm did relate to the Messias we are able to prove from the Jewish Doctors, who do acknowledge it: And therefore when it was alledged to this purpose they cannot say that it was an allegation out of a place which did not belong to the Messias. The Apostle applies these words to this sense; he assures us that God hath fulfilled His promise in that He *hath raised up Jesus again*, as it is also written in the second Psalm, *Thou art my Son*, &c. It being confessed by the Jews themselves that the Psalm out of which these words are cited, is to be understood of the Messias; I need not go about to justify and make good that it belongs to the matter for which it is alledged. I shall only consider how fitly these words are applied to the resurrection of the Messias. For, *Thou art my Son, this day have I begotten Thee*, seem rather to relate to the birth than to the resurrection of the Messias.

'For the clearing of this matter it is to be considered, that it is no unusual thing to call the *earth* our Mother, as well as our *Parent* from whom we are born; it is very common to call each of these by the same name: the earth, out of which we are *taken*, and to which we *return*, is our Mother, as well as our Parent from whom we spring....Philo the Jew tells us that the earth seems to be a Mother, and that thence it was among the Ancients it was called by a word[2] that at once signifies the *Earth* and *Mother*. ... After this manner do the writers of the Old Testament speak, with whom the grave which receives the dead is called the *womb;* and therefore a resurrection from hence may well be called a new birth...And we find among the Jewish writers that the Mother's womb

---

[1] *Demonstr. Messias*, I. 289.   [2] Δημήτηρ.

is called a *sepulchre*. He that is born, and dies, and is buried, does but pass from *one* Tomb to *another*. And he that rises out of the *womb* of the *earth*, or his *grave*, may be said to be *born anew;* and therefore it may well be said of our Saviour, when He rose from the dead, that He was then begotten. And when the Apostle applies those words, *this day have I begotten Thee*, to our Saviour's resurrection, he does but speak the language of the Hebrew writers; and the Jews, who own this Psalm to belong to the Messias, have no reason to complain that those words of it should be applied to His resurrection.' In further confirmation of this usage, the same writer instances *the sign of the prophet Jonas*[1], 'who was *three days and three nights* in the *whale's belly*, to which the heart of the earth, in which *Jesus* was, and from which he rose, answers.'

V. An expression in the forty-fifth Psalm, quoted in Heb. i. 8, has given rise to much controversy, and is confessedly difficult, not from any peculiarity in the words themselves or in their arrangement, but from the relations of the clause, in itself simple, to the context. If the original of the clause in question had occurred only as a fragment, and the remainder of the Psalm had not been preserved, there would have been no difficulty in accepting the words, '*Thy throne, O God, is for ever and ever*,' as a literal rendering of the passage cited: but, seeing that the original context diminishes the naturalness of the rendering, it may be well first to state some of the conjectures to which the passage has given rise; and secondly to examine the context of the citation, with a view to determining whether the argument depends upon the disputed word, so exclusively as is now commonly supposed.

1. The Psalmist thus opens his address to the King, whose praises are his theme: 'Thou art fairer than the children of men: grace is poured into thy lips: therefore *God hath blessed thee for ever;*' and, further on, occur the

---

[1] See Note A, p. 165.

words, as commonly translated, '*Thy throne, O God, is for ever and ever:* the sceptre of thy kingdom is a right sceptre. Thou lovest righteousness, and hatest wickedness: therefore *God*[1], *thy God, hath anointed thee* with the oil of gladness above thy fellows' (Ps. xlv. 6, 7). If the vocative rendering ['O God'], which is supported by the concurrent testimony of antiquity, be correct, there are still two modes of application to be distinguished. The clause may either be taken as a parenthetic address to God breaking in upon the address to the King, to whom the *second person* is appropriated in the context; or it may be an address to the King (*as* God) who is spoken of before and after as blessed and anointed *by* God. There is no difficulty, apart from the context, in this application of the title *God* to the King. The word *Elohim* stands in parallelism with *rulers*, in Ex. xxii. 28 : 'Thou shalt not revile the gods, nor curse the ruler of thy people;' and in a passage quoted by Rashi (who adopts the explanation, 'Thy throne, O *prince* and *judge*') it is said by the Lord to Moses: 'See, I have made thee a *god* to Pharaoh' (Ex. vii. 1). It occurs too in Ps. lxxxii. 1, and again in ver. 6, which is cited by our Lord in Joh. x. 33—36: 'The Jews answered him saying, For a good work we stone thee not; but for blasphemy; and because that thou, being a man, makest thyself God. Jesus answered them, Is it not written in your law, I said, *Ye are gods?* If he called them *gods*, unto whom the word of God came, and the Scripture cannot be broken; say ye of Him, whom the Father hath sanctified, and sent into the world, Thou blasphemest; because I said, I am the Son of God?' But although there may be no difficulty in the application of the word *God*, taken singly, the context seems repugnant to either of the vocative renderings.

Another rendering, frequently adopted, supposes an ellipsis, thus: 'Thy throne is *God's*,' it is a throne Divine. This view of R. Aben Ezra is thought [Kimchi] to be supported by 1 Chron. xxix. 23: 'Then Solomon sat on the

---

[1] See Note B, p. 166.

The sure Mercies of David. 163

throne of the LORD as King instead of David his father.' Others, with slight variation, render, 'Thy God-throne *is* for ever,' but there is some force in the objection of Dr Ewald[1], that elsewhere in the Psalm, the phrase, *for ever* is not used as a predicate, but as qualifying a statement upon which it follows, thus: 'God hath blessed thee *for ever*' (ver. 2); 'Therefore shall the people praise thee *for ever.*' It may be mentioned, in passing, that the rendering, '*Deus ipse est sedes tua,*' is given by Erasmus, and thus paraphrased by Grotius: 'Deus te semper in regno sustentabit.'

The meaning, 'Thy throne *shall* God *establish*[2],' is indeed well suited to the context; but by what construction is it to be obtained? Such a meaning might be arrived at by the (unsupported) conjecture, that the word for *thy throne*, elsewhere occurring only as a noun, is here to be taken as a verb: 'God *hath enthroned thee.*' This rendering of the disputed clause agrees very well with the antecedent and following statements; 'God *hath blessed thee*' (ver. 2); 'God, thy God, *hath anointed thee.*' Again, a parallelism is developed between the sixth verse and the seventh. 'God hath enthroned thee for ever.' *And wherefore?* (it may be asked in the words of Rashi). *Because 'the sceptre of thy kingdom is a right sceptre;' &c.* Thus the sixth verse corresponds, by introversion, to the seventh: 'Thou lovest righteousness, and hatest wickedness: therefore God, thy God, hath anointed thee with the oil of gladness above thy fellows.'

2. It remains to consider what rendering is required, or admitted, by the context of the citation in Heb. i. 8. 'But unto the Son he saith, Thy throne, *O God*, is for ever and ever;' where the vocative rendering of 'the LXX. and all the old versions' is adopted. The rendering 'Thy throne is *God's*' would also harmonize with the context, although not agreeing literally with the rendering there adopted. This latter form of words would but assert indirectly what is im-

---

[1] 'Das *ewig immer*, ist auch in unserm liede immer bloss begleitend, nie selbst prädicat, &c.'

[2] והגאון אמר כסאך יבין אלהים

plied by the direct use of the title *God*. But the conjectural rendering (of the Hebrew) which stands last in order, seems at first sight irreconcileable with the argument of Heb. i. 8, where the chief stress is usually laid upon the application of the Divine name to Christ. The application is, however, parenthetical, and does not seem to be absolutely essential to the argument, which ought therefore to remain unimpaired when the words, '*O God*,' are omitted[1] as in the subjoined transcript of Heb. i. 5—14.

'For unto which of the angels said he at any time, Thou art my Son, this day have I begotten thee? (Ps. ii. 7). And again, I will be to him a Father, and he shall be to me a Son? (2 Sam. vii. 14). And again, when he bringeth in the first-begotten into the world, he saith, And let all the angels of God worship him[2] (? Ps. xcvii. 7). And of the angels he saith, who maketh his angels spirits, and his ministers a flame of fire (Ps. civ. 4.) But unto the Son he saith, Thy throne ...is for ever and ever: a sceptre of righteousness is the sceptre of thy kingdom. Thou hast loved righteousness, and hated iniquity; therefore God, even thy God, hath anointed thee with the oil of gladness above thy fellows (Ps. xlv. 7, 8). And, thou, Lord, in the beginning hast laid the foundation of the earth: and the heavens are the works of thine hands: They shall perish; but thou remainest; and they all shall wax old as doth a garment; and as a vesture shalt thou fold them up, and they shall be changed: but thou art the same, and thy years shall not fail. (Ps. cii. 26—28). But to which of the angels said he at any time, Sit thou on my right hand, until I make thine enemies thy footstool? (Ps. cx. 1). Are they not all ministering spirits, sent forth to minister for them that shall be heirs of salvation?'

The angels pass to and fro to do His bidding; the Son sits enthroned eternally. They are coordinated with the

---

[1] They are omitted only to test their essentiality to the argument. Their use amounts to an assertion of our Lord's divinity. But see, on the passage, Pusey, *Daniel the Prophet*. Further remarks on the Psalm will be found in Note C, p. 166.

[2] Deut. xxxii. 43 (LXX).

agencies of perishable nature ; Thou art the unchanging LORD, and Maker of all. The words, '*Thy throne is for ever*,' sustain the argument, independently of the omitted parenthesis, and would seem, moreover, to appropriate the chief emphasis of the clause itself, when taken singly, and viewed without reference to the context. Lastly it may be asked, are not ver. 13, 14, a brief *résumé* of the argument, thus expounded ? To the Son—*Sit thou on my right hand;* to the angels—*Go forth and minister*.

It is doubtless intended in Heb. i. 8, to address Christ as God, but it may be questioned, as above, whether the words ὁ Θεός, are the *characteristic* of the citation. If not, they may still, according to the common usage, have been retained, as appropriate in themselves, and in harmony with the special purpose of the citation, yet without furnishing 'a key to the interpretation of the whole Psalm.' All that could be implied by the form of address ὁ Θεός, is implied unequivocally by ver. 10, 'Thou Lord, in the beginning, &c.'

The word *Lord* does not indeed occur in the particular verse here cited, but, except as regards perspicuity, it is immaterial whether the word be expressed or understood, the significant fact being, that the hundred and second Psalm is addressed throughout to JEHOVAH, as the Redeemer of Israel, and is, in Heb. i. 10, transferred to Christ.

NOTES ON CHAPTER VI.

A. When our Lord shadows forth His resurrection by a reference to the history of Jonah, is He attaching a new meaning to the familiar narrative; or is He applying it in a way that would be recognized by His hearers, as in harmony with its original significance? The latter view derives strong confirmation from the words of the Prophet's prayer. He substitutes, *belly of hell*, for *bowels of the fish;* and describes his deliverance in words borrowed from the Psalms, as a return from death to life. ' Out of the belly of hell cried I, and thou heardest my voice...I went down, to the bottoms of the mountains; the *earth* with her bars was about me for ever: yet hast thou brought up my life from corruption, O Lord my God' (Jon. ii. 2, 6).

B. If משחך אלהים אלהיך, were rendered: 'Thy God, O God, hath anointed Thee;' the abruptness of the preceding אלהים, taken vocatively as an address to the king, would be diminished. Pearson, *Creed, Art. II.*, quotes from Jerome *in loc.:* 'Duas personas, ejus qui unctus est Dei et qui unxit, intellige.' 'Quod sequitur, *Unxit te, Deus, Deus tuus*, primum nomen Dei vocativo casu intelligendum est, sequens nominativo; quod satis miror cur Aquila non, ut cœperat in primo versiculo, vocativo casu interpretatus sit, sed nominativo, bis nominans Deum, qui supradictum unxerit Deum.'—See Field's *Origenis Hexaplorum quæ supersunt.*—But against this vocative rendering it may be urged, that the repetition, *God, even Thy God*, has its counterpart in other places where a like collocation occurs; *e. g.* 'Then will I go unto the altar of God, unto God my exceeding joy: yea upon the harp will I praise thee, *O God, my God*,' (Ps. xliii. 4); 'I am *God, even thy God*,' (l. 7); '*God, even our own God*, shall bless us,' (lxvii. 6). See li. 14; lxiii. 1; lxviii. 8; lxxii. 18.

C. Saadiah's rendering of Ps. xlv. 6 [p. 163, note] might be explained as follows. In ver. 8 the true construction is perhaps a *zeugma*, thus: 'myrrh, &c.—all thy garments: [myrrh, &c.] have gladdened thee;' where some verb governing 'garments,' and having 'myrrh, &c.' for its nominative, is to be anticipated from שמחוך. So in ver. 7, 8 there may be a *zeugma:* 'God—thy throne...God, thy God, hath anointed thee;' where a verb (e. g. *hath established*) applicable to 'throne,' is to be anticipated from משחך. But this would be further complicated by the explanatory parenthesis: 'Thou hast loved righteousness, &c. &c.' For the verb-rendering of כסאך, all that is to be said is, that it agrees with the context of the Psalm, and that כסא, elsewhere a noun, is of the same form as the 3rd pers. past piel. This is far from convincing to the writer, and seems only sufficiently plausible to be recorded; regard being had to the acknowledged difficulty of the passage. The possessive rendering is ill-supported. The vocative rendering, adopted in Heb. i. 8, is, grammatically, as Dr Pusey contends, no doubt the simplest.

P.S. Scaynus Salodiensis writes: 'etiam sic Filius super Angelos insinuatur, ut *ille cujus Thronus sit Deus*.'

CHAPTER VII.

He gave gifts unto men.

Ps. lxviii. 18; Eph. iv. 8.

THE difficulties of this citation are fully recognized by commentators, and by none more fully than by Bishop Ellicott; who, comparing Eph. iv. 8, with the LXX. rendering of the clauses corresponding to it in Ps. lxviii. remarks, that 'the difference in St Paul's citation is palpable, and, we are bound in candour to say, does not appear diminished by any of the proposed reconciliations.'

The citation is thus introduced:—'There is one body, and one Spirit, even as ye are called in one hope of your calling ... But unto every one of us is given grace, according to the measure of the gift of Christ. Wherefore he saith, *When he ascended up on high, he led captivity captive, and gave gifts unto men*[1]. (Now that he ascended[2], what is it but that he also descended first into the lower parts of the earth? He that descended is the same also that ascended up far above all heavens, that he might fill all things.) And *he gave* some, apostles; and some, prophets; and some, evangelists; and some, pastors and teachers; for the perfecting of the saints, for the work of the ministry, for the edifying of the body of

---

[1] διὸ λέγει, Ἀναβὰς εἰς ὕψος ᾐχμαλώτευσεν αἰχμαλωσίαν, καὶ ἔδωκεν δόματα τοῖς ἀνθρώποις.

[2] τὸ δὲ ἀνέβη. See note A, p. 175.

Christ: Till we all come in the unity of the faith, and of the knowledge of the Son of God, unto a perfect man, unto the measure of the stature of the fulness of Christ' (Eph. iv. 4—12).

The Apostle here substitutes ἔδωκεν for the LXX. ἔλαβες, which corresponds more directly to the original expression. This variation it is usual to account for as *explanatory*, and intended to set forth explicitly the implied meaning of the Hebrew. In the Authorized Version, which presents the received arrangement of the clauses, the verse runs as follows: 'Thou hast ascended on high, thou hast led captivity captive, *thou hast received gifts for men;* yea, for the rebellious also, that the LORD God might dwell among them;' and it is admitted that the receiving of gifts *for* men, and the giving of gifts *to* men, are so intimately connected, that the latter expression might naturally replace the former. The real difficulty arises in the reconciliation of either of the foregoing with the original Hebrew. It is usual to cite passages in which the word *to take* imports a taking with *the intention of giving* to another; thus, in Gen. xviii. 5: 'I will *fetch* a morsel of bread, and comfort ye your hearts;' and in Ex. xxvii. 20: 'And thou shalt command the children of Israel, that they *bring thee*[1] pure oil-olive beaten for the light, to cause the lamp to burn always.' But such illustrations are insufficient, not to say illusory; shewing only that the word may mean generally *to take, fetch, obtain,* &c. (for one's own use or for another's, *as the context may require*) but not establishing its practical equivalence to δοῦναι in such a context as that of Ps. lxviii. where the preposition following is *in*, not, *to* or *for*. Moreover, when the usual explanation of these particular words is accepted, there remains a general inconsecutiveness, best evinced by the many attempts which have been made to force the clauses of the verse into harmonious sequence. It seems best therefore to reconsider the whole verse *ab initio*,

[1] ויקחו אליך.

and in particular to subject the clause above considered to a fresh analysis.

The preposition *in* does not follow naturally upon the word, *to take*, in the sense required by the Authorized Version : 'Thou hast received gifts for men.' To receive *among*[1] (i. e. *from*) would be a more natural rendering, and some accordingly have taken this to be the true construction; but an abruptness would still attach itself to the concluding words, and the whole verse would present itself as ill-balanced and unsymmetrical. If the extreme clauses of the verse be read in close connection, and the last mentioned explanation of the *reception* of gifts *in* men be adopted, the whole verse will run as follows: '*Thou hast* gone up on high—Thou hast led captives captive; Thou hast received gifts from men; yea from the rebellious also—to dwell, O LORD God[2].' But the rendering is still abrupt and unsymmetrical; and since much of the difficulty felt in adopting it arises from its lack of symmetry, it may be asked whether a rearrangement of the clause, be not possible. Is it necessary to join the words, *Thou hast received gifts*, with the following expression, *among men?* would not the latter read better in connection with the word *to dwell* (which now stands elliptically), as serving in that connection to define the locality wherein the LORD God is about to dwell?

The expression 'to *dwell* among men,' is aptly illustrated by Ps. lxxviii. 60, where the same verb is used : 'So he forsook the tabernacle of Shiloh the tent which *he had placed* among men[3];' and again, no less explicitly, by Rev. xxi. 3: 'And I heard a great voice out of heaven saying, Behold, the

---

[1] 'Thou art gone up into Thy sanctuary on high ; Thou hast led Thy captivity captive; Thou hast received gifts among men, yea even the refractory, that the LORD God may be lodged.' *Mudge.*

[2] 'Hunc versum, parum feliciter a superioris ætatis interpretibus tractatum, ...primus recte explicavit Schnurrerus : *Conscendisti altum, captivos ducens victos hostes, accipiens munera inter homines, rebelles etiam, ut habites hic* JAH, *Deus.*' (Rosenm.)

[3] אהל שכן באדם.

tabernacle of God is with men, and he will dwell with them, and they shall be his people, and God himself shall be with them, and be their God.' The same thought is expressed[1] in Ex. xxv. 8: 'And let them make me a sanctuary; that I may dwell among them;' and again, in Ex. xxix. 45, 46: 'I will dwell among the children of Israel, and will be their God.' While in other passages, this 'dwelling' is predicated of the same locality as in Ps. lxviii. 18, viz. of 'Zion, my holy mountain' (Joel iii. 17, 21; Zech. viii. 3; Ps. lxxiv. 2). Moreover, the rendering, '*to dwell among men*,' which is thus abundantly illustrated, falls in with a more symmetrical arrangement of the verse before us:

> Thou hast gone up on high—
> Hast led captives captive,
> Hast received gifts—
> With men[2], yea backsliders,
> O LORD God, to dwell[3].

Where the primary allusion is to the ascent of the Ark from the house of Obed-Edom to 'the tabernacle that David had pitched for it' (2 Sam. vi. 17) on Mount Zion; while the typical allusion is to the celestial heights, in accordance with the analogy of Ps. lxxviii. 67—69: 'Moreover He refused the tabernacle of Joseph, and chose not the tribe of Ephraim: But chose the tribe of Judah, the Mount Zion which He loved. And he built his sanctuary like high palaces[4], like the earth which he hath established for ever;' where for 'high palaces,' should be read (as one word) *high-places*, in the sense of *heavens*, as the parallelism suggests. This is the interpretation of Rashi, who remarks quaintly, that, as it is written: 'Mine *hand* also hath laid the foundation of the earth, and my *right hand* hath spanned the heavens' (Is. xlviii.

---

[1] Compare Numb. v. 3; xxxv. 34; 1 Kings vi. 13; Is. xxxiii. 5; Ezek. xliii. 9; Zech. ii. 11.

[2] בָּאָדָם. In the books אֱמֹ"ת, *Ethnach* is often a slight stop, like the colon in our Prayer-Book Psalms. See ver. 9, 14, 21, 22, 29.

[3] Or: 'that JAH God may dwell.'

[4] כמו רמים. Cp. למרום, *supra*, Ps. lxviii. 18.

He gave gifts unto men.

13), earth and heaven being described as each the work of a single hand; whereas the Sanctuary is described as the work of both hands, thus: 'Thou shalt bring them in, and plant them in the mountain of thine inheritance, in the place, O LORD, which thou hast made for thee to dwell in, in the Sanctuary, O LORD, which *thy hands* have made' (Ex. xv. 17); so in Ps. lxxviii. 69, the Sanctuary is compared at once to both heaven and earth, the fabrics of the separate hands. It may be further remarked, that, in Ex. xxv. 8 (*supra*), the building of a sanctuary is connected with the dwelling of God among men: 'Let them make me a sanctuary; that I may dwell among them;' a verse expressing the same collocation of ideas as Ps. lxviii. 18: 'Thou hast gone up on high [to the mountain of the sanctuary]...*to dwell among* men.'

The occasion of the composition of Ps. lxviii. has been much disputed, and, indeed, the Psalm itself is allowed to be one of the most difficult in the whole Psalter. The majority of interpreters suppose it to have been written at the time when the Ark was removed from the house of Obed-Edom to Mount Zion, 2 Sam. vi. This view, says Hupfeld, though not adopting it himself, 'gives incontestably the best sense; in fact, it is the only one which suits, not only the mention of Zion, in opposition to Sinai and the heights of Basan, and the historical glance at the earlier leading of God from Sinai onwards, as introductory to this triumphal entry, but also the lofty utterances and prospects connected with it[1].' A full account of the arguments and opinions of commentators would shew that there is no very strong case made out as yet against the view here adopted[2];

---

[1] Perhaps, however, the circumstances of Solomon's bringing up of the Ark into the temple would suit as well. Compare ויעלו, 2 Chron. v. 5, with עלית, Ps. lxviii. 18. This is perhaps favoured by ver. 28: but see Perowne, on Ps. v. 7. It is unimportant, so far as the citation is concerned, to distinguish between these two occasions.

[2] 'Satis probabilis est interpretum complurium conjectura, hoc carmen a Davide compositum esse ex occasione illius solennitatis, qua circa sacra ex ædibus Obededomi in arcem Zioniticam ad locum ei paratum transferretur.' Rosenmüller.

it may suffice therefore to dismiss the point with slight notice.

The Psalm opens with the words: 'Let God arise, let his enemies be scattered: let them also that hate him flee before him;' and that the Psalm deals with a procession of the Ark, is suggested by the correspondence of these its opening words with those addressed to God in the wilderness as the Ark was setting forward on its several journeyings, viz.: 'Rise up, LORD, and let Thine enemies be scattered; and let them that hate Thee flee before Thy face' (Numb. x. 35). The eighteenth verse is applicable, as above, to the settlement of the Ark on Mount Zion; and again, the general tenour of the Psalm is in harmony with the circumstances of that time, which was a time of victory and wealth, a time when 'the fame of David went out into all lands; and the LORD brought the fear of him upon all nations' (1 Chron. xiv. 17). It was a time when 'kings with their armies did flee and were discomfited,' and the victor, enriched with spoil, bethought himself of the unworthy housing of the Ark: 'Lo, I dwell in an house of cedar, but the Ark of the covenant of the LORD remaineth under curtains' (1 Chron. xvii. 1, 2). The enrichment by the spoil of conquered kings, which helped to stir in David the desire to find a habitation for the God of Jacob—and in truth to build that house which it was reserved for Solomon to build—is expressed in the verse cited: 'Thou hast led captives captive; Thou hast received *gifts*;' i.e. spoils and tributary offerings from vanquished foes[1]; or, it may be, offerings from the children of Israel, consequent upon their enrichment by those

---

[1] 'As on Sinai God had ordered Moses (and somewhat like this from the spoils of the Midianites) to receive contributions for His tabernacle, of which the spoils of the stubborn Egyptians made no small share; so here from Zion God had been collecting, by the hands of David, contributions for a Temple, that He might have a fixed residence: He had raised them from the rebellious enemies as well; for the spoils of enemies, as well as the gifts of the people, David had consecrated to that purpose.' *Mudge.*

spoils. The result of this triumphal ascent to the holy Mount was that God became a dweller among men, in the sense already set forth; and thus, while the gifts spoken of are not gifts from God, but offerings to Him, yet the mention of these is but accessory to the great gift of the Divine Presence, which HE, by there fixing His habitation, was to give to men. Zion was to become the central source of celestial graces, wherefrom Apostles, Prophets, and Evangelists should issue forth and impart the gifts of the Holy Spirit to mankind; an explanation ultimately coincident with that of the Targum, followed by Rashi, where a like conclusion is arrived at, though by a very different process; the Psalm being referred to the ascent of Moses 'into the firmament,' to his possessing himself of the captive Law, and receiving gifts from the Supernals to give them to the sons of men[1].

In St Paul's citation, Christ is depicted as a conqueror, with a captive train, bestowing gifts, *sc.* from the spoils of victory, as may be illustrated by a reference to the circumstances of a Roman triumph. In the preceding verse, our Lord is spoken of emphatically as the *Giver*—'According to the measure of the gift of Christ.' In the eleventh verse this emphasis is sustained: 'And *He, αὐτός*, gave;' and thereupon follows a specification of the gifts, which are no less than the gift of the Holy Spirit, dwelling in holy men, in strict, though not literal, accordance with the purport of the original Hebrew as above explained: 'And He gave some, apostles; and some, prophets; and some, evangelists; and some, pastors and teachers.' That St Paul is intentionally departing from the phraseology of the original, as regards the expression, *He gave gifts*, is suggested by the repetition of the word, *He gave*, in ver. 11, where it would be unnatural *in a rendering of the passage into Hebrew* to use the same word of which the preceding 'gave' is supposed to be the

---

[1] שנית שבי את התורה ולקחת מתנות מן העליונים לתתם לבני אדם

counterpart. The apostle, we may say, expressed the *idea*[1] of the Hebrew in Greek, and then proceeded to develop its application in the latter language, without further verbal reference to the original. Such a practice argues thoroughness of acquaintance with the general purport of the original, and a consequent disregard of possible charges of misapplication, taking their rise from *prima facie* incongruities in this and that detail.

St Paul's citation being admitted to represent the purport of the original, it is still to be asked whether its formal variations from the Hebrew can be accounted for. It would be natural to adopt the familiar Targumic version, if it contained a suitable rendering of the clause. If however the citation was drawn, as some think, from a Septuagintal source, it may be asked why the important change from *take* to *give* was introduced; a change whereby the citation is made to express clearly what the LXX. could only be said to imply obscurely, if at all. The necessity for the variation is apparent. The LXX. describe a captive train, and gifts received, as accessories to the triumph of Him who ascends; the original lays chief stress on the sequel to the ascent, for which the apostle quotes the passage, viz., *a bestowal of spiritual graces*, and God's dwelling among men. The original, be it added, is, after the manner of *types*, partial, and corresponds but inadequately to the antitypical idea. The citation is an application of a type thus partial, and hence some difficulty in details must needs present itself. In the Psalm, the ascent to heaven is represented under the figure of a going up to a sanctuary on mount Zion, and, as a result of this typical ascent, God dwells among men. In the application the Ascension is viewed a *departure* from men, and thus stands out in marked contrast with the ascent

---

[1] 'The rendering of the Apostle... may be perhaps a free rendering of the passage, ἔδωκε δόματα τοῖς ἀνθρώποις. It is remarkable that the Chaldee has the same, יהבתא להון מתנן לבני נשא. As the Targum on the Psalms is manifestly composite, some portions being much earlier than others, this rendering *may* have been earlier than the time of the Apostle.' *Perowne.*

spoken of in the Psalm; but the Ascension is supplemented by the Mission of the Comforter to dwell in men, and thus by two steps the direct conclusion of the original is reached.

NOTE ON CHAPTER VII.

A. Dr Lightfoot remarks, on τὸ Ἄγαρ, Gal. iv. 25, that 'it need not necessarily mean, *the word* Hagar; compare for instance Eph. iv. 9, τὸ δὲ ἀνέβη τί ἐστιν; where τὸ is the statement, for the preceding *word* was not ἀνέβη, but ἀναβάς.' But this is inconclusive, for neither was the preceding *statement* ἀνέβη. It might have been written that τὸ ἀναβάς implies καταβάς, but for greater simplicity ἀναβάς is resolved into ἀνέβη καί, and the καί being dropped, there follows τὸ δὲ ἀνέβη, κ.τ.λ. This resolution is *a returning to the form of the original*, where only past tenses, עָלִיתָ, שָׁבִיתָ, לָקַחְתָּ, are used.

It may be remarked that, just as ἀνέβη, with the Apostle, implies κατέβη, so *take* (LXX.) may have implied *give*, as many have supposed. Dr Wordsworth understands בָּאָדָם to mean, 'in His character as man,' and adds:—'The reception of those gifts in Him and by Him, in His humanity, as our second Adam, virtually implied the donation of those gifts to us, who are mystically united as one body in Him.'

CHAPTER VIII.

A body hast Thou prepared Me.

Ps. xl. 6; Heb. x. 5.

THIS word *body* occurs in the LXX. rendering of Ps. xl. 6; but neither in the present Hebrew text, nor in the versions of Aquila, Symmachus, or Theodotion, where ὦτια replaces σῶμα. The Authorized Version, following the Masoretic text, reads: 'mine ears hast Thou opened.' (1) Some would account for the occurrence of cωma as a transcriber's mistake for ωτια, the c being repeated from the preceding ηθελησας. (2) To others, '*ears*' and '*body*' are alike suggestive of obedience and service. (3) A third explanation supposes a reference to *the boring of a servant's ear* in token of perpetual enslavement; but the form of the clause (not merely the use of the dual, *ears*) is opposed to this explanation. In the passages referred to, it is provided, that 'if he [the servant] say unto thee, I will not go away from thee: because he loveth thee and thine house, because he is well with thee; Then thou shalt take an aul, and thrust it through his ear unto the door, and he shall be thy servant for ever. And also unto thy maid-servant thou shalt do likewise' (Deut. xv. 16, 17.; Ex. xxi. 6). But in the Psalm, it is written, not precisely as in the Authorized Version, '*mine* ears hast thou opened,' but 'ears hast thou opened [digged] for me.' (4) Others again suppose the change from *ears* to *body* to have been made intentionally, in order to express more fully the prophetic meaning of the passage. The foregoing suppositions seem at first sight mutually exclusive; but, to pass by the third, it may be said that a modification of the last is not irreconcileable with the first and second. The reading σῶμα may have owed its origin to an error of transcription, but, when found in the text, may have been adopted deliberately, as associating itself with the thought of *obedience*, and the working of the Father's will. Dean Alford concludes his note with a remark which recognizes the twofold nature of the difficulty presented. First of all, it has to be inquired how the reading arose; and, secondly, why it has been retained. 'As Christian believers, our course is plain. How the word σῶμα came into the LXX. we cannot say: but being there, it is now sanctioned for us by the citation here: not as *the* (or even *a*) proper rendering of the Hebrew, but as a prophetic utterance, equivalent to, and representing, that other.'

I. The fortieth Psalm is not ascribed in the New Testament to any specific author; the formula of citation being the indefinite λέγει. 'Wherefore, when he cometh into the world, *he saith.*' In the Hebrew it is styled a David-psalm; but this title being in itself not altogether free from ambiguity, it was perhaps not intended originally to designate David as the author; and moreover, even if the inscription amounted to a clear affirmation of Davidic authorship, it might still be rejected, if at variance with internal evidence, as being (like the subscriptions of the apostolic Epistles) of no canonical authority. No satisfactory explanation having been suggested on the theory of Davidic authorship, it is here assumed, provisionally, that the reference is to a time of captivity.

The central revelation of the Psalm follows as a sequel to the discovery that there was no inherent efficacy in the sacrifices of the Law; and this teaching was pre-eminently the teaching of exile and captivity. Faith in the God of Israel then survived, when it had become impossible to join, as of old, in the temple service; and from this it followed necessarily that JEHOVAH could be served without sacrifice or hand-built shrine. But so long as the legal system remained accessible[1], the worshipper was less likely to attain to a full appreciation of its barely typical significance. This truth would be best taught by an intermission of the temple service; for when the worshipper, far away, it may be, in Babylon, was under a physical incapacity of offering sacrifice, his heart was thereby prepared for other consolations; his ear opened to the new, or as yet unheeded, teaching, that the sacrifice of praise would find acceptance. 'What period in the history of the Jews was more propitious [than that of the captivity] for the circulation of these truths? So long as all the ordinances of the Law were celebrated with their former regularity, the worshipper might seldom realize the possibility of fundamental changes in the system under which he lived. But when the sanctuary itself was levelled with the ground, when the sacrifices were no longer offered... how much was there in an emergency like this to lift their thoughts above the legal institutions, and constrain them to reflect on better things to come[2].'

II. The Psalm thus commences: 'I waited patiently for the LORD; and He inclined unto me, and heard my cry. He brought me up also out of an horrible pit, out of the miry clay, and set my feet upon a rock, and established my goings. And he hath put a new song in my mouth, even praise unto our God.' Further on, the subject of the 'new song' is specified. From the mire of despondency the Psalmist has been raised to a sure ground of hope, unmoved by external shocks. He has learned the spirituality of true religion. The temple may be in ruins, but God's truth still reigns. Old things have passed away, and a strange song is put into his mouth—the song of praise. The discovery of the spirituality of true worship is overwhelming. Words

---

[1] In 1 Sam. xv. 22, obedience is preferred to sacrifice. But *circumstances*, which set the two in opposition, gave rise to this teaching also. See note A.

[2] Hardwick, *Christ and Other Masters*, Part I. p. 149.

A body hast Thou prepared Me. 179

cannot express the grandeur of the conception. 'Many, O LORD my God, are Thy wonderful works which thou hast done, and thy thoughts which are to us-ward: they cannot be reckoned up in order unto thee: if I would declare and speak of them, they are more than can be numbered. Sacrifice and offering Thou didst not desire ... burnt-offering and sin-offering hast Thou not required.'

Between these last clauses come the disputed words: 'ears hast Thou digged for me;' i.e. *Thou hast revealed to me* the truth that the blood of bulls and goats avails not; that 'sacrifice and offering Thou didst not desire.' Thou hast taught me that for which I had no ears before. The expression, *ears hast Thou digged*, is indeed unique, but may be regarded as an intensification of either of two expressions, which might be used in the sense assigned. One of these is exemplified by 1 Sam. xx. 2: 'Behold, my father will do nothing either great or small, but that he will *shew it me*' [lit. *uncover my ear*]; the other by Is. l. 5: 'The LORD God hath *opened mine ear*, and I was not rebellious, neither turned away back;' where the first hemistich affirms that *instructions were given*[1]; and the second that they were obeyed. In Is. xlviii. 8 the same mode of expression is adopted, but there seems rather to imply *obedience*. There is no reason for excluding either of these two usages, each of which seems appropriate in its context; it may be concluded therefore that there is the same ambiguity in this *digging of ears* as in the common word to *hear*; which implies in some contexts *obedience*, but in others, no more than the bare aptitude for *hearing*.

In Ps. xl., the meaning adopted by many commentators is 'that the *truth just stated had been communicated* to Messiah by the Almighty[2];' while others interpret the clause of

---

[1] 'אדני פתח לי אזן, certiorem me fecit mei officii et mandata mihi dedit.' Rosenmüller. פתח, *to open*, is a stronger expression than גלה, *to uncover*, and may be equivalent to כרה in Ps. xl. It is used of *engraving*. Cp. Ex. xxviii. 9, 36.

[2] French and Skinner. *Transl. of Psalms.* So Mudge: 'Sacrifice and offering Thou didst not choose; (Thou insinuatedst into my ears) burnt-offering and sin-offering Thou didst not ask.'

an awakening to the necessity of *obedience*, as contrasted with ceremonial observances: 'Behold, to obey is better than sacrifice.' Against the latter rendering it may be urged that no antithetic particle intervenes[1], such as might have been looked for, if the intention had been to exhibit (in this verse) a contrast between sacrificial celebrations and the open ear of obedience. For this reason, the interpretation: 'Sacrifice and offering Thou didst not desire, *but* mine ears hast Thou opened,' seems objectionable: nor is this the sole, or even the strongest, objection that is to be urged against it. The seventh verse commences with an emphatic *Then*. 'Then said I, Lo, I come: in the volume of the book it is written of me, I delight to do Thy will, O my God: yea, Thy law is within my heart.' And this word, *Then*, appears to mark off the first *destructive* lesson that sacrifice was 'not required,' from the *constructive* teaching of the following verses, viz. that the real desideratum was conformity to the divine will. To interpret, '*mine ears* hast Thou opened,' of obedience, breaks the continuity of negative statement, and anticipates the positive teaching of the following verses, which seem marked off expressly from the former. The explanation above adopted is free from this objection. It preserves the unity of the sixth verse, and leads up naturally to the contrast introduced in the next verse by τότε εἶπον. 'Sacrifice and offering Thou desirest not—this Thou hast taught me—burnt-offering and sin-offering thou dost not require.' *Then,*—when I had unlearned my former error—*then said I, Now have I arrived at*[2] the truth that had been veiled by previous misconceptions. Having learned what was *not* required, I then came to understand what *was* required, and *what in the volume of the book is enjoined upon me,* viz. 'to do Thy will, O my God.'

In the preceding paraphrase, an unfamiliar application of the Hebrew word, *I come,* has been adopted. The usual ren-

---

[1] The LXX. has σῶμα δέ, but there is nothing in the Hebrew text corresponding to δέ.

[2] אז אמרתי הנה באתי במגלת ספר
כתוב עלי.

derings may be described as lacking structural coherence; and this suggests the enquiry, whether some variation in the construction might not result in a closer connection of the adjacent clauses. The word *bâthî*, like words of motion in the classical languages, may be followed by a simple accusative, thus: 'Now have I *come to* what is written;' or, to go back to the primitive meaning[1] of the Hebrew word: 'Now *have I entered into* what is written.' The analogy of our own and other languages suggests for the meaning of the above literal rendering: 'Now have I *entered into* (or arrived at) *the purport of*[2] what is written.' Thus much being premised, it remains to compare the latter hemistich of this seventh verse, with a strikingly similar passage in 2 Kings xxii. 13:—'Great is the wrath of the LORD that is kindled against us, because our fathers have not hearkened unto the words of this book, *to do according unto all that which is written concerning us*.' Following the clew here given, we may thus render Ps. xl. 7, 8—

Then said I, Now I understand:
What in the roll of the book is enjoined upon me.
To do Thy will, O LORD, is my delight:
Yea Thy law is within my heart.

Thus the central revelation of the Psalm consists in two particulars:—

[i.] Sacrifice is not required. (ver. 6).
[ii.] Obedience is required. (7, 8).

The concluding portions of the Psalm fall in with the hypothesis that the whole refers to a time of captivity. In the first half the allusion is to a spiritual revelation, and to a rock of truth whereon the feet of the waverer had been set; in the second to the innumerable physical evils that encompassed the Psalmist, and from which he still had need to be delivered. 'Be pleased, O LORD, to deliver me: O LORD, make haste to help me...Let all those that seek Thee rejoice and be glad in Thee; let such as love Thy salvation say con-

---

[1] As preserved *e. g.* in the expression for sunset. The sun is said to *go out* and *go in*, when it rises and sets. For the construction, see Ps. cv. 18, *et passim*.

[2] See note B, p. 185.

tinually, The LORD be magnified. But I am poor and needy; yet the LORD thinketh upon me: Thou art my help and my deliverer; make no tarrying, O my God.'

III. *On the purport of the citation.* In Heb. x. the frequent legal sacrifices of victim after victim are contrasted with the single oblation of the One. 'The law having a shadow of good things to come, and not the very image of the things, can never with those sacrifices which they offered year by year continually make the comers thereunto perfect ... But in those sacrifices there is a remembrance again made of sins every year. For it is not possible that the blood of bulls and goats should take away sins. Wherefore, when He cometh into the world[1], He saith, Sacrifice and offering Thou wouldest not, but a body hast Thou prepared me: In burnt offerings and sacrifices for sin Thou hast had no pleasure. Then said I, Lo, I come (in the volume of the book it is written of me) to do Thy will, O God.' (Heb. x. 1—7.)

Then follows an analysis of the passage cited:

By first saying—'Sacrifice and offering and burnt-offerings and offering for sin Thou wouldest not, neither hadst pleasure therein; which are offered by the law;'—and next saying—'Lo, I come to do Thy will, O God—He taketh away the first' (the legal sacrifices), 'that He may establish the second,' i.e. *the will of God.* 'By the which will we are sanctified through the offering of the body of Jesus Christ once for all' (ver. 10); where the sanctification is effected *by* or *in* the 'will,' and *through the medium of* 'the offering.'

The citation thus analyzed gives prominence to the same 'first' and 'second' points as does the original; but the 'second,' relating to the divine will, is supplemented by a specification of the *means* whereby that will is wrought. If the mention of the σῶμα be thus supplementary to, and not at variance with, the teaching of the Hebrew Psalm, it becomes a question of secondary moment, how the word σῶμα first

---

[1] See note C, p. 186.

found its way into the LXX. text. Being there, and admitting an interpretation not at variance with the original, it may have been adopted, not as an exact rendering of any Hebrew word there occurring, but simply as a truthful element of the familiar version, which may have found its way into that version as a textual corruption, or may have been adopted, in the first instance, as corresponding paraphrastically to the translator's view of the thought expressed.

On the relation of σῶμα to the argument.

Bishop Horsley, after mentioning the emendation[1] whereby Mr Pierce seeks to bring the Hebrew into accordance with the LXX., thus continues his annotations on Ps. xl. :—

The interpretation of the LXX. may seem, in some degree, confirmed by St Paul's quotation. Pierce's conjecture is approved by Bishop Lowth. Bishop Horne, however, very justly remarks, that, 'if the Apostle's argument turned on the word σῶμα, such an emendation might seem necessary. But that word is not essential to the argument, which seems to stand clear and full, whatever the meaning of σῶμα κατηρτίσω μοι.' He might have added, that the Apostle's argument would be complete, if these words were expunged, or if they had been omitted in the citation. Archbishop Secker was clearly of the same opinion. 'It is not certain,' says the Archbishop, 'that the Apostle argues from the word σῶμα at all. He quotes the translation of the LXX. as he found it in his copy; lays a stress on what is in the Hebrew, but none on the rest; either knowing it not to be there, or being restrained by the Spirit of God from making use of it.'—

This however is an extreme statement; though it may be admitted on the other hand that σῶμα occurs only as a medium for the operation of the θέλημα, and must be viewed in close and inseparable connection therewith. The inefficacy of the ancient sacrifices, evinced by their multitudinousness

---

[1] אזנים for אז נוה.

(ver. 2), followed from the lack of voluntariness in the offering. They were offered *according to the law*[1], and so on compulsion; but the offering of Christ's life was voluntary: 'I lay it down of myself' (Joh. x. 18); 'Himself He offered through the eternal Spirit' (Heb. ix. 14). But the σῶμα was a pre-requisite to His complete submission, and obedience μέχρι θανάτου (Phil. ii. 8), to the θέλημα wherein we are sanctified.

NOTES ON CHAPTER VIII.

A. The fifty-first Psalm plainly inculcates the need of spirituality in worship. 'Thou desirest not sacrifice' (ver. 16); 'The sacrifices of God are a broken spirit' (ver. 17). But, despite its inscription, it is not clear that this Psalm is to be referred to the age of David. If the rendering, *Against Thee, Thee only, have I sinned* (ver. 4) be correct, it is a strong argument against retaining the title: 'To the chief Musician. A Psalm of David, when Nathan the Prophet came unto him, after he had gone in to Bath-sheba.' And, again, the natural interpretation of ver. 18, 19, seems to point to a later age than David's. 'The two last verses seem plainly to shew this Psalm to have been written during the captivity, and therefore the title to be wrong...At present God could not accept any offering, because the temple and altar were destroyed: but, would He in mercy restore them, he would that moment do all those honours to God which He had required in His law.' *Mudge.* (For counter arguments see Phillips *in loc.*) But even if these two difficulties could be explained away, it would still be more natural to suppose that the Psalmist had come at length, after sore perplexity, to feel his sinfulness, although it had not broken out into such open acts as murder or adultery. At length he learns that God's sentence is just (ver. 4). He prays for 'a clean heart,' and 'a right spirit.' The words: 'Deliver me from blood-guiltiness,' are not such as might be

---

[1] There is a reading κατὰ νόμον, which would further emphasize the *compulsoriness* of the old sacrifices.

Notes on Chapter VIII. 185

expected, after the prayer for a perfect inward purity (ver. 7); but a prayer to be delivered from the violence (דָּמִים) of others would be appropriate. With this agree the immediately following expressions, *God of my salvation* [Ps. cxliv. 10], and, *Thy righteousness* [xxii. 31]. Compare Ps. lix. 3.

B. An attempt to make the clauses of ver. 8 more coherent, suggested this construction of כתוב as an *accusative of motion towards;* thus [i.] '*I have come to* what is written,' or [ii.] '*I have entered into* &c.' I find a like conjecture about the *meaning* of בָּאתִי in Dr Geddes' translation of the Psalm, where the word is rendered: —*Now I come at thy meaning.* The second clause would be *prosaically,* הַכָּתוּב עָלַי בִּמְגִלַּת הַסֵּפֶר, but the *poetical* inversion brings about the omission of the article before כתוב.

This derived use of בָּאתִי is not frequent in the Bible, but it may be illustrated by Eccl. iii. 22: מִי יְבִיאֶנּוּ לִרְאוֹת. *Who shall bring him* to see? Cp. בָּא לִפְנֵי (Gen. vi. 13). May not the difficult words אָבוֹא בִּגְבֻרוֹת אֲדֹנָי יְהוִה (Ps. lxxi. 16), mean that, *I will enter upon* (the contemplation or recital of) the mighty acts of the LORD God? With this meaning of אָבוֹא, which agrees well with the context, [and with the construction of Job iii. 6], the verse has been rendered by French and Skinner:

> The greatness of the Lord JEHOVAH shall be my theme;
> THY mercies, Thine only, will I commemorate.

So Bp Horsley: 'I will enter upon [the subject of] the Lord Jehovah's great might.' There is another derived use of בא (with עַד) in 2 Sam. xxiii. 19, where it is said that Abishai 'did not attain unto [*Angl.* come up to] the three.' From the meaning: 'attain unto *in prowess*,' to the preceding: viz. 'attain unto *in knowledge,*' the transition is easy. The adjective קָרוֹב is used, (1) of local proximity; (2) of mental proximity, *within reach of the understanding;* as when the law is described as 'not in heaven,' beyond man's reach, but *nigh,* yea even in his heart. It is quite as natural *a priori* for בא, as for קָרוֹב, to have this double application. In later Hebrew, הִשִּׂיג is *very commonly* used as in the following examples:—'But the truth of the matter the human intellect cannot comprehend nor *attain unto.*' 'What then was that which Moses our Rabbi sought *to attain unto*. .

he sought to know the truth of the existence, &c.' Bernard's *Maimonides*, p. 77. For the use of באתי, compare Rashi's paraphrase of אגידה וג' (Ps. xl. 5): אם באתי להגיד ולדבר עצמו מספר.

C. With a different division of words we might read, διὸ εἷς, ἐρχόμενος [for εἰσερχόμενος] εἰς τὸν κόσμον, λέγει, κ.τ.λ., or with a slight change: διὸ ὁ εἷς, ἐρχόμενος κ.τ.λ. In favour of the alteration it may be urged that :—

[i.] It gives a grammatical *definiteness* to the sentence.

[ii.] The use of εἷς, or ὁ εἷς [διὰ τοῦ ἑνός. Rom. v. 17, 19], has a special appropriateness in a passage which gives marked prominence to the contrast between the many and the ONE.

[iii.] The Messiah is elsewhere spoken of as ὁ ἐρχόμενος [not εἰσερχόμενος] εἰς τὸν κόσμον. The phrase εἰσέρχεσθαι εἰς τὸν κόσμον is used of *Sin* (Rom. v. 12), and of the κενοδοξία ἀνθρώπων (Sap. xiv. 14); but seems *not to be used of persons*, either in the Canonical Books, or in the Apocrypha. It occurs in the *textus receptus* of 2 Joh. 7, but the true reading is probably ἐξῆλθον κ.τ.λ. See (for ἔρχεσθαι εἰς τὸν κόσμον) Joh. i. 9; vi. 14; ix. 39; xi. 27; xii. 46; xvi. 28; xviii. 37; 1 Tim. i. 15. For ἐρχόμενος in connection with ἥκω (ver. 7), see ver. 37.

CHAPTER IX.

The Allegory of Hagar.

Gen. xvi., xxi.; Gal. iv. 21—31.

IN seeking to fix the meaning of the word by which the Apostle introduces the 'Allegory' of Hagar, it is natural first of all to have recourse to the Hellenistic authors, with whom the terminology of allegorism was in common use; and of them, especially to one, 'who lived at a time which renders his works peculiarly valuable for the purpose of our enquiry.' Of the works of PHILO, so much has come down to us, that we are in a position not only to discover therefrom the nature of his allegorical deductions, but to estimate their attractiveness to the mind of the writer, and the extent to which they are to be regarded as components of his system. Had fragments of those works alone remained, it could not have been affirmed with full assurance that, whereas 'they [the Christian Fathers] occasionally allegorize, he never misses the opportunity:' that while 'they in a few instances supersede the historical meaning, he can scarcely be said to allow the historical meaning to stand at all:' and that 'they were almost as far as any modern historian from the dreamy inconsecutive apprehension of historical facts which we find in Philo, who is as entirely devoid of the historical sense as an Indian philosopher.' These however we may now admit to be fair statements; and, the prevalence of such extravagance in interpretation being established, it remains to investigate how far the author of the Epistle to the Galatians is to be regarded as adopting or sanctioning this method of the Hellenists: and, again, how far the usages of the Old Testament Scriptures may have suggested, what their interpreters—Rabbinic and Alexandrian—had developed, and were further developing, to an extravagance of absurdity.

I. St Paul's express words first demand attention. Much learning has from time to time been brought to bear upon them, but with less decisive results than might have been anticipated; and that chiefly, as it would seem, because of the undue prominence which has been given to one detail of the 'allegory.' The chief verbal discussion has centred in St Paul's reason for identifying Hagar with Mount Sinai, or the former covenant; whereas this identification is but a detail, and the chief point which challenges enquiry is the mode and purport of his antecedent transition from history to allegory. Though the key-word of the passage is not Ἄγαρ, but ἀλληγορούμενα, the grammatical difficulties attendant upon the usual rendering of this latter have been very commonly depreciated or overlooked. The right understanding of the word is the first pre-requisite for the interpretation of the passage. With it the Apostle passes from history to allegory; and it is the mode and purport of this transition which it is the commentator's chief aim to elucidate. Have we therein an argument whereby the folly of the Judaizers is to be refuted; or an illustration whereby the writer's meaning is to be impressed upon the imagination of his hearers? To such enquiries diverse answers have been given.

[i.] Dr Lightfoot expresses the opinion that, 'whereas with Philo the allegory is the whole substance of his teaching, with St Paul it is but an accessory. He uses it rather as an illustration than an argument; as a means of representing in a lively manner the lessons before enforced on other grounds.'

[ii.] It is the view of Professor Jowett, that 'to an Alexandrian writer of the first century (may we not say therefore to St Paul himself?)' the distinction between an illustration and an argument 'could hardly have been made intelligible.

That very modern distinction ... was precisely what his mind wanted to place it on a level with the modes of thought of our own age. We must therefore find some other way of characterizing the passage. It is neither an illustration nor an argument, but an interpretation of the Old Testament Scripture, after the manner of the age in which St Paul lived; that is, after the manner of the Jewish and Christian Alexandrian writers.'

[iii.] Others, as Dr Wordsworth, so far agree with the preceding statement as to regard the passage in the light of 'an interpretation;' not however a merely fanciful and subjective one. The words of the sacred narrative 'have a second spiritual sense; the holy Apostle does *not take away the History*, but he teaches us what is spiritually signified by it.' 'The Apostle here instructs us how to allegorize aright,—namely to preserve the truth of the history, while we elicit from it its spiritual sense. Abraham, he says, had two sons, from two wives; here is the *History*. He then tells what was their spiritual meaning; there is the *Allegory*.'

There is an ambiguity of application in Dr Lightfoot's statement [i] as it stands. The passage now under discussion consists of two main divisions:

a. The historical citation.

'Tell me, ye that desire to be under the law, do ye not hear the law? For it is written, that Abraham had two sons, the one by a bondmaid, the other by a freewoman. But he who was of the bondwoman was born after the flesh; but he of the freewoman was by promise.' (Gal. iv. 21—23.)

b. Its allegorical application.

'Which things are an allegory: for these are the two covenants; the one from mount Sinai, which gendereth to bondage[1], which is Agar. For this Agar is mount Sinai in Arabia, and answereth to Jerusalem which now is, and is in

---

[1] Cf. υἱοὶ τῆς διαθήκης (Acts iii. 25).

bondage with her children. But Jerusalem which is above is free, which is the mother of us all. For it is written, Rejoice, thou barren that bearest not; break forth and cry, thou that travailest not: for the desolate hath many more children than she which hath an husband. Now we, brethren, as Isaac was, are the children of promise. But as then he that was born after the flesh persecuted him that was born after the Spirit, even so it is now. Nevertheless what saith the scripture? Cast out the bondwoman and her son: for the son of the bondwoman shall not be heir with the son of the freewoman. So then, brethren, we are not children of the bondwoman, but of the free' (ver. 24—31).

The *whole passage* is, or *seems* to be, viewed in the statement (i) as 'a means of representing in a lively form the lessons before enforced on other grounds;' the term 'allegory' being taken to include the narrative, as the groundwork of the allegorical superstructure. In (ii) there is less ambiguity. St Paul's whole treatment of the history is classed with current modes of 'interpretation,' and is viewed as an appeal to the imagination rather than to the judgement of his hearers. The statement (iii) is chiefly objectionable in respect of the expression, '*second* (i.e. spiritual) sense.' The 'spiritual sense'—as will be maintained below—is identical with the true significance of the history; and *the allegorical application* is but 'a means of representing in a lively form the lessons' which might have been, and *are* elsewhere[1], enforced by way of direct and non-allegorical inference from the history.

The great difficulty is in the twenty-fourth verse: '*which things are an allegory, &c.;*' where the statement that the foregoing narrative is 'an allegory' seems to be explained or justified by what follows: '*for* these are the two covenants, &c.' Whether Ἄγαρ should be retained or not, in the following verse, is a matter of detail, and of slight importance in comparison with the interpretation of the clause, ἅτινά

---

[1] Rom. x. 6—16, *infra*.

ἐστιν ἀλληγορούμενα. Bishop Ellicott renders the disputed clause: 'which things *are allegorized;*' and further explains the rendering as equivalent to: 'which things *are allegorical;*' 'by the which things another is meant' (*Genev. Transl.*). Dean Alford adopts the rendering: 'which things *are allegorical;*' and adds: 'i.e. to be understood otherwise than according to their literal sense.' Mr Conybeare's rendering is: 'all this *is allegorical.*' No one of the preceding translations differs materially from that of the Authorized Version, which is adopted by Professor Jowett, and explained as meaning: 'which things are spoken in one way, but designed to be understood in another.' By one and all it seems to be affirmed that there the passage has an allegorical meaning discrete from, and at least equally authoritative with, its direct historical significance.

It may be urged moreover that all renderings which make ἀλληγορούμενα a 'primary predicate[1],' present the general statement, '*which things are an allegory,*' as deduced from or justified by an intricate series of assumptions about *details;* whereas it would have been a more natural order of proceeding to begin with the general assumption that the passage was, in this or that sense, allegorical, and afterwards to apply the proposed method of interpretation to particulars. To the *English reader*, at any rate, it will appear that the Apostle thus inverts the natural order of proceeding, when he writes—or is represented as writing—'which things are an allegory; *for*[2] these are the two covenants; the one from Mount Sinai,... which is Agar, &c.'

On the meaning and construction of ἀλληγορούμενα.

There are two established usages of the word ἀλληγορεῖν, viz.:

---

[1] Donaldson, *Greek Gram.* p. 360.
[2] This *might* be said to imply the broad statement that, the two women being two covenants, all the circumstances of their history were therefore to be allegorized. The use of γάρ assumed above is not the only use possible: perhaps it may not be the most appropriate: but suffice it to have called attention to the point.

1. To speak in an allegory.
2. To treat or interpret as an allegory.

The former is adopted in the Vulgate rendering, *per allegoriam dicta;* but this requires the perfect participle, rather than the present (ἀλληγορούμενα), which actually occurs.

The latter is more frequently adopted, and the clause is rendered: 'which things *are allegorized.*' This might import, grammatically, either that the things in question were *then* being expounded allegorically (sc. by the Apostle), or that they were *habitually* so expounded. The former does not commend itself as appropriate, although perhaps involved in Dr Wordsworth's statement, that the things 'are *not* an allegory... but they *are allegorized*, or allegorically *expounded.*' The latter is required by the majority of the received renderings, which make ἀλληγορούμενα practically equivalent to ἀλληγορικά. It may be remarked, however, that this quasi-adjectival use needs explanation, and that it leaves in full force the above-mentioned objection from the context—αὗται γάρ εἰσιν κ.τ.λ.

If the received *construction* of the disputed clause be the true one, the words ἅτινά ἐστιν ἀλληγορούμενα are approximately equivalent to ἅτινα ἀλληγορεῖται[1]. Considering it thus, we may be helped to a different explanation of the force of the participle. The expression, ἅτινα ἀλληγορεῖται, is immediately suggestive of such phrases as, ὄφις ἀλληγορεῖται ἡδονή[2], where it is not stated barely that ὄφις *is allegorized*, or has an allegorical significance; but the thing (ἡδονή) is added, to which ὄφις is allegorically equivalent. A like usage of the *active* occurs in Κρόνον ἀλληγοροῦσι τὸν χρόνον[2]. Can the construction in Gal. iv. 24 be assimilated to the foregoing?

In *translating*, as it were, from the language of history to the language of allegory, we may reasonably have recourse to the analogy of translation from any one language, as Hebrew, to any other, say Greek. A suitable example is

---

[1] See note A, p. 204.   [2] See Ellicott *in loc.*

afforded by the second Gospel, where the Saviour's words: 'Eloi, Eloi, lama sabachthani?' are first transcribed, and then rendered into Greek. The formula of transition is: ὅ ἐστι μεθερμηνευόμενον, '*which is, being interpreted;*' and then follow the equivalent Greek words: ὁ θεός μου, ὁ θεός μου, εἰς τί με ἐγκατέλιπες; If St Paul's formula of transition from history to allegory were rendered analogously, it would import that the narrative, *being allegorized*, i.e. *if* or *when* allegorized, assumed such and such a form. It may be added that the position of the substantive verb, which *precedes* the participle, favours the rendering: 'the which *are*, being allegorized, &c.' The next clause is a parenthetic explanation of the Apostle's reason for applying the allegorical form of representation. 'For these be [the] two covenants'—αὗται γάρ εἰσιν [αἱ] δύο διαθῆκαι. St Paul, having premised certain historical facts about Abraham's 'two wives,' undertakes to identify the one with Judaism, the other with the gospel covenant; first of all assuming that his readers were familiar with the thought that the two wives typified the two covenants. Starting with this *general* assumption, he undertakes to work out the *details* of the allegory; and thus, from an admission which his readers would readily make, he leads them to a conclusion which they had not foreseen:—

'The which are, being allegorized,—
For these be the two covenants [as all allow]—
The one from mount Sinai...which is Hagar...
Whereas we, brethren, like Isaac, are the children of promise.'
Gal. iv. 24, 28.

The change from the neuter, ἅτινα, to the feminine, ἥτις ἐστὶν Ἁγαρ, if felt at all as a difficulty, may be sufficiently accounted for as brought about by the intervention of the parenthetic, αὗται γάρ εἰσιν αἱ δύο διαθῆκαι, where αὗται may be a feminine *attracted* by διαθῆκαι, or may mean 'these *women*.' The primary predicate of the main sentence now follows, and, as frequently happens, is so far modified by the parenthesis, that it might, structurally, be regarded as a continuation of it.

After the mention of Hagar (ἥτις ἐστὶν Ἁγάρ) follow more parentheses, up to the commencement of ver. 28, which introduces the second main division of the allegory. Here the connection with the remote ἅτινά ἐστιν (ver. 24) is broken off[1], and the categorical mode of statement is adopted: ὑμεῖς δὲ... ἐπαγγελίας τέκνα ἐστέ.

The above outline of the allegory exhibits a correspondence between its two main divisions and the two chief points in the history; but the correspondence of each to each is not precisely the same in the second case as in the first; for the name of one wife, Hagar, finds place in the allegory, but not so the name of Sarah. This omission is significant. 'He who was of the bondwoman was born after the flesh; but he of the freewoman was by promise.' And accordingly, the one κατὰ σάρκα γεννῶσα, is mentioned in the allegory; but the name of Sarah is omitted, *because it is St Paul's aim to throw fleshly descent into the background.* For this reason the earthly mother is passed by, and the accepted sons are described emphatically as ἐπαγγελίας τέκνα, children of Promise.

The proposed construction of the introductory formula—ἅτινά ἐστιν ἀλληγορούμενα—would remove a difficulty, which some now feel, in accepting the statement that the narrative is not *an allegory*, but that it is *allegorized;* that St Paul is 'not denying [or overlaying] the historical truth of the narrative,' but only presenting its actual teachings in a form calculated to impress its inner truth indelibly upon the mind. The argument is wholly historical, and dependent upon the *fact* that a descent from Abraham, κατὰ σάρκα, was not, as the Judaizers contended, the ground of acceptance before God. This the narrative shews plainly; for it introduces a progeny 'born after the flesh,' and not accepted; and another, the sole ground of whose acceptance was 'the Promise.'

---

[1] Or the case may be put thus. The neuter ἅτινα alludes to the *circumstances* of the narrative; and it is only when a disturbing parenthesis has intervened, that it is followed up by the name of the woman Hagar. The form of expression in ver. 28 [*not* ἑτέρα δέ, corresponding to μία μέν] indicates a recovery from the disturbing effect of the now remote parenthesis.

The Allegory of Hagar. 195

The points are then represented in the allegorical form, the better to impress them upon the reader's imagination; but the argument is summed up in the history itself, and would remain *entire* if denuded of its allegorical adornment. The same argument, be it noted, is deduced directly, in a subsequent[1] epistle, from the narrative which underlies this allegory of Hagar. In the passage alluded to, St Paul is contending that God did not once for all limit His election by a promise to one line, κατὰ σάρκα, but still reserved to Himself the prerogative of having mercy 'on whom I will have mercy,' and of having compassion 'on whom I will have compassion.' This reservation was further shewn, argues St Paul, in the preference of Jacob to the firstborn Esau, on whom the election, if merely κατὰ σάρκα, must have fallen:—

'For they are not all Israel, which are of Israel: neither, because they are the seed of Abraham, are they all children: but, *In Isaac shall thy seed be called* (Gen. xxi. 12). That is, they which are the children of the flesh, these are not the children of God: but the children of the promise are counted for the seed. For this is the word of promise, *At this time will I come, and Sarah shall have a son* (Gen. xviii. 10). And not only this; but when Rebecca also had conceived by one, even by our father Isaac; (For the children being not yet born, neither having done any good or evil, that the purpose of God according to election might stand, not of works, but of Him that calleth;) it was said unto her, *The elder shall serve the younger* (Gen. xxv. 23). As it is written, *Jacob have I loved, but Esau have I hated* (Mal. i. 2, 3). What shall we say then? Is there unrighteousness with God? God forbid. For he saith to Moses, *I will have mercy on whom I will have mercy, and I will have compassion on whom I will have compassion* (Ex. xxxiii. 19). So then it is not of him that willeth, nor of him that runneth, but of God that sheweth mercy.' (Rom. ix. 6—16.)

---

[1] If the allegorical accessories had been introduced in the *later* epistle, it might have been thought that they added something to the argument. As it is, their disuse confirms the view that they are not only non-essential, but contain no additional argument.

Here the call of the Gentiles is declared to be in strict accordance with that very law by which the Jews sought to establish the exclusive privileges of Abraham's fleshly descendants: granting indeed that they might be communicated, but to those only who should conform as proselytes to the ordinances of Judaism. The *promise* was the one efficient cause of Isaac's acceptance, as again of Jacob's; and God's purpose would still continue to manifest itself in unimagined forms, 'As he saith also in Osee, *I will call them my people, who were not my people.*' (Rom. ix. 25.) In Gal. iv. the argument is similar, and differs only by being represented allegorically. 'You have misread the history,' argues St Paul, 'and have given undue prominence to what was non-essential. You should have laid stress, not on the κατὰ σάρκα, but on the διὰ τῆς ἐπαγγελίας, and then you would not thus have mistaken the nature of the divine election. The two mothers correspond, as you will grant, to the two covenants. Consider the matter in detail; and I will shew you that Jewish externalism corresponds to the natural descent of the outcast Ishmael; while the accepted progeny were then, temporally, sons of Sarah, but then, and now, and eternally, the seed of *Promise.*'

II. Of the two points which remain to be considered, the distribution of the clauses in ver. 25—28 next demands attention.

After concluding that Hagar 'answereth to Jerusalem which now is, and is in bondage with her children,' St Paul continues: 'But Jerusalem which is above is free, which is the mother of us all' (ver. 26). It is commonly supposed that this verse is an elliptical 'completion of the parallel,' and hypothetically susceptible of expansion into some such form as is below indicated;—

'Now all this is allegorical; for these two women are the two covenants;

The first (μία μέν) given from Mount Sinai, whose children are born into bondage, which is Hagar, (for the word Hagar in Arabic signifies Mount Sinai); and she answers to the earthly Jerusalem, for she is in bondage with her children.

But [*Sarah is the second covenant in Christ, and answers to the heavenly Jerusalem; for*] the heavenly Jerusalem is free which is the mother of us all. And so it is written, Rejoice thou barren that bearest not; break forth into shouting, thou that travailest not; for the desolate hath many more children than she which hath the husband (Is. liv. 1). Now we (ἡμεῖς δέ), brethren, like Isaac, are children [born not naturally, but] of God's promise.'

The above is extracted from Mr Conybeare's translation of the Epistle. Dean Alford, again, remarks that ἡ δὲ ἄνω (ver. 26) is not opposed to μία μέν (ver. 24), 'which as Meyer observes, is left without apodosis, the reader supplying that the other covenant is Sara, &c.' So Dr Lightfoot, on μία μέν— 'The true antithesis would have been ἑτέρα δέ, but it melts away in the general fusion of the sentence.' The imperfection of the correspondence between ver. 26 and the second portion of the *narrative* is very plainly allowed too by Professor Jowett, who observes *in loc.*: 'Here St Paul drops the figure, and compares the heavenly Jerusalem with Jerusalem that now is. What we expect to follow is—*But the other covenant is Sarah the freewoman, whose children are free.* Instead of this the Apostle only works out the idea of freedom.' If then the conclusion of the allegory is not found in ver. 26, should it not rather be sought, as above, in ver. 28? It would have been quite in accordance with St Paul's habit of 'going off at a word,' if at the mention of 'Jerusalem which now is,' he had dismissed the narrative from his thoughts, and passed on, by way of contrast to 'Jerusalem which is above.' As it is, we may suppose the mention of the heavenly Jerusalem to have suggested itself in connection with 'Jerusalem which now is, and is in bondage with her children;' but the antithesis thus suggested is *subordinated* to the history, and made to lead up to the second main point in the allegory: 'Now we, brethren, as Isaac was, are the children of Promise.' This promise (*sc.* to the Gentile Church) is recorded in the preceding verse:

The Allegory of Hagar.

Rejoice thou barren that bearest not, &c. 'So then, brethren, [being thus *by promise*, ver. 23] we are not children of the bondwoman, but of the free' (ver. 31).

III. The most perplexing (though not most important) question remains, viz.: How comes Hagar to be identified with mount Sinai and the Jewish polity? The MS. authority and later editors being not very unequally divided[1] about the admission of the word Ἄγαρ, in ver. 25, it will be necessary to consider the two subjoined readings, whereof the latter (that of the *textus receptus*) is perhaps to be preferred.

[i] τὸ γὰρ Σινᾶ ὄρος ἐστὶν ἐν τῇ Ἀραβίᾳ·
[ii] τὸ γὰρ Ἄγαρ Σινᾶ ὄρος ἐστὶν ἐν τῇ Ἀραβίᾳ·

A consideration of some importance in deciding between these two classes of readings is, that τὸ Ἄγαρ, though quite grammatical (in the sense, *the word Hagar*), is, notwithstanding, a combination of rare occurrence[2], and hence, owing to its strangeness, likely to have been omitted, but very unlikely to have been inserted by error of transcription, or foisted into the text as an emendation. The last word of the preceding verse being Ἄγαρ, it would be remarkable if from

ΗΤΙϹ ΕϹΤΙΝ ΑΓΑΡ ΤΟ ΓΑΡ ΑΓΑΡ

something had not been lost in transcription, through *homœoteleuton*. If γάρ were omitted, δέ would naturally be supplied; which accounts for the existent reading τὸ δὲ Ἄγαρ. And again, from the tempting omission of the second Ἄγαρ, the simpler τὸ γὰρ Σινᾶ would take its rise.

[i] With this reading, the meaning of the clause can scarcely be, that 'mount Sinai is in Arabia[3].' 'As it is, the

---

[1] So Jowett *in loc.* See also note B, p. 205.

[2] With Ἄγαρ, the feminine article would be expected, the more so that ἥτις ἐστὶν Ἄγαρ precedes.

[3] Would not this necessitate the changed order, ἐν τῇ Ἀραβίᾳ ἐστίν? Moreover, if the rendering, *for Sinai is a mountain in Arabia*, were adopted, would there not be a stress on the ὄρος? the order being, ὄρος ἐστὶν ἐν τῇ Ἀραβίᾳ, not ὄρος ἐν τῇ Ἀραβίᾳ ἐστίν, which would be required to make ὄρος 'unemphatic.'

law of emphasis would require it to be rendered, *For Sinai is a mountain in Arabia;* information which the Judaizing Galatians would hardly require.'

[ii] Professor Jowett, with the received reading, thus connects Hagar with mount Sinai: 'For this Hagar is mount Sinai, *in the land of the children of Hagar.*' To the same effect Dr Lightfoot: 'Such too seems to be the most probable account of his meaning, *even if,* with the received text, we retain Hagar: *This Hagar is mount Sinai in Arabia,* i. e. it represents mount Sinai, because mount Sinai is in Arabia, the land of Hagar and her descendants. It is not ἡ Ἄγαρ, the woman Hagar, but τὸ Ἄγαρ, the thing Hagar, the Hagar of the allegory, the Hagar which is under discussion.' If, however, the reader's first impression, viz. that τὸ Ἄγαρ points to an etymological[1] connection, be the right one, there is no necessity for assuming that the *current* etymological explanation is to be received. According to this view 'Hagar' contains an allusion to a local Arabic name of Mount Sinai: τὸ δὲ Σινᾶ ὄρος οὕτω μεθερμηνεύεται τῇ ἐπιχωρίῳ αὐτῶν γλώττῃ. This citation is from Chrysostom, who goes on to speak of the mountain as, ὁμώνυμον τῇ δούλῃ. 'To the same effect writes Theophylact, who is often a mere echo of Chrysostom, as do one or two anonymous commentators in the Œcumenian Catena, without doubt deriving their information from the same source.' And further: 'Even if it be granted that his hearers were acquainted with the fact which was the key to his meaning, is ἐν τῇ Ἀραβίᾳ at all a likely expression to be used by any writer for ἐν τῇ Ἀραβικῇ γλάσσῃ or Ἀραβιστί, unless it were made intelligible by the context?' If the explanation be etymological, is it not more likely *a priori* to

---

[1] See note A, p. 175. It is not disputed that τὸ Ἄγαρ may mean 'the *word* Hagar;' it is only asserted by some that it does not of necessity mean that. Any other meaning would, however, need illustration from allegorical or other writings. In τὸ ἀνέβη, the etymological substratum of the word is alluded to; but, independently of that, we require analogous usages of *proper names,* to justify the explanation of τὸ Ἄγαρ which is adopted *e. g.* by Dr Lightfoot.

have been drawn not from Arabic, but from Hebrew, which was at once the sacred tongue, and the language in which the narrative in question was written?

To recapitulate the results arrived at :—

1. It has been argued, on merely textual grounds, and independently of any preconceived *explanation*, that the reading τὸ Ἄγαρ is to be retained.

2. τὸ Ἄγαρ probably means 'the *word* Hagar.'

3. The explanation of the word is to be drawn from a Hebrew source; the process being either *literal*[1], or *etymological*; probably the latter. But it must not be taken for granted that the explanation is now *discoverable*. Subjoined, however, is a quasi-etymological interpretation that may be worth considering, if not for the result, at least for the process by which it is obtained.

An Interpretation of the word Hagar.

In seeking for an explanation of a proper name, it must be borne in mind that according to the usages of Biblical (not to say of Rabbinic) Hebrew, the required derivation may be *altogether fictitious;* and, secondly, that *a compound derivation* is quite as appropriate as one from a single root. It suffices, on the one hand, that the form of the name to be analyzed should resemble the form of certain words with which it is compared; and, secondly, that the name should *suggest*, rather than contain, the word or words which are regarded as its *quasi-constituent* parts. To take two familiar examples :—SAMUEL is variously interpreted as, *heard of God*, and as *asked of God;* but on neither supposition is the 'derivation' fully exhibited in the name. The name ISSACHAR exhibits the transitional phenomenon of a consonant *written*, but *unvocalized*, and therefore unpronounceable; and it thus leads up by two stages to such elliptic compounds as *Samuel*,

---

[1] In Rabbinical writings, letters are sometimes interchanged according to certain empirical laws. Two words, or sets of words, are then said to be equivalent, when their letters can be interchanged in accordance with one of these laws. See *Introduction*.

from which one consonant at least has dropped out in the process of combination[1].

The name HAGAR may be very simply explained on the above principles as an elliptical compound. The accent being on the second syllable, and the vowel having a broader sound than is commonly given to it in English, the word *Hagár* differs but slightly in pronunciation from *Hargár*: much less, certainly, than *Darmesek* (2 Chron. xxviii. 5) from the usual form, *Dammesek* [Damascus]. *Hagar* would thus suggest, by its first syllable, the common word for ὄρος, and by its second, the common word for *pilgrimage*[2] or *sojourning*. The tendency to pronounce *ar* as *a* is observable alike in ancient and modern languages. In a Talmudic form of the Hebrew *amar* (to say), the *r* is replaced by a quiescent consonant [א]. On the other hand, such quadriliteral Hebrew words as *qardom* are formed by the insertion of *r*; while in Syriac, *barth* e.g. is written with the *linea occultans* (the mark of quiescence) under the *r*, and is thus phonetically equivalent to its Hebrew synonym, *bath*. As this Syriac word is phonetically *bath*, but grammatically *barth*, so *Hagar* may, with etymological intent, be regarded as equivalent to *Hargar*.

The article before Ἀραβία has to be noticed. St Paul, when speaking of his visit to Arabia (Gal. i. 17), leaves the name indefinite: 'I went εἰς Ἀραβίαν, and returned again εἰς Δαμασκόν.' Is there any significance in the use of τῇ before Ἀραβίᾳ in iv. 25? It might be said that it is a matter indifferent whether the article be here used or not; it is, however, accordant with Old Testament usage to regard ἡ Ἀραβία[3] as suggestive of the *Arabah* or *wilderness*. If this allusion be assumed in the passage before us, we have in the explanation of Hagar's name above set forth an expressive reference to

---

[1] Compound words other than proper names are in like manner defective. Thus פרשׁו is explained as compounded of פרשׁ and פרו; ערפל, of ערב and אפל; and the letter ב has disappeared from רמפשׂ. Proper names might be expected to be still more abbreviated.

[2] It is sometimes said that the whole name means simply *wanderer* or *wandering*: but the root הגר is not used in Hebrew.

[3] See Tromm. *Concord. in LXX.*

the historical associations of the covenant which she represents. 'This *Hagar*, or *mount of sojourning*, is mount SINAI, in the wilderness;' where there is the same emphasis on *Sinai* as on *Sion*[1] in Heb. xii. 22. The wilderness was the scene of Israel's wanderings, and mount Sinai in that wilderness represents *Jerusalem that now is;* 'for here have we no continuing city, but we seek one to come.' Mount Sion, on the contrary, corresponds to the heavenly Jerusalem, and is contrasted with Mount Sinai: 'For ye are not come unto the mount that might be touched, and that burned with fire...But ye are come *unto mount Sion*, and unto the city of the living God, the heavenly Jerusalem' (Heb. xii. 18, 22).

IV. The foregoing explanation of the clause τὸ γὰρ Ἅγαρ κ. τ. λ. is purely conjectural, and rests upon no authority. Whether it commends itself as plausible or not, we again urge the merely secondary nature of this part of the investigation. The all-important question is, How does the Apostle introduce the allegory? and the answer to this question depends upon the construction of ἀλληγορούμενα. If it be used as above suggested, the argument is clearly based upon the history, and the allegory is not, nor is it supposed to be, of the essence of the argument. In using such a form of representation, the Apostle is adapting his teaching to the receptivity of his Galatian converts, and imitating the patriarchal expedient of associating names and things, in such a way that the name of HAGAR might ever afterwards recall the great spiritual lesson that he purposed to impress upon his disciples.

The forced verbal argumentations of the Rabbins, and their pernicious use of 'the letter that killeth,' may be referred doubtless, in some degree, to a misplaced reverence for each constituent element of the sacred language. It was inconceivable to them that an inspired writer should have used the most ordinary of expressions without some recondite reason for not having used another that might have served as well;

---

[1] Σιὼν ὄρει.

and hence it came to be agreed amongst them, that in very forms and arrangements of the letters, the highest mysteries lay enshrined[1].

It may be granted, however, that the example of the sacred writers themselves must have conspired with other causes to influence the interpretations of the allegorists, of whatever school; and accordingly, it may be surmised that the peculiar significance of the Biblical names was a starting point for diverse extravagances of exegesis; whilst, on the other hand, it is obvious that such extravagances involve a total misconception of the principles from which they took their rise. In the sacred narrative the names of individuals are, ever and anon, adapted to, or explained in accordance with, the most noteworthy circumstances in the lives and conditions of those who bear them. Sometimes, a child is named after the attendant circumstances of his birth; sometimes, a patriarchal blessing is commemorated by a pointed reference to the name of him upon whom it was bestowed. But mark the perversions of the hyper-allegorists. They credited names, not with a marvellous significance, but with a mystic power. They said in effect that Moses was rescued from the water because named Moses; Samuel, asked of the Lord because named Samuel, rather than so named in commemoration of the mother's prayer. Names come thus to be exalted above things, and are viewed as the symbols of transcendental mysteries; while the historical circumstances from which they borrow their significance are cast into the shade, if not utterly forgotten.

Philo, like St Paul, has an allegory of Hagar, but one which reduces the historical personages into mere philosophical abstractions. The subjoined sketch is borrowed from Dr Lightfoot, *Galatians*, ed. 2, p. 195.

"Abraham—the human soul progressing towards the knowledge of God—unites himself, first with Sarah, and then with Hagar. These two alliances stand in direct opposition

---

[1] See pp. 129, 130.

the one to the other. Sarah the princess—for such is the interpretation of the word—is divine wisdom. To her therefore Abraham is bidden to listen in all that she says. On the other hand Hagar, whose name signifies *sojourning* (παροίκησις), and points therefore to something transient and unsatisfying, is a preparatory or intermediate training—the instruction of the schools—secular learning, as it might be termed in modern phrase. Hence she is fitly described as an Egyptian, as Sarah's handmaid. Abraham's alliance with Sarah is at first premature. He is not sufficiently advanced in his moral and spiritual development to profit thereby. As yet he begets no son by her. She therefore directs him to go in to her handmaid, to apply himself to the learning of the schools. This inferior alliance proves fruitful at once. At a later date, and after this preliminary training, he again unites himself to Sarah; and this time his union with divine wisdom is fertile. Not only does Sarah bear him a son, but she is pointed out as the mother of a countless offspring. Thus is realized the strange paradox that *the barren woman is most fruitful.* Thus in the progress of the human soul are verified the words of the prophet, spoken in an allegory, that *the desolate hath many children.*"

NOTES ON CHAPTER IX.

A. The clause ἅτινά ἐστιν λόγον μὲν ἔχοντα σοφίας (Col. ii. 23), is, in like manner, usually rendered as if ἔχει replaced ἐστιν ἔχοντα. But, in this case also, it seems best to include the participle, &c. in a parenthesis. See Conybeare and others *in loc.* Where does the parenthesis end? It seems best to make it include ἐν τιμῇ τινι. On this hypothesis, we remark that the chief (instinctive) objection to the parenthetic construction seems to arise from the comparative length of the parenthesis; and that, if this be so, then, to state the objection clearly, is to remove it; regard being had to the involved and protracted parentheticism of the Apostle's style. If the paren-

Notes on Chapter IX.

thesis were abbreviated thus: ἅτινά ἐστὶν, λόγον μὲν ἔχοντα σοφίας, πρὸς πλησμονὴν τῆς σαρκός, there would probably be no difficulty in accepting some such rendering as: 'The which *are*, though having indeed a repute for wisdom, *for* (πρός) the glutting of the flesh.' Cp. ἐστὶν εἰς φθοράν (Col. ii. 22). The words ἐν ἐθελοθρησκείᾳ, κ.τ.λ., which follow upon σοφίας, shew *the element wherein* the repute for wisdom is attained. The clause, καὶ ἀφειδίᾳ σώματος οὐκ ἐν τιμῇ τινι, would seem to be best explained by referring οὐκ ἐν τιμῇ τινι to the σῶμα. For this we have the authority of the Greek commentators, and it gives the most natural meaning to ἐν τιμῇ. The parts of the clause are consecutive: the body, being held in no honour, is recklessly abused—it being in the nature of things that are not valued to be used unsparingly. The meaning of the whole passage (on which Dr Wordsworth has some excellent remarks) would thus be, that such wilful, supererogatory enactments as 'Touch not, taste not, handle not' things meant for use and consumption, are, notwithstanding their show of 'wisdom,' for the gratification of the carnal propensities in man's mind. 'The which are (with all their repute for spirituality, in will-worship, and humility, and unsparingness of the body, as of no value, *lit.* held *not in any honour*) for the satiating of the flesh.' This rendering gives a natural *position* and *an antithesis* to the μέν, which the non-parenthetic readings fail to do.

B. Dr Lightfoot has tabulated the MS. authorities for the various readings of the clause τὸ γὰρ Ἀγὰρ κ.τ.λ. (*Galatians*, ed. 2, p. 189.) The last of the four readings there given being neglected, ought not the preceding to be arranged, not in *three* classes, but *four* or *two*? The reading placed first is (i) τὸ γὰρ Σινᾶ ὄρος ἐστίν. 'So it is read in אCFG...Augustine, Jerome...and probably *all* the Latin fathers. This is also the reading of the Gothic Version, except that it omits γάρ... The MS. א after ἐστίν adds ὄν, in which respect it stands alone, &c.' Next in order, Dr Lightfoot places (ii) τὸ δὲ Ἀγὰρ Σινᾶ ὄρος ἐστίν, and (iii) τὸ γὰρ Ἀγὰρ Σινᾶ ὄρος ἐστίν. If, however, (ii) and (iii) are to be separated, ought not א, with its remarkable interpolation after ἐστίν, to stand alone? Thus the testimony in favour of (i) would be diminished. But it seems more natural in balancing the authorities for and against the omission of the word Ἀγὰρ, to neglect minor variations, and to weigh (i), not against (ii) and (iii) taken separately, but against the two combined. We should have then in favour of retaining Ἄγαρ, the authority of 'ABDEKLP with the vast majority of cursive manuscripts, with both Syriac Versions, and with the Greek commentators generally...;' and it would be necessary to reconsider the statement, that 'the strongest, because the most varied, testimony is in favour of the first of these readings.' It is difficult to account for the unexpected occurrence of the word Ἄγαρ, following upon the neuter article, if it formed no part of the original reading. On the other hand, from the reading (iii), the variations (i), (ii) might (or, so to say, *must*) have arisen through *homœoteleuton*.

P.S. ἅτ. ἐστ. ἀλληγορούμενα] ' *Quæ alio quodam sensu sunt*, sub. *talia:* vel, *Quorum allegoria* (quam ὑπόνοιαν veteres vocarunt) *talis est.*' Poli Synops. v. 710. f.

γεννῶσα] Mr Pater notices, in its bearing upon the Allegory, the avoidance or indirect use of this verb when the mother of JESUS is spoken of. Contrast Matt. i. 16, 20, 21, 23; Luke i. 31, 35; ii. 5, 7 with Luke i. 13, 57. Compare Luke xxiii. 29; Joh. xvi. 21. Bengel remarks on τὸ γεννώμενον (Luke i. 35): 'Vocabula abstracta, et neutro genere expressa, initiis illis valde congruunt.'

CHAPTER X.

The Apology of St Stephen.

Amos v. 25—27; Acts vii. 2—53.

'THE speech of St Stephen is in itself an ample field of study, demanding of us much meditation before we can master either the general argument or the meaning and connection of the parts, and giving occasion for researches into Jewish history, Rabbinical traditions, and Egyptian customs.' It contains a brief abstract of the sacred narrative—from the call of Abraham to the building of Solomon's temple—interspersed with more or less direct citations from the original sources; and its twofold aim, as gathered from antecedent circumstances, is to preach Jesus as the Messiah, and to defend the speaker from the charge of blasphemy 'against Moses, and against God.' False witnesses had said of him: 'This man ceaseth not to speak blasphemous words against this holy place, and the law: For we have heard him say, that this Jesus of Nazareth shall destroy this place, and shall change the customs which Moses delivered us' (Acts vi. 13, 14); and it is in answer to the high-priest's question, 'Are these things so?' that the address now before us was delivered.

I. Of the citations with which this address abounds, one stands out, by general consent, as its *characteristic*, and gathers round it a greater complication of difficulties than any other. It is taken from Amos v. 25—27, and is introduced as follows: 'And they made a calf in those days, and offered sacrifice unto the idol, and rejoiced in the work of their own hands. Then God turned, and gave them up to worship the host of heaven; as it is written in the book of the prophets, *O ye house of Israel, have ye offered to me slain beasts and sacrifices by the space of forty years in the wilderness? Yea, ye took up the tabernacle of Moloch, and the star of your god Remphan, figures which ye made to worship them: and I will carry you away beyond Babylon*' (Acts vii. 41—43).

1. For the question, *Have ye offered &c.?* diverse answers have been assumed. Some infer that the Levitical sacrifices were *not* offered in the wilderness; or, at least, that the system was (owing to the difficulties of the situation) in partial abeyance. Others, as Dr Pusey, emphasize the pronoun, and maintain that the sacrifices were not offered to God. 'God does not say that they did not offer sacrifice at all, but that they did not offer unto *Him*. The *unto Me* is emphatic. If God is not served wholly and alone, He is not served at all.' Not dissimilarly Jerome, seeking '*quomodo hostias et sacrificium non Deo obtulerint in deserto*,' concludes that after the making of the golden calf, '*omnia quæ fecerunt, non Deo, sed idolis fecisse monstrantur. Et quod, postea, quædam Domino eos legimus obtulisse, non voluntate, sed pœnarum fecerunt metu... Dominus autem non ea quæ offeruntur, sed voluntatem respicit offerentium.*' It is commonly held that the answer to the question, Μὴ σφάγια καὶ θυσίας προσηνέγκατέ μοι; must be negative, but it is disputed whether the negation is to be made absolute or relative: whether the '*No*' means 'Not then [from the nature of the case] *as in after time;*' or with implied reproach, 'Not to *Me*.' With the latter explanation, the sequence is as follows: 'Have ye offered to *Me* slain beasts...? Not so, but ye took up the tabernacle of Moloch... And I will carry you away beyond Babylon.' The third clause here follows naturally upon the second, but the rendering of καὶ ἀνελάβετε is harsh. Mr Humphry combines the first and second clauses more harmoniously, by making both interrogative. 'Did ye sacrifice to Me forty years in the

wilderness, and yet adopt the worship of Moloch?' But the words καὶ μετοικιῶ ὑμᾶς, do not follow very smoothly upon this. It might indeed be conjectured that this harshness in the Greek has arisen from the literal transference of Hebrew idioms into a strange language, while in the original the same harshness has no place. But the original, *as usually explained*, is scarcely more harmonious than the Greek; its abruptness being fairly represented by our Authorised Version: 'Have ye offered unto me sacrifices and offerings in the wilderness forty years, O house of Israel? But [*lit.* and] ye have borne the tabernacle of your Moloch...Therefore will I cause you to go into captivity beyond Damascus' (Amos v. 25—27). It is possible, however, so to render the passage as to avoid this appearance of abruptness.

2. The first verb of Amos v. 26 is *in the same tense* as that which stands at the commencement of ver. 27, and which is taken by the LXX. and others as a future. The Hebrew commentator Rashi has, accordingly, adopted the expedient of rendering the former also of these verbs in the future: '*Ye shall bear.*' If ver. 25 be now dismissed for a while as parenthetic, a close connection is apparent between the verses which precede and follow, thus: 'And judgement shall run down as waters, and righteousness as a mighty stream. And ye shall take up the tabernacle of your Moloch...And I will cause you to go into captivity beyond Damascus.'

3. The coherence of these verses with the preceding may be made more complete by rendering the word for '*Take thou away*' (ver. 23), as an infinitive (rather than as an imperative), although it is not denied that the received imperative rendering is equally grammatical. Two arguments however may be advanced in favour of the infinitive rendering. (*a*) It makes the parallelism still more complete (the infinitive serving, as it well may, for a quasi-future); and (*b*) the *putting away* is best ascribed to God Himself, who, in ver. 22, 'will not accept though ye offer.'

4. There remain some points to be noticed in the twenty-sixth verse.

The word translated *Moloch* cannot be a proper name, for if so, it could not be joined with a possessive affix (*your*). This however does not stand in the way of an indirect reference to Moloch, as 'your *king*' (*melech*). *Chiun* should also be taken as a noun substantive, in the sense, *pedestal* (of your images). So Jerome and Theodotion[1], as seems required moreover by the parallelism, for otherwise, '*perit rhythmicus ille verborum concentus.*' In the next clause, for 'star of your gods,' may be read *star-gods*, in accordance with a not uncommon usage[2], illustrated by Gen. xvi. 12, where Ishmael is called a *wild-ass of a man*, and by Hos. xiii. 2, where *sacrificers of men*, are not such as sacrifice men, but *men who sacrifice* (Kimchi). The verse in question may be taken as describing, first of all, the idols' paraphernalia; and secondly, in parallelism with this, the star-gods themselves, whose *canopies* and *pedestals* had been mentioned separately. The whole passage, with the exception of the parenthetic twenty-fifth verse, may now be rendered as below.

'Woe unto you that desire the day of the LORD! to what end is it for you? the day of the LORD is darkness, and not light. As if a man did flee from a lion, and a bear met him; or went into the house, and leaned his hand on the wall, and a serpent bit him. Shall not the day of the LORD be darkness, and not light? even very dark, and no brightness in it? I hate, I despise your feast-days, and I will not smell the savours of your solemn assemblies. Though ye offer me burnt-offerings, and your meat-offerings, I will not accept them: neither will I regard the peace-offerings of your fat beasts. But will put away from me the noise of thy songs; and will not hear the noise of thy viols. And judgement shall run down as waters, and righteousness as a mighty stream... And ye shall take up the tabernacle of your king, and the

---

[1] Pusey *in loc.* See note A, p. 222.
[2] This being also a Greek construction it might be asked whether the LXX. ἄστρον τοῦ Θεοῦ ὑμῶν, might not also be rendered your '*star-god.*' This is doubtless a non-natural rendering of the Greek; but regard should be had to the extreme literalness with which the LXX. often rendered difficult sentences or expressions.

pedestal[s] of your images, your star-gods, which ye made for yourselves. And I will cause you to go into captivity beyond Damascus, saith the LORD, whose name is The God of Hosts' (Amos v. 18—27).

The judgement and justice which they had neglected and cast down to the ground (ver. 7), should burst forth, after long repression, and sweep them away as with a flood (ver. 24). The idols wherein they trusted should be found unavailing in their calamity; themselves must swell the captive train. In other passages, God is depicted as bearing and carrying the infant Israel; here, by way of contrast, the idols need to be carried. They are no helpers in distress, but a dead weight and an accession to their makers' burdens. You made them 'to yourselves;' you must *take them up* and carry them. This word *take up*[1] (Amos v. 26) is from the same root as the word for *burden* in Is. xlvi., where the same contrast between God and the idols is expressed. 'Bel boweth down, Nebo stoopeth, their idols were upon the beasts, and upon the cattle: your carriages were heavy loaden; they are a *burden*[2] to the weary (beast). They stoop, they bow down together; they could not deliver the burden, but themselves are gone into captivity. Hearken unto me, O house of Jacob, and all the remnant of the house of Israel, which are borne by me from the belly, which are carried from the womb: And even to your old age I am he; and even to hoar hairs will I carry you: I have made, and I will bear; I even I will carry, and will deliver you. To whom will ye liken me, and make me equal, and compare me, that we may be like? They lavish gold out of the bag, and weigh silver in the balance, and hire a goldsmith; and he maketh it a god: they fall down, yea they worship. They bear him upon the shoulder, they carry him, and set him in his place, and he standeth; from his place shall he not remove: yea, one shall cry unto him, yet can he not answer, nor save him out of his trouble' (Is. xlvi. 1—7. Cp. Jer. xlix. 3).

[1] ונשאתם. [2] משא.

According to the interpretation which these verses illustrate, there is no allusion in Amos v. 26 to sacrificial celebrations in honour of Moloch, in contradistinction to the sacrifices spoken of in ver. 25. The *grammatical objections* to any such contrast will appear from an analysis (*infra*) of the last-mentioned verse; but, independently of these, the expressions used in ver. 26 do not naturally convey the notions of sacrifice, &c. This is well brought out by Dr Pusey, who, while arguing in favour of this contrast, intimates the inadequacy of the words used to express it. 'But whether *the king*, whom the Israelites worshipped in the wilderness, was the same as the Ammonite Molech or no, those dreadful sacrifices were then no part of his worship; else Amos would not have spoken of the idolatry as *the carrying about his tabernacle* only. He would have described it by its greatest offensiveness.'

5. The parenthesis (ver. 25), thus far omitted, has next to be considered. It may be rendered literally, with due regard to *emphasis:* 'Sacrifices and oblations offered ye me in the wilderness forty years, O house of Israel?' a negative answer being presupposed, as in Gen. xvii. 17, where the arrangement is similar: 'Unto him that is an hundred years old shall a child be born?' A still closer parallel is afforded by 2 Sam. vii. 5: 'Shalt thou build me an house for me to dwell in?' which is replaced in 1 Chron. xvii. 4 by the direct negation: 'Not thou shalt-build-me the house to dwell in.' As in the passage from 2 Sam. vii., the vocative 'thou' is emphatic, and the 'me,' being joined to its governing verb, is devoid of emphasis. So in Amos v. 25, there is an emphasis on 'sacrifices and oblations,' but none on the pronoun 'me,' which is joined here also to its verb, and would thus seem to be degraded, so far as emphasis is concerned, to the level of a pronominal affix. The Hebrew is fairly represented by the LXX: μὴ σφάγια καὶ θυσίας προσηνέγκατέ μοι, οἶκος Ἰσραήλ, τεσσαράκοντα ἔτη ἐν τῇ ἐρήμῳ; and the question, thus put, seems to require a negative answer, and to exclude the supposition that the pronoun is to be emphasized. The question

comes in passing as an impassioned expostulation: 'Sacrifice and oblation offered ye me during the forty long years of wandering in the wilderness?' God's favour was graciously bestowed, not purchased by vain oblations, through that most notable crisis, that spring-time of national existence (Hos. ii. 15). 'Ye offered me then no oblations; think not that my favour is to be purchased by them now.' One more consideration confirms the parenthetic rendering of ver. 25. The following verses being referred to idolatries *prevalent in the time of Amos*, and to judgements *then impending*, it is no more than natural to separate them from a verse which alludes to the circumstances of a long-past age. It might indeed be worth while to ask whether this consideration could not be explained away, *if* grammatical considerations pointed to a connection (of sequence or of direct contrast) between the twenty-fifth and twenty-sixth verses; but, as it is, such a connection can scarcely be brought about, except by departure from the laws of emphasis, and by a non-natural use of particles. The rendering (Rashi's) above adopted, which makes ver. 26 a declaration of coming judgement, and connects it with ver. 24, is free from the like grammatical objections. The rapid rush of denunciation is interrupted for a moment, and only for a moment, by the expostulation: 'Sacrifices and oblation offered ye me in the wilderness?' The answer is so obvious, or, from another point of view, the reproof is so unanswerable, that no pause is made for a reply. The course of judgement is no longer stayed. 'And ye shall take up and carry the idols that your own hands have made, and I will cause you to go into captivity beyond Damascus, saith the LORD, whose name is The God of hosts.'

The virtual statement that sacrifices were not offered in the wilderness may be taken, as above remarked, with a certain latitude. It is competent, some would say, to affirm that *the richness and magnificence* of the later sacrifices are alone excluded. 'Ye offered not then these costly sacrifices.' Sacrifice was not then, as it came afterwards to be considered, the staple of divine service; a meritorious ground of acceptance, and the price of God's favour. Some, with Lightfoot, are of opinion that though *public* sacrifices were at times offered, yet individuals seldom or never rivalled, in their oblations, the display of later times—and that from the difficulty of obtaining victims in the wilderness. This hypothesis makes due allowance for the mention of *coals upon the altar* (Numb. xvi. 5, 9, 10), and for the peculiar nature of Korah's sin, which consisted in the usurpation of sacerdotal functions. Dr Pusey remarks, that the sacrifices in the wilderness were 'not the freewill offerings of the people, but the ordinance of God performed by his priests. The people, in that they went after their idols, had no share in, nor benefit from, what was offered in their name.' By others the 'forty years' is taken as a round number for $38\frac{1}{2}$; and it is held that during the interval '*post vitulum confectum et explorationem Cananæ*' no sacrifices at all were offered. The general ordinances about sacrifice are thought, by advocates of this last view, to refer by anticipation to the time of settlement in the promised land. But it would suffice, perhaps, to grant that the sacrificial system was not fully developed in the wilderness, and that the one main point insisted upon was the fulfilment of the moral law. There would then be no need to gloss over the sacrifices of Sinai; which were no part of an established system, but an exceptional celebration, for the ratifying of a covenant. 'And Moses took the blood, and sprinkled it on the people, and said, Behold the blood of the covenant, which the Lord hath made with you concerning all these words' (Ex. xxiv. 8). An important declaration of Jeremiah is calculated to throw further light upon this subject. 'For I spake not unto your fathers, nor commanded them in the day that I brought them up out of the land of Egypt, concerning burnt-offerings or sacrifices: But this thing commanded I them, saying, Obey my voice, and I will be your God, and ye shall be my people: and walk ye in all the ways that I have commanded you, that it may be well unto you' (Jer. vii. 22, 23).

II. *The Apology.*

Against the HOLY PLACE, and against the LAW, 'this man ceaseth not,' said the false witnesses, 'to speak blasphemous words.' The centre of the law was *Sacrifice;* and the law was in abeyance when the daily sacrifice was taken away. We should expect then to find in the *Apology*, a formal and direct notice of the sacrificial system and of the holy place, and not mere '*digressions*' respecting the idolatries of the Jews, and concerning the temple. MOSES, their lawgiver, was to be superseded, and the customs which he delivered them to be changed: such is the final clause of the indictment, standing in parallelism with what precedes.

The defence opens with an allusion to the call of Abraham, and the divine revelations to their great progenitor; and this is followed up by a brief sketch of the people's history, till the time when Moses came to free them from Egyptian bondage. 'Seeing one of them suffer wrong, he defended him, and avenged him that was oppressed, and smote the Egyptian: For he supposed his brethren would have understood how that God by his hand would deliver them: *but they understood not.* And the next day he shewed himself unto them as they strove, and would have set them at one again, saying, Sirs, ye are brethren; why do ye wrong one to another? But he that did his neighbour wrong thrust him away, saying, Who made thee a ruler and a judge over us? Wilt thou kill me, as thou diddest the Egyptian yesterday? (Ex. ii. 14). Then fled Moses at this saying, and was a stranger in the land of Madian...This Moses whom they refused, saying, Who made thee a ruler and a judge? the same did God send to be a ruler and a deliverer by the hand of the angel which appeared to him in the bush.... This is that Moses, which said unto the children of Israel, *A prophet shall the Lord your God raise up unto you of your brethren, like unto me; Him shall ye hear*...To whom *our fathers would not obey*, but thrust him from them, and in their hearts turned back again into Egypt.' Moses 'received the *lively oracles* to give unto us,' but the people demanded visible objects of worship: 'Make us gods to go before us.' Sacrifices and oblations were not required (ver. 42); but they, not content with a spiritual service, made for themselves images to worship. The (portable) *tabernacle* of Moloch suggests the '*tabernacle* of witness' (ver. 44); and this, by contrast, the fixed habitation built by Solomon for the mighty God of Jacob (ver. 47). 'Howbeit the most High dwelleth not in temples made with hands; as saith the prophet, Heaven is my throne, and earth is my footstool: what house will ye build me? saith the Lord: or what is the place of my rest? Hath not my hand made all these things? Ye stiffnecked and uncircumcised in heart and ears, ye do always resist the Holy Ghost: as your fathers did, so do ye. Which of the prophets have not your fathers persecuted? and they have slain them which shewed before of the coming of the Just One; of whom ye have been now the betrayers and murderers: who have received the law by the disposition of angels, and have not kept it.'

The opening of the speech was calculated to conciliate the populace, by its implied assurance that the sacred traditions were after all not repudiated by the speaker; while at the same time, it embodies the important truth that the Promise was prior to and independent of the Law. But the thirty-seventh verse contains the central point of the argument. It is said that Moses foretold the advent of a prophet like unto himself. That prophet, St Stephen affirms to be JESUS of Nazareth; and thus, far from desiring to subvert the Mosaic institutions, he is but urging upon his fellow-countrymen the injunction of Moses: 'Unto Him shall ye hearken.' The coming Prophet was to *be like unto Moses*, with whom accordingly JESUS is compared in two particulars, corresponding to the two main charges of blasphemy, against the Temple, and against the Law. The second charge is refuted by the expostulatory interrogation of Amos: 'Sacrifices and oblations offered ye me in the wilderness forty years, O house of Israel?' The sacrificial system was not in force under the rule of Moses; hence JESUS, in requiring a spiritual service, and dispensing with sacrifice, *was like Moses*, 'who received the *lively oracles*¹ to give unto us,' and gave to obedience its due exaltation above ritual. Again, 'our fathers had [only] the *tabernacle of witness* in the wilderness,' for the 'house' was not yet built. 'I have not dwelt in an house since the day that I brought up Israel unto this day; but have gone from tent to tent, and from one tabernacle to another' (1 Chron. xvii. 5). Under the rule of *Moses* there was no temple, and the Divine Presence was not thought of as localized; JESUS, therefore, *was like Moses*, for He taught that 'the hour cometh, when ye shall neither in this mountain, nor yet at Jerusalem, worship the Father. But the hour cometh, and now is, when the true worshippers shall worship the Father in spirit and in truth' (Joh. iv. 21, 23). This argument from the non-existence of the temple in the time of Moses, is supplemented in the following verses. David, 'who found favour before God,' desired to build a temple: but his longing was not to be gratified; it was reserved for Solomon to build the 'house.' The word Solomon² being emphasized, this point in the argument is brought out. The nation had subsisted till that time—had passed through its greatest crises, and outlived its most fondly remembered rulers—and still...no *house* was built. It was *Solomon* who built it;... and even then, it was not in temples made with hands that God deigned to dwell.

A third point in the comparison is to be noted.

To Moses it was said: 'Who made thee a ruler and a judge over us?' Him 'our fathers would not obey, but thrust him from them.' JESUS, therefore, *was like Moses*, because he was rejected by the people. 'As your fathers did so do ye...And they have slain them which shewed before of the coming of the Just One; of whom ye have been now the betrayers and murderers.' Thus the Apology is completed, and the charges brought against St Stephen's teaching are turned into corroborative arguments. 'You reject the doc-

---

¹ See note B, p. 223.   ² Σολομῶν δὲ ᾠκοδόμησεν αὐτῷ οἰκίαν.

trine of JESUS of Nazareth, because He dispenses with the temple and its sacrifices. But it is for this reason that you should the rather enrol yourselves as His followers; for by the spirituality of His teaching He is designated as *like unto Moses*, in whose day the sacrificial system was in abeyance, and the temple was not yet built. By your rejection of Him, you liken Him still further to that great lawgiver, '*to whom our fathers would not obey, but thrust him from them.*'

III. *The Gospel before the Law.*

1. The Promise to Abraham contained the Gospel in itself, and thus the Gospel was before the Law. In connection with this subject a remarkable verbal argument is used by St Paul. 'Now to Abraham and his seed were the promises made. He saith not, And to seeds, as of many; but as of one, And to thy SEED, which is CHRIST' (Gal. iii. 16). The plural of this Hebrew word for seed occurs once only in the canonical writings, viz. in 1 Sam. viii. 15: 'And he will take the tenth of your seed[s], and of your vineyards, and your oliveyards, even the best of them, and give them to his servants;' where the plural, *seeds*, must be taken to mean *grain* or *crops*, probably with reference to *different* kinds of crops. In strict accordance with this application of the plural, is the ordinary use of the singular, viz. as a collective expression for *descendants*, implying the unification of a multitudinous posterity in a *single line.* 'It has been urged,' writes Dr Lightfoot *in loc.*, 'that the stress of the argument rests on a grammatical error; that as the plural of the word here rendered σπέρμα is only used to signify *grain* or *crops*, the sacred writer could not under any circumstances have said, *seeds as of many*... But the very expression in St Paul, which starts the objection, supplies the answer also. It is quite as unnatural to use the Greek σπέρμα with this meaning, as to use the Hebrew זרעים. Avoiding the technical terms of grammar, he could not express his meaning more simply than by the opposition, *not to thy* SEEDS, *but to thy* SEED. A plural substantive would be

inconsistent with the interpretation given; the singular collective noun, if it admits of plurality (*as it is interpreted by St Paul himself*, Rom. iv. 18; ix. 7), at the same time involves the idea of unity. The question therefore is no longer one of grammatical accuracy, but of theological interpretation.' In Gen. xv. 5, the collective singular, 'seed,' implies, on the one hand a multiplicity of individual descendants, and on the other a unity and limitation; for the promise is *restricted* (Gen. xxi. 12) to the line of Isaac—'in Isaac shall thy seed be called.' The singular expresses *one line* of posterity, as in Gen. iv. 25, where Eve exclaims, in reference to the birth of Seth: 'God hath appointed me *another seed* instead of Abel, whom Cain slew.' That St Paul did not build his argument upon a grammatical misconception, is made sufficiently obvious by his express words, shortly following:—' For as many of you as have been baptized into Christ have put on Christ. There is neither Jew nor Greek, there is neither bond nor free, there is neither male nor female: for *ye are all one in Christ Jesus*. And if ye be Christ's, *then are ye Abraham's* SEED, and heirs according to the promise' (Gal. iii. 27—29). The Apostle here explains what is meant by the *oneness* of the seed spoken of in ver. 16. It is a oneness of *kind*, harmonizing an infinity of diverse individualities; Jew and Greek are made one IN CHRIST, and, being thus unified by being made 'part of Christ,' they are included in that *one* seed whereon the promise rested[1].

Referring to Heb. ii. 11, where the sanctified are called brethren of the Sanctifier, Professor Jowett remarks—with perhaps over nice regard to uniformity of statement—that ' Christ is not the same as His Church, however close may be the connection between them.' This consideration however has no *special* bearing on St Paul's argument from the singular σπέρμα, in connection with which it is adduced by the above-named commentator. If St Paul's representation of Christians

---

[1] 'Ye are all *one man* in Christ; and if ye *are part of Christ*, then are ye Abraham's *seed* and heirs according to promise.' (Lightfoot.)

as *one* in Christ, be inaccurate in Gal. iii. 28, then consistency demands the repudiation of other allusions to Christ's *mystical body*, as illogical and erroneous. If however the reality of the idea be presupposed, due allowance must be made for its concurrence with the view of the singular (σπέρμα) propounded in ver. 16. We are familiar with the former method of representation, but less familiar with the latter: and it is from this inequality that our difficulty in interpretation arises. The two pictures must be viewed at once and with like appliances, before they will combine inseparably as a life-like whole.

2. In the Divine purpose, wherein the Law had exhibited itself from the first as temporary and conductive, the Gospel was before the Law: but in what particulars (it may be asked) is this Divine order manifested to human intelligence? Two such particulars are dwelt upon (*supra*) by St Stephen, who, as regards *Sacrifice* and the *Temple*, maintains that the Gospel system existed before the Law. A third, not indeed independent of the preceding, is the catholicity of the promise to Abraham:—'And the scripture, foreseeing that God would justify the heathen through faith, preached before the gospel unto Abraham, saying, In thee shall all nations be blessed' (Gal. iii. 8). As the taking away of the daily sacrifice favoured the growth of a more spiritual conception of true worship; so the destruction of the temple, and the dispersion of the chosen race, concurred with a greater diffusiveness in their hopes and anticipations. 'Rising above the exclusiveness which marred the greatness of the Israelite,' the later Psalmists 'would extend the rights of Abraham's children to all; for have not all, who are in heart the true servants of Jehovah, been born again as citizens of Jerusalem[1]?' These late approximations to the spirit of the Gospel were then brought about by a return to a state of things more or less resembling what had pre-existed, when the law was yet future. When St Paul thus writes:—'Moreover,

---

[1] *The Psalms chronologically arranged.* By four Friends. In this work Dr Ewald's theories are given.

brethren, I would not that ye should be ignorant, how that all our fathers were under the cloud, and all passed through the sea; and were all baptized unto Moses in the cloud and in the sea; and did all eat the same spiritual meat; and did all drink the same spritual drink: for they drank of that spiritual Rock that followed them: and that Rock was Christ' (1 Cor. x. 1—4)—it is thought by some that he attributes to the Jews of the age referred to, such a spiritual conception of Christ as was lacking in the Apostle's times. However this may be, the circumstances of the former time were in some respects favourable to the more spiritual frame of mind. When an elaborate ritual system was established, there would be a not unnatural tendency to satisfy its express requirements more and more perfunctorily, and thus to glide, in lapse of time, into sensuous conceptions of Divine worship. The temple again, and the narrow localization of their chief acts of worship, would tend to materialize the Jews' conception of the Divine nature. To what end then served the law? Narrowing this broad question to the point at issue, we may answer, that what was lost in spirituality was gained in definiteness. There may have been oscillations in the chosen people's religious progress; but to assume an absolute retrogression would seem to imply, in some sort, a negation of a divinely fore-ordained plan. In earlier times, the Promise may have presented itself with more of spirituality; in later times, with more of definiteness: it remained for those who, like St Paul, could look back upon the historical CHRIST, to combine the utmost diffusiveness and spirituality with a sure personal appropriation of the Promise.

3. 'It will greatly heighten the interest of this speech, if we can see reason to believe that it left permanent impressions on the mind of one of the hearers, the young man Saul; and that though it failed to convince him at the time, yet he dwelt on it after his conversion, as the Apostles, after the Resurrection, called to mind some of the sayings of our Lord. That this was actually the case, is rendered highly probable by the circumstance that St Paul often falls upon

the same arguments, and uses the same expressions (not very common ones), which are here attributed to St Stephen[1].' Having exemplified this statement, Mr Humphry concludes that 'These coincidences, taken separately, might not have much force; but when joined together, they are surely strong enough to warrant the belief that the seed which was now sown in the Apostle's mind, was afterwards quickened and brought forth fruit, and that the arguments and expressions of Stephen never passed from his memory. Indeed, it is not unlikely that we owe the preservation of the speech, as we have it in this chapter, to St Paul. For among the hostile audience of the martyr, who besides would be likely to treasure it up, or to communicate it to the Evangelists?'

From the apology of St Stephen, may not St Paul have derived a thought on the priority of the Gospel to the Law?

NOTES ON CHAPTER X.

A. The occurrence of the name Remphan (not found in the Hebrew) has to be accounted for. There are various readings of the word, one being 'Ραιφάν. Some suppose the LXX. to have read ריון (for כיון), and thence to have obtained 'Ραιφάν by transliteration. So Gesenius: 'LXX. interpretes כיון nomen proprium numinis esse censuerunt, licet hoc (כ et ר inter se permutatis, cf. v. c. באש Nah. i. 6, LXX. ἀρχάς = ראש) corrupte scriberent 'Ραιφάν, 'Ρηφάν; moxque magis etiam corrumperent librarii in 'Ρεμφάν, 'Ρεμφᾶ' (*Thesaur.* 670 a). Against this view, it is urged that ו would not have been replaced by φ ['Ut taceamus, ריון illos potius per 'Ρωυάν expressuros fuisse.' *Rosenmüller.*] So Montfaucon—quoted by Rosenmüller—'Litera *Vau* nunquam consonantis vice fungitur in fragmentis per Græcos descriptis, nec fungi posse videtur, quandoquidem initio vocum exprimitur per οὐ (οὐαεεί, ויחי, *et vixit*; οὐεσσακή, וישקרן, *osculatus est*). In medio autem et fine vocum modo per οὐ; modo, et quidem frequentius, per ω redditur.' But,

---

[1] Humphry *on Acts vii.* See Conyb. and Howson's *St Paul.*

on the other hand, it should be noted, that the LXX. were much given to transliterating difficult words; and hence arises a presumption that Ῥαιφάν has resulted *somehow or other* from transliteration. Another explanation is, that the word כיון was read as an Arabic word, and replaced by a Coptic synonym for *the planet Saturn*. But, supposing the translators to have been acquainted with some such word as Ῥαιφάν, or Ῥεφάν, actually existing, may we not conjecture that they would have attempted to force the difficult Hebrew word under consideration into agreement with this seemingly appropriate Ῥαιφάν? Would not this suffice to account for a rare, or unique, consonantal rendering of the letter ו, elsewhere replaced [Montfaucon, *supra*] by ου, or ω? Other transliterative solutions might however be suggested.

B. In Acts vii. 38—41, it is said that:
(i) Moses ἐδέξατο λόγια ζῶντα δοῦναι ἡμῖν.
(ii) The people said, ποίησον ἡμῖν θεούς. And they rejoiced ἐν τοῖς ἔργοις τῶν χειρῶν αὐτῶν.
In the citation (ver. 42, 43):
[i] Sacrifice offered ye me in the wilderness?
[ii] Ye took up τοὺς τύπους οὓς ἐποιήσατε προσκυνεῖν αὐτοῖς.
Here a parallelism is observable.

Moses is mentioned (i) as the institutor of a spiritual worship: God declares [i] that He required no sacrifice in the time of Moses.

But the people (ii) craved for a sensuous worship, and made themselves a calf, &c.: Ye took up [ii] the images which ye had made to worship. [In Amos the expression is '*which ye made for yourselves.*' Cp. ἐν τοῖς ἔργοις τῶν χειρῶν αὐτῶν.]

There are two main differences between Amos v. 25—27, and St Stephen's citation. (*a*) In the former there is no mention of Moloch and Remphan. (*b*) St Stephen, as it would seem, notwithstanding the mention of Babylon, refers καὶ ἀνελάβετε to the forty years; whereas the corresponding Hebrew word points onward from the time of Amos. But neither variation affects the general sense of the passage cited; whereof the main purport is to proclaim the inefficacy of a merely external worship, and to illustrate this inefficacy by an allusion to the circumstances of the forty years.

CHAPTER XI.

The Imprecations of Psalm LXIX.

A FEW passages, conspicuous for their sustained severity of denunciation, are fatal (some think) to certain theories, which might otherwise have seemed not inapplicable to the imprecations of the collective Psalter. 'We find in the Psalms terrible denunciations of the writer's enemies, withering anathemas, imprecations so awful that we almost tremble to read them. How are we to explain the occurrence of such prayers for vengeance? Are they justifiable? Are they, not the mere outbursts of passionate and unsanctified feeling, but the legitimate expression of a righteous indignation? Or are they Jewish only, and not Christian? And if so, then how are we to reconcile this with a belief in the Divine authority and inspiration of the Scriptures? Such language is certainly very different from anything we meet with in the New Testament; and yet, if it is not legitimate, if we may not use it ourselves, then how can it be said to be given by inspiration of God?'

Having thus stated the difficulty, Mr Perowne goes on to notice the 'non-natural' interpretations of those who argue that 'such language could be lawfully used now, only with reference to the enemies of our souls' peace;' and adds: 'Yet it is obvious how impossible it is to carry out this principle of interpretation. How, for instance, in wrestling with spiritual enemies, could we adopt with any definite meaning such words as these:—Set Thou a wicked man over him, and let Satan stand at his right hand. When he shall be judged, let him be condemned; and let his prayers become sin. Let his days be few, and let another take his office. Let his children be fatherless, and his wife a widow, &c.?—It is manifestly out of the question: the gulf is too wide between the original sense and the attempted application.' The illustration is from the hundred and ninth Psalm, which, 'in the awfulness of its anathemas, *surpasses everything of the kind in the Old Testament.*' But second only to this in deliberateness of detailed invective, and in some particulars almost surpassing it, is the sixty-ninth Psalm. Both of these are cited in the New Testament, and come, therefore, within the scope of the present enquiry: to both, moreover, a *special* explanation is perhaps applicable. It is proposed therefore to devote to each a separate section, wherein their peculiar difficulties may be discussed; independently of the general comparison which will be entered upon subsequently, between the Ethics of Christianity and the Ethics of Judaism.

I. *The structure of Psalms lxix., cix.*

Not to mention the theory which represents the maledictions contained herein as calm and unimpassioned statements of the evils that await the sinner; it should be noted, that an apparent breach of continuity results, in each case, from treating the disputed expressions as IMPRECATIONS proper, so long as the received translations are retained.

1. The sixty-ninth Psalm 'was written under circumstances of great and unmerited suffering, by one who was persecuted for righteousness' sake...In the former part of the Psalm we have the fact of this persecution detailed, in the form of a humble complaint to God, together with an earnest prayer for deliverance. In the latter part *there is a marked change of feeling.* The sad, humble, subdued, entreating tone in which he had spoken, turns suddenly into a strong outburst of indignant execration. One curse is heaped upon another, till the whole terrible series is completed in the

prayer that those who have persecuted and mocked God's afflicted servant, may have their names blotted out of His Book of Life[1].' But to render the analysis of the Psalm less incomplete, it should be added, that after this marked change of feeling, the Psalmist—dropping all mention of his persecutors—gives expression to 'joyful hopes and vows of thanksgiving for God's mercy,' as in other Psalms, *with which that in question has been compared.* Psalms xxii. and cii. describe like circumstances, and express like hopes, with Ps. lxix.; but the medial curses of this last have no counterpart in the former two. In Ps. xxii., the utmost malice is simply deprecated, and the Psalmist hopes for the *conversion* of the heathen (ver. 27). In Ps. lxix., no less than Psalms xxii. and cii., the salvation of God's servant is contemplated as a theme for universal gratulation. Without straining this consideration, we may say, that it removes any *a priori* presumption which might be conceived to exist, in favour of the commonly received application of the curses in Ps. lxix.

2. There is a still greater seeming incongruity in Ps. cix. The plaintive tone of its opening verses is thrown aside at ver. 6; to be taken up again at ver. 20. The intermediate section alludes to an INDIVIDUAL; but before and after, the Psalmist makes no allusion to any specific enemy—*not even in the verse which sums up the imprecations supposed to be directed against the one foe singled out*[2]. This Psalm too, like others above-mentioned, 'closes with the confident and joyful anticipation that his prayer is heard and answered.' There is a way of accounting for the change from the plural to singular and back again, which gives a greater consistency to the representation, and obviates the necessity of presupposing violent transitions in tone and feeling. It is thought by Dr Sykes, Dr Kennicott, and by the renowned Hebrew commentator Mendelssohn, that the imprecations proceed *from the Psalmist's enemies to himself;* not, as is commonly supposed, from him to them. Subjoined is an attempt to apply a like

---

[1] Perowne, on Ps. lxix.
[2] 'Let it thus happen from the Lord unto mine *enemies*, &c.'

method to Ps. lxix.: but before entering upon the discussion, it may be well to illustrate, by a few examples out of many, the characteristic of the Hebrew style upon which this explanation depends.

II. *Marks of citation, wanting in Hebrew.*

"As there are not in Hebrew any marks, like our inverted commas, to shew where a train of thought is interrupted by a quotation—as when a speaker introduces abruptly the words of another person, or of himself at a previous time—passages sometimes occur in which it is requisite to supply such marks in a translation; and so, at times a dialogue will be found, without anything to point it out as such in the Hebrew Text, but the alternate members of which must, in the translation, be each enclosed in inverted commas. Thus [Numb. xxiii. 7] Balaam says, *Balak the king of Moab hath brought me from Aram, from the mountains of the east:*

'Come, curse me Jacob,
And come, defy Israel.'

How shall I curse, &c.?

[Prov. xxiii. 34, 35]. *And thou shalt be as one lying in the midst of [the] sea, even as one lying on the top of a mast:*

'They have stricken me, [yet] I felt no pain;
They have beaten me, but I perceived it not,' &c.

where it will be observed that the words enclosed in inverted commas, are supposed to be uttered by the drunkard[1]."

In certain contexts, the English language will bear the like sudden and unmarked transitions. Thus in Is. xxii. 13[2], it is sufficiently obvious, without typographical intimation, that the words: 'Let us eat and drink; for to-morrow we shall die;' are a quotation, not an expression of the Prophet's

---

[1] Mason and Bernard, *Hebrew Grammar*, Vol. II. p. 163.

[2] Quoted by St Paul: 'If after the manner of men I have fought with beasts at Ephesus, what advantageth it me, if the dead rise not? *Let us eat and drink; for to-morrow we die.*' (1 Cor. xv. 32.)

own frame of mind. But in many other places, there would be a considerable risk of putting words into the mouth of a wrong speaker, and thereby perverting and misapplying them. The risk is less in Hebrew, only because this abruptness of transition from one speaker to another is a recognized peculiarity of the language[1]. In our Authorized Version citations are frequently introduced by words printed in italics, to shew that there is nothing in the Hebrew corresponding to them. Thus: 'The kings of the earth set themselves, and the rulers take counsel together, against the LORD, and against His anointed, *saying*, Let us break their bands asunder, and cast away their cords from us' (Ps. ii. 2, 3). 'All they that see me laugh me to scorn: they shoot out the lip, they shake the head, *saying*, He trusted on the LORD that He would deliver him: let Him deliver him seeing he delighted in Him' (Ps. xxii. 7, 8). The true construction of Ps. x. 4 appears to be:—

> The wicked, such is his pride, [*imagines that*]
> 'HE will not require.'
> [*That*] 'There is no God,'
> Is all his thought.

'Set the trumpet to thy mouth,' writes the Prophet: and in immediate sequence follow the words of proclamation: '*As an eagle against the house of the* LORD' (Hos. viii. 1). 'They flee [*amid cries of*] Stay, stay,' is briefly expressed, in Nah. ii. 8, by the words, 'They flee, Stay, stay.' And a bold ellipsis in Habakkuk (i. 11) is well supplied by our translators: 'He shall pass over, and offend, *imputing* this his power unto his god.'

III. *Introductory remarks on the sixty-ninth Psalm.*

There are two series of denunciations in this Psalm which must be considered separately. The former are contained

---

[1] This abruptness is chiefly observable in poetical passages. But see 1 Sam. i. 20: 'and called his name Samuel, Because [*said she*] I have asked him of the LORD.' See further, Mason and Bernard, Vol. II. p. 167, on 1 Kings iii. 16—28.

The Imprecations of Psalm LXIX.

in ver 22—25; the latter (which are of greater severity), in ver. 27, 28.

1. The twenty-sixth verse, which separates the two series, stands thus in the Authorized Version:

For they persecute *him* whom thou hast smitten;
And they talk to the grief of those whom thou hast wounded.

It is intended to express thereby, that the preceding curses were imprecated by the Psalmist upon his enemies, in return for their persecution of him. It is however to be observed, that the original is simply: 'For whom thou hast smitten &c.' where the relative might, irrespectively of the context, be either singular or plural; but, to judge by the parallelism, is plural¹. This consideration removes (*infra*) an antecedent objection to the proposed transference of the foregoing curses, from the mouth of the Psalmist to the mouth of his enemies.

2. The expression, 'TALK TO the grief of &c.' in the second hemistich of 26, occurs once only elsewhere, viz. in Ps. ii. 7: 'I WILL DECLARE the decree: the LORD hath said unto me, Thou art my Son; this day have I begotten thee.'

In this latter case, *the thing declared follows upon the words, 'I will declare.'* In the former case we might look for an analogous specification of the words which the enemy *talks, to* the grief of (*i. e.* so as to grieve²) the divinely afflicted. Thus:

They talk to the grief of those whom thou hast wounded:
'Add iniquity unto their iniquity:
And let them not come into thy righteousness.
Let them be blotted out of the book of the living,
And not be written with the righteous.'

3. It may be objected that the whole weight of authority is against the proposed rendering of ver. 26; but it is found,

¹ אמר רבי משה ולהכא״ב תללי״ך יספרו את העם הזה אשר אתה הכית רדפו (*Rashi*). זה לזה שאנחנו מוכים וחללים (*Aben Ezra*). See note A. p. 242.

² This construction is adopted in the following comment:

upon examination, that there is precisely that disagreement among commentators which paves the way for a new rendering, by shewing the unsatisfactoriness of such as have been proposed. It is a significant fact that the Hebrew text has been denounced as *obviously corrupt* in its reading of the passage, and as needing to be assimilated to the LXX. προσέθηκαν. Of modern commentators, Dr Ewald agrees to the proposed alteration, and expresses his acquiescence with characteristic decision[1]. Others, with Rosenmüller, would elicit a like meaning from the text as it stands[2]. It seems then, that there is no such concurrence of testimony, as at first sight appears, in favour of the received view of these imprecations and against that suggested in the foregoing paragraph: but, on the contrary, to those who regard the vexed clause from the usual standpoint, its words seem to need elaboration before a suitable sense can be extracted from them.

Translation of the sixty-ninth Psalm[3].

1. Save me, O God : for the waters are come in, even unto my soul.

2. I am sunk in deep mire, where no ground is : I am come into deep waters, so that the floods run over me.

3. I am weary of my crying (my throat is dry : mine eyes have failed) while I wait upon my God.

4. They that hate me without a cause are more than the hairs of my head : they that would destroy me[4], being mine enemies wrongfully, are many in number : when I had not robbed I must restore.

---

[1] 'Ist für יספרו deutlich (auch nach LXX. προσέθηκαν) יספי zu lesen, die dichterische form von יסף = הפפה; denn dass sie bloss von den göttlichen strafen erzählen hat bei weitem nicht die sträfflichkeit als wenn sie, wie hier der zusammenhang schon fordert, durch eigne thätliche angriffe und schläge jene noch aufs fühlbarste vermehrten.'

[2] 'Ad dolorem eorum qui a te sunt sauciati annumerant;' is the reading of Rosenmüller, who testifies to the want of an accusative after יספרו, by adding, '*scil.* plures alios.'

[3] In this translation (which is inserted chiefly for convenience of reference) departures from the familiar phraseology have been avoided, in many doubtful cases. So with the translation of Ps. cix. in the following chapter.

[4] For, '*my destroyers,*' some read, '*more than my locks,*' as suggested by

The Imprecations of Psalm LXIX.

5. O God, Thou knowest my foolishness : and my trespasses are not hid from Thee.

6. Let not them that trust in Thee, O Lord God of hosts, be ashamed through me: let not them that seek Thee be confounded through me, O God of Israel.

7. For for Thy sake have I suffered reproof : shame hath covered my face.

8. I am become a stranger unto my brethren : and an alien unto my mother's children.

9. For the zeal of[1] Thine house hath eaten me : and the rebukes of them that rebuked Thee are fallen upon me.

10. And I fasted, and wept sore[2] : and it was made a reproach unto me.

11. I made sackcloth also my clothing : and became a by-word unto them.

12. They that sit in the gate speak against me : and the drunkards make songs upon me.

13. Yet is my prayer to Thee in an acceptable time[3] : O God, in the abundance of Thy loving-kindness, answer me with Thy sure salvation.

14. Deliver me from the mire, that I sink not : let me be delivered from them that hate me, and out of the deep waters.

15. Let not the water-flood whelm me, neither let the deep swallow me up : and let not the pit shut her mouth upon me.

16. Answer me, O Lord, for Thy loving-kindness is good : turn Thee unto me according to the abundance of Thy mercies.

---

the parallelism. So Mendelssohn: 'Fester als gewund'ne Locken.' Ewald (after the *Peschito*): 'Zahlreicher als meine knochen;' a reading which, 'gibt zugleich ein wortspiel.' Cp. '*all* my bones' (Ps. xxxv. 10).

[1] That is, 'zeal or longing *for* the temple and its services,' from which the Psalmist is cut off. A noteworthy use of the genitive occurs in Jer. l. 28; li. 11: 'the vengeance of His temple.'

[2] This rendering [Ewald and others] gives the general sense, but probably not the construction. Rosenmüller : 'Et quum flevi et in jejunio anima mea est.' The difficulty is merely grammatical.

[3] 'And this was my prayer, viz. O God, &c.' (*Aben Ezra. Kimchi.*)

17. And hide not Thy face from Thy servant; for I am in a strait : O haste Thee, and answer me.

18. Draw nigh unto my soul, and save it : O deliver me because of mine enemies.

19. Thou hast known my reproach, and my shame, and my dishonour : mine adversaries are all in Thy sight[1].

20. Reproach hath broken my heart and I am full of heaviness[2] : and I looked for some to have pity, but there was no man, and for comforters, but I found none.

21. And they mixed gall with my portion[3] : and gave me vinegar for my thirst.

22. Let their table before them become a trap : and a snare[4] when they are at peace.

23. Let their eyes be darkened, that they see not : and make their loins continually to shake.

24. Pour out Thine indignation upon them : and let the furiousness of Thine anger overtake them.

25. Let their habitation be desolate : and let none dwell in their tents[5].

26. For[6] whom Thou hast smitten, they have persecuted : and to the grief of Thy plagued ones do they talk[7]:

27. Add iniquity to their iniquity : and let them not come into Thy righteousness.

28. Let them be wiped out of the book of the living[8] : and not be written among the righteous.

---

[1] May not this verse rather mean : 'Thou knowest my reproach on Thine account from all mine enemies?' i. e. more fully expressed; 'the reproach which I suffer on Thine account; a reproach wherewith all mine enemies assail me.' Cp. ver. 7. From one point of view the construction resembles that of Ps. lxxxix. 50: 'How I do bear in my bosom [the reproach of] all the mighty people.'

[2] Aben Ezra takes אנושה as 1 pers. fut. from אנש, with א for י, as in הם יוסיפון. Ex. xviii. 26.

[3] See p. 117, note 2.

[4] מוקש would seem to mean properly a *lure* or *decoy*, leading into destruction, not itself consummating it. So in 1 Sam. xviii. 21 : 'that *she* may be *a snare* to him, and that the hand of the Philistines may be against him.' In the Psalm, the food is not distasteful, but insidiously grateful; calculated to stupefy, and thus prepare for destruction.

[5] On St Peter's application of this, together with Ps. cix. 8, see Chap. xii.

[6] See note B. p. 242.

[7] 'They talk, *sc.* as follows, *Add iniquity to their iniquity, &c.*'

[8] See note C. p. 243.

The Imprecations of Psalm LXIX.

29. But afflicted as I am and pained[1] : Thy salvation, O God, shall set me up on high.

30. I will praise the name of God with a song : and magnify it with thanksgiving.

31. And it shall better please the Lord than ox : than bullock horned and hoofed[2].

32. The humble shall see this, and be glad : and your heart shall live that seek God.

33. For the Lord heareth the poor[3] : and hath not despised His prisoners.

34. Let heaven and earth praise Him : the sea and all that moveth therein.

35. For God will save Zion, and build the cities of Judah[4] : that men may dwell there, and have it in possession.

36. And the seed of His servants shall inherit it : and they that love His name shall dwell therein.

IV. On the Subject of the Psalm.

In ambiguous cases, where words might grammatically be attributed to one or other of two personages, it is well to inquire into the characteristics of the speakers, and hence to gather, as far as may be, from whose mouth the disputed utterances would the more naturally proceed. In the case before us, who and what are the speakers? What is the subject of the Psalm?

---

[1] Mr Perowne writes on this clause: 'BUT AS FOR ME, placing himself emphatically in contrast to those who had been the object of his imprecation.' But does not אֲנִי give *distinctness* rather than *emphasis*? the construction would be incomplete without it. Emphatic contrast is scarcely so suitable in Ps. xl. 17, as: 'Mean though I am, let not the LORD neglect me.' Cp. Ps. lxx. 5. In lxxxvi. 1; lxxxviii. 15; cix. 22; the order is different.

[2] That is, *of fit age for sacrifice*: 'not over small' (*Aben Ezra*). The exaltation of praise over sacrifice favours the view that this is a Captivity Psalm.

[3] 'אֶבְיוֹנִים *pauperibus*, uti עֲנָוִים *afflictis*, ver. 32, sæpe in Psalmis Hebræi *exilii* miseriis oppressi designantur. *Rosenmüller.*

[4] 'Non dubitamus adstipulari iis interpretibus, qui et hunc Psalmum ex persona Judæorum, qui in Babylonem fuerant abducti, dictum putant, præsertim quum *captivorum, urbiumque Judææ dirutarum* diserta fiat mentio.' *Rosenmüller.*

The opinion that it relates to a time of captivity is advocated by Rashi, who takes Israel—'As the *lily*[1] among thorns'—for the speaker, and explains, 'waters' (ver. 1), by 'the nations:' Aben Ezra concludes, that an allusion to the captivity gives the best sense[2] in ver. 33; and Kimchi explains the singular, 'Save *me* &c.,' as used, either collectively or distributively, by the captive people. The initial imagery is not unsuited to this hypothesis. The evil plight of the Psalmist is made a reproach to the God of Israel, who seems to the heathen persecutor to have cast off His people (ver. 6, 7): the temple is inaccessible (ver. 9), but thanksgiving shall find acceptance, and 'please the LORD better than ox or bullock that hath horns and hoofs' (ver. 31): the final deliverance is to be of world-wide interest: 'Let the heaven and earth praise Him...For God will save Zion, and will build the cities of Judah' (ver. 34, 35).

We may conclude then, provisionally, that the Psalm deals with two characters:—

(*a*) A captive Israelite, recording his individual experience of the national calamity; conscious that what befel him was devised against others too, and expectant of no merely personal deliverance.

(*b*) Heathendom, plotting the subversion of the Jewish polity.

To which of these are the imprecatory utterances of ver. 22—25, and of 27, 28, best referred?

1. It is usual to explain the connection of ver. 21, 22, as follows. 'They had given him gall and vinegar for his food: let their food, their table, with all its sumptuousness and all its luxury, become a snare to take them;' where 'vinegar' is regarded as unwholesome, or at least distasteful. But it is granted that 'vinegar' is well suited to quench thirst[3]; nor does it stand for a thing distasteful *e.g.* in Ruth

---

[1] This refers to the title: 'upon Shoshannim.'

[2] וחס על בני הגלות יותר נכון.

[3] Rosenmüller, attempting to apply the received theory about these imprecations, urges that the meaning, *acetum*, must be rejected: '*nihil enim melius promtiusque sitim restinguit aceto.*'

ii. 14: where 'Boaz said unto her, At meal-time come thou hither, and eat of the bread, and dip thy morsel in the vinegar.' In Psalm lxix., it must not be assumed arbitrarily that the 'vinegar' is distasteful. Why may it not there too be a thing grateful to the palate of one athirst? tending, it may be, to inebriation[1]; but perhaps altogether harmless.

2. It is hard to determine precisely the nature of the 'gall.' Gesenius citing, 'papaveris *capita*' (Liv. I. 54), supposes it to be the poppy; which favours the hypothesis that it was calculated to induce stupefaction. 'Water of gall' denotes a stupefying drug in Jer. viii. 14; 'The LORD our God hath put us to silence, and given us *water of gall* to drink;' and a like meaning of 'gall' seems not inappropriate in Ps. lxix. 21. The *vinegar*, insidiously grateful to the palate, is drugged with *gall*, and thus proves a snare to the unsuspecting. The sufferer,—one of many[2]—receives drugged potions from the enemy; who would have '*their*' table become a trap to them in their security. Reft of sense and power, may they prove an easy prey. 'Let their habitation be desolate; and let none dwell in their tents.' So plot they, 'For they persecute [them] whom Thou hast smitten; &c.'

3. The enemy devise evil, not against an individual, but against the whole chosen people. The Psalmist, in the character of one of them, describes the outrage heaped upon himself, in the execution of their general plan; and hence the change from the singular ver. 21, to the plural in the following verses is accounted for. If this transition does not take place at the beginning of the first series of cursings, it must take place at its conclusion; or else, as seems still less suitable, in the middle of ver. 26. 'The plural in the second clause of the verse,' writes Mr Perowne, 'passes from the individual instance to the general conduct of these men, but implies at the same time that there are some few others exposed to the like treatment with himself.' Few or many, they are spoken of in

---

[1] Numb. vi. 3.

[2] He speaks as an ordinary Israelite: the calamity was national: the plot is not laid against him personally, but he comes within its range, and describes what he himself undergoes.

the plural, till in ver. 29 the one sufferer stands out as before, and then again is lost sight of finally in ver. 32.

V. *Other points in the Imprecations calling for Special Notice.*

1. In ver. 22, those on whom the curse lights are represented as *at peace*[1], if not *men of peace*. In Ps. lv. 20, the same word is applied to inoffensive sufferers, and it is said of the enemy: 'He hath put forth his hands against *such as be at peace* with him: he hath broken his covenant.' Elsewhere, the notion of *peace*, implies not unfrequently a certain moral excellence, thus:

> Mark the perfect; behold the upright:
> For there is a futurity to a man of *peace*.

Whereas the futurity of the wicked shall be cut off (Ps. xxxvii. 37, 38). The Psalmist is '*peace*,' in Ps. cxx. 7; his enemies, 'for war.' 'They speak not *peace:* but they devise deceitful matters against them that are quiet in the land' (Ps. xxxv. 20). In accordance with such usages as the foregoing, it is more natural to apply the description, *at peace* (Ps. lxix. 22), to the persecuted Israelites, than to their heathen persecutors. In other words, it is natural to suppose the first series of imprecations uttered *against*, not *by*, the Psalmist.

2. An objection to this view may be thought to arise from ver. 24. Is it likely that the heathen persecutors would curse the suffering Israelite in the form of an address to JEHOVAH? thus: 'Pour out thine indignation upon them: and let the furiousness of thine anger overtake them.' It may be granted that it is not likely. But the Psalmist is not giving the actual words of his enemy: the representation is subjective: the ills brought about by heathen instrumentality are referred to their first cause, and viewed as a Divine infliction; and the enemy, while compassing what is viewed as a manifestation of God's anger, may well be represented as praying that *the furiousness of that anger* may be displayed. A like remark applies to ver. 27, 28. The form of the curses

---

[1] לשלומים, '*tranquillis*.'

The Imprecations of Psalm LXIX.

is here too that in which they present themselves to the mind of the Psalmist, in whose view sin goes hand in hand with punishment; and whereas the enemy curses in *deed*, by striving to aggravate the calamities of Israel, the Psalmist—with his vivid conception of sin as necessarily involving punishment—depicts the enemy as praying that the LORD would add to his people's iniquities.

3. It is unnatural to say of heathens, *qua* heathens, 'Let them not come into *Thy righteousness;*' for God's 'righteousness' was the especial hope of the chosen people. God's 'righteousness' may include (or stand in parallelism with) salvation and deliverance, from *Captivity*, as from other evils. The following passages serve to illustrate this usage. 'Deliver me in *Thy righteousness*, and cause me to escape: incline Thine ear unto me, and save me...My mouth shall shew forth *Thy righteousness* and thy salvation all the day; for I know not the numbers thereof' (Ps. lxxi. 2, 15). 'Deliver me in *Thy righteousness*' (xxxi. 1). 'In Thy name shall they rejoice all the day: and in *Thy righteousness* shall they be exalted. For Thou art the glory of their strength: and in Thy favour our horn shall be exalted. For the Lord is our defence; and the Holy One of Israel is our king' (lxxxix. 16—18). 'Quicken me, O LORD, for Thy name's sake: for *Thy righteousness*' sake bring my soul out of trouble. And of Thy mercy slay mine enemies, and destroy all them that afflict my soul: for I am Thy servant' (cxliii. 11, 12). 'Behold, the days come, saith the LORD, that I will raise unto David a righteous Branch, and a King shall reign and prosper, and shall execute judgement and justice in the earth. In his days Judah shall be saved, and Israel shall dwell safely: and this is the name whereby he shall be called, THE LORD OUR RIGHTEOUSNESS' (Jer. xxiii. 5, 6). 'They shall come, and shall declare *His righteousness*' (Ps. xxii. 31). In this last passage, the primary reference is to *restoration from captivity*, as that whereby God's 'righteousness' displays itself. In Ps. lxix. 27 we have then, it might be conjectured, curses not against Gentiles but against Jews, for:

(a) Gentiles, as such, would not have been thought of at all as having hope to enter into God's righteousness.

(b) Another possible explanation is unnatural; for to say, 'Let them not come into Thy righteousness;' in the sense, 'Let them not be converted, and become objects of Thy mercy,' is out of harmony with the conclusion of the Psalm itself (ver. 34), not to say, with Psalms xxii., cii., &c. Whereas, on the other hand, a complete consistency is given to the Psalm, if the imprecations proceed from the enemy. They had plotted how their unsuspecting prey might be treacherously disabled:—'Let their habitation be desolate. Let them not experience the salvation of Thy righteousness, but be blotted out of the book of the living.'—In ver. 29 comes the assurance that these plots will fail. 'Poor as I am and sorrowful, Thy salvation shall set me up on high. For Thou wilt save Zion, and build the cities of Judah, and they that love Thy name shall dwell therein.'

VI. *Imprecations cited by St Paul from Psalm lxix.*

Some verses of this Psalm are quoted by St Paul, in Rom. xi. 9, 10, in his argument against the inference that God had cast away His people which He foreknew. The case of Elias leads up to the citation from the Psalm. 'Wot ye not what the Scripture saith of Elias? how he maketh intercession to God against Israel, saying, Lord, they have killed thy prophets, and digged down thine altars; and I am left alone, and they seek my life. But what saith the answer of God unto him? I have reserved to myself seven thousand men, who have not bowed the knee to the image of Baal. Even so then at this present time also there is a remnant according to the election of grace....What then? Israel hath not obtained that which he seeketh for: but the election hath obtained it, and the rest were blinded (according as it is written, God hath given them the spirit of slumber, eyes that they should not see, and ears that they should not hear;) unto this day. And David saith, Let their table be made a snare, and a trap, and a stumblingblock, and a recompense unto them: Let their eyes be darkened that they may not see, and bow down their back alway. I say then, Have they stumbled that they should fall? God forbid: but rather through their fall salvation is come unto the Gentiles, for to provoke them to jealousy' (Rom. xi. 2—11).

If we might argue back from the Apostle's citation of Ps. lxix. 22, 23, to the primary allusion of the verses cited, two considerations would suggest themselves.

1. Whether these imprecations proceed from the Psalmist or from his enemies, it takes away from their *prima facie* virulence, to note that they are not only temporal but *temporary*, in their nature. It is not the total ruin of persons cursed which, in St Paul's application of them, is contemplated, but the removal of an obstruction which opposes itself to the attainment of an all-important end. 'Have they stumbled that they should fall? God forbid.'

2. 'According to Rom. xi. 9, 10,' it has been said, 'the rejection of Israel may be best described in the words of Ps. lxix. 22, 23.' This being granted, it might be inferred, as not improbable, that the Psalm deals with those historical[1] circumstances which are most closely analogous to the rejection of the Jews, and the admission of the Gentiles to the Gospel covenant; and hence arises a retrospective argument in corroboration of the view already propounded, that Ps. lxix. refers to the Captivity. Between the Captivity and the later casting-off of Israel there is the intimate correspondence of type and antitype. The Jews were not, argues the Apostle, cast off for ever; but their rejection was for the reconciling of the world; and finally, by their restoration, there should be as life from the dead. In the season of captivity, it is notorious that their minds were opened to the spirituality of their religion and the non-essentiality of its external rites. Then, more distinctly than before, they contemplated the universality of the inheritance, which they had counted

---

[1] Other references in the context (e.g. that to Elias) being *historical*, it might be surmised that the reference in the Psalm is in like manner *historical*.

theirs alone; and to the hope of national restoration they added the loftier aspiration that all the ends of the world might turn to JEHOVAH, and all the kindreds of the nations bow before Him. Thus was the fall of them the riches of the world, and the diminishing of them the riches of the Gentiles.

3. The word κατάνυξις[1] (Rom. xi. 8) is used to describe the effect of *a stupefying draught;* the same word being used by the LXX. in connection with ποτίζω. In the original of the passage cited, the corresponding word is that for 'a deep sleep;' but, at the same time, there is an explicit contrast of the condition described with that of the *drunkard.* 'Stay yourselves, and wonder: cry ye out, and cry: they are drunken, but not with wine; they stagger, but not with strong drink. For the Lord hath poured out upon you the spirit of deep sleep' (Is. xxix. 9, 10). In Ps. lx. 3, κατάνυξις is again used with ποτίζω. 'Thou hast made us to drink the wine of astonishment.' By St Paul, this πνεῦμα κατανύξεως is represented as taking away sight and hearing (ver. 8), and as, in fact, working out the curse of Ps. lxix. 23, 'Let their eyes be darkened, that they may not see, and bow down their back alway.' It would seem then, so far as may be argued from St Paul's citation, that the darkening of eyes, &c. spoken of in Ps. lxix. was such as would result from a stupefying potion; and this seems to corroborate the opinion that a stupefying draught is described in the verse: 'They gave me also *gall* for my meat (?); and in my thirst they gave me vinegar to drink.' *i.e.* they drugged my food, contriving that my table might become a snare to take myself withal, &c. The objection to this explanation, which arises from the use of the plural (*their* table) rather than the singular, has been already adverted to. In its favour is its avoidance of an abrupt transition in the tone of the Psalmist, and the lack of any particle

---

[1] 'κατάνυξις h. l. notat πάθος ex frequentissima *punctione* in stuporem desinens' (Bengel). See Wratislaw, *Notes and Diss.* But may it not denote a *throbbing* and confusion of the brain, indicative of intoxication; or the internal *pricking* sensation which accompanies some forms of numbness?

to mark such transition. It may be well to reiterate, in conclusion, that the application of these curses is to be discussed independently of the *second* series, in ver. 27, 28; and that if the former proceed from the Psalmist, this of itself is no argument for assigning to him the latter also. The question of the application of the latter is mainly grammatical, and *not dependent upon any hypothesis with regard to the subject of the Psalm.* A certain phrase introduces these imprecations. The phrase is used once more, and once only, viz. in Ps. ii. 7. If this phrase is to be applied analogously in the two cases, then the imprecations of Ps. lxix. 27, 28 must be attributed to the Psalmist's enemies, and the Psalmist himself be taken as one against whom they are imprecated.

VII. *Further Citations from Psalm LXIX.*

'When it is said (Joh. xv. 25), that the enemies of Jesus hated Him without a cause, and this is looked upon as a fulfilment of Scripture, the reference,' writes Mr Perowne, 'is probably to ver. 4, though it may be also to xxxv. 19. To Him, and the reproach which he endured for the sake of God, St Paul refers the words of this Psalm (ver. 9), when he writes: For even Christ pleased not Himself; but, as it is written, *The reproaches of them that reproached Thee fell on me*' (Rom. xv. 3). The Cleansing of the Temple brings to the disciples' remembrance those other words of ver. 9: 'The zeal of *Thine house hath eaten me up*' (Joh. ii. 17). The 'zeal *of* &c.' in the Psalm, may have a similar meaning to, 'vengeance *of* &c.' above cited from Jer. l., li.; or it may mean more generally 'zeal for the honour of...;' 'zeal for God's service and worship.' Perhaps the former meaning of '*indignation*,' is the more appropriate; but, in any case, the profanation of the Temple by heathen violence which the Psalmist deplored, presents an analogy to its later profanation, which stirred the righteous 'zeal' of JESUS. 'In ver. 12,' continues Mr Perowne, 'we have a foreshadowing of the mockery of our Lord by the soldiers in the prætorium (Matt. xxvii. 27—30); in ver. 21, the giving of the vinegar and the gall found their counterpart in the scenes of the Crucifixion[1] (Matt. xxvii. 34). In Joh. xix. 28, there is an allusion, probably, to ver. 21 of this Psalm, and to xxii. 15. The imprecation in ver. 25 is said, in Acts i. 20, to have been fulfilled in the case of Judas Iscariot, though, as the words of the Psalm are plural, the citation is evidently made with some freedom.' Some MSS. however read '*their* (for *his*) habitation' in Acts i. 20, and with reference to this Dr Henry Owen writes in his *Modes of Quotation*:—'There is in this quotation, it must be acknowledged, some difficulty. And this difficulty I know not how otherwise to solve, than by observing that Judas is not here specified as the only traitor, though the chief and most infamous; but as the *guide* of *them* that took Jesus. And as the prophecy was now singularly fulfilled in Judas, the head; so, with reference to its plural construction, it was a plain presage, that the rest, the body of the Jews, would surely meet with the like fate—which fate they wofully experienced not long after.'

NOTES ON CHAPTER XI.

A. The rendering of Ps. ii. 7: 'I will declare *for* (i.e. so as to be) a decree,' is well supported. [With this use of אל חק, compare אל נכון, '*for* certain;' אל חנם '*to* no purpose.'] But whether this, or the usual rendering be right, it may be argued, that, as in Ps. ii., אספרה אל חק, '*I will declare &c.*' is followed by the actual words of the speaker's declaration; so in Ps. lxix., אל מכאוב חלליך יספרו, '*they declare &c.*,' might be expected to be followed by the actual words of the Psalmist's enemies, who are there represented as the speakers. It is more usual to render אל, *concerning*. Gesenius and Fuerst bring *one* example (Ps. xxii. 31) to prove a like meaning for ל, following ספר. But it may be suggested in passing, that יספר לאדני *perhaps* means, 'He shall be accounted for, or as, LORD [to

[1] See pp. 114—119.

that generation].' Thus, the verse may be freely rendered: 'A seed shall serve Him; the generation to come shall own Him for their LORD.'

B. It might appear that the received interpretation of this clause is more natural: this makes ver. 22—25, curses uttered by the Psalmist against his enemies. 'Let their table &c. *For*, or *because*, they have persecuted those whom Thou hast smitten.' Ps. xxxv. 7 might be quoted to support this:—'*For*...without cause have they digged a pit for *my soul*.' Perhaps the next verse in Ps. xxxv. should be attributed to the Psalmist's enemies, as Mr Mason suggests, thus:—'*saying*, Let destruction come upon him at unawares...' 'But *my soul* [ונפשי],' continues the Psalmist, 'shall exult &c.' The change to the singular, 'upon *him*,' favours this transference. The analogy of Ps. xxxv. thus explained, would favour the attributing of Ps. lxix. 22—26 to the Psalmist, and ver. 27, 28 to his enemies. But though the first imprecations in the two Psalms are not unlike ['Let their way be dark and slippery,' xxxv. 6; lxix. 23], there are some special arguments (*supra*) for supposing the persecutors to be the speakers in Ps. lxix. 22—26.

C. Let them be wiped out of the book *of the living*, or *of life*]. 'The figure is borrowed,' as Mr Perowne notes, 'from the civil lists or register in which the names of the citizens were enrolled. To be blotted out of this denotes exclusion from all the blessings and privileges of the theocracy, and therefore from all hope of salvation, as is evident from the next clause...the *righteous* being the true *Israelites* as in Hab. ii. 4.' This text has been much discussed with reference to predestination. [See Poole *in loc.*] But as regards the form of representation, the names of the persons spoken of would seem to be actually written in the book of life. They are not thought of as heathens, but as Israelites. Thus the argument of § 3, p. 237, is confirmed.

CHAPTER XII.

The Imprecations of Psalm CIX.

BEFORE referring to the original of this Psalm, it may be well to note some of the most striking features of the familiar English versions, from which the subjoined translation differs only in details, and those comparatively unimportant for our present purpose.

The Psalmist's enemies have overwhelmed him with false accusations (ver. 2), and rewarded him evil for good; but in his unmerited sufferings, he gives himself wholly and unreservedly to prayer[1]. 'Deliver me, for I am helpless and poor; and my heart is wounded within me. I go hence like the shadow that departeth; and am driven away as the grasshopper ... *Though they curse, yet bless* THOU; and let them be confounded that rise up against me, but let Thy servant rejoice' (ver. 21—28). The Psalmist is 'helpless and poor,' and an object of derision to his enemies; who are described in ver. 20, as 'those that speak evil against my soul.' If, then, they are expressly styled his cursers, and his resource is prayer to JEHOVAH for deliverance; it would seem *a priori* natural to assign the curses specified, not to the Psalmist as speaker, but to his enemies. This distribution of its parts seems to give to the Psalm a more complete structural consistency than do the usual renderings, which assume a sudden change of tone at ver. 6, and a return, at ver. 21, after a series

---

[1] ואני תפלה might be rendered idiomatically: 'but I [am all] prayer.'

of distinct imprecations, to the resigned prayerfulness of the opening verses. But with the proposed rearrangement, we have 1. An appeal to God against the malice and the false accusations of his adversaries. 2. A specification of the curses which they utter, and of the false charges (ver. 16—18) which they bring against him. 3. A contrast between the treatment which the persecuted man trusts to experience at the Lord's hand, and that which his adversaries desire for him. The concluding verses, whether imprecatory or predictive, express the Psalmist's joyful anticipation of his adversaries' discomfiture, and would thus seem to exclude any necessity for regarding him as the utterer of the former curses[1]. The curses, moreover, are directed against an individual; while—to except the disputed verses—there is no trace of any individual adversary, who stands out from the main body; not even, as before noticed, in ver. 20, which sums up the imprecations. In this verse, be it observed moreover, there is no direct expression of a wish; as the Bible version shews by its significant arrangement of the type. '*Let* this *be* the reward of mine adversaries &c.' The words in italics not occurring in the original, a more exact rendering would be: 'This [is] the reward &c.' This verse, which will be considered more at length below, constitutes the main objection to the proposed transference of the Imprecations; but, on examination, it will be found to be ambiguous in itself, and dependent, therefore, upon the context for its interpretation, as regards those of its words which contain the ambiguity. A general view of the Psalm being required to complete the argument, a version of it, amended in some particulars, is subjoined.

I. *Translation of the hundred-and-ninth Psalm.*

1. Hold not Thy tongue, O God of my praise.

2. For the mouth of the ungodly, yea the mouth of the deceitful is opened upon me : and they have spoken against me with false tongues.

---

[1] The Psalm being supposed structurally complete and symmetrical, the fact that the Psalmist's curses are found in one place serves (*pro tanto*) for a proof that they are not to be sought in another.

3. They compassed me about also with words of hatred: and fought against me without a cause.

4. For my love they are mine adversaries: but I [am all] prayer.

5. And they have rewarded me evil for good: and hatred for my love.

6. Set Thou a wicked man over him: and let Satan[1] stand at his right hand.

7. When he shall be judged, let him be condemned: and let his prayer be faulty.

8. Let his days be few: and let another take his office.

9. Let his children be fatherless: and his wife a widow.

10. Let his children wander continually (to beg and to seek *bread*[2]) out of their desolate homes.

11. Let the extortioner consume all that he hath: and let strangers spoil his labour.

12. Let there be none to extend mercy unto him: neither let there be any to favour his fatherless children.

13. Let his posterity be cut off: and in the next generation let his name be blotted out.

14. Let the iniquity of his fathers be remembered with the LORD: and let not the sin of his mother be blotted out.

15. Let them alway be before the LORD: that He may cut off the memory of them from the earth.

16. Because that he remembered not to shew mercy: but persecuted the afflicted man and needy, and the broken in heart, to death[3].

17. And he loved cursing, and it came unto him[4]: and he delighted not in blessing, but it was far from him.

18. And he clothed himself with cursing, like as with

---

[1] "In Zech. iii. 1: 'and he shewed me Joshua the High Priest standing before the angel of Jehovah, and the adversary (or, the Satan) *standing at his right hand* to be an adversary unto him,' Satan himself is doubtless meant. ...On the whole I prefer the more general word *adversary*,...especially as the same root occurs several times in the Psalm." (*Perowne*).

[2] *Lit.*: 'and let them seek and beg:' a semi-parenthetic sequel to ינועו, which is taken with מחרבותיהם.

[3] למותת, *to slay*.

[4] Cursing was familiar to him, and he to it.

The Imprecations of Psalm CIX. 247

his garment: and it came into his bowels like water, and like oil into his bones[1].

19. Let it be unto him as the cloke that he hath upon him: and as the girdle that he is alway girded with.

20. This is the reward of mine adversaries from the LORD[2]: and of those that speak evil against my soul.

21. But THOU, God, the LORD[3], deal-with-me according unto Thy name: because Thy mercy is good, O deliver me.

22. For I[4] am afflicted and needy: and my heart is wounded within me.

23. I am gone like a shadow when it declineth: I am shaken off[5] as a grasshopper.

24. My knees are weak through abstinence[6]: my flesh is dried up for want of fatness.

25. And I[7] am become a reproach unto them: when they look upon me they shake their head.

26. Help me, O LORD my God: O save me according to Thy mercy.

27. That they may know that this is Thy hand: that Thou, LORD, hast done it.

28. Though they curse, yet bless[8] THOU: and let them

---

[1] He drank it in thirstily (that is), and grew sleek upon it.

[2] זאת פעלת שטני מאת יהוה. 'Diess wirkten gern vom Herrn mir meine Feinde aus, Die meiner Seele Untergang geschworen. Aber du Herr! Ewiger! Thu' mir um deines Nahmens Willen.' (*Mendelssohn.*)

[3] Or, 'God *my* LORD' [Ps. xxxv. 23; xvi. 2]. 'This they imprecate against me from the LORD: but Thou art *my* LORD, &c.'

[4] Perhaps (in contrast with ver. 16): 'It is I that am afflicted...' The full form אנכי is used.

[5] 'Also I *shook* my lap, and said, So God shake out every man from his house, and from his labour, &c.' (*Neh.* v. 13.)

[6] If צום (Esth. v. 16) denotes abstinence in general—being לשון קיבוץ (*Kimchi*)—there may be a double contrast, in צום [cognate with צמא], and שמן; with the '*water*' and the '*oil*' of ver. 18.

[7] In ואני הייתי, the emphasis may be: 'Far from revelling in oppression, as they say, *I* am become a reproach unto *them*.'

[8] But perhaps it is better to make this an expression of trust, and not an imperative. 'Thou wilt bless, and (mine adversaries having been put to confusion) Thy servant shall rejoice.' See ver. 30, where the verbs are likewise futures.

be confounded that rise up against me : but let Thy servant rejoice.

29. Let mine adversaries be clothed with shame : and let them cover themselves with their own confusion as with a cloke[1].

30. I will greatly praise the LORD with my mouth : yea, I praise Him among the multitude.

31. For He shall stand at the right hand of the poor : to save him from those that condemn his soul[2].

II. In seeking to determine the true application of the curses in ver. 6—19, we shall consider :—

a. The introductory formula of ver. 5.

b. The retrospective summation of them, in ver. 20.

The collective Psalm will then be analyzed, and its corresponding parts compared one with another.

(*a*) As in Ps. xxii. 7, 8 a quotation is introduced without any introductory formula :—

> All they that see me laugh me to scorn :
> They shoot out the lip, they shake the head,
> 'He trusted on the LORD that He would deliver him :
> Let Him deliver him, seeing He delighted in him.'—

So it would be quite grammatical to refer Ps. cix. 6, &c. to the adversaries before spoken of, thus :

> And they have rewarded me evil for good :
> And hatred for my love,
> 'Set Thou a wicked man over him :
> And let Satan stand at his right hand, &c.'

More than this, the reference to an individual ['over *him,* &c.'], not to mention the lack of any adversative or transitional particle [e.g. '*Therefore* set Thou,' &c.], seems to mark the above as the obvious and *prima facie* meaning of the verses cited. The objection to this view, which will be next

---

[1] Contrast ver. 19.   [2] Contrast ver. 6, 7.

considered, is extraneous to the passage itself, being drawn from the supposed exigencies of a subsequent verse.

(*b*) The verses immediately following the imprecations are rendered in the Prayer-Book in a way commonly supposed to be a more or less faithful paraphrase of their meaning :—

'Let it thus happen from the Lord unto mine enemies: and to those that speak evil against my soul. But deal Thou with *me*, O Lord God, according unto Thy name: for sweet is Thy mercy.'

The more literal: 'This *is* the reward &c.,' *as explained by Mr Perowne and others*, differs little from the preceding; for, in each case, the Psalmist has been represented as imprecating direct curses upon an enemy; and the distinction between: 'Let this be the reward &c.;' and 'This is, or shall be, the reward;' seems, under the circumstances, little more than formal. If, however, the order of the words (ver. 20, 21) and their natural emphasis be attended to, the possibility of a very different explanation suggests itself. Mr Perowne preserves (*infra*) the order of the Hebrew:

This is the reward of mine adversaries from Jehovah,
And of them that speak evil against my soul.
But THOU, O Jehovah Lord, deal with me for Thy Name's sake,
For Thy loving-kindness is good: deliver Thou me.

From this it would seem that the contrast is not between 'mine adversaries,' and 'me,' but between those adversaries and evil speakers, and 'THOU, O Jehovah Lord:' not between their destruction and the Psalmist's deliverance, but between the curses which they imprecate and the loving-kindness of the Lord. Mr Perowne's form of words being retained, the required meaning may be elicited, by understanding 'the reward *of mine adversaries*' as a subjective genitive. This is mine adversaries' award unto me: this the sentence that they would procure against me from Jehovah, when they pray: 'Set Thou a wicked man over him. Let the iniquity of his fathers be remembered with Jehovah;

and let not the sin of his mother be blotted out; but let them always be before the Lord.'

That a person's wages or reward may mean not what he receives but what he bestows, is illustrated by the following passages. 'The wages *of* Sin[1] is death; but the gift *of* God is eternal life through Jesus Christ our Lord' (Rom. vi. 23). 'Lo, children are an heritage *of* the Lord: and the fruit of the womb is *His* reward' (Ps. cxxvii. 3). 'Behold, I come quickly; and *my* reward is with me, to give every man according as his work shall be' (Rev. xxii. 12).

III. *Isaiah xl. 10; lxii. 11, compared with Psalm cix. 20.*

In these verses of Isaiah, the word for '*reward*,' in Ps. cix. 20, is rendered '*work*.' 'Behold, the LORD God will come with strong hand, and His arm shall rule for Him: behold His reward is with Him, and His *work* before Him' (xl. 10). 'Behold, the LORD hath proclaimed unto the end of the world, Say ye to the daughter of Zion, Behold, thy salvation cometh; behold, His reward is with Him, and His *work* before Him' (lxii. 11). This meaning 'work' is indeed primary, but the meaning 'reward of labour' is well authenticated, and is by some applied in the verses quoted from Isaiah. Thus, Rosenmüller's rendering of the last clause of Is. xl. 10 is: '*et operæ pretium ejus coram facie sua;*' and Dr Henderson has in the same place: 'and His *recompense* before Him.'

1. If *recompense* be the true rendering, the verses in question seem to illustrate the construction which is required in Ps. cix. 20; '*His* recompense' being not what He is to receive, but what He is to bestow. So Rosenmüller, who explains the second hemistich, in each case, as a declaration that Jehovah has a recompense in store for His pious worshippers, and continues: 'Sistitur autem hic Deus ut imperator, cui, victori e bello reduci, præferuntur præmia inter probatæ fidei milites ab ipso dividenda.' Dr Henderson

---

[1] Sin being personified (ver. 16).

indeed remarks, on the other side, that 'The reward and recompense following are not those which the Messiah would bestow on others, but his own—what he himself had merited;' and affirms that this is the only sense of which the Hebrew word in question will admit. The question however is about the use of the pronoun '*His*.' Does He receive or bestow the recompense[1]? If the latter, then 'my enemies' recompense' might mean analogously the recompense to be bestowed by them; and, as in Isaiah it is said, 'His reward is with Him,' so here in Ps. cix. the recompense proceeds from (lit. *from-with*) Jehovah. From Him would they procure it for me.

But it introduces no essential variation, to take the primary meaning of the word for *recompense*, in Ps. cix. 20, and to explain the verse accordingly: 'This is my enemies' treatment of me;' *i.e.* the treatment which they would procure for me, from Jehovah. This meaning is, in a measure, favoured by the contrast: 'But THOU, *deal*, or *do*, with me &c.'

IV. *Outline of Psalm cix.*[2]

The foregoing explanations develop an intimate correspondence between the various portions of the Psalm.

It opens with an invocation of Divine help by one assailed with imprecations (ver. 3), and false charges (ver. 2), which are yet insufficient to rouse in him feelings of revenge, or to extinguish the memory of his former love (ver. 4).

Now follow

[i] The words of hatred (ver. 6—15, 19).
[ii] The false accusations (ver. 16—18).

'Thus,' writes the Psalmist, 'would my evil speakers have it done unto me. But Thou, Lord God, deal mercifully.'

We have next a refutation of the calumnious charges (ver. 22—25); and lastly, a deprecation of curses, with specific allusions to the several imprecations, superadded to a

---

[1] See note A, p. 258. [2] See note B, p. 258.

general prayer (or expression of trust) that the curses may turn to blessings (ver. 28, 30, 31); the discomfiture of the enemy being contemplated only as a necessary prelude to the Psalmist's deliverance (ver. 29).

V. *Comparison of ver. 16—18, with 22—25.*

1. They say that I remembered not to shew mercy; but persecuted the *afflicted and needy* to the last extremity. But it is I that am *afflicted and needy;* my heart is wounded within me: I go hence like the shadow that declineth; I am shaken off like a grasshopper.

2. They say that I revelled in oppression: that cursing was as water to my thirsty soul; as marrow and *fatness* to my bones. Alas! my knees are frail through abstinence: my flesh is dried up for want of *fatness*. Far from being the lordly contemner of others, I am a reproach, and an object of derision to them.

The Prayer-Book rendering of ver. 16, 17, is, indeed,

'His delight was in cursing, and it shall happen unto him: he loved not blessing, therefore shall it be far from him. He clothed himself with cursing, like as with a raiment: and it shall come into his bowels like water, and like oil into his bones.'

But (*a*) all the verbs must be rendered in the same tense, thus: 'He loved cursing, and it came unto him. He delighted not in blessing, and it stood aloof from him: &c. &c.'

And (*b*) the received explanations of the similes, 'like water,' 'like oil,' are scarcely accordant with the certain well-known biblical usages. *Water* is more commonly the symbol of something delicious; and *oil* is used in a good sense, even in such expressions as, 'smoother than oil,' applied to the words of the wicked; for it is the attractiveness of the words which is there described. In Job xv. 16, it is said: 'How much more abominable and filthy is man, which drinketh iniquity like water?' *i.e.* with delight, and greedily. And again, in Job xxxiv. 7: 'What man is like Job, who drinketh up scorning like water?' With the clause, 'and like oil into his bones;' may be compared, Prov. iii. 7, 8; xv. 30; and, by way of contrast, Prov. xvii. 22: 'Be not wise in thine own eyes: fear the Lord, and depart from evil. It shall be health to thy navel, and marrow to thy bones.' 'The light of the eyes rejoiceth the heart: and a good report maketh the bones fat.' 'A merry heart doeth good like a medicine: but a broken spirit drieth the bones.' See too Ps. lxxiii. 6, 7, 10.

VI. *Comparison of ver. 6—15, 19, 20, with 26—31.*

In ver. 20 it is said, with reference to the preceding curses: '*This* is the reward of mine adversaries from the Lord;' and in ver. 27, by way of contrast: 'Let them know that *this* [*i.e.* this salvation¹] is Thy hand. Though they curse, yet bless Thou.' Instead of an early grave, desolation, and oblivion, grant me to praise Thee among the multitude. Leave me not comfortless, but give me the comfort of Thy *grace* (ver. 12, 21). Appoint thou no wicked one to have charge over me. Let God, not Satan, stand at my right hand.

VII. To recapitulate some of the chief arguments in favour of this transference of the imprecations:

1. It is at least as natural, grammatically, to assign ver. 6 &c. to the Psalmist's enemies as to himself.

2. The persistent use of the singular, 'over *him*, &c. &c.' is thus explained; whereas, according to the more commonly received theories, there is some difficulty in accounting for it. In certain cases indeed, and those not rare, a collective or distributive singular may replace a plural; but such substitutions are not made altogether at random. In the present instance, although it is not affirmed that the singular is incapable of being explained in accordance with the usual hypothesis; it may be said that its explanation is less easy when that hypothesis is retained, than when it is rejected.

3. The verse (20) wherein lies almost the only difficulty in the way of accepting the view here adopted, is found upon examination to depend for its emphasis upon a contrast be-

---

¹ Aben Ezra. Kimchi.

tween the *animus* of the Psalmist's adversaries, and the mercy of the LORD. Moreover, it describes those adversaries in express terms as *speakers of evil*, which makes it more natural to attribute the preceding curses to them, than to one who was all 'prayer.'

4. Lastly, not only are violent transitions in tone and feeling thus avoided, but an intricate antistrophic correspondence is developed. After some prefatory verses, come specifications of

>   (*a*)   The words of hatred.
>   (*b*)   The false charges.

Next in order (ver. 20, &c.) there is a contrast between 'mine adversaries,' and 'Thou, God the LORD.'...Then follow, in inverse order,

>   (β)   An answer to the false charges.
>   (*a*)   A deprecation of the curses.

The concluding prayer corresponds to the initial curses; and, in general, (*a*) to (*a*), and (β) to (*b*); while at the turning point of the Psalm (as it may be called), to ver. 20 corresponds ver. 21.

VIII. *St Peter's citation from Psalms lxix; cix.*

In Acts i. 16, &c. we read that 'in those days Peter stood up in the midst of the disciples, and said ... Men and brethren, this Scripture must needs have been fulfilled[1], which the Holy Ghost by the mouth of David spake before concerning Judas, which was guide to them that took Jesus. For he was numbered with us, and had obtained part of this ministry. Now this man purchased a field with the reward of iniquity; and falling headlong, he burst asunder in the midst, and all his bowels gushed out. And it was known unto all the dwellers at Jerusalem; insomuch as that field is called in their proper tongue, Aceldama, that is to say, The field of blood. For it is written in the book of Psalms, Let his habita-

---

[1] ἔδει πληρωθῆναι.

tion be desolate, and let no man dwell therein: and his bishopric let another take. Wherefore of these men which have companied with us all the time that the Lord Jesus went in and out among us, beginning from the baptism of John, unto that same day that He was taken up from us, must one be ordained to be a witness with us of His resurrection.'

1. There is a difficulty in explaining the import of ὅτι, in the clause: '*For* he was numbered with us.' Some commentators have resorted to the expedient of rendering it, *although.* The Scripture must needs have been fulfilled in Judas, although he was among the chosen twelve.

2. Dr Wordsworth writes as follows:

ὅτι.] *Because* he was their ὁδηγός, or leader; *because*, being one of us, 'he knew the place' (Joh. xviii. 2) where, and the time when, He might be taken: and *because* it had been prophesied that one of His familiar friends should betray Christ (Ps. xli. 9).

3. 'There may be,' writes Dean Alford, 'an ellipse:— *guide to them that took Jesus: but this was not his only character—;* or the ὅτι may have reference to the substance of the prophecy, and serve to explain, ἡ ἔπαυλις αὐτοῦ, and ἡ ἐπισκοπὴ αὐτοῦ.' This last view leads to a plausible explanation, if the ὅτι be taken as explanatory, not of πληρωθῆναι τὴν γραφήν, but of προεῖπεν τὸ πνεῦμα τὸ ἅγιον. How, it may be asked, come the words cited to be applied to Judas? of whom, at first sight, they seem to make no mention. It might, indeed, be said that St Peter's application of them is a sufficient answer to the enquiry; but, the allusion to Judas, independently of Apostolic authority, being by no means obvious, it might have been expected that St Peter—arguing for instant action, and speaking to be understood—would explain the words cited, where ambiguous, and remove the difficulties, which to his hearers might appear to beset his application of those words. Nor does such an expectation rest upon mere surmise. In the following chapter of the Acts, another address by the same Apostle is recorded; and therein he is careful to explain in what way it comes to pass that a certain

Psalm (xvi) from which he quotes is applicable to the Messiah. 'The patriarch David being dead and buried, his words: *Neither wilt* THOU *suffer Thine holy one* . . . ; were unfulfilled in him, &c.;' and hence, they are to be applied to Christ[1]. In like manner, we may, perhaps, explain the clause, ὅτι κατηριθμημένος ἦν κ.τ.λ. How is 'this Scripture' applicable to Judas ? *Because* (ὅτι), by being numbered with us, he came into possession of an ἐπισκοπή. '*Ratio*, sub qua Judas hic memoratur, quia habuerat *munus*.'

4. How, again, is ἔδει πληρωθῆναι to be understood ?

Perhaps its *prima facie* meaning would be, that 'this Scripture' *ought to have been*[2] fulfilled, but was not—'ἔδει dicitur de eo quod fieri *debet*, nec tamen fit[3].' But there is a reading δεῖ, for ἔδει, which is not indeed comparable with the received reading in weight of MS. authority, but leads to an explanation which is in some respects simpler than that of ἔδει πληρωθῆναι. If δεῖ were the original reading, it would be easy to account for the change into ἔδει, as brought about by *assimilation* to the construction of Luke xxiv. 26 ; where our Lord, conversing with the two disciples on their way to Emmaus, demands, whether Christ *ought not to have suffered?* οὐχὶ ταῦτα ἔδει παθεῖν τὸν Χριστόν ;

5. Before proceeding to apply the foregoing variation, it should be remarked, that the Citation from the sixty-ninth Psalm is in the *singular*, whereas the original is *plural:* 'Let *their* habitation be desolate, &c.' It might occur to the commentator that perhaps, the Apostle here cites in its primitive form a passage which in the present Hebrew text is corrupt: but there is no ground for the surmise that the Hebrew text errs as regards the *plural* which it exhibits; for, whatever view of Citations generally, and of their relations to the original passages, be adopted, this same passage is cited again, viz. by St Paul in his Epistle to the Romans[4], and the *plural* (as

---

[1] See p. 148.

[2] ἔδει σε οὖν βαλεῖν (Matt. xxv. 27): ἔδει μὴ ἀνάγεσθαι (Acts xxvii. 21). With *relative* sentences the case is different. See Luke xxii. 7.

[3] This is very frequently implied. But see Joh. iv. 4. *Winer*.

[4] See § VI. p. 238.

in the Hebrew) there occurs. We may assume then, that St Peter has substituted the singular for the plural, on some principle of adaptation, which remains to be determined. One solution of the difficulty presented is, that the words cited, not without modification, from the sixty-ninth Psalm, are but preparatory to the words next cited, viz. from the hundred-and-ninth Psalm: 'His bishopric let another take.' On the assumption, that these last words are the *characteristic* of St Peter's citation, the argument may be stated as below.

The Ordination of St Matthias.

'That the disciples should have proceeded to this election after the departure of Christ, and before the coming of the Holy Spirit, is a proof that in the interval they felt no sense of desertion, no want of guidance for their own internal economy.' This remark of Mr Humphry contains a clew to the right understanding of St Peter's first address. The disciples, not yet 'endued with power from on high,' might well shrink from the grave responsibility of choosing a successor to fill up the number of THE TWELVE. The Apostle's advice is to proceed at once with a task from which they would fain draw back, and he urges, accordingly, as the most potent of incentives, that 'the Scripture must be fulfilled'[1]; $\delta\epsilon\hat{\iota}\ \pi\lambda\eta\rho\omega\theta\hat{\eta}\nu\alpha\iota\ \tau\grave{\eta}\nu\ \gamma\rho\alpha\phi\acute{\eta}\nu$. The argument is not without its parallels. The Apostle contends *a priori* for a certain course of action, because the Scriptures must needs be fulfilled: so, JESUS had addressed them *a priori*: 'How then shall the Scriptures be fulfilled that so it must be?' (Matt. xxvi. 54) Attention is arrested by St Peter's opening words: their explanation follows. What saith the Scripture on this matter? It has indeed an application to Judas, seeing that 'he was numbered with us[2], &c.:' from that estate he has fallen: the divine decree is $\lambda\acute{\alpha}\beta o\iota\ \acute{\epsilon}\tau\epsilon\rho o\varsigma$, 'his bishopric *let another take.*' This being the case, there must needs be chosen one to take his place, and

---

[1] 'It behoueth that the Scripture be fillid.' *Wiclif.*
[2] Compare Ps. xli. 9.

witness with us to the Lord's Resurrection[1]. The argument at once prevails: they choose out two: and the lot falls upon Matthias.

NOTES ON CHAPTER XII.

A. 'Is. xl. 10—his reward and the recompense of his work] That is, the reward and the recompense which he bestows, and which he will pay to his faithful servants: this he has ready at hand with him, and holds it out before him, to encourage those who trust in him, and wait for him.' *Lowth.*

B. To the same effect Green, Keate, Partridge and others.

1. Sykes, *Epistle to the Hebrews*, Introduction, p. xxxii:—

'Psalm cix.] Take this Psalm as containing a recital of the curses and imprecations of very slanderous men against the Psalmist himself, from ver. 5th to the 20th, and all is clear. David says, ver. 3, that they compassed him about with words of hatred; and, ver. 2, the mouth of the wicked and the mouth of the deceitful are opened against him, They have spoken against me with a lying tongue. And when he had urged his love and good actions to these enemies of his, ver. 4, 5, then follow the evil wishes they expressed against him to ver. 20. And at length, ver. 27, he says, Let them curse, but bless thou.'

2. Kennicott, *Remarks on Select Passages in the Old Testament:—*

'Psalm cix.] 'The thanksgiving of an innocent man, against whom an accusation had been brought by his adversaries for some capital crime, and whose ruin was thought so certain, that they already began to triumph over him as if condemned; when, by some remarkable interposition, his innocence is made to appear, the falsity of the accusation is manifested, and his adversaries are clothed with shame and disgrace.

---

[1] Compare δεῖ πληρωθῆναι, δεῖ οὖν μάρτυρα γενέσθαι (ver. 16, 21, 23); λαβέτω, λαβεῖν (ver. 20, 21).

'ver. 5] I render with the Arab. version, *imprecati sunt*, Arab. סוֹם or שׂוּם, *flagitavit*. This rendering makes the Psalm consistent; the curses being put in the mouth of the enemies of the Psalmist, to whom they certainly belong.

'ver. 20] The literal rendering is, *hæc est actio adversariorum meorum apud Jehovam*. For פְּעֻלָּה signifies *actio, molimen*. This is the subject-matter of their prayer.'

[Another rendering may be proposed for consideration. If, '*from* the Lord,' could mean, 'with the Lord's permission,' then ver. 20 might signify: 'This, God willing, is the reward of my adversaries...' i. e. *This would be their award, if He permitted.*]

3. Dr Sykes was answered by Dr Randolph, who lays chief stress upon the exigencies of ver. 20, but does not allude to any such proposed interpretation thereof as that adopted by Mendelssohn (p. 247, note), and in the text of the present Chapter.

4. Mr Perowne, who adopts the more usual explanation, writes on the Imprecatory Psalms :—

'An uninstructed fastidiousness, it is well known, has made many persons recoil from reading these Psalms at all. Many have found their lips falter when they have been called to join in using them in the congregation, and have either uttered them with bated breath and doubting heart, or have interpreted them in a sense widely at variance with the letter...But after all, whatever may be said of particular passages, the general tone which runs through the two covenants is unquestionably different. To deny this is not to honour Moses, but to dishonour Christ (Matt. v. 43, xix. 8). On the other hand, we must not forget that these imprecations are not the passionate longing for personal revenge: the singer undoubtedly sees in his enemies the enemies of God and His Church. They that are not with him are against God. And because the zeal of God's house even consumes him, he prays that all the doers of iniquity may be rooted out. The indignation therefore is righteous, though it may appear to us wrongly directed, or excessive in its utterance.'

CHAPTER XIII.

Christian and Jewish Ethics.

Lev. xix. 18; Deut. vi. 5; Matt. xxii. 37—40.

SOME special imprecatory passages having been considered in preceding sections, it is still to be sought, in what way the varied (though individually less striking) denunciations which are found elsewhere in the Old Testament, and may be said to pervade the Psalter, are to be reconciled with the forgiving spirit of the Gospel and the counsels of CHRIST. Do they indicate, as many affirm, a contrariety of principle between the Gospel and the Law? or do the two agree essentially, and differ only in phase; the one presenting certain principles in their most elementary form; the other exhibiting a later and continuous development of the same?

I. *Comparisons of Old and New Testament Language.*

1. The imprecations which abound in the Psalms would doubtless seem, for the most part, out of place, if transferred to the pages of a Gospel, or an Apostolic Epistle. This might be said, *e. g.* of such passages as:—' Lead me, O Lord, in Thy righteousness because of mine enemies; make Thy way straight before my face... Destroy Thou them, O God; let them fall by their own counsels; cast them out in the multitude of their transgressions; for they have rebelled against Thee' (Ps. v. 8, 10). 'Give them according to their

deeds, and according to the wickedness of their endeavours: give them after the work of their hands; render to them their desert. Because they regard not the works of the LORD, nor the operation of His hands, He shall destroy them, and not build them up' (xxviii. 4, 5). 'Let me not be ashamed, O LORD: for I have called upon Thee: let the wicked be ashamed, and let them be silent in the grave. Let the lying lips be put to silence; which speak grievous things proudly and contemptuously against the righteous' (xxxi. 17, 18). 'Let them be confounded and put to shame that seek after my soul: let them be turned back and brought to confusion that devise my hurt. Let them be as chaff before the wind: and let the angel of the LORD chase them. Let their way be dark and slippery; and let the angel of the LORD persecute them. For without cause have they hid for me their net in a pit, which without cause they have digged for my soul' (xxxv. 4—7). 'Let them be ashamed and confounded together that seek after my soul to destroy it; let them be driven backward and put to shame that wish me evil. Let them be desolate for a reward of their shame that say unto me, Aha, aha' (xl. 14, 15). 'But Thou, O LORD, be merciful unto me, and raise me up, that I may requite them. By this I know that Thou favourest me, because mine enemy doth not triumph over me' (xli. 10, 11).

2. But, on the other hand, there are passages comparable with these in the New Testament itself. Thus (not to mention our Lord's denunciations of the scribes and Pharisees, in Matt. xxiii.) we may instance St Paul's words: 'Alexander the coppersmith did me much evil: the LORD reward him according to his works' (2 Tim. iv. 14). Here ἀποδώσει should perhaps be rendered as a simple future, and not optatively. But the variation thus introduced is less important than such variations are sometimes thought to be; for the optative rendering would represent the Apostle as desiring that such and such a retribution might overtake the gainsayer; while, with the simple future, he would seem to contemplate the like issue as one to be desired. In any case,

St Paul's words may be compared with those denunciatory passages in the Psalms which are to the same extent ambiguous, and may even be set down as, not improbably, a free citation of Ps. xxviii. 4: δὸς αὐτοῖς κατὰ τὰ ἔργα αὐτῶν. The denunciatory expressions in the New Testament may be comparatively few; but the occurrence of even one would indicate either the recognition, in Christian theology, of principles in harmony with the severity of the former Dispensation; or a departure, under special circumstances, from the general law of Christ, which would require explanation, and might give rise to the conjecture that, in the Old Testament also, special considerations may be adducible in explanation of imprecatory passages.

3. That the difference in this matter between the Old Testament and the New is not one of principle, is further shewn by direct statements in the former, which are in complete harmony with the forgiving spirit of the latter. Thus, the Book of Proverbs dissuades from unseemly exultation over a fallen enemy, declaring it hateful in the sight of God: 'Rejoice not when thine enemy falleth, and let not thine heart be glad when he stumbleth, lest the LORD see it, and it displease Him, and He turn away His wrath from him' (Prov. xxiv. 17, 18). So in Job xxxi. 29, 30: 'If I rejoiced at the destruction of him that hated me, or lifted up myself when evil found him: Neither have I suffered my mouth to sin by wishing a curse to his soul.' Again: 'Thou shalt not hate thy brother in thine heart: thou shalt in any wise rebuke thy neighbour, and not suffer sin in him. Thou shalt not avenge, nor bear any grudge against the children of thy people, but thou shalt love thy neighbour as thyself: I am the LORD' (Lev. xix. 17, 18). In Deut. xxxii. 35, JEHOVAH speaks: 'To Me belongeth vengeance, and recompense; their foot shall slide in due time: for the day of their calamity is at hand, and the things that shall come upon them make haste.' The first part of this verse is quoted, in Heb. x. 30, as predictive of Divine retribution to such as have 'done despite unto the Spirit of grace,' 'For we know Him that hath said, *Vengeance*

belongeth unto Me, I will recompense, saith the LORD. And again, *The Lord shall judge His people* (Ps. cxxxv. 14). It is a fearful thing to fall into the hands of the living God.' But in Rom. xii. 19, the same passage from Deuteronomy is cited as a dissuasive from vindictiveness: 'If it be possible, as much as lieth in you, live peaceably with all men. Dearly beloved, avenge not yourselves, but rather give place unto wrath: for it is written, *Vengeance is mine, I will repay,* saith the Lord.' The Law then contains the Gospel teaching; the Gospel illustrates the practice of the Law. What is the relation of the doctrine to the practice? How is Christian charity to be reconciled with legal severity?

II. *An Interpretation of Rom. xii. 20, 21; Prov. xxv. 21, 22.*

A solution of the difficulty above propounded is contained in the vexed passage: 'Therefore, if thine enemy hunger, feed him; if he thirst give him drink: for in so doing thou shalt heap coals of fire on his head. Be not overcome of evil, but overcome evil with good' (Rom. xii. 20, 21). Bishop Patrick remarks, not quite conclusively, upon the *coals of fire,* &c.: 'If he have the least spark of goodness in him, it will work a change in his mind, and make him throw off all his enmities; or, if it have the contrary effect, he shall have so much the sorer punishment, and thou shalt not lose thy reward, which the Lord himself shall give thee.' Dean Alford thus states the case: 'The expression ἄνθρακας πυρός occurs repeatedly in Ps. xviii., of the *Divine punitive judgments.* Can those be meant here? Clearly not, in their bare literal sense. For however true it may be that ingratitude will add to the enemy's list of crimes, and so subject him more to God's punitive judgment, it is impossible that to *bring this about* should be set as a precept, or a desirable thing among Christians. Again, can the expression be meant of the *glow and burn of shame* which would accompany, even in the case of a profane person, the receiving of benefits from an enemy? This *may* be meant; but it is not probable, as not sufficing for the majesty of the subject. Merely to *make an enemy ashamed of himself*, can hardly be upheld as a motive for action. I understand the words, *For in* this doing, you will be taking the most effectual vengeance; as effectual as if you heaped coals of fire on his head.' Although the above seems on the whole unsatisfactory, yet *to heap coals of fire*, &c., is most naturally taken as expressive of vengeance and destruction, as *e. g.* in Ps. xi. 6: 'Upon the wicked He shall rain snares, fire and brimstone, and an horrible tempest: this shall be the portion of their cup.' Hence, it is not likely that 'the expression is used in a good sense,' as some think, and as the following remarks of Dr Macknight express: 'The metaphor,' writes this commentator, 'is supposed to be taken from the melting of metals, by covering the ore with burning coals. This being understood, the meaning will be, In so doing, thou wilt mollify thine enemy, and bring him to a good temper. This no doubt is the best method of treating enemies. For it belongs to God to punish the injurious, but to the injured to overcome them, by returning good for evil.' Augustine concludes: 'ut intelligas, carbones ignis esse urentes pœnitentiæ gemitus, quibus superbia sanatur ejus, qui dolet se inimicum fuisse hominis, a quo ejus miseriæ subvenitur.'

There is, however, another way of explaining the difficult verse in question, which allows its most natural meaning to the phraseology employed. To heap coals of fire upon an enemy, would imply an uncompromising enmity, not to be satisfied by anything less than the extermination of the foe. In some sense, the Christian is supposed to desire such a consummation, and is encouraged in the attempt to compass it: nor does any difficulty arise in reconciling this with such precepts as, 'Love your enemies,' if it be remembered that the latter are plain practical directions for the conduct of life, while the verse under discussion deals more directly with first principles and the nature of things. In it the word 'enemy' stands, in part, as an abstraction, and signifies rather enmity and antagonism, than the individual in whom the enmity resides. The Christian may, or must, desire to root out the enmity; and when this is done, the enemy, *qua* enemy, will have been destroyed. The individual (never himself the object of hatred) remains, but the enemy has disappeared, and his place knows him no more: he who was an enemy before, has, *qua* enemy, passed out of being; a deadly vengeance has been exacted; coals of fire have been heaped upon his head. Or, to put the case rather differently: The word enemy symbolizes the complex notion of a person in relation with certain qualities not inherent; and when that relationship comes to an end, then, by its dissolution, the complex being, 'enemy,' is *ipso facto* destroyed. Not unlike, from one point of view, is the case of an *idol*, which 'is nothing in the world.' The essence of an *idol* is an imaginary relationship between *e.g.* 'a stock of a tree' and certain qualities; and the idol is *ipso facto* destroyed when the worshipper's regard for that 'stock of a tree' has vanished. Conversely, the idol is not necessarily destroyed by the burning of the 'stock,' seeing that the false idea of it may still remain: and, in like manner, an 'enemy' is not annihilated by the physical destruction of a person hated, unless the *idea* of the enemy then vanishes. But even thus, if the enmity does indeed cease with the death of the enemy, his physical destruction will but have induced a change of mind in the survivor (which might have been effected by some other means), and will not have contributed in any direct way to the destruction of the 'enemy.' In popular language, *to kill an enemy*, is to kill a *person*, whether or no the idea of enmity survives; but, strictly speaking, the destruction of an enemy can be effected only by the eradication of enmity; a process which stands in no direct relation to the physical destruction of an opponent[1]. St Paul, following the Parœmiast, is *not* using popular language, when he affirms that, to succour a distressed enemy is to heap coals of fire upon his head.

[1] St Paul contemplates a *destruction* of enemies, which is a reversal of the process of *making* enemies.

III. *On the Christian duty of Forgiveness.*

There are some confused popular notions on the subject of the Christian duty of forgiving enemies, which take their rise from the assumption that there is some inherent virtue in an unprincipled mercy, and that charity should be cognisant of no distinction between light and darkness. But WHY *are we to forgive our enemies?*

1. Charity, taking the form of compromise, is a condition of imperfection: for in an ideal state of existence which shews things as they are, there is no room for charity which 'thinketh no evil,' and for the nice adjustment of essential contrarieties. Right must enter upon the contest without misgiving, and engage in a war of extermination with wrong absolute and irreclaimable. And such must be our mode of representation, when the principles and workings of good and evil are to be set forth as abstractions, though in a concrete form. But in actual life we find none absolutely good, and none whom we can declare absolutely and irreclaimably bad; and hence, precepts for guidance in practical affairs may differ conspicuously from such as relate to abstract good and evil, and presuppose an ideal state of things. Christian Charity, hoping all things, allows for the existence of latent good, and has faith in a Divine Power which can reclaim those in whom evil most preponderates: but if the Christian's enemies were absolutely evil, and known of a certainty to be incapable of amendment, his rightful attitude would be one of uncompromising hostility, and there would be no place for the injunction: 'Love your enemies.'

2. Not to desire the discomfiture of an enemy is *contrary to nature*. The Apostle, granting this, and making it the groundwork of his argument, shews what is the most efficacious weapon that can be employed: the benignant treatment of an enemy is the readiest way to overcome him: 'In so doing thou shalt heap coals of fire on his head. Be not overcome

of evil, but overcome evil with good;' *i.e.* perhaps: 'I say not, that you should yield and allow yourselves to be overcome by evil; but rather that you should resist and overcome it; and that, by the most potent weapon, *good.*' The Psalmist takes it as evidence of God's favour towards him, that 'mine enemy doth not triumph over me;' CHRIST himself by His passivity and non-resistance evinces no desire that His enemies may triumph over Him, nor indifference as to the issue of their antagonism: in a word, wherever the mutual relations of persons and things can be symbolized under the form of a contest, the desire to discomfit one's enemy must of necessity enter as one element into the representation.

IV. *Distinction between practical and ideal Ethics.*

It has been remarked above, that our Lord's *practical* precepts are, in some cases, unsuited for an ideal state of things; and it follows as a natural consequence, that representations which presuppose such an ideal state may be *prima facie* at variance with, while yet not actually opposed to, the doctrine of CHRIST. The Psalmists being for the most part conversant with an ideal condition of affairs, the above remark is applicable to their compositions. The characters which they introduce are, in certain cases, absolutely good, or absolutely evil: they depict sin, truth, purity, ungodliness, &c. in the abstract: the Psalmist, if not an embodiment of righteousness, is at least *on the side of right*, the object of Jehovah's care, calling to Him for aid: his enemies are 'the wicked,' 'the workers of iniquity,' 'the blasphemer;' and hence, it is only natural that a Psalmist should pray, not *for*, but *against*, his enemies, and that he should desire their destruction; seeing that they are regarded as embodiments of evil, and are not thought of as capable of amendment.

Again, the figure of a contest being presupposed, it is scarcely necessary to remark, that the success of one implies the discomfiture of another; and that in the description of a battle it is, so to say, immaterial from which point of view the issue is regarded. It has been thought however that the directness with which the Psalmists contemplate the destruction of their enemies is out of harmony with the Christian spirit, which would choose rather to dwell upon the victory of faith, and to cast into the back-ground the implied defeat of the opposing powers of evil. It has been thought too, that if the latter is to be dwelt upon at all, it should be with less of detail than the Psalms exhibit. (*a*) As a practical answer to the former of these two objections, it may be urged that the discomfiture of enemies is prayed for, in no unchristian sense, in our National Anthem:

>Scatter her enemies,
>And make them fall:

and in *A Prayer for the Queen's Majesty*: 'strengthen her that she may vanquish and overcome all her enemies.' (*b*) But the objections to certain imprecations in the Psalms may be said to spring almost entirely from their particularity and detail. Is not this at least at variance with the tenour of Christian teaching? The answer to this is obvious. The thing objected to is essential to the completeness of the broad concrete representations of Hebrew poetry, which are very far removed from euphemistic abstractions of modern phraseology; and not only so, but parallel representations are found in the work of a Christian Apostle, which concludes the Canon.

V. *The Curse of Babylon, Ps. cxxxvii.* 8; *Rev. xviii.* 6.

Of all denunciatory passages in the Psalms not as yet specially considered, the most striking is the curse of Babylon in Ps. cxxxvii. 8, 9: 'O daughter of Babylon, who art to be destroyed; happy shall he be that rewardeth thee as thou hast served us. Happy shall he be that taketh and dasheth thy little ones against the stones.' Whatever the true explanation of the difficulty which the foregoing passage raises, it may be remarked that the Apocalypse contains passages which may well be compared with it. The description of the fall of Babylon in Rev. xviii. is cast in the Old Testament mould, and borrows one of its expressions from the Psalm in question:—'*Reward her even as she rewarded you*[1] (Ps. cxxxvii. 8), and double unto her double according to her works: in the cup which she hath filled fill to her double. How much she hath glorified herself, and lived deliciously, so much torment and sorrow give her: for she saith in her heart, I sit a queen, and am no widow, and shall see no sorrow. Therefore shall her plagues come in one day, death, and mourning [ἀτεκνία καὶ χηρεία, Is. xlvii. 9], and famine; and she shall be utterly burned with fire: for strong is the Lord who judgeth her... Rejoice over her, thou heaven, and ye holy apostles and prophets; for God hath avenged you on her.' As regards sustained severity of tone, the passage of which this forms a part can scarcely be said to fall short of 'the varied, deliberate, carefully constructed, detailed anathemas of the Psalms.'

VI. *The Psalms, being poetical, are to be interpreted non-naturally.*

1. The opinion that the Psalmists' denunciations were directed against their spiritual enemies has been maintained by some as the means of accounting for the semblance of vindictiveness which attaches itself to some of them: but on the other hand this explanation has been characterized as *non-natural*, and on that account to be rejected. Advocates of the theory in question (which is at least plausible) have sometimes indeed exaggerated its non-naturalness, by taking the characters introduced in the Psalms for more complete abstractions than they are, and neglecting the natural element altogether. For David, contemplating the destruction of his enemies, is not a mere abstraction; though, on the other hand, to his *natural* feelings he superadds the consciousness that he is the favoured of Jehovah: 'The Lord is on my side.' 'Zion,'

---

[1] The original, את גמולך שגמלת לנו (*Thy reward* wherewith thou hast rewarded us), illustrates the use of the genitive in Ps. cix. 20. See p. 250.

again, is not the advanced abstraction of a later age but the Psalmist speaks of it with the feelings of a patriot, yet all this notwithstanding, he feels, at the same time, that it is the Holy City[1]. The descriptions in the Psalter are something more than natural, even if not altogether spiritual; and, being moreover poetical and ideal, they are to be compared with the Apocalyptic Vision, rather than contrasted with the Sermon on the Mount. To characterize an interpretation of a poetical passage as non-natural is not always to condemn it, for such interpretations are, in many cases, plainly necessary, and to admit none but such as are natural would lead ofttimes to ludicrous results.

2. It has been urged above that the Psalms are to be treated as poetical and ideal, and their interpretation, especially as regards some imprecatory passages, to be modified accordingly. All this notwithstanding, it may be, that those who used the Psalter, in a manner misapplied it; and that, through faulty and restricted notions of God's purpose, and a wrong estimate *e.g.* of the place of the literal Zion in the Divine economy. This consideration, be it remarked, is an important element in the distinction between the Ethics of Christianity and the Ethics of Judaism.

VII. *Representative Characters described in the Psalms.*

A recent commentator thus sets forth the difficulty presented by the Old Testament imprecations:—

'Now the real source of the difficulty lies in our not observing and bearing in mind the *essential* difference between the Old Testament and the New. The older dispensation was in every sense a sterner one than the new. The spirit of Elias, *though not an evil spirit*, was not the spirit of Christ

---

[1] It is a part of the Hebrew style to express spiritual ideas by types. Thus in Rev. ii. 20, an evil principle is denounced under the name of Jezebel. So, by Zion and Babylon are understood their suprasensual counterparts. It is hard to assign limits to the *natural* and the *spiritual* in the conceptions which such typifications suggested to a Jew.

(Luke ix. 55). "The Son of Man came not to destroy men's lives, but to save them." And through Him His disciples were made partakers of the same spirit. But this was not the spirit of the older economy[1]. The Jewish nation had been trained in a sterner school. It had been steeled and hardened by the discipline which had pledged it to a war of extermination with idolaters, and however necessary such a discipline might be, it would not tend to foster the gentler virtues; it is conceivable how even a righteous man, under it, feeling it to be his bounden duty to root out evil wherever he saw it, and identifying, *as he did*, his own enemies with the enemies of Jehovah, might use language which to us appears unnecessarily vindictive. To men so trained and taught, what we call "religious toleration," was a thing not only wrong, but absolutely inconceivable[2].'

So far, however, as a righteous man identifies 'his own enemies with the enemies of Jehovah,' and has no misgiving about the accuracy of his estimate; it is clearly incumbent upon him to dismiss the thought of compromise and toleration; nor do even extreme measures render him amenable to the charge of *unnecessary vindictiveness*. But a more enlightened view of things, and a clearer insight into the failings and the capacities of man's moral nature, shews the necessity for that toleration (with a view to amendment) which Christianity enjoins. Christianity, no less than Judaism, is 'pledged to a war of extermination with idolaters,' and with every kind of evil: but the former differs as regards its mode of warfare from the latter; inasmuch as it has a clearer insight into the complexities of human character, and the difference between the sinner and his sin. 'Resist, be not overcome by, evil,' is their common teaching; but the former counsels the more excellent way. Charity (it proclaims) is the most effectual disintegrant, whereby the evil may be separated from the good.

[1] Psalms lxix, cix, cxxxvii have been thought plain proofs of 'the essential difference &c.' But, as cited by SS. Peter, Paul, and John, they must be regarded as capable of a New Testament application.

[2] Perowne, on Ps. xxxv. 22.

VIII. *The Growth of Charity.*

There are two ways in which knowledge may affect conduct, and contribute to that charitableness which Christianity requires.

1. The Psalter is adapted to an ideal and absolute state of things, and its language is such as we recognize as appropriate, when spiritual things and the final separation of good and evil are contemplated. It has indeed been urged, that their comparative ignorance of all that related to the future state and the workings therein of the Divine judgements, led the Psalmists to desire, and express a longing-for, the temporal destruction of the wicked. Thus, Mr Perowne:—'Once more, the very fact that a dark cloud hid God's judgment in the world to come from the view of the Old Testament saints, may be alleged in excuse of this their desire to see Him take vengeance on His enemies here. How deeply the problem of God's righteousness exercised their minds, is abundantly evident from numerous places in the Psalms. They longed to see that righteousness manifested. It could be manifested, they thought, only in the evident exaltation of the righteous, and the evident destruction of the wicked here.' They used temporal imagery to express the spiritual idea of the Divine judgements, and exhibited the working of those judgements in time, rather than in eternity. Hence must arise an apparent (but not real) contrariety of principle between the Old Dispensation and the New; for Christian Charity, as in the parable of the Tares, contemplates a final separation between good and evil, and tolerates the admixture of evil in time, only that it may the more effectually, and without injury to the good, be cast away in eternity. This would seem to contribute somewhat to the understanding of the Psalmists' frame of mind; or, if so much be not granted, it at least justifies the *Christian use and application* of certain passages objected to. Many other passages in the Psalter, such as those which portray the peaceful issue of righteousness, are

expressed in terms strictly applicable only to the life in the flesh; and are yet more broadly interpreted by Christians (and that without hesitation) to the spiritual life. Why should not certain imprecatory passages be treated likewise? It is usual to apply a 'non-natural' interpretation to the former[1]: why not to the latter? But, to conclude, this one thing will perhaps be granted: that the prospect of a future retribution tends to induce longsuffering in the present, and thus Christian Charity is naturally *developed* from Legal severity; and that, by the clearer Revelation of Divine Truth.

2. It has already been remarked, that, so long as a Psalmist *e.g.* viewed himself as on the Lord's side, it was permissible, not to say required, that he should use expressions which may seem 'unnecessarily vindictive,' to those who view him as other than a representative of truth and righteousness, and his enemies as neither worse nor better than ordinary men. It might however be asked, what was the practical effect of such representations upon the Jewish mind, and whether exclusive and exaggerated views of their religious *status* were not thereby encouraged; for while in ideal representations intolerance is a necessity, in life and practice it is a product of ignorance and prejudice; seeing that in the one case good and evil are supposed discernible; while in the other they are confusedly joined together. In earlier times, doubtless, if the Jew did not exterminate the idol-worshippers, their idolatry would have corrupted the Jew; and hence it was necessary to maintain uncompromisingly certain broad distinctions, and to sanction intolerance, as a concession to acknowledged weakness. This fostered, doubtless, a spirit of exclusiveness, and was directly favourable to that confusion

---

[1] Cp. Ps. xxxvii. 25: 'I have been young, and now am old: yet have I not seen the righteous forsaken, nor his seed begging bread.' Such passages are not taken to mean, that good men escape outward ills and privations. One of two *non-natural* interpretations must be accepted. Either (1) ills are no ills, but "all things work together for good to them that love Him;" or (2) the ideally righteous man is described, and the Psalmist intends only to express that the ultimate *tendencies* of virtue are sufficiently indicated by the course of nature. Compare Pss. xxxiv. 10; lxxiii. 2 sqq.

between positive precepts and negative, which led to the development of: 'Thou shalt love thy neighbour;' into: 'Thou shalt love thy neighbour, and hate thine enemy.'

3. The ancient precept contained the common principle of the old and the new moralities, which differed as regards the largeness of their interpretations of the one word, 'neighbour.' The word was an expansive one, interpretable, in the first instance, in the most restricted sense; but equally applicable in the broadest sense which increased knowledge and experience could suggest. As, in the individual, there is a continuous growth of the affections, through the several phases, domestic, social, &c.—their sphere widening continually—so the narrowest interpretation of the precept: 'Thou shalt love *thy neighbour*,' was historically the undeveloped form of its Christian acceptation. To interpret it, at any time, as implying that, 'thy neighbour *only*' was to be loved, was to reverse its tendency, by importing into it a negative element from without. The like may be said of other Mosaic precepts which have not passed unchallenged; as, for example, of that to which our Lord thus refers, by way of contrast: 'Ye have heard that it hath been said, An eye for an eye, and a tooth for a tooth' (Ex. xxi. 24) : 'But I say unto you, That ye resist not evil: but whosoever shall smite thee on thy right cheek, turn to him the other also' (Matt. v. 38, 39). It seems, at the first glance, that the Christian principle, in the matter of retaliation, is here contrasted with that of Mosaic law; but a distinction drawn above should be once more applied. CHRIST is giving practical precepts to the multitude, and teaching them that, whereas by Mosaic law it was permitted to exact an equivalent for an injury—eye for eye, tooth for tooth—in the Christian code the spirit of vindictiveness was not recognized, except as evil. Thus there is the *practical* difference and contrast, that Moses gave 'eye for eye, &c.:' but not so CHRIST. But in *principle* there is no contrast, as St Augustine admirably sets forth. The injunction was not imposed as an incentive to revenge, but as a restriction of it: '*non fomes sed limes furoris est.*' 'Who

would rest content, in a moment of anger, with a mere equivalent for injury received? Do not we see men who have been but slightly injured, thirsting for the blood of the offender, and not to be satisfied by anything short of his death?' The *Lex Talionis* was instituted to limit this extravagant vindictiveness: 'lex, justum modum figens, pœnam talionis instituit: hoc est ut qualem quisque intulit injuriam, tale supplicium pendat.' Moses, then, does not here encourage vindictiveness, but propounds in an elementary form that same principle of self-restraint which Christianity develops.

4. The above may suffice to illustrate, how the moral precepts of our Lord are to be reconciled with the system of 'the Law and the Prophets,' of which they are, and indeed professedly, developments. The Mosaic precepts are to be interpreted not statically, so to say, but dynamically: not as fixed and stereotyped results in legislation, but as signs which register the extent of a still continuing progress: or as special manifestations of a vital power, in due time to be embodied in a higher organism. It is easy to gather from examples, the possibility of reconciling directly opposite courses of conduct with one and the same principle of action; the contrariety being brought about solely by difference of knowledge. There is a zeal according to knowledge, and there is a zeal not according to knowledge: and the two may lead to opposite courses of conduct, in persons whose *animus* and intention is the same. It is notorious that in common affairs ignorance is continually prompting men to act in ways in which but for ignorance they would never have acted; and, in particular, that it gives occasion to harsh judgements, and severities of procedure, which would have been abstained from if the results of after experience could have been anticipated. Where knowledge fails, 'Charity,' allowing for the lack of knowledge, 'thinketh no evil;' but 'beareth all things, believeth all things, hopeth all things, endureth all things' (1 Cor. xiii. 5, 7).

IX. *The Originality of Christian Ethics.*

The old problem of the Originality of Christian Ethics has been much discussed from age to age, and various solutions of it have been attempted. A full discussion of the difficulty being here impracticable, it may suffice to call attention to a few particulars.

1. By our Lord, as by His Apostles, the Old Testament is referred to as the ground of Christian Ethics. They make no profession of inventing precepts which are not contained implicitly in the existing code. 'Think not that I am come to destroy the law, or the prophets: I am not come to destroy, but to fulfil' (Matt. v. 17). And, again, the saying quoted, almost more than any other practical precept, as characteristic of our Lord's teaching, is enforced by the argument that it is a gathering up of what the Law and the Prophets contained. 'Therefore *all things whatsoever ye would that men should do to you, do ye even so to them*[1]*:* for this is the law and the prophets' (Matt. vii. 12). St Paul uses the same argument, that '*it is written*,' when he would enforce the duty of forgiveness, 'Avenge not yourselves... *for it is written*, Vengeance is mine; I will repay, saith the Lord. Therefore if thine enemy hunger, &c.' (Rom. xii. 19, 20).

2. It might seem that our Lord's teaching was novel in respect of its exhibiting the twofold Law of Love as the sum of Old Testament morality. Thus, in Matt. xxii. 40, Christ is represented as answering to the lawyer's question: 'Thou shalt love the Lord thy God with all thy heart, and with all thy soul, and with all thy mind. This is the first and great commandment. And the second is like unto it, Thou shalt love thy neighbour as thyself. *On these two commandments hang all the law and the prophets.*' But the addition in St Mark's account (xii. 32): 'Master, Thou hast said the truth;'

---

[1] See also Luke vi. 31.

might imply that the answer to that oft-mooted question was no new one, but rather that which was *recognized* as true. In another passage—introductory to the Parable of the Good Samaritan—'a certain Lawyer,' gives the two commandments, *To love God*, and, *To love one's neighbour*, as a summary of the law. He is asked: 'What is written in the law? how readest thou?' And he answers: 'Thou shalt love the Lord thy God with all thy heart, and with all thy soul, and with all thy strength, and with all thy mind; and thy neighbour as thyself' (Luke x. 26, 27). But the fact that St Paul grounds this equivalence on reason solely, goes far to prove that he did not regard the mere statement of it as a characteristic novelty in the Christian scheme. 'Love,' writes the Apostle, 'worketh no ill to his neighbour: *therefore* love is the fulfilling of the law¹' (Rom. xiii. 10).

3. A modern advocate of the Talmud has, in the course of an attractive Article², enlarged the popularity of a celebrated anecdote of Hillel and thereby caused perplexity to some, who had been accustomed to set down the supposed invention by our Lord of the precept already quoted from Matt. vii. 12, as evidence of the Divine origin of Christianity. The anecdote referred to runs as follows:—'One day a heathen went to Shammai... and asked him mockingly to convert him to the law while he stood on one leg. The irate master turned him from his door. He then went to Hillel, who received him kindly and gave him that reply—since so widely propagated—*Do not unto another what thou wouldest not have another do unto thee. This is the whole Law, the rest is mere commentary³*.' But without the aid of Talmudic lore, it may be seen that the substance of Christ's precept had been already expressed; for, shades of difference apart,

---

¹ In Joh. xiii. 34, the words, 'A *new* commandment I give unto you, That ye love one another,' might seem to imply, that the law of mutual love was put forward as new. But the words following explain wherein lay the novelty: '*As I have loved you*, &c.'

² *Quarterly Review*, No. 246.

³ דעלך סני לחברך לא תעביד זו היא כל התורה כולה ואידך פירוש היא. Buxt. *Lex.* 1508. Lightfoot, Matt. vii. 12.

Hillel's saying (the converse of our Lord's precept) agrees with Tobit iv. 15: '*Do that to no man, which thou hatest.*' It should be noticed, however, that, whereas the saying of Hillel, as above rendered, is couched in the familiar phraseology of the Gospels, its more literal rendering: '*That which is hateful to thyself* do not to thy neighbour,' would bring it into a very exact coincidence with the saying in Tobit, ὃ μισεῖς μηδενὶ ποιήσῃς. But suffice it to remark, that the English reader may find in our Authorized Version of the Apocrypha (*loc. citat.*), a precept which is the direct converse of our Lord's precept: 'as ye would that men should do to you, do ye also to them likewise' (Luke vi. 31). Further, is it not patent, that both precepts are readily deducible from the 'second great commandment,' which enjoins that 'thou shalt love thy neighbour as thyself'? For *the one does but enjoin a course of conduct agreeable to that commandment; while the other deprecates the plainly inconsistent opposite course.*

4. Our Lord Himself and His Apostles referred persistently to the Old Testament for principles of action, and did not rest the claims of the new Dispensation upon the invention of new Precepts. The Gospel claims to be a lifegiving power rather than a formal system of morality, and its claims are therefore undisturbed by possible discoveries of approximations from without to the principles of what we understand by Christian Ethics. On any other hypothesis, it would be difficult to account for the phenomena *e.g.* of St Paul's Epistles, which contain but scanty allusions to those ethical *formulæ* whereon some have attempted to raise a superstructure of Christian Evidences. St Paul himself must be supposed familiar with the principles of contemporary Rabbinism, nor did he regard the acceptance of them as precluding the necessity of conversion to CHRIST; and hence, to those whose faith is based in any degree upon the evidence of St Paul, it will be so far a question of comparative unimportance, whether or no such and such approximations to the *formulæ* of Christian Ethics were in vogue with the Jews at or before the commencement of the Christian Era. With

St Paul, the Gospel is CHRIST: that name gives the tone and meaning to his writings, as to his life: and their entire power and significance would be confessedly lost, if all direct references to the personal CHRIST could be supposed blotted out. While, on the other hand, the forms of his moral teaching and exhortations might be supposed to vary indefinitely from their acknowledged standard; yet still, so long as the all-pervading $\dot{\epsilon}\nu$ $X\rho\iota\sigma\tau\hat{\omega}$ remained, it would be felt that the essential characteristic of his Epistles was preserved, and we should still trace therein the familiar features of the Apostle of the Gentiles. Such a statement seems scarcely to need formal confirmation: the attention, however, may be directed to St Paul's singular faculty of assimilating extraneous conceptions by the solvent power of his devotion to CHRIST. Things external, practices that prevail around, current thoughts and maxims—one and all are transfigured into their spiritual antitypes. The panoply of the Roman sentinel becomes 'the whole armour of God:' the athlete's garland, a crown incorruptible: the Stoic's $a\mathring{v}\tau\acute{a}\rho\kappa\epsilon\iota a$, a self-sufficiency in CHRIST[1]. 'I have learned, in whatsoever state I am, therewith *to be content*... I can do all things through CHRIST which strengtheneth me' (Phil. iv. 11, 13). And thus, all forms reflect his one indwelling thought; and all aspirations of poets and philosophers converge towards, and find their joint realization through, the one Name CHRIST.

[1] See the Dissertation on *St Paul and Seneca* in Lightfoot's *Philippians*.

CHAPTER XIV.

The Symbolism of Sacrifice.

Gen. xv. 17; Matt. xxvi. 28; Heb. ix. 16.

THE representative theory of sacrifice having been applied by Mr Wratislaw to the case of covenants, it is proposed to consider the ordeal by which the Promise was confirmed to Abraham (Gen. xv. 8 sqq.) with a reference to its bearing upon the doctrine of Theanthropic Mediation. The analogy of the New Covenant to the Old is dwelt upon by our Lord Himself and His Apostles with considerable minuteness of detail, and it will be assumed in the present investigation that retrospective inferences may be drawn from such comparisons, with regard to the nature of the Old Covenant and its attendant ceremonial. The argument will thus depend, in great measure, upon the New Testament representations of the Mediation and Death of CHRIST.

I. *The New Covenant ratified in the Blood of Christ.*

1. One writer upon the Atonement and Satisfaction has summed up the results of his Scriptural research in the three propositions following:—

'Firstly: That our Lord never describes His own work in the language of atonement and sacrifice.

'Secondly: That this language is a figure of speech borrowed from the Old Testament, yet not to be explained by the analogy of the Levitical sacrifices; occasionally found in the writings of St Paul; more frequently in the Epistle to the Hebrews; applied to the believer at least equally with his Lord, and indicating by the variety and uncertainty with which it is used that it is not the expression of any objective relation in which the work of Christ stands to the Father, but only a mode of speaking common at a time when the rites and ceremonies of the Jewish law were passing away, and beginning to receive a spiritual meaning.

'Thirdly: That nothing is signified by this language, or at least nothing essential, beyond what is implied in the teaching of our Lord Himself. For it cannot be supposed that there is any truer account of Christianity than is to be found in the words of Christ.'

But, firstly, not to mention His appropriation to Himself of Is. liii., our Lord very clearly describes the last culminating act of His mission under the figure of an expiatory sacrifice, not without reference to the sacrificial sanctions of the former covenant (Matt. xxvi. 28). Moreover, the ordinance thus instituted upon the basis of sacrificial analogy was to be perpetually conjoined with the commemoration of His death. (1 Cor. xi. 24 sqq.) And secondly, while the legal sacrifices, so far as they were merely external, were inefficacious observances, it must not be assumed hastily that they were devoid of inner meaning—difficult as it might be to elucidate their true significance. One thing at least may be affirmed, *viz.* that if St Paul regarded CHRIST as the End of the Law, there must have seemed to him to be some reality shadowed forth by that Law, and consummated in CHRIST. If again, as well may be surmised, sacrifice was the central ordinance of the legal system, it would follow that it was viewed as having a deep esoteric significance; and this being granted, it is incredible that sacrificial analogies should have been lightly used. In the Epistle to the Hebrews, the analogy of CHRIST'S sacrifice to the Levitical sacrifices is expressly and particularly dwelt upon, and much of the Epistle is taken up with shewing that their mutual relation was that of type and antitype. Thus much is plain, but much still remains obscure: nor does it commend itself as an exhaustive answer to the enquiring mind, that the former sacrifices were simple prophecies of the latter and had no *direct* significance; no meaning except such as might be reflected upon them from their Antitype. 'We seem to be very much in the dark,' writes Bishop Butler[1], 'concerning the manner in which the ancients understood atonement to be made, *i.e.* pardon to be obtained by sacrifices;' but that their sacrifices conveyed some idea to them originally, however soon the full primitive meaning thereof may have lapsed into oblivion, is a point that will perhaps be conceded as axiomatic, or will at any rate be assumed in the present enquiry.

With regard to the Levitical sacrifices in particular, it may be taken for granted, at least provisionally, that they were not solely prophetical, but had a meaning of their own; nor does the fact that the Pentateuch leaves their import unexplained militate in the slightest degree against the assumption that they *had* a meaning; for it is not to a code of practical regulations (such as those parts of the Books of Moses which deal with sacrifice) that we should naturally have recourse, when our aim is to determine the symbolism of the outward acts prescribed. It is assumed therein without explanation, that there is *e.g.* a purifying efficacy in sprinkling with blood, but from the lack of explanation it could not be inferred that no *direct* meaning was attached to it; and the like may be said of sacrifice in general, whereof the form, rather than the meaning, would naturally be sought in the Levitical code. Whence then is the explanation to be gathered? One way, that of theory and hypothesis, is sufficiently obvious: but may not the truth of conjecture be brought to the test of Apostolic teaching? may not retrospective conclusions be drawn, as above assumed, from the New Testament language? might it not be inferred from the later sacrificial analogies—drawn out, be it remarked, *deliberately* by those who had been trained in

---

[1] *Analogy*, Part II. Chap. 5.

the school of Moses—what was the actual and direct significance of the rites from which those analogies were drawn? This principle of retrospective inference will be seen to confirm the view that it was a function of the covenant-victim or 'mediator' *to represent or symbolize the union in itself of the two covenanting parties.*

2. A disputed passage in the Epistle to the Hebrews will be mainly dwelt upon. The passage is for the most part thought to require that $\delta\iota\alpha\theta\acute{\eta}\kappa\eta$[1] should be rendered 'testament;' but not to say that this usage, *qua* Hellenistic, is perhaps altogether post-Biblical, the mention of a 'testament' is allowed to be so far inappropriate, that it reduces the whole passage to a mere play upon the double meaning of a word which signifies in one dialect a *covenant*, and in another a *will*. The rendering 'testament' has indeed been imported herefrom into some few other passages, and especially into the narratives of our Lord's institution of the Eucharist; but it is a strong argument against such a rendering in those places, that the mention of a *new* $\delta\iota\alpha\theta\acute{\eta}\kappa\eta$ implies a reference to one that had gone before and was clearly *not* a 'testament.' Moreover the death spoken of, as in Matth. xxvi. 28, is expiatory, and is thus altogether out of harmony with the mention of a will. 'This,' says our Lord, 'is my blood of the new $\delta\iota\alpha\theta\acute{\eta}\kappa\eta$, which is shed for many *for the remission* of sins.' The same expression, 'blood of the $\delta\iota\alpha\theta\acute{\eta}\kappa\eta$,' occurs in Ex. xxiv. 8 (the passage alluded to), and there means, the blood by which the *covenant* is ratified: in Zech. ix. 11 the same idea is expressed: but in Heb. ix. 20, where the passage from Exodus is distinctly cited, the same formula is incongruously rendered, 'blood of the *testament;*' whereas the Authorized Version of its original has *covenant* for *testament*. But the testamentary sense is now very commonly abandoned, except in the passage from Heb. ix.; nor are there wanting those who regard that one exception as apparent, and who consider that even there 'covenant will probably

[1] See *Test. XII. Patr.* (Sinker, p. 31).

make the more pertinent sense[1].' Assuming then that there are but slight independent grounds for the testamentary sense in any other passage, we proceed to shew that there are serious objections to that sense in the one passage where it has been strongly supported.

II. *General view of the Argument in Heb. viii., ix.*

The eighth chapter of the Epistle to the Hebrews commences with a summation of the arguments which precede, and sets forth as the point whereto all converge, that 'We have such an high priest, who is set on the right hand of the throne of the Majesty in the heavens. A minister of the sanctuary, and of the true tabernacle, which the Lord pitched, and not man.' The Levitical analogy is further dwelt upon: the priests and their offerings served unto the example and shadow of heavenly things; but CHRIST hath obtained a more excellent ministry, 'by how much also He is the Mediator of a better Covenant, which was established upon better promises. For if that first [Covenant] had been faultless, then should no place have been sought for the second. For finding fault with them He saith, Behold, the days come, saith the Lord, when I will make a new Covenant with the house of Israel and with the house of Judah: Not according to the Covenant that I made with their fathers in the day when I took them by the hand to lead them out of the land of Egypt; because they continued not in my Covenant, and I regarded them not, saith the Lord. For this is the Covenant that I will make with the house of Israel after those days, saith the Lord; I will put my laws into their mind, and write them in their hearts: and I will be to them a God, and they shall be to me a people: And they shall not teach every man his neighbour, and every man his brother, saying, Know the Lord: for all shall know me, from the

---

[1] Browne, *On the Articles* (XXVIII). See Professor Scholefield's '*Hints for a New Translation.*' The same view is advocated in Stroud's *Physical Cause of the Death of Christ;* and Wratislaw's *Notes and Dissertations*, to which I have several times referred in the present Chapter. For other authorities, see Alford *in loc.*

least to the greatest. For I will be merciful to their unrighteousness, and their sins and their iniquities will I remember no more (Jer. xxxi. 31—34). In that He saith, A new [Covenant], He hath made the first old. Now that which decayeth and waxeth old is ready to vanish away' (Heb. viii. 6—13). The ninth chapter, as a whole, is taken up with detailed comparisons between the work of Christ and the Mosaic types. 'Then verily the first [Covenant] had also ordinances of divine service, and a worldly sanctuary. For there, &c.' 'But CHRIST being come an high priest of good things to come, by a greater and more perfect tabernacle, not made with hands, that is to say, not of this building; neither by the blood of goats and of calves, but by His own blood He entered in once into the Holy place, having obtained eternal redemption for us. For if the blood of bulls and of goats, and the ashes of an heifer sprinkling the unclean, sanctifieth to the purifying of the flesh: How much more shall the blood of Christ, who through the eternal Spirit offered Himself without spot to God, purge your conscience from dead works to serve the living God?' (Heb. ix. 11—14).

III. *Objections to the usual rendering of Heb. ix. 15—18.*

1. This vexed passage, as commonly rendered, is hard to reconcile with its context; although in the passage itself (ver. 15—18) a superficial simplification is introduced by the disuse of the word Covenant—thus far consistently adopted as the rendering of διαθήκη—and the temporary intrusion of another meaning, whereof many great authorities affirm unhesitatingly that there is no trace elsewhere throughout Holy Scripture.

The meaning alluded to is *Testament* or *Will;* the former word being adopted in the Authorized Version. Since however this word has lost much of its definiteness by its theological usage in the passage before us, and still more by its employment as a designation of the Canonical Books; it may not be amiss to transcribe the vexed passage, using *Will* for *Testament,* and thereby exhibiting perhaps more strikingly the marked change, not to say incongruity, which is brought about by the departure from the rendering of διαθήκη which is used both before and after.

As a conclusion following upon ver. 14, we should thus read :—

'And for this cause He is the Mediator of the new Will, that by means of death, for the redemption of the transgressions that were under the first Will, they which are called might receive the promise of eternal inheritance. For where a Will is, there must also of necessity be the death of the testator. For a Will is of force after men are dead: otherwise it is of no strength at all while the testator liveth. Whereupon neither the first Will was dedicated without blood. For when Moses had spoken every precept to all the people according to the law, he took the blood of calves and of goats, with water and scarlet wool, and hyssop, and sprinkled both the book, and all the people, saying, This is the blood of the Will which God hath enjoined unto you. Moreover he sprinkled with blood both the tabernacle, and all the vessels of the ministry. And almost all things are by the law purged with blood: and without shedding of blood there is no remission. It was therefore necessary that the patterns of things in the heavens should be purified with these; but the heavenly things themselves with better sacrifices than these' (Heb. ix. 15—23).

There are several difficulties in the way of reconciling the passage, if thus rendered, with the context.

a. Three significant words are common to Heb. viii. 6 and ix. 15, viz. *Promise, Covenant,* and the remarkable technical word, *Mediator;* yet whereas in the former verse JESUS is styled 'the Mediator of a better *Covenant*,' in the latter He is said to be the 'Mediator of the new *Will*,' although the same Greek word represents in both cases that whereof He is the Mediator.

b. After detailed allusion to sacrificial atonement and purgation we read that, 'For this cause He is the Mediator of the new Will, that by means of death for the redemption of transgressions, &c.' But in the case of a Will, there is no 'redemption of transgressions:' the testator does not offer himself up as a sacrifice for those in whose favour the will is made.

c. With regard to a will being of no strength at all while the testator liveth, we may remark (1) (with Codurcus[1]) that a disposition of property, as in the case of the Prodigal Son (Luke xv. 12), is none the less valid for the Father's being alive; and (2) that the Prodigal seems to have regarded the portion asked for as one which would have fallen to him of right, and without testamentary disposition (Deut. xxi. 17), on the death of his Father. Moreover the Hebrew word which the LXX. render by διαθήκη certainly does not mean a Will; and many have affirmed that the very idea of a Will (the *classical* διαθήκη) was altogether foreign to ancient Jewish modes of thought. 'The very idea of a Will or Testament,' argues Mr Wratislaw, 'is unknown throughout the Hebrew Scriptures, and was probably unknown in the ordinary life of the Jews, as such, in our Lord's earthly lifetime, although King Herod the Great left both a will and codicils attached to it.'

d. What is meant by the Mediator of a Will? It would seem that (1) there is no third party concerned in such cases; and (2) if there were, he (the μεσίτης) must be identical with the διαθέμενος (ver. 15, 16). Who, then, are the other two?

e. The second διαθήκη, like the first (ver. 18), must be dedicated not without blood. This first is elsewhere alluded to as a *Covenant*, and is here made by some to be a *Will*, by the reverse process of *assimilation* to the second '*Will*;' although it is apparently the aim of the writer to shew that the second has a detailed antitypical correspondence with the first, whereof the ceremonial sanctions are supposed familiar to the reader. But, granted that διαθήκη is here a Will, what is meant by 'the *blood* of the Will[2];' for how does blood, as a

---

[1] *Critici Sacri*, Vol. VII. p. 4278.

[2] The *blood of* a διαθήκη is spoken of in Ex. xxiv. 8; Zech. ix. 11; Heb. x. 29; xiii. 20: also in Matt. xxvi. 28; Mark xiv. 24; Heb. ix. 20. Cp. Luke xxii. 20; 1 Cor. xi. 25. In the first series of passages διαθήκη is rendered *covenant*; in the second, *testament*; the *identity* of Ex. xxiv. 8 and Heb. ix. 20 notwithstanding.

symbol of death by *violence*, enter into the conception of a Will?

f. Codurcus, dismissing the supposition that God the Father is the 'Testator,' goes on to remark that '*neque* CHRISTUS *mortuus est quasi Testator, quasi dominus bonorum: sed quasi vas et sponsor, tanquam debitor, tanquam obnoxius, tanquam reus,...tanquam damnatus, tanquam servus.*' And to this it may be added, that through His humiliation unto death CHRIST obtained to Himself a kingdom, and did not leave by way of testamentary bequest a kingdom of which He had been previously in possession (Phil. ii. 8—11).

g. There is perhaps little to be urged directly in favour of 'Testament' as a rendering of διαθήκη in the passage before us, except (1) the implied death of the testator (ver. 16); and (2) the use of the word κληρονομία in the preceding verse. The former analogy is a but slight one, seeing that the death in question is *violent* and *expiatory:* the latter—*prima facie* plausibility notwithstanding—is equally inconclusive, as may be shewn by the comparison of passages wherein the like collocation of διαθήκη and κληρονομία occurs. One such passage is Gal. iii. 15, 18, where, in the opinion of Dr Lightfoot, 'the mere mention of the inheritance is not sufficient to establish the sense *a Testament*, which is ill-suited to the context.' Dean Alford to the same effect: 'not *Testament*...for there is no introduction of that idea: the promise spoken to Abraham was strictly a *covenant*, and designated διαθήκη in the passages which were now in the Apostle's mind.' Thus we are brought round once more to the same Covenant of Promise with Abraham which is alluded to in Heb. vi. 13—18, and into which the idea of κληρονομία enters, but not so (it will be granted) that of testamentary bequest. In Gen. xv. 7, 8, we read with respect to it :—'I am the LORD that brought thee out of Ur of the Chaldees, to give thee this land to *inherit* it. And he said, LORD God, whereby shall I know that I shall *inherit* it?' And thereupon follows the sacrificial ratification of the *Covenant*. If then in this, the original account, 'inheritance' does not import a testamentary sense into διαθήκη, it cannot be inferred from the same collocation in *citations of the passage* that διαθήκη must mean not *covenant* but *will*.

2. The foregoing objections shew the meagreness of the analogy between the old Covenant and the new so-called 'Testament;' which is further granted, not only by those who make this their non-correspondence an argument against the rendering 'Testament,' but by others who here adopt the meaning Testament, while yet regarding it as unique and unprecedented in Holy Scripture. Thus Dr Lightfoot *loc. cit.:*—

διαθήκην] *a covenant.* This word in classical writers almost always signifies, 'a will,' 'a testament'...On the other hand in the LXX. it is as universally used of a covenant, whether as a stipulation between two parties (συνθήκη, 'a covenant' in the strict sense) or as an engagement on the part of one. Nor in the New Testament is it ever found in any other sense, with one exception. Even in this exceptional case, Heb. ix. 15—17, the sacred writer starts from the sense of 'a covenant,' and glides into that of 'a testament,' to which he is led by two points of analogy, (1) the *inheritance* conferred by the covenant, and (2) the *death* of the person making it. 'The disposition in this case,' he says in effect, 'was a testamentary disposition or will.'

Le Clerc too regards the passage as a rhetorical play upon the word διαθήκη, 'ex qua nihil philosophice colligas.' But it seems incredible that the sacred writer should here turn from his course to pursue a slight lateral analogy, and should dwell with strong emphasis upon the *natural* death which concurs with a testamentary bequest, when the central argument of the context is made to depend upon Christ's *expiatory* and *sacrificial* death. With this remark we pass on to a passage which is sometimes adduced in favour of the testamentary rendering in Heb. ix. 15 sqq.

IV. *On the meanings of* διαθήκη *and* διαθέσθαι.

1. A particular passage, wherein CHRIST on the eve of departure claims to be in some sense a διαθέμενος, has been

adduced, on the hypothesis that the implied διαθήκη is testamentary, as corroborative of the usually-received interpretation of Heb. ix. 16, 17. But whatever be the precise nature of the διαθήκη in Luke xxii. 29, it is obvious from its immediate context that it is not such as implies the death of the testator, and therefore not such as is contemplated in the Epistle to the Hebrews, *loc. citat.* According to the Authorized Version, the Lord says to His disciples: 'Ye are they which have continued with me in my temptations. And I *appoint* unto you a kingdom, as my Father *hath appointed* unto me; that ye may eat and drink at my table in my kingdom, and sit on thrones judging the twelve tribes of Israel' (Luke xxii. 28—30); where CHRIST does not represent Himself as about to suffer death in the capacity of 'testator,' but rather as on the point of entering upon a kingdom purchased by His sufferings and death, and as granting to His faithful followers a share in the glorious issue which is all but consummated. Thus much is sufficiently clear from the Authorized Version, which is here, however, scarcely equal in perspicuity to the rendering of Theophylact. It seems at first sight that a kingdom is transmitted from Christ to His disciples, in the same sense as that in which a kingdom had been appointed for CHRIST by God the Father; but this is scarcely coincident with the promise to the disciples, to eat and drink 'at my table in *my* kingdom.' A closer consistency is gainêd by reverting to the order of the Greek original and thus arranging the clauses: 'And I appoint unto you (as my Father hath appointed unto me a kingdom) that ye may eat and drink at my table in my kingdom.' To the same effect, St Paul: 'As ye are partakers of the sufferings, so shall ye be also of the consolation' (2 Cor. i. 7): and again: 'If we suffer, we shall also reign *with* Him' (2 Tim. ii. 12).

2. Of the meanings of διαθήκη one, viz. *Testament*, has been above considered in relation with Heb. ix. 15—18, and seems there inappropriate, as being not only extra-Biblical, but out of harmony with the context. Setting this meaning aside, we have two others, viz. (*a*) *Covenant* proper, where two

covenanting parties and a Mediator are involved; and (*b*) the general and abstract meaning *dispositio*, derived from the preceding through the assignation of special prominence to one of the covenanting parties, who dictates the terms. In this way the Divine covenant with man is commonly conceived of, and is described as a διαθήκη, rather than as a συνθήκη[1] or compact of equality. In this second class of usages there are several degrees of abstractness and departure from the full primal significance of the covenantal sanction, whereas, in Heb. ix. 15—18 much depends upon the symbolism of the ordinance; and indeed by the argumentative particularity of the allusion in that passage, we are apparently restricted to the primary acceptation of διαθήκη[2], and are thus led back successively to the covenant of Ex. xxiv. 6—8, and, further, to that still more primitive form of covenant whereby the promise was confirmed of God to Abraham. What was the significance of its attendant ceremonial?

V. *The Confirmation of the Promise to Abraham.*

In answer to the patriarch's doubt, 'Whereby shall I know that I shall inherit it?' the LORD said to him, 'Take me an heifer of three years old, and a she-goat of three years old, and a ram of three years old, and a turtle-dove, and a young pigeon.' 'And he took unto him all these, and divided them in the midst, and laid each piece, one against another: but the birds divided he not. And when the fowls came down upon the carcases, Abram drove them away. And when the sun was going down a deep sleep fell upon Abram: and, lo, an horror of great darkness fell upon him....And it came to pass, that, when the sun went down, and it was dark, behold a smoking furnace, and a burning lamp that passed between those pieces. In the same day the LORD made a covenant with Abram, saying, Unto thy seed have I given this land'

---

[1] Compare the composite formula συνθώμεθα διαθήκην (1 Macc. xi. 9).
[2] The LXX rendering of ברית.

(Gen. xv. 8—18). The burning lamp is here taken to be the symbol of the Divine presence; but although the LORD alone thus symbolically passed between the pieces we may assume doubtless with Menochius that, *transiit et Abraham*[1], as the subjoined parallel from Jeremiah suggests. 'And I will give the men that have transgressed my covenant, which have not performed the words of the covenant which they made before me, *when they cut the calf in twain, and passed between the parts thereof*, The princes of Judah, and the princes of Jerusalem, the eunuchs, and the priests, and all the people of the land, *which passed between the parts of the calf;* I will even give them into the hand of their enemies, and into the hand of them that seek their life: and their dead bodies shall be for meat unto the fowls of the heaven, and to the beasts of the earth' (Jer. xxxiv. 18—20). We may assume then, from these passages jointly—and the assumption is further justified by classical analogies—that the two covenanting parties were required to pass between the pieces into which the victim had been divided, and that so the covenant was ratified. Thus far all is plain; but what was the meaning of the symbol?

VI. *The Symbolism of the Covenant.*

It is commonly said, that the death of the victim symbolized the consequences which would ensue upon the breaking of the covenant. But this can scarcely be said to exhaust the esoteric symbolism of Abraham's sacrifice; for (1) whereas it was natural to contemplate, in ordinary cases, the breaking of the treaty by either party, and his actual death consequent thereupon, yet in Gen. xv. 17 chief stress is laid upon the passing of the 'burning lamp,' the symbol of the Divine Presence, between the pieces, and it is not mentioned (though doubtless implied[1]) that Abraham likewise passed between; (2) it would not be surprising if something of the primal symbolism of sacrifice had come in later times to be forgotten, and if, by consequence, so ancient a sacrifice as that

---

[1] But see note A, p. 3.

of Abraham had a significance which could not be fully brought out by the reflex process of *a posteriori* illustration; and (3) bearing this in mind, we must not overlook the particularity of detail in that sacrifice, wherein, not only is it essential to pass between the pieces, but the parts of the several beasts are *adjusted carefully*, and laid each over against its fellow (ver. 10). It might be assumed that this had its meaning, and that meaning was perhaps *the introition of the covenanting parties* into the being of the mediator or victim, which was intended to be the actual representative of the parties concerned; and this identification with the victim would imply not a potential death in the future, but an instant participation in the fate and conditions of the victim. Hence the ceremony may be said to signify, that:—

[i] The covenanting parties then and there died *in* the victim, which implied the irrevocability of mutual engagement, and did not merely represent a potential and future death, consequent upon non-fulfilment of their covenanted duties.

[ii] By identification with one and the same victim, the two parties (previously, it might be, at variance) became εἰς ἕν and so at peace with one another[1].

[iii] In the case of a covenant between God and man the ideas of expiation and purgation would enter necessarily into the preceding, for man *qua* sinner, must have died before becoming εἰς ἕν with God.

The second of these three symbols contains the idea of the Incarnation in its bearing upon the Sacrifice of Christ, for it imports the unification of the two covenanting parties, God and Man, in the person of one Covenant-Victim; while light is reflected upon the third symbol by the sacrificial language of the New Testament, elsewhere remarked upon.

VII. *The symbolical Resurrection of Isaac.* Heb. xi. 19.

This principle of Representation is easily discernible, as Mr Wratislaw remarks, in the case of the Passover, where

[1] 'Transibant per medias partes, ut sanctius in unum corpus coalescerent, sacrificio simul juncti' (Vatablus).

'a lamb was taken for every family, representing the firstborn of that family. The firstborn of the Egyptians suffered a real death in their own proper persons; those of the Israelites a symbolical death in the substituted lambs.' And again, on the great Day of Atonement it is provided, that 'Aaron shall lay both his hands upon the head of the live goat, and confess over him all the iniquities of the children of Israel, and all their transgressions in all their sins, *putting them upon the head of the goat*, and shall send him away by the hand of a fit person into the wilderness: And the goat shall bear upon him all their iniquities into a land not inhabited' (Lev. xvi. 21). Here too the principle of Representation is exemplified; the individuality of the people, *qua* sinners, being transferred to the goat; and the whole symbolizing a renunciation of the sinful Self. But a still more striking example is afforded by Heb. xi. 19 (taken as a comment upon the narrative of Gen. xxii. 1—14), where Abraham is described as having received back Isaac from the dead 'in a figure' or symbolically. This difficult passage yields at once to the alternative rendering of Chrysostom, taken in connexion with the foregoing theory, which it incidentally corroborates; and when thus explained, it throws much light upon the expression which has been thought to militate most effectually against the non-testamental rendering of διαθήκη in the great *crux* of Heb. ix. 15—18. The ram, as Chrysostom suggests, was a 'figure' of Isaac, and represented him in its death; and by consequence, when Abraham received back Isaac, whose death had been symbolically represented, he received him symbolically from the dead[1]. In the light of this remarkable Scripture so strikingly elucidated, we proceed to attempt a direct exposition of the passage in the Epistle to the Hebrews, not without a reservation of some points for a fuller subsequent discussion.

[1] 'Chrysostom himself afterwards, in recapitulating, gives this very interpretation as an alternative: ὥσπερ γὰρ παραβολὴ ἦν ὁ κριὸς τοῦ Ἰσαάκ.' Alford *in loc.*

VIII. CHRIST *the Mediator of the New Covenant.* Heb. ix.

It has already been remarked, and is sufficiently obvious, that in the immediate context the most sacred sacrificial rites of the Old Covenant are dwelt upon as introductory to the Mediatorial work of CHRIST, and that the central point of the argument is to evince the strict analogy of New to Old. The Old is regarded as a 'figure' of the New (ver. 9), where, be it noted, the same word is used to express the analogy as in Heb. xi. 19 (*supra*) : 'Accounting that God was able to raise him up, even from the dead; from whence also he received him *in a figure.*' In accordance with this analogy, it is proposed to interpret the argument: 'For where a covenant is, there must also of necessity be implied[1] the death of the covenanter. For a covenant is in force over corpses[2]: otherwise it is of no strength at all while the covenanter liveth. Whereupon neither the first covenant was dedicated without blood' (Heb. ix. 16—18).

On the foregoing it has to be remarked, that:

Whereas in the authorized version we read, that 'there also must of necessity *be* the death of the testator,' yet the expression is not γενέσθαι (ver. 15), but φέρεσθαι, which has been well explained as meaning, that 'there must be necessarily something done that *implies* the Death of the Covenanting Party[3].' Now, as in ch. xi. 19, ὅθεν, referring to ἐκ νεκρῶν,

---

[1] θάνατον ἀνάγκη φέρεσθαι τοῦ διαθεμένου.

[2] διαθήκη γὰρ ἐπὶ νεκροῖς βεβαία. A covenant can only be ratified over the bodies of slaughtered victims. Dr Stroud quotes Ps. l. 5 : 'those that have made a covenant with me ἐπὶ θυσίαις.' This clause, taken in connexion with the following, 'otherwise it is of no force, &c.', is a good instance of a particular affirmative implying a general negative. Cp. 'So then faith cometh [not except] by hearing...For how shall they believe in him of whom they have not heard?' (Rom. x. 17, 14.)

[3] Thus we need not with Dr Stroud make the διαθέμενος to be the covenant-victim. See Wratislaw. Or perhaps we may say that Abraham's covenant was an imperfect type, and that in the ideal covenant the victim would be a person, and at once the μεσίτης, ἔγγυος, and διαθέμενος.

includes the double meaning of (1) an actual death, viz. of the animal victim, and (2) the implied death *in* that victim of the person represented by it; so in ch. ix. 16, 17, it is affirmed that a covenant is not of force otherwise than over the body of a representative victim actually slaughtered, and thus with the implied death of the Covenanting Party. 'Whereupon neither the first covenant was dedicated without blood. For when Moses &c.' Then follow further allusions to expiation and purgation by the blood of the first covenant; and the 'holy places made with hands' are again set forth, as in the opening of the chapter, as 'figures of the true.'

IX. *What is the fundamental idea in Mediation?*

1. A mediator is said to be a 'go-between,' who interposes between two contending parties, and negotiates a reconciliation; but although this is doubtless the later form of the idea of mediation, it may be questioned whether something more may not have been once included therein: whether in fact the later meaning is not degenerate[1], and ultimately referable to a fuller and more expressive original. The word μεσίτης is used by Suidas to explain μεσέγγυος (a depositary of mutual pledges), and by implication attributes a quasi-*representative* function to the μεσίτης, which may be a relic of a more complete *personation* formerly involved in the conception of a mediator. A passage wherein the covenantal sanctions are dwelt upon argumentatively may well be chosen as a point of departure in an attempt to trace the archetypal significance of mediation. Starting, accordingly, from Heb. ix. 15, we remark (1) that the *death* of the mediator was an element in the covenantal sanction: 'For this cause He is the *Mediator* of the new covenant, that by means of *death*, for the redemption of the transgressions that were under the first

---

[1] An attempt is here made to investigate the primary idea of *mediation*; not that of the *words* μεσίτης, &c., which may have come into use when the primary idea had degenerated. Thus a secondary idea might with reference to the words themselves be primary.

covenant, they which are called might receive the promise of eternal inheritance.' And (2) that the mediator represented the covenanters, inasmuch as the real death of the former implied (ver. 16) the death of the latter. Moses, indeed, who was in some sense a mediator, and is called a μεσίτης by Philo, does not fulfil this condition literally in his own person; but his mediation, too, which will be further considered in the sequel, was not unattended by sacrifice. (Ex. xxiv. 8; Heb. ix. 18.)

2. Meanwhile we may revert to the covenant with Abraham, in quest of a fuller explanation of the term μεσίτης: a course of proceeding suggested by the use of the rare word ἐμεσίτευσεν, in reference to God's twofold confirmation of the promise to Abraham. The Authorized Version, which does not make it clear what were the two elements of confirmation, runs as follows: 'Wherein God, willing more abundantly to shew unto the heirs of promise the immutability of His counsel, *confirmed it by an oath:* That by two immutable things, in which it was impossible for God to lie, we might have strong consolation, who have fled for refuge to lay hold upon the hope set before us' (Heb. vi. 17, 18). The words italicized correspond to ἐμεσίτευσεν ὅρκῳ, where the verb perhaps refers, as Mr Wratislaw suggests, to the sacrificial confirmation of Gen. xv. For, not to mention that the English rendering, and that of the Vulgate, 'interposuit jusjurandum,' are philologically, so to say, unsatisfying, it may be urged, further, that the oath is probably to be regarded as a contemporaneous expression of the promise (ver. 13, 14), rather than as a second confirmation of that whereof the *promise itself* was the first. And again it would be remarkable indeed if there were no implied allusion to so prominent a feature of the narrative as the incident of Gen. xv. 9, sqq., which is an *express confirmation* of the promise, following closely upon the misgiving of the Patriarch: 'LORD God, whereby shall I know that I shall inherit it?' We may assume, then, that in ἐμεσίτευσεν ὅρκῳ there is the double allusion (1) to the sacrificial confirmation, and (2) to the subsequent oath of Gen.

xxii. 16, 17. The meaning of the verse in question would thus be that the *oath* was the second confirmation of the promise, whereof the *sacrifice* was the first. The promise that, as the stars of heaven 'So shall thy seed be,' is recorded in Gen. xv. 5, and in immediate sequence follows its covenantal sanction: the like promise, 'I will multiply thy seed as the stars of heaven,' is recorded in Gen. xxii. 17, in connexion with the oath for confirmation, 'By myself have I sworn.' And with reference to this twofold sanction, it is said in the Epistle to the Hebrews, that God, willing more abundantly to shew the immutability of His counsel, ἐμεσίτευσεν ὅρκῳ, covenanted *with* an oath, or superadded the assurance of an oath to the covenantal sanction.

3. If then it be allowed to assume that ἐμεσίτευσεν refers to the covenant made with Abraham by sacrifice, we may glean from the sacred narrative a suggestion with regard to the meaning of the word. The covenant was ratified when the Divine symbol 'passed between those pieces;' and in Jer. xxxiv. 18, 19, not dissimilarly, the ratification seems to consist in passing between the parts of the severed calf. It may be, then, that μεσιτεύειν signifies to submit oneself to an ordeal whereof the distinctive feature is a passing ἀνὰ μέσον τῶν διχοτομημάτων, and the word, being applicable to the two covenanting parties, would thus have a simple and intelligible application to God Himself as sharing in the covenant.

4. A meaning above suggested for the symbol is, that the two covenanting parties *coalesced* in the person of the mediator: in other words, that the mediator (or covenant-victim) *included* rather than *came between* the parties engaging in the covenant. And this interpretation will appear to be confirmed by the language of St Paul, if the thoughts expressed thereby be regarded as a light thrown back upon the past, rather than as novelties intruded upon, and superadded to, the true and primæval idea of the mediatorial function. Thus, in Eph. ii. 14—16 the reconciliation of those at variance is thought of as effected by joining the two together *in one body*, whether the reconciliation be that of Jew to Gentile,

or of man to God. 'For He is our peace, who hath made both *one*, and hath broken down the middle wall of partition between us; Having abolished in His flesh the enmity, even the law of commandments contained in ordinances; *for to make in Himself of twain one new man*, so making peace; And that he might reconcile both unto God *in one body* by the cross, having slain the enmity thereby.' Nor is it improbable that the same idea of *inclusion*[1] lies at the root of the argument in a difficult passage of the first Epistle to Timothy: 'For there is one God, and one *Mediator* between God and man, the man Christ Jesus; Who gave Himself a ransom for all, to be testified in due time' (1 Tim. ii. 5, 6). Supposing however that the primary idea of a mediator was one of *inclusion* rather than of *intervention*, it would naturally degenerate into the latter, when the form of the covenantal sanction was changed from that of Gen. xv. 17 to that of Ex. xxiv. 8.

X. *The Blood of Sprinkling.*

1. Moses did not fully discharge the function of mediator in his own person, but stood between God and the people *with* the blood of the victim. 'And Moses took half of the blood, and put it in basons: and half of the blood he sprinkled on the altar...And Moses took the blood, and sprinkled it on the people, and said, Behold the blood of the covenant, which the LORD hath made with you concerning these words' (Ex. xxiv. 6, 8). In Lev. xvi. 15 we read further of a sprinkling of blood within the vail, on or towards the mercy-seat: 'Then shall he kill the goat of the sin-offering, that is for the people, and bring his blood within the vail, and do with that blood as he did with the blood of the bullock, and sprinkle it upon the mercy-seat and before the mercy-seat.' Nor must the sprinkling of the Paschal blood upon the door-posts (Ex. xii. 7) be left unnoticed.

It is difficult to see how the idea of purification could have

---

[1] CHRIST is said to 'mediate' or stand *between* God and man in virtue of His *being* both God and Man. But this is to make the idea of *standing between* secondary, and that of *inclusion* primary.

attached *primarily* to the sprinkling with blood, nor indeed is the same language used with reference to this Paschal sprinkling, as was used subsequently of the like ceremony, *e.g.* in Lev. xvi. and Heb. ix. But if we attempt to collate the ceremonies of the covenant in Ex. xxiv. with the earlier forms of Gen. xv., and assume that the one is a modification of the other, an explanation of the sprinkling at once suggests itself; one which is strikingly confirmed by our Lord's mode of inauguration of the New Covenant, not to say by the remarkable passage in the Epistle to the Ephesians which has already been in part alluded to.

2. In the covenants of Gen. xv. and Jer. xxxiv. the two covenanting parties *coalesce* in the *one body* of the 'mediator' or victim, and this is symbolized by their passing between its parts, and so *into the body of the victim*. If then with this introition, which was the main feature of the ceremony, be identified the *sprinkling* of altar and people in the covenant of Ex. xxiv., it would follow that by that sprinkling the parties to the covenant—heaven and earth—were joined together in the body of the covenant-victim. The people sprinkled with the blood, 'which is the life,' of the victim, become thereby partakers of the individuality of the victim, and are joined *in one body* with him. So in the ratification of the Christian Covenant, man becomes one with the mediating θεάνθρωπος by assimilating the Body and the Blood of CHRIST, the Covenant-Victim[1]. (Matt. xxvi. 26, 27.) And once more, if the sprinklings in the Law symbolized an incorporation into the *one body* of the 'mediator,' we have a simple explanation of the difficult expression ἐν τῷ αἵματι, which in the two subjoined passages stands in connexion with the being joined *in*

---

[1] In Luke xxii. 20 and 1 Cor. xi. 25 the expression 'testament *in my blood*' is used. Purification is not the primary notion in the making of a covenant, but rather the conjoining of the covenanters. It may be remarked, that it is not here intended to affirm anything with regard to the *essence* of the Sacraments, which would be to enter upon a subject not directly associated with the present inquiry. The *form of representation* is all that I have ventured to consider. This remark is applicable, more or less, to the whole Chapter.

one body to the Theanthropic Mediator, and thereby having access to and being one with God.

(*a*) 'But now in Christ Jesus ye who sometimes were far off are made nigh *in* the blood of Christ...who hath made both one...that He might reconcile both unto God in one body by the cross' (Eph. ii. 13—16).

(*b*) 'Having therefore, brethren, boldness to enter into the holiest *in* the blood of Jesus, by a new and living way, which He hath consecrated for us, through the veil, that is to say, His flesh...Let us draw near with a true heart in full assurance of faith, having our hearts sprinkled from an evil conscience, and our bodies washed with pure water' (Heb. x. 19—22).

3. We may conclude then the idea of purgation by sprinkling was not improbably a secondary and derived idea, to be referred back to the archetypal sacrifice of Abraham, wherein the coalescence of the covenanters was symbolized by their introition into the body of the victim or mediator; and that, in aftertime, the blood of the victim being sprinkled upon the covenanters symbolized the same coalescence of those 'who sometimes were far off,' in the 'one body' to which the blood of sprinkling appertained. In like manner, a share in the New Covenant is appropriated by an assimilation of the Body and Blood of CHRIST the Mediator. It is not difficult to see that the idea of purgation by sprinkling is involved in, and derived from, that which is conjectured above to be primary and inherent.

XI. *St Paul's conception of Membership in Christ.*

1. To pass from the case of covenants to the case of sin-offerings, we remark that the same theory of Representation explains a marked characteristic of St Paul's phraseology, which in turn bears out the assumption that the victim was regarded as an impersonation of him by whom it was offered. 'The soul that sinneth, it shall die' (Ezek. xviii. 4) was the unalterable decree, in accordance wherewith the death of the offender was symbolized by that of the offering. Death was

the penalty of sin, and when that penalty had been paid, the man was thereby justified, from sin (Rom. vi. 7); but without death to sin he could not be freed from sin[1]. The thought of being *in* CHRIST is the corner-stone of the Apostle's theology. The context of the last mentioned passage is built up upon it. 'How shall we, that are dead to sin, live any longer therein? Know ye not, that so many of us as were baptized into Jesus Christ were baptized into His death? Therefore we are buried with Him by baptism into death[2]: that like as Christ was raised up from the dead by the glory of the Father, even so we also should walk in newness of life. For if we have been planted together in the likeness of His death, we shall be also in the likeness of His resurrection. Knowing this, that our old man is crucified with him, that the body of sin might be destroyed, that henceforth we should not serve sin. For he that is dead is freed from sin' (Rom. vi. 2—7). So in Gal. ii. 20, he speaks again of being crucified with Christ; and in Col. ii. 20, of being dead with Christ to the rudiments of the world; not to mention numerous other passages wherein the inclusion in Christ and the being part of Christ are spoken of. All such expressions are simply explained upon the hypothesis of a symbolical introition by the sacrificers into the sacrificial victims of the law; and this being presupposed, the ideas of being *in* CHRIST, and *one with* CHRIST, and of sharing the death and resurrection of Christ, would naturally suggest themselves to one with whom CHRIST was the End and Antitype of the law and its ceremonial. The Sacrifice of CHRIST is thus viewed as *representative;* and—whatever may be the precise meaning of the expression—He is set forth as the Saviour of those who are '*in* HIM,' rather than of those whose life and being are independent of His own.

2. There are indeed other modes of statement wherein Christ is represented broadly as suffering in the place of others—the Just for the unjust; and it is to such representations

---

[1] Wratislaw *in loc.*
[2] Cp. 2 Cor. v. 15: If One died (ἀπέθανεν) for all, then all died (ἀπέθανον).

as these that exception has sometimes been taken by opponents of Christianity, on the ground that an injustice is involved in punishing the innocent for the guilty; a view of the case which is distinctly recognised by Holy Scripture itself in such passages as: 'The soul that sinneth, it shall die. The son shall not bear the iniquity of the father, neither shall the father bear the iniquity of the son: the righteousness of the righteous shall be upon him, and the wickedness of the wicked shall be upon him. But if the wicked will turn from all his sins that he hath committed, and keep all my statutes, and do that which is lawful and right, he shall surely live, he shall not die. All his transgressions that he hath committed, they shall not be mentioned unto him: in his righteousness that he hath done he shall live. Have I any pleasure at all that the wicked should die? saith the LORD God: and not that he should return from his ways, and live?' (Ezek. xviii. 20—23.)

3. With this principle, that each must bear his own sin and not another's is to be compared the complementary sentence of the Decalogue: 'I the LORD thy God am a jealous God, visiting the iniquity of the fathers upon the children.' The former is at once accepted as obviously just; while the latter is seen to involve no contradiction thereunto, but to follow as a consequence of the organic oneness of the race, whereby the sins of one portion are entailed upon another. The one principle is abstract; the other practical: and to argue from analogy, so far as the individuals of a race are separate and independent one of another—which they are not *absolutely*—so far and no farther, does natural justice seem to require that one should not be made to suffer for another: but on the other hand, if the human race can be regarded as a continuous unit, so far is it in accordance with the moral sense that one part thereof should suffer, as one member of a body suffers, for the act of another.

St Paul is careful to set forth the work of CHRIST in a way accordant with this analogy. CHRIST suffers for and saves man, inasmuch as He includes humanity. 'As in Adam all die (all as members of one body sharing a common fate), even so *in* CHRIST shall all be made alive' (1 Cor. xv. 22). And again, in the preceding verse: 'Since by man came death, by man came also the resurrection of the dead;' where it is implied, that the race which had sinned must pay the penalty of its own sin, and was not to be freed therefrom by the sufferings of an altogether separate and *unrelated* substitute.

XII. *Summary of Results.*

(α) If the representative theory of sacrifice be applied to covenants, it follows that the covenant-victim (or mediator), by representing each covenanting party separately, represents the union of the two in its one body[1]: and this may have been symbolised by the ceremony of passing between the parts of the victim, pp. 293, 298.

(β) Mediation may have referred originally to this passing between the parts of the victim[2], and only secondarily to the standing between[3] the covenanters, p. 298.

(γ) In the form of ratification used in Gen. xv. the covenanters passed between the parts of the victim; but in the covenant of Ex. xxiv. it was necessary to find a substitute for this form, seeing that the symbols of the Divine Presence were *fixed* and localized. It thus became necessary for an administrator (in this case Moses) to intervene: and one main feature of the ceremony was then the sprinkling of the blood

---

[1] A remarkable confirmation of the theory that covenants were ratified by symbolical assimilation and conjunction in one body, is afforded by Herod. I. 74. There the form mentioned is *the licking up of one another's blood.* τὸ αἷμα ἀναλείχουσι ἀλλήλων. This unification is even more completely symbolized by the ceremony described in Tacit *Annal.* XII. 47. 'Mos est regibus, quotiens in societatem coëant, implicare dextras, pollicesque inter se vincire nodoque præstringere: mox ubi sanguis in artus extremos suffuderit, levi ictu cruorem eliciunt, atque invicem lambunt.' May not compounds of ἀλλάσσειν, used of reconciliation, refer back to the symbolical *change of individuality* which took place in the ancient covenantal sanction? Cp. such usages as that in 2 Cor. v. 18, where the reconciliation takes place through a Mediator. [τοῦ καταλλάξαντος ἡμᾶς ἑαυτῷ διὰ Χριστοῦ.]

[2] ἀνὰ μέσον τῶν διχοτομημάτων. Gen. xv. 17; Jer. xxxiv. 18 (Aquila).

[3] κἀγὼ εἱστήκειν ἀνὰ μέσον Κυρίου καὶ ὑμῶν. Deut. v. 5.

i.e. the *application thereof to the covenanting parties*. By this was symbolised, as in the more ancient form, their being joined together in the one body to which the blood appertained, p. 301.

(δ) Priest and victim in the later form of covenant answered to the victim alone in the primitive form; and hence when CHRIST is represented as discharging a twofold function as Mediator, the idea is not novel but archetypal—the two lines of thought, which had a common origin, once more converging, p. 299.

(ε) The idea of being *in* CHRIST, which in one form or other pervades the New Testament, is an expression of the inner symbolism of the ancient sacrifices, wherein the victim *represented* the covenanter or the person for whom atonement was made, pp. 298, 301.

NOTE ON CHAPTER XIV.

A. The statement that *transiit et Abraham* requires further consideration; but it may suffice to remark that the main argument of the chapter depends upon a *general view* of the covenantal sanction, and not specially upon the covenant of Gen. xv. The sanction in this case is assumed however to be of the same class as in Jer. xxxiv., even though abnormally developed in one direction. The chapter was indeed written on the assumption that *transiit et Abraham;* and thus undue prominence may seem to have been given to some points in the account of the covenant in Gen. xv. But this will not impair the argument, if it be granted that the ordeal was implicitly the same there as in the general case.

CHAPTER XV.

The LXX. as a Medium of Citation.

THE intrinsic value of the original Septuagint Version, the state of preservation of its text, and the estimation in which it was held by our Lord and His Apostles, are questions which have entered largely as controversial elements into the momentous and widely-ranging subject of Citation in the New Testament from the Old.

1. Some have inferred from the frequent use made of the LXX. in the New Testament, that the Version is authorized and declared immaculate, not only in passages cited, but throughout. Discrepancies between portions of the Hebrew text and the corresponding Greek citations have been thought to prove a corruption, by wilfulness or by negligence, of the former; and again, from the palpable inadequacy of the existing LXX. renderings in numberless instances, it has been argued that the text of the LXX. has likewise suffered, and that, from the same cause or causes as the Hebrew. Thus Dr Henry Owen, after attributing a high degree of excellence to the original Septuagint, proceeds as follows:—

'Whilst the Jews therefore employed such diligence about it, the genuine purity of the *Septuagint* Version must needs have remained in a great degree at least, if not entirely, unblemished. For few, if any, errors could creep into their

Copies in that early age, when they were carefully transcribed, critically examined, and publickly read in their Synagogues. And since no occurrence appears to have happened for a length of time, that could induce them either to remit their care, or to make alterations in this version; we may reasonably conclude, that it continued in a pure, uncorrupted state, and in general agreement with the Hebrew Original from which it was derived, quite down to the days of our Saviour.'

The same writer supposes the LXX. to have been since corrupted, partly by Christians[1], who, 'to serve a turn, have daringly interpolated, altered, or expunged, as best suited their purposes;' and partly by Jews, when pressed by arguments from the Greek Version, to which they allowed a certain authority, by their adoption of it in their Synagogue worship.

'Can we suppose, that the Jews...could strictly adhere to the Septuagint Version, when they saw it produced so frequently against them?...must we not rather on the contrary imagine, that such a circumstance would have provoked their resentment, and set them entirely against this version? This is certainly the most natural conclusion. And IRENÆUS assures us, that they were so enraged on this very account, that, "if they had known the Christians would have arisen, and brought such Testimonies from the Scriptures against them, they would have made no scruple themselves to have burned their own Scriptures"—meaning thereby the *Septuagint copies*: for the Testimonies alleged, or the Quotations produced by the ancient Christians, were drawn from *them* only.'

2. Others have contended for the *Hebraica veritas*, or practical perfection of the Masoretic text, and have thought more or less slightingly of the LXX. The Hutchinsonian

---

[1] This statement is exemplified by the reading of the *Alexandrine*: ἐν ὕδατι οὐκ ἐλούσθης τοῦ Χριστοῦ μου (Ezek. xvi. 4). The latter words may have arisen as a Christian *midrash* from למשיחי. *An Enquiry into the Present State of the LXX.* (p. vi).

school of Hebraists held high mystical views of the Hebrew, and depreciated the Greek Version. 'They conceived that Greek terms were totally inadequate to represent the mysteries contained under the corresponding words in the Hebrew; and that it was out of mere condescension to the Gentiles, the New Testament was written in Greek. Viewing, therefore, the Greek Version, *as a Targum rather than a literal translation*, they would not admit, strictly speaking, there were any quotations from the LXX. *Neither doth the use the writers of the New Testament make of the LXX.* (writes Spearman) *stamp any authority on that version, or entitle it to impose the sense of the Greek words and phrases on the Hebrew*[1].' Surenhusius, again, argues learnedly for a Hebrew original of the New Testament citations, while fully recognizing the divergences which have to be accounted for. In his treatise on the subject he undertakes (as the title-page announces) to harmonize the quotations and their originals in accordance with Rabbinic usages in citation and modes of interpretation.

3. A third class of harmonists assert the co-ordinate canonicity of the Hebrew and the Septuagint. '*Spiritus qui in Prophetis erat*,' writes St Augustine, '*quando illa dixerunt; idem ipse erat in LXX. viris quando illa interpretati sunt.*' This side is espoused by Mr Grinfield, who, in his *Apology for the Septuagint*, lays chief stress upon the use made of that version by our Lord; remarking, that 'nearly all the quotations made by JESUS Himself from the Old Testament are taken *verbatim* from the LXX., and occasionally, where they differ from the Hebrew; whilst several quotations made by the Evangelists, differ from the LXX. and agree with the Hebrew.'

I. *Results of Investigation with Inferences therefrom.*

The persevering advocacy with which mutually exclusive theories on the immediate sources of the citations have been

---

[1] See Grinfield's *Apology for the Septuagint*, where frequent references to the literature of the subject may be found.

The LXX. as a Medium of Citation.

defended, has been instrumental in shewing clearly the difficulties which have to be surmounted, and has suggested simultaneously, as the only safe course to be pursued, that the phenomena of the various cases should be noted carefully, while *a priori* theories of reconciliation are abstained from. Space forbids the attempt to treat this broad question exhaustively: it may suffice therefore to state generally some of the results which seem to have been established by the labours of successive harmonists; and to consider one or two cases of citation, which have a marked and special bearing on the point at issue.

(α) *A large proportion of the Citations are taken from the LXX.*

(β) *The LXX. is sometimes followed where it differs considerably from the Hebrew.*

(γ) *In some few cases the Greek, being clearly inadequate, is replaced by another rendering of the original Hebrew.*

Bishop Horne, in his Preface to the Psalms, expresses the reasonable conclusion to which many have been led by the above results:—'It may be considered, that the Apostles generally cited from the Greek of the LXX. Version, and took it as they found it, making no alteration, when the passage as it then stood was sufficient to prove the main point which it was adduced to prove;' and closely connected with this is the important canon of interpretation, not unrecognized by Jerome, that the general purport, rather than the mere words, should be considered, and that the Apostles may be thought, in their citations, '*sensum scripturæ posuisse, non verba.*'

Dr Owen, in his *Modes of Quotation*, gives reasons why the Septuagint should have been adopted, for the most part, as the source of citation:—

'It is allowed on all hands, that, as the Old Testament Prophecies were delivered in *Hebrew*, and the Gospels were penned in *Greek*, the Evangelists must either have translated for themselves, or else have adopted the *Septuagint* Version, which was the only one extant at that time. *Both* these methods lay equally before them, and they might make choice of either as they thought proper. Now, if we suppose that they chose the first and always translated the Hebrew for themselves, we shall find them exposed to many difficulties which otherwise they might have easily avoided; and which prudence indeed would have directed them to avoid. (1) In the first place it would have been an useless, unnecessary undertaking; for the translation was already made to their hands with great care and acknowledged fidelity. And therefore they seem, generally speaking, to have had nothing more to do but to adopt and apply it as occasion required. (2) In this way, no objections could be formed against them; whereas, had they gone in the other, and translated for themselves, the Jews would have disputed the authority of their version, would have perpetually charged it with errors and corruptions, and brought the other that was highly esteemed, and in common use, to support the charge against it. (3) Besides, had the Evangelists rejected the Septuagint Version,...they would have first discouraged their converts from reading it, and then have precluded themselves from the advantage of appealing to it in their frequent conferences with the *Hellenistick* Jews, &c.—To obviate, therefore, these cavils and inconveniencies, the Evangelists, we may presume, chose rather to follow, *in general*, that common version, against which the Jews had *then* nothing to object, and for which the *first converts* had a high veneration.'

But, granted, further—as some would have it—that to the Apostles and Evangelists themselves, the Septuagint was what the Authorized English Version is to us; granted, that they were acquainted with the Hebrew Scriptures only as we may be acquainted with the Scriptures in any language which is not vernacular; it still would not follow—nay, it is implicitly denied by these very assumptions—that their ultimate appeal was to the Septuagint. For from our Authorized Version it is customary, and no less natural within certain limits, to draw illustrations and arguments without critical

The LXX. as a Medium of Citation. 311

reference to the Hebrew of the passage from which the argument or illustration may be drawn: but beyond those limits —*i.e.* if an inference from the version should seem *unscriptural*—none would insist upon the argumentative value of the English except so far as it is, or is assumed to be, a faithful rendering of the original Hebrew. To apply this principle to the New Testament citations from the Septuagint—

(i.) *If the Greek sufficiently proves the main point at issue, and thus far agrees with the Hebrew, the accuracy of the Greek rendering is not thereby vouched for in particulars which have no well-defined bearing on the general argument.*

A striking illustration hereof is afforded by St Stephen's citation from Amos, in Acts vii. 42, 43, where the point to be proved is, that the service required of the Israelites in the Wilderness was not ritual but spiritual. This the citation proves by its opening clauses; and seeing that their counter-bias towards a sensuous worship was sufficiently evinced by the history of the Golden Calf, it becomes a question of merely critical and archæological importance, whether at any time—and if so, when—they betook themselves to the worship of a god called Remphan. This citation would seem then not to guarantee the accuracy of the LXX. rendering in respect of '*Remphan*' or '*Raiphan*,' whereof there is no mention in the Hebrew.

(ii.) *A citation of a Septuagint rendering does not guarantee its accuracy, even when it contains important accessions to the argument, whereof no trace is found in the existing Hebrew text.*

An illustration is supplied by Heb. x. 5, where the word 'body' is quoted from the LXX. and incorporated into the argument, but is not found in the Hebrew text, as it has come down to us. This addition to the Hebrew is made subservient to the general argument of the Psalm, which is preserved *entire;* and the fact that there is nothing in the familiar Greek version which does not harmonise with the original may be described as a sufficient reason why the Greek should be retained, rather than replaced by a *strange* rendering more literally exact. There are cases, however, in which the

Septuagint would fail to convey the meaning of the Apostle or Evangelist, and in such cases the original Hebrew is resorted to.

II. *Non-Septuagintal Citations.* *Joh. xix.* 37; *Rev. i.* 7.

To pass by the striking deviations from the LXX. which have been already commented upon in Chapters IV. and VII.[1], we proceed to notice the citation from (or allusion to) Zech. xii. 10, which occurs in St John's account of the Crucifixion: 'And again another Scripture saith, *They shall look on Him whom they pierced*' (Joh. xix. 37); and which is incorporated in Rev. i. 7: 'Behold, He cometh with clouds; and *every eye shall see Him, and they also which pierced Him:* and all kindreds of the earth shall wail because of Him.' The original passage is thus rendered in the Authorized Version: 'And I will pour upon the house of David, and upon the inhabitants of Jerusalem, the Spirit of grace and of supplications: and *they shall look upon Me whom they have pierced*, and they shall mourn for Him, as one mourneth for his only son, and shall be in bitterness for Him, as one that is in bitterness for his first-born.'

This passage was anciently interpreted of *the* MESSIAH *the son of Joseph;* and it is quoted by the Evangelist, argues Calvin, as an assertion of the Divinity of the Crucified: '*ut ostendat Christum esse Deum illum, qui olim conquestus fuit per Zachariam, sibi pectus a Judæis transfodi.*' But the allusion to the Crucifixion could not have been expressed by the rendering of the LXX.[2], which is accordingly rejected, and replaced by a more exact rendering of the original Hebrew.

The error of the LXX. is very naturally attributed by St Jerome to their accidental transposition of two letters which very closely resemble one another[3]; and seeing that like errors have arisen in numberless passages of little or no con-

---

[1] Compare 1 Cor. xv. 54. In Rom. xii. 19, where the argument depends upon the *emphasis*, the Hebrew is resorted to. See Deut. xxxii. 35.
[2] ἀνθ' ὧν κατωρχήσαντο.
[3] Reading וְרָקְדוּ for וְדָקְרוּ.

troversial interest, it must be confessed that there is a strong presumption in the favour of the explanation which he has propounded. Some, however, with Dr Henry Owen, have charged the Jews with a wilful corruption of the LXX., in this as in other places:—'When the Jews began to censure and condemn the Septuagint Version, and, in consequence thereof, to correct and model it to their Hebrew Copies; there is reason to suspect, that in some remarkable places where a word, by similarity of letters, was capable of being read differently, they changed the Greek to the worse Reading, in order both to pervert the sense, and to bring contempt on the old Translators and the Version they had made. Thus, I conceive, the Septuagint Version was altered by them in that noted passage of ZECHARIAH, chap. xii. 10, where the Greek is at present ἀνθ' ὧν κατωρχήσαντο...whereas it appears from undoubted testimonies, that the original Greek was εἰς ὃν ἐξεκέντησαν.. For the Syriac Version has *quem transfixerunt;* and the Vulgate, *quem crucifixerunt.* IGNATIUS and JUSTIN MARTYR read ὄψονται εἰς ὃν ἐξεκέντησαν. IRENÆUS, *videbunt in quem compunxerunt.* And TERTULLIAN, *cognoscent eum, quem pupugerunt.*' The charge however must be regarded in this case as ill-supported; for while, on the one hand, the reading κατωρχήσαντο may have arisen from one of those slight misreadings of the Hebrew, of which so many instances are afforded by the Septuagint Version; on the other, the testimonies cited by Dr Owen for the reading ἐξεκέντησαν are altogether neutralized by the consideration, that this reading would have been adopted on the authority of St John's citations, even though no trace of it were discoverable in the Septuagint.

Again, it has been urged that in Hos. xi. 1 the LXX. was wilfully corrupted by the Jews, into ἐξ Αἰγύπτου μετεκάλεσα τὰ τέκνα αὐτοῦ, and that they did this, either to exclude St Matthew's application of the passage to the infant Saviour, or to bring discredit on the LXX. Version. But against the first supposition it is to be noted, that in their own later Greek versions the form of the citation is approximated to; and against the second, that their Targum has points of contact with the Septuagint rendering of the passage in question. In these cases, then, the hypothesis of wilful corruption may be regarded as inadequately sustained. Other causes, however, have contributed to the palpable deterioration of the LXX. text (whatever may have been its original value as a rendering of the Hebrew), and to some of these it may be well to advert.

III. *Assimilations of the Septuagint to the New Testament.*

In the Prayer-Book Version of the Psalter, which agrees in general with that of the LXX., the following passage occurs as a rendering of Ps. xiv. 1—7:

1. The fool hath said in his heart: There is no God.
2. They are corrupt, and become abominable in their doings: there is none that doeth good, *no not one.*
3. The Lord looked down from heaven upon the children of men: to see if there were any that would understand, and seek after God.
4. But they are all gone out of the way, they are altogether become abominable: there is none that doeth good, no not one.
5. *Their throat is an open sepulchre, with their tongues have they deceived: the poison of asps is under their lips.*
6. *Their mouth is full of cursing and bitterness: their feet are swift to shed blood.*
7. *Destruction and unhappiness is in their ways, and the way of peace have they not known:* there is no fear of God before their eyes.

The Bible rendering, which is taken directly from the Hebrew, contains no trace of the part italicized. How then (it may be asked) is this great difference in the two versions to be accounted for?

An answer is easily found. In Rom. iii. 10—18, a succession of verses are cited from the Old Testament: 'As it is written, There is none righteous, no, not one. There is none that understandeth, there is none that seeketh after God. They are all gone out of the way, they are together become unprofitable; there is none that doeth good, no, not one. &c.' To the end of ver. 12, the citation is from Ps. xiv.; and it has been assumed incautiously, that the remaining verses must have been drawn from the same source, and that the LXX. therefore had need to be corrected by the insertion of the words cited in Rom. iii. 13—18, in immediate sequence upon those cited from the Psalms. Hence has arisen the interpolation, or supposed correction, whereby the Vatican text of Ps. xiv. is distinguished from the Masoretic. Nor is this a full statement of the argument for the hypothesis of interpolation; for, in one clause of the citation, which *is* drawn from the Psalm, there is a marked departure from the form of Hebrew and LXX. alike. In the original, 'the LORD looked down...*to see if there were any that would understand;*' in the citation the categorical form of statement, '*There is none that understandeth &c.*' is anticipated from the following verse.

Thus far, then, St Paul's words *do not agree exactly with the LXX.*, although expressing faithfully its general purport. But with the following verses the case is different; the LXX. agreeing word for word with the citation in the New Testament, and thereby favouring the hypothesis, that the verses in question, viz. those not occurring in the Hebrew, have been interpolated from Rom. iii. 13—18.

The true account of St Paul's citation is, that it is composed of detached passages from various parts of Holy Scripture, which were freely rendered (being perhaps cited from memory), and brought into combination, as illustrative of like particulars. The citation and the corresponding passages as rendered in the Authorized Version are subjoined: references being given in the notes to some of the Greek renderings.

Rom. iii. 10 There is none righteous[1], no, not one: Eccl. vii. 20. For there is not a just[1] man upon earth,

[1] δίκαιος.

11 There is none that understandeth, there is none that seeketh after God.

12 They are all gone out of the way, they are altogether become unprofitable; there is none that doeth good², no, not one.

13 Their throat is an open sepulchre; with their tongues they have used deceit⁴; the poison of asps is under their lips:

14 Whose mouth is full of cursing and bitterness⁵:

15 Their feet are swift to shed blood:

16 Destruction and misery are in their ways:

17 And the way of peace they have not known:

18 There is no fear of God before their eyes.

that doeth good¹, and sinneth not.

Ps. xiv. 2, 3³ The LORD looked down from heaven upon the children of men, to see if there were any that did understand, and seek God. They are all gone aside, they are altogether become filthy: there is none that doeth good, no, not one.

Ps. v. 10 Their throat is an open sepulchre; they flatter⁴ with their tongue.

Ps. cxl. 3 Adders' poison is under their lips.

Ps. x. 7 His mouth is full of cursing and deceit⁵ and fraud.

Prov. i. 16 For their feet run to evil, and make haste to shed blood.

Is. lix. 7, 8 Their feet run to evil, and they make haste to shed innocent blood: their thoughts are thoughts of iniquity; wasting and destruction are in their paths. The way of peace they know not.

Ps. xxxvi. 1—4 The transgression of the wicked saith within my heart, that there is no fear of God before his eyes &c.

---

¹ ἀγαθόν.
² The same as Ps. lii. 3, 4 (LXX.), except in having χρηστότητα for ἀγαθόν.
³ χρηστότητα.
⁴ ἐδολιοῦσαν.
⁵ πικρίας.

The LXX. as a Medium of Citation. 317

It would seem, then, that the text of the LXX. has here been very greatly disturbed by forced assimilation to the New Testament; and this being granted, it might be supposed that numberless minor corruptions have arisen from the same cause.

IV. *Further Remarks on the Corruption of the LXX.*

Amongst causes of deterioration, other than mere inaccuracy of transcription may be further mentioned:—

(1) A desire to bring the Greek text into conformity with the Hebrew by alterations and interpolations, which may be evinced by a comparison of the Vatican and Alexandrine MSS. (2) A tendency to simplify Hebraisms or difficult constructions; as, perhaps in 1 Sam. xvii. 53, where εκκλινοντες οπισω may be a corruption of εκκαιοντες οπισω, which would agree more literally with the corresponding Hebrew phrase. This phrase signifies in another passage (Gen. xxxi. 36), *to pursue hotly after;* the verb meaning literally, *to burn*, and its participle being rendered by καιομένοις, in Ps. vii. 14. (3) Another fruitful source of error has been the existence of *double renderings*, an alternative rendering (or explanation) being first written in the margin and then introduced into the text, while the former rendering was still retained. This was probably the origin of the confusion in Gen. ix. 20, where a literal rendering would be ἄνθρωπος γῆς, in the sense, *a man of the ground*, or *husbandman;* but, an explanatory word or second rendering being absorbed into the text, there results the existent reading ἄνθρωπος γεωργὸς γῆς. So in Deut. xxxii. 40, where the Hebraism '*to lift up the hand*' is used in the sense, *to swear*, we have first the literal rendering, ἀρῶ εἰς τὸν οὐρανὸν τὴν χεῖρά μου, and in immediate sequence, a fragment of a like expression (with δεξιάν for χεῖρα) confusedly joined with an explanatory ὀμοῦμαι, thus, καὶ ὀμοῦμαι τὴν δεξιάν μου. These causes alone would account for a very great deterioration of the Septuagint original, which may or may not have been as nearly perfect as some have presumed; and, this being the case, it would seldom

be necessary to resort to the hypothesis of wilful corruption by controversialists, although some changes may have owed their origin to a predisposition and bias in favour of such and such views and interpretations.

V. *On the Hellenistic Dialect as Vernacular.*

The question of the Apostles' comparative familiarity with the Hebrew and the Greek might be variously answered; but the inference from their frequent citation of the LXX. is rendered to a great extent precarious by a consideration already dwelt upon, viz. that the desire to speak and write *so as to be understood* would induce a preference for the Greek version, as being very generally adopted. Professor Jowett, after a general survey of St Paul's citations, draws the following conclusion:—' None of these passages offer any certain proof that the Apostle was acquainted with the Hebrew text. That he must have been so can hardly be doubted; yet it seems improbable that he could have had a familiar knowledge of the original without straying into parallelisms with the Hebrew, in those passages in which it varies from the LXX.... The inference is that the Greek and not the Hebrew text must have been to the Apostle what the English version is to ourselves.' But this conclusion—to whatever extent plausible—has only an indirect bearing on the value of the LXX. as an ultimate appeal; for, to revert to the analogy suggested by Professor Jowett, a person acquainted with the English version alone may hold the original of the Old Testament in no less esteem than would the most accomplished Hebraist, and may be equally ready to appeal thereto in cases of difficulty, or of supposed *inadequacies* of rendering which are of sufficient importance to vitiate an argument. The Septuagint might be so used freely for illustration, and even for verbal argumentation, as to seem, at first sight, the one medium of evangelistic citation; yet a single case of departure therefrom, where in some important particular it fails to express the meaning of the Hebrew, would suffice to degrade that version from its ideal supremacy: while, on the other hand, no amount of deviation from the Hebrew in the direction of the Septuagint (provided only that the results be *true* and *scriptural*) could do more than evince the esteem in which the Septuagint was held *as a generally recognised and familiar rendering*.

While however some (with Mr Grinfield) have laid perhaps undue stress on the quasi-vernacular knowledge of the LXX. which the New Testament citations evince, it must be admitted that the thought and expression of the New Testament have been very largely contributed to by that first Greek version of the Old. To pass by professed citations (whereof some, as perhaps those in Rom. iii. 10—18, are made from memory), we find cases in which citations and adaptations occur without acknowledgement; nor is it always obvious, whether we are dealing with conscious citations or unconscious adaptations, especially when fragments of two or more distant unconnected verses of the Old Testament are blended into a single sentence or phrase. But, to pass on from more or less unconscious assimilations of whole clauses or passages, there is yet another way in which the Septuagint translation has entered largely into the composition of the New Testament Scriptures.

The doctrinal terminology of the New Dispensation owes much to the Hellenistic version of the Hebrew Scriptures; nor is it easy to over-estimate the importance of this consideration. The terms Repentance, Faith, Justification, &c. drew their theological significance from Hellenistic usage, and the composite language of the Dispersion became an *instrument of thought* to Apostles and Evangelists, as it had been for ages to no mean portion of the civilized world. One unflinching advocate of the Sacred Tongue[1] thus concedes the indebtedness of the New Testament to the existing Greek rendering of the Old:—'Had there not been a translation of the Old

---

[1] Spearman, quoted by Grinfield (*Apology*, p. 27).

Testament into Greek before this time, I do not see how they could have wrote the New Testament in Greek; for as they must have used Greek words in a different sense from what they were used in the Greek authors, there could have been no standard by which to have tried them, had not the LXX. Version been made. I think I am justified in saying, that, if there had not been a translation in Greek of the Old Testament, made and received by sufficient authority, a proper time before the advent of our Saviour, I do not see how the penmen of the New could have written Greek.'

Conversely, an acquaintance with the LXX. is rightly commended by Bishop Pearson, as a key to the New Testament style and diction:—'for the sacred penmen, not only frequently produce testimonies out of the Old Testament, but also accommodate Moses and the Prophets to the doctrines of Christianity: and hence it will needs happen, that the mode and manner of expression, or the phraseology of the Hebrew, which was unknown or at least unusual amongst the Grecians, must, to such as only understand Greek, render the Apostolic writings more obscure than they would otherwise have been. Neither can this obscurity be taken away or cured by any other means than by the knowledge of the Hebrew idiom, in which the Old Testament is written; upon which the Apostles everywhere keep an eye, and which, a little varied from its original purity, the Jews spake in the time of our Saviour, to whose customs and manner of speaking they accommodated their discourses. For which reason, the Greek Version of the Old Testament will of necessity be of very great use in understanding the apostolic writings; since in that Version all the idioms of the language were transplanted, as well as the soil would bear them; in that, the sense of the prophetic writings was explained, as well as the Greek tongue and the skill of the translators would permit; and to that the Grecians, with whom the Apostles had most concern, had long been accustomed. And it is reasonable to believe, that this translation, by Divine Providence, was at first made to be the instrument and means of preparing the minds of the nations, who everywhere had it among them, for the better and more kindly reception of the doctrines of CHRIST and His Apostles.'

VI. *General Conclusion on the Authority of the LXX.*

The Hellenistic dialect was to a large proportion of converts the sole medium whereby the truths of Christianity and its relation to Mosaism could have been communicated; and it must be admitted to have served as *an instrument of thought*, and *a groundwork of theological conceptions*, if not so much to the preachers, at least to no mean array of hearers of the Gospel. It followed as a natural consequence that theological *ideas* were developed through the instrumentality of the Septuagint; words and expressions occurring in the Greek to which nothing can be found precisely equivalent in the Hebrew. Thus Dr Lightfoot concludes[1], after an investigation into the origin and growth of the Hellenistic conception πίστις, that *the word 'Faith' can scarcely be said to occur at all in the Hebrew Scriptures of the Old Testament*. As the Gospel to the Law, so is the plastic dialect of the Dispersion to its Hebrew archetype. The New may pass the limits of the Old, but the Old must contain the rudimentary principles of the New. Though the Hellenistic dialect may have been to the preachers of the Gospel a quasi-vernacular language; though they may have thought *in* and *by* it, and adopted therefrom words and phrases which could not have been simply and adequately retranslated into Hebrew; the ultimate appeal might (and would) still be from the Greek, as from any other vernacular rendering, to the original. The product of Greek thought must be a legitimate development from the Hebrew; the Hebrew must enfold the germ of the Hellenistic development. *Granted that Hellenistic Greek was the vernacular language of Citation, analogy requires that we should presuppose a reservation—however seldom to be exemplified—in favour of the Hebrew.*

[1] *Galatians*, ed. 2, p. 1, 6.

VII. *Styles of Citation.*

1. Seeing that the LXX. rendering is sometimes rejected in citation, and sometimes retained, the enquiry suggests itself whether the New Testament writers may not have differed, as in their styles of composition, so in their Styles of Citation from the Old Testament Scriptures; and if so, whether arguments may not be deduced therefrom, evincing *identity* or *diversity* of authorship in cases where external (and other) evidences are conflicting. In illustration, it may suffice to call attention to a remark of Dr Wordsworth on the passage from Zechariah above considered. In the Apocalypse the Septuagintal ἀνθ' ὧν κατωρχήσαντο is replaced by εἰς ὃν ἐξεκέντησαν, and by the same form of words in the fourth Gospel. Hence arises an argument for identifying the author of the fourth Gospel with the author of the Apocalypse—an argument the strength whereof is proportionate to the infrequency of such departures from the familiar phraseology of the LXX.

2. It may be remarked in further confirmation of this identification, that a prominent feature in the Apocalypse is the representation of CHRIST as the ἀρνίον ὡς ἐσφαγμένον, while the author of the fourth Gospel is careful to point out the fulfilment of the Paschal Type, ὀστοῦν οὐ συντριβήσεται αὐτοῦ[1], and to record the saying of the Baptist: 'Behold the *Lamb* of God.' In this case indeed ἀμνός not ἀρνίον is used, but the change of word is perhaps sufficiently accounted for by the difference of subject and accessories in the two compositions; and more than this, in the one case the description is the Evangelist's, and in the other the words are cited from the Baptist[2]. But, be this as it may, CHRIST stands out prominently as the Sacrificial *Lamb*, in the fourth Gospel and the Apocalypse alike; and hence a corroboration of the argument whereby it is sought to prove that the fourth Gospel was written by the author of the Apocalypse, ST JOHN.

[1] See Note A, p. 323.
[2] ἀρνός, &c. are commonly used for the oblique cases of ἀμνός.

3. The Hellenistic idiom and that singular admixture of the Old and the New which characterize the New Testament Scriptures, fix (within certain limits) the date, and may aid in determining the authorship of compositions in which they occur. This is well expressed by the subjoined remarks of Professor Jowett, with which we conclude :—

'Vestiges of Old Testament language are so numerous as to admit of an argument from their occurrence to the genuineness of the Epistles. If the same interpretation of new and old phraseology occurs in the Epistle to the Ephesians that we find in the Epistles to the Romans, Corinthians, and the Galatians, here is considerable reason for supposing that they are writings of the same author, or at any rate of the same date. A new argument from coincidence arises, for no one would imagine that it could have occurred to a forger of a later age to imitate the manner in which St Paul used the language of the LXX.'

NOTE ON CHAPTER XV.

A. The notice of the efflux of 'blood and water' (Joh. xix. 34) is a strong testimony to the writer's having been an eye-witness of the Crucifixion. The phenomenon is at any rate a very rare one, and one therefore which was unlikely to have been thought of by any but an eye-witness, and more unlikely to have been mentioned, seeing that it must necessarily give rise to great perplexities. Some have assumed it to be wholly miraculous and of mystical import. For a striking investigation see Stroud's *Physical Cause of the Death of Christ*. Death ensued preternaturally soon (ver. 33), and that, some conjecture, from previous exhaustion. Against this is the fact, that JESUS *cried with a loud voice* when on the point of yielding up the ghost (Matt. xxvii. 50; Mark xv. 37; Luke xxiii. 46). Dr Stroud's theory accounts for this fact, which St John does not mention, and at the same time for the very singular phenomenon which he alone records.

CHAPTER XVI.

Miscellanea.

I. Ps. cxvi. 11; Ps. li. 4; Rom. iii. 4.

'Yea, let God be true, *but every man a liar;* as it is written, *That Thou mightest be justified in Thy sayings, and mightest overcome when Thou art judged.*'

1. THE words πᾶς δὲ ἄνθρωπος ψεύστης (Ps. cxvi. 11), which precede the formula of citation, are perhaps no more than an instinctive adaptation of a familiar phrase. The reference in the original is to man's weakness and frailty; and commentators have illustrated the Psalmist's meaning by such passages as: 'Vain is the help of man' (Ps. lx. 3); 'Surely men of low degree are vanity, and men of high degree are a *lie;* to be laid in the balance, they are altogether lighter than vanity' (lxii. 9); 'Put not your *trust* in princes, nor in the son of man, in whom there is no help' (cxlvi. 3). The meaning of the words 'All men are liars' would thus be, that men, owing to their frailty and inability to help, are deceivers of those who put trust in them. A further illustration might be drawn from a passage in which Job describes the failure of his friends' attempts to comfort him:—'My brethren have *dealt deceitfully* as a brook, and as the stream of brooks they pass away ... What time they wax warm, they vanish; when it is hot, they are consumed out of their place ... The troops of Tema looked, the companies of Sheba waited for them. They were confounded because they had hoped; they came thither, and were ashamed. For now ye

are *nothing;* ye see my casting down, and are afraid' (Job vi. 15—21).

Perhaps, however, the Psalmist is describing not the inability of others to help him, but his own frailty :—' I said in my extreme affliction, Man's life is a shadow, a phantom, an *unreality.*'

2. To pass by the *Syriasm* 'overcome,' we have to reconcile the following ἐν τῷ κρίνεσθαί σε (usually rendered passively) with the original Hebrew, where the corresponding verb is active, and the justice of God's sentence is acknowledged :—' that thou mightest be justified when Thou speakest, and be clear when Thou *judgest*' (Ps. li. 4). An explanation frequently adopted is, *That Thou mightest be acknowledged righteous, when the justice of Thy dealings is called in question.* But some think a *middle* rendering of κρίνεσθαι more suitable. Thus Bengel :—' Simul Deus et κρίνει et κρίνεται. Κρίνεται, media significatione, qualem habere soleat verba *certandi.* Κρίνονται, qui in jure disceptant. LXX., Es. xliii. 26. Jud. iv. 5; Jer. xxv. 31. Exemplum Mich. vi. 2 s. necnon 1 Sam. xii. 7. Ineffabilis benignitas, qua Deus ad hominem disceptandi causa descendit.'

II. Gen. xviii. 10; Rom. ix. 9.

The citation differs from the LXX. in a detail involving merely critical considerations. In the former we read: 'At *this time* will I come, and Sarah shall have a son;' while the LXX. uses the fuller expression, κατὰ τὸν καιρὸν τοῦτον εἰς ὥρας. The Hebrew is literally, *at the living season*[1], *i.e.* according to the analogy of χρόνῳ τῷ ζῶντι καὶ παρόντι (Soph. *Trach.* 1169)—*at the present season,* sc. of next year. Nor does there seem to be any necessity for assigning to the adjective *living* the unusual sense *reviving.* The latter meaning is not established by such passages as : '*and* . . . the spirit of Jacob their father *revived*[2]' (Gen. xlv. 27) ; 'If a man die *shall he live again*[3]?' (Job xiv. 14) ; 'They are dead, *they shall not*

[1] כעת חיה   [2] ותחי   [3] היחיה

live[1]' (Is. xxvi. 14); for the fact that a *tense* of a verb may mean, *to become alive* (sc. *again*), does not prove that reviviscence is expressed radically by the verb 'to live.' It would seem, then, that the Hebrew phrase in question means *at the living* (*i.e.* present) *season*, and that it is fully and sufficiently rendered by κατὰ τὸν καιρὸν τοῦτον. On the other hand, the citation may be a direct *abbreviation from the LXX*.

III. Hos. i. 10; ii. 23; Rom. ix. 25, 26; 1 Pet. ii. 10.

One expression in the citation calls for critical remark. 'As he saith also in Osee, I will call them my people, which were not my people; and her beloved, which was not beloved. And it shall come to pass, that *in the place where it was said unto them*, Ye are not my people; *there* shall they be called the children of the living God.'

The phrase italicized is taken from the LXX.: καὶ ἔσται ἐν τῷ τόπῳ οὗ ἐρρέθη κ.τ.λ., and it is also a literal rendering of the Hebrew: but a difficulty arises in explaining the local reference, which is further marked by the subsequent ἐκεῖ. Dean Alford's comment illustrates the difficulty :—' By ἐν τῷ τόπῳ... ἐκεῖ must not, I think, be understood, in any particular place, as Judæa; nor among any peculiar people, as the Christian Church: but as a general assertion, that in every place where they were called, *not His people*, there they shall be called, *His people*.' The original[2] might, however, be rendered literally: 'in place of that they should be called;' *i.e.* 'instead of their being called;' which appears to satisfy the requirements of the context better than the *local* rendering, and to agree better with the *general* statements of a subsequent verse: 'And I will have mercy upon her that had not obtained mercy; and I will say to them which were not my people, Thou art my people; and they shall say, Thou art my God' (Hos. ii. 23).

It remains to ask whether the citation is susceptible of a like general rendering; and it may be suggested in answer,

[1] בל יחיו.   [2] במקום אשר יאמר להם, Hos. ii. 1, *Heb.*

that the Greek ἐν τῷ τόπῳ κ.τ.λ. may have been intended originally as a simply *literal* (and therefore unidiomatic and *non-natural*) rendering. Thus much being premised, we remark that, τόπος (like *locus*) may mean *a passage*, or place *in a book*, as in Luke iv. 17: 'when he had found the PLACE where it was written[1].' With a very similar non-local sense of τόπος, St Paul's citation may be explained to mean, that 'where, or whereas, they used to be called οὐ λαός μου, they should be called υἱοὶ θεοῦ ζῶντος.'

IV. Deut. xxxii. 43; Rom. xv. 10.

This is one of the places in which the Jews have been suspected of corrupting the text of the original; and, whatever may be the grounds of the accusation, there is certainly a wide divergence between the Hebrew and the Greek. The citation occurs in connection with some others of which the characteristic word is ἔθνη—'Now I say that Jesus Christ was a minister of the circumcision for the truth of God, to confirm the promises made unto the fathers: And that the Gentiles might glorify God for His mercy; as it is written, For this cause I will confess to Thee among the GENTILES, and sing unto Thy name (Ps. xviii. 49). And again He saith, *Rejoice ye* GENTILES, *with His people* (Deut. xxxii. 43). And again, Praise the Lord, all ye GENTILES; and laud Him, all ye people (Ps. cxvii. 1). And again, Esaias saith, There shall be a root of Jesse, and He shall rise to reign over the GENTILES; in Him shall the GENTILES trust (Is. xi. 10).'—In the Hebrew of the passage in Deuteronomy, it is said: 'Rejoice, ye nations, His people;' which will bear the same application as St Paul's '*with His people;*' for in the original the nations are addressed *as* His people, while in the citation, they are numbered *with* His people. And moreover the hypothesis of a very simple case of double-rendering would go far to account for the Septuagintal reading, regarded as a development out of a briefer original.

[1] τὸν τόπον οὗ ἦν γεγραμμένον.

The Authorized Version, following the Hebrew, reads:—

'Rejoice, O ye nations, His people: for He will avenge the blood of His servants, and will render vengeance to His adversaries, and will be merciful unto His land and to His people'

and the Greek:—

εὐφράνθητε οὐρανοὶ ἅμα αὐτῷ, καὶ προσκυνησάτωσαν αὐτῷ πάντες ἄγγελοι θεοῦ· εὐφράνθητε ἔθνη μετὰ τοῦ λαοῦ αὐτοῦ, καὶ ἐνισχυσάτωσαν αὐτῷ πάντες υἱοὶ θεοῦ· ὅτι τὸ αἷμα τῶν υἱῶν αὐτοῦ ἐκδικᾶται, καὶ ἐκδικήσει καὶ ἀνταποδώσει δίκην τοῖς ἐχθροῖς, καὶ τοῖς μισοῦσιν ἀνταποδώσει· καὶ ἐκκαθαριεῖ κύριος τὴν γῆν τοῦ λαοῦ αὐτοῦ.

Against the view that the Greek here represents the genuine Hebrew text, it may be urged that the whole passage in the Greek is apparently an expansion, and is not sufficiently concise to represent the original; so far at least as may be judged from the remaining portions, wherein no such wilful corruption is suspected. It is not only to the former part of the passage cited from the LXX. that there is nothing correspondent in the Masoretic text, but the like may be said of the latter part, where a tampering with the text would have been aimless and superfluous. If there is an accidental double-rendering of the clause, *will render vengeance*, the like may be the case with the preceding clauses; nor is evidence in confirmation of this hypothesis altogether lacking. Thus, whereas the literal rendering of the third word in the Hebrew[1] is ὁ λαὸς αὐτοῦ, its literal rendering if pointed differently would be, ἅμα αὐτῷ, or μετ᾽ αὐτοῦ, the former whereof occurs in the first clause of the Septuagint rendering, while a confusion of the latter with ὁ λαὸς αὐτοῦ might have led to the μετὰ τοῦ λαοῦ αὐτοῦ.

Further, it is well known that the LXX. in many cases vacillate between υἱοὶ θεοῦ and ἄγγελοι θεοῦ, as renderings of one and the same expression; and hence (not to mention that in another reading of *this* passage the two expressions

---

[1] עמו.

are transposed) it seems more than probable that we have here too a case of double-rendering. The apostrophe to the heavens, εὐφράνθητε οὐρανοί, may have been suggested by the opening words, ver. 1: 'Give ear, O ye heavens, and I will speak;' and, in connection with this, the language of Ps. xcvi. 6—8 (LXX.) may have contributed to the interpolation. In particular, the words προσκυνησάτωσαν αὐτῷ πάντες ἄγγελοι θεοῦ have been compared with the seventh verse of the Psalm, προσκυνήσατε αὐτῷ πάντες ἄγγελοι, and if, as some think, the citation in Heb. i. 6 is referable directly to the Psalm, the interpolation in the LXX. may have come to pass through the medium of the citation, as in the case of Ps. xiv., which has been already discussed[1]. Lastly, it may be noted that if ἅμα αὐτῷ and μετὰ τοῦ λαοῦ αὐτοῦ have indeed arisen from a single Hebrew word, the fact that καὶ προσκυνησάτωσαν κ.τ.λ. *intervenes* goes far to prove it an interpolation, and with it the corresponding clause καὶ ἐνισχυσάτωσαν κ.τ.λ. must stand or fall. We may conclude then that the LXX. cannot safely be adduced as evidence that the Masoretic text of Deut. xxxii. 43 has been, wilfully or otherwise, corrupted.

V. Is. xxv. 8; Hos. xiii. 14; 1 Cor. xv. 54, 55.

Two more or less direct citations are joined together in the last-named passage:—'Then shall be brought to pass the saying that is written, Death is swallowed up in victory. O death, where is thy sting? O grave, where is thy victory?'— but it might be questioned, whether the formula of citation applies in the outset to both passages, or to the former only; the latter being supposed to follow as an adaptation of Hos. xiii. 14, suggested by the foregoing. It may be well to notice the passages separately.

1. In the Authorized Version Is. xxv. 7, 8 is rendered as follows: 'And He will destroy in this mountain the face of the covering cast over all people, and the vail that is spread over all nations. *He will swallow up death in victory;* and the LORD God will wipe away tears from off all faces; and

[1] See pp. 314—317.

the rebuke of His people shall He take away from off all the earth: for the Lord hath spoken it.' The LXX. rendering[1], being altogether inadequate, is rejected, and (a) the verb signifying *to swallow up* is rendered, as it should be, in the past: (b) the *passive* form, instead of the active, is adopted: (c) a Hebrew expression, meaning *for ever*, and for which Symmachus *e.g.* has εἰς τέλος, is by St Paul rendered εἰς νῖκος.

To obtain the passive κατεπόθη the Apostle may have rendered the active (which seems well suited to the original context) indefinitely, and thus have obtained idiomatically: (1) *one hath swallowed up death;* (2) κατεπόθη ὁ θάνατος. But supposing God to be the subject, the general sense is the same with the active as with the passive. As regards the expression εἰς νῖκος, its *natural* meaning is fairly expressed by the Authorized Version; it is, however, a translation of a phrase signifying *for ever*, in which sense εἰς νῖκος is not unfrequently used elsewhere, and especially by Aquila[2]. The two renderings being ultimately coincident, it has only to be observed that St Paul adopts the *literal* rendering εἰς νῖκος (which is an Aramaizing periphrasis for *in perpetuum*), and then, as is his wont, goes off at a word, viz. νῖκος, which leads up, not unnaturally, to the citation from Hos. xiii. 14.

2. The following is the Authorized Version of Hos. xiii. 9—14: God thus addresses Israel:—'O Israel, thou hast destroyed thyself; but in me is thine help. *I will be* thy king: *where* is any other that may save thee in all thy cities? and thy judges of whom thou saidst, Give me a king and princes? I gave thee a king in mine anger, and took him away in my wrath. The iniquity of Ephraim is bound up: his sin is hid. The sorrows of a travailing woman shall come upon him: he is an unwise son; for he should not stay long in the place of the breaking forth of children. I will ransom them from the power of the grave; I will redeem them from

---

[1] κατέπιεν ὁ θάνατος ἰσχύσας.

[2] Aquila reads καταποντίσει τὸν θάνατον εἰς νῖκος. Theodotion, the same as St Paul. 'Pro נצח et לנצח Aquilae proprium est εἰς νῖκος' (Field, *Orig.*

Hexapl. Ps. xii. 1). Cp. 2 Sam. ii. 26 (LXX.): μὴ εἰς νῖκος καταφάγεται ἡ ῥομφαία; num in perpetuum devorabit gladius? (Schleusner, *Lex. Vet. Test.*)

death: *O death, I will be thy plagues; O grave, I will be thy destruction:* repentance shall be hid from mine eyes.'

This rendering is perhaps not quite accurate in some particulars. (1) To pass by the difficult ninth verse (which seems to be a reproach for forgetting that the LORD is the sole helper), it may be remarked that the word for 'I will be' signifies, in all probability, *where*, and is best taken in connection with the interrogative particle which follows the word 'thy king,' and is rendered 'where' in our English Version. The sense then would be that Israel had forgotten wherein lay their true help; ' *Where* now is thy king to save thee[1]? where thy judges, whom thou askedst for?' (2) The word italicized recurs in the verse from which St Paul's citation is drawn; and many (following the Septuagint) assign to it the same meaning, '*where*,' both in that verse and in the tenth. To say: 'O death, I will be *thy plagues*,' appears somewhat strange and unnatural; and it may be well to ask whether the substitution of '*where*' for '*I will be*,' might not lead to a more satisfactory adjustment of the passage.

3. The word *deber* or 'plague' probably means an *arrow;* and hence, secondarily, the *arrow of pestilence*, as may be illustrated, not only from Hebrew, but from Greek[2], Arabic, &c. A discussion of the root will be found in the second number of the *Journal of Philology*[3]: it may suffice therefore to adduce a single passage, which illustrates, not only the meaning of *deber*, but the very collocation of the words,'*plague*,' or pestilence, and '*destruction*,' as in Hos. xiii. 14. The passage is as follows: ' Thou shalt not be afraid for the terror by night; nor for the *arrow* that flieth by day; nor for the *pestilence* that walketh in darkness; nor for the *destruction* that wasteth at noonday' (Ps. xci. 5, 6). Here the two words in question occur in parallelism with one another, and with *arrow*, which favours the hypothesis that their primitive meanings are, *dart* and *goad*, or the like. These meanings will be recognized as appropriate in Hos. xiii.

---

[1] אהי מלכך אפוא ויושיעך. In some copies there are two slightly different pointings for אהי in ver. 10, 14. Some suppose that this word has arisen, by accidental transposition, from איה, *where*. But compare the Chaldee אהיא.

[2] *Iliad*, 1. 47.

[3] November, 1868, p. 56.

14; for Death is ofttimes represented as armed with missiles or other implements of destruction. 'I will ransom them,' is the Divine promise, 'from the power of the Grave; I will redeem them from Death.' And, as in ver. 10, Israel had been asked, —' *Where* now is thy king, that he may save thee?'—so the promise of deliverance in ver. 14 is followed up by the quick parenthetic interrogations—' *Where*, Death, thy darts? *Where*, Grave, thy goad? Wherewithal wilt thou oppose Me?'—and lastly by the asseveration, that '*repentance* shall be hid from mine eyes;' the LORD hath sworn, and will not *repent*[1].

The foregoing seems better suited to the context than does the rendering '*I will be* &c.;' and it agrees, further, with the LXX. and the citation, except as regards the use of the one word νῖκος. Different methods of reconciliation have been applied to this particular; but it may suffice to suggest, that we are perhaps not dealing with *a formal* citation, and if so, we are under no obligation to harmonize the several clauses of 1 Cor. xv. 55 with the original Hebrew, but need only shew that there is a general agreement between them. In the citation, be it remarked, there is a doubt about the order of the words νῖκος and κέντρον. Placing νῖκος first (although the variation is unimportant), we may thus explain the allusions in 1 Cor. xv. 54, 55.

[i.] St Paul adduces Is. xxv. 8, *rejecting the LXX. rendering as inadequate.*

[ii.] He *goes off at the word* νῖκος, which occurs in a phrase meaning *in perpetuum.*

[iii.] He passes on to Hos. xiii. 14 (wherein *a victory* over death is described), taking up the preceding νῖκος, and thus incorporating it into the passage: 'O grave, where is thy victory?'

[iv.] He concludes, in the Prophet's words: 'O Death, where is thy sting?'

VI. Ex. xxxiv. 33; 2 Cor. iii. 13.

By the insertion of the word 'till' in the Authorized Version, the meaning of the passage cited seems to be misrepre-

---

[1] 1 Sam. xv. 29; Ps. cx. 4.

sented. According to the literal rendering of Ex. xxxiv. 33, it appears that, when Moses had done speaking with them, he put a veil on his face; this being done, that they might not see the quenching of its transitory radiance. 'The use of this veil,' writes Delgado[1], 'was to cover from the people the Shechinah, or glory, that was on Moses' face: but *that* he did not dare to do while he was rehearsing the Lord's words to them; for that glory was his credentials, as if the Lord was speaking to them through his mouth.' But with regard to the putting on of the veil, the true explanation seems to be the former, viz. that they might not scrutinize the ending of his intermittent glory[2].

St Paul's application of this text has occasioned much difficulty. In the Authorized Version, the word 'vail' being inserted, ver. 14 is thus rendered:—'But their minds were blinded: for until this day remaineth the same vail untaken away in the reading of the old testament[3]: which [vail] is done away in Christ[4].' But it is *a priori* more natural to refer the last clause (as does Bengel) to the abolition of the Old Testament, and thus to interpret the καταργεῖται of ver. 14 analogously to the καταργούμενον of ver. 13. With one other alteration we may render the clause in Bengel's words, though not altogether with his meaning, *Quia in Christo aboletur*, 'because it is abolished in Christ.' The connection between ver. 13, 14, may now be exhibited as follows: 'Moses put a veil upon his face that the fading of its transitory radiance might not be looked into: The Jews veil their hearts, and will not gaze upon the fading glories of the Old Covenant; they will not look closely into it, because of their instinctive feeling that it is being done away in Christ.' And this is indeed the application which we should *anticipate* from the way in which the allusion is introduced. 'Much more *that which remaineth* is glorious. Seeing then that we have *such hope* (viz. in the durability of the new dispensation), we use

---

[1] See Barrett's *Synopsis*.
[2] πρὸς τὸ μὴ ἀτενίσαι τοὺς υἱοὺς Ἰσραὴλ εἰς τὸ τέλος τοῦ καταργουμένου.
[3] On the doing away of the *old* covenant, see Heb. viii. 13.
[4] ὅτι ἐν Χριστῷ καταργεῖται.

great plainness of speech: And not as Moses, &c.' (2 Cor. iii. 11—13). We use πολλῇ παῤῥησίᾳ, trusting that our 'glory' will endure: they veil their hearts, for the lack of that same confident assurance[1].

VII. Ps. cxvi. 10; 2 Cor. iv. 13.

The Apostle quotes from the LXX.: 'I believed, and therefore have I spoken;' where articulate expression is viewed as indicative of strong conviction. Do the Hebrew words yield any such meaning as this? Various renderings have been given; but suffice it here to suggest that the connection in the Psalm *may* be as follows. The Psalmist describes the extremity to which he had been reduced. 'I was greatly afflicted: I said in my haste, All men are liars.' The vexed clause immediately precedes, and might be rendered: *I believed, for I must needs speak*[2]*;* and thereupon follow the words spoken, which express the greatness of his affliction. With this interpretation, the speaking is an evidence of belief: the fact that he must needs speak testifies to the strength of his conviction: and thus the sense is the same as in the inverted rendering of the LXX. which the Apostle cites.

VIII. Ps. iv. 4; Eph. iv. 26.

The meaning in the Psalm is, apparently, 'stand in awe and sin not;' but the citation (from the LXX.) seems to mean, '*Be ye angry*, and sin not.' Mr Sinker suggests, however, that ὀργίζεσθε, which has naturally *one* meaning of the Hebrew *ragaz*, may be intended by the LXX. to represent it generally, and thus to include a variety of emotions; for *ragaz*, as meaning primarily *to tremble*, may imply the tremulousness of *fear, &c.*, equally with the tremulousness of *anger*. In Gen. xlv. 24, the LXX. have ὀργίζεσθε, where the meaning, '*Fear*

---

[1] In this explanation, καταργούμενον, καταργουμένου, καταργεῖται (ver. 11, 13, 14) are referred to one and the same thing, viz. the glory of the old διαθήκη. Also the κάλυμμα μὴ ἀνακαλυπτόμενον of ver. 15 is contrasted, as seems philologically simplest, with the ἀνακεκαλυμμένῳ προσώπῳ of ver. 18.

[2] האמנתי כי אדבר.

not by the way,' seems more appropriate than, '*Fall* not *out* by the way:' and a stronger argument may be based upon Ex. xv. 14: 'The people shall hear, and *be afraid;*' unless the Alexandrine reading ἐφοβήθησαν is to replace ὠργίσθησαν[1].

IX. Gen. xlvii. 31 ; Heb. xi. 21.

The LXX. by change of pointing, read 'staff' for 'bed,' and their rendering is adopted in the citation. The Authorized Version has, doubtless, the true rendering of the original: 'And Israel bowed himself *upon the bed's head*[2];' where, moreover, there is an ambiguity in the word *bowed*, which may import, that he *worshipped*, or only that, 'se rursus ad caput lectuli requiem captaturus *inclinârit*[3].' The bed's *head*, it may be remarked, is a Hebraism for the *top* or *surface* of the bed[4]; and thus the meaning is, that he prostrated himself upon the bed, after having strengthened himself, and sat up, as in Gen. xlviii. 2. In the similar passage, 1 Kings i. 47, the word *head* is omitted, and it is recorded simply, that the King bowed himself *upon* the bed ; where, however, the word for 'bed' is different. In Gen. xlviii. 2 the same Hebrew word occurs, and is rightly rendered κλίνην by the LXX. These two passages combined almost suggest the suspicion that the text of the LXX. in Gen. xlvii. 31, may have been corrupted ; but, in any case, the Greek of 1 Kings I. 47, should be taken as a guide to the true construction in the passage cited, and it is evidently unfavourable to the rendering of the Vulgate : 'et adoravit fastigium virgæ ejus.'

It remains however to be asked, whether Jacob's bowing down of himself signified worship, in accordance with the *prima facie* meaning of the citation : and the parallel case of David (*loc. citat.*) suggests that worship is at any rate implied, even if not expressed by the word 'bow down;' for in immediate sequence, comes the prayer of the King : '*Blessed*

---

[1] Schleusner, *Lex. Vet. Test. s. v.* ὀργίζομαι.
[2] The word is על ראש המטה.
[3] Poli *Synops. in loc.*
[4] The rendering, 'upon the bed's *head*,' though literal, is misleading. It means no more than *on the top of*, or simply *on*, the bed.

be the LORD God of Israel, which hath given one to sit on my throne this day.'

X. *Latent Citations.*

Of unacknowledged citations, or such as occur without any introductory formula, there are many which occasion no difficulty, but are at once recognized as containing more or less direct allusions to doctrines of the ancient Scriptures, or to the circumstances, it may be, of the Old Testament history. But an allusion may at times presuppose a very exact acquaintance with the documents referred to, and be set forth accordingly with an indirectness and obscurity which would render it a matter of no slight difficulty to find traces of any reference or citation at all. And it is obvious moreover that the traces of any such reference might be disguised not only by its obliquity and intrinsic indefiniteness, but, in cases of special difficulty, by our imperfect comprehension of (1) the passage in which the allusion occurs, or (2) that to which allusion is made. This remark may be illustrated by the help of R. Shalom ben Abraham's rendering of an obscure verse, Prov. xxi. 8, which we proceed to consider; premising that, even if the rendering proposed should be incorrect, it may still serve to illustrate the nature of a difficulty which has sometimes to be encountered.

1. The Authorized Version reads in the place referred to: 'The way of man is froward and strange: but as for the pure, his work is right' (Prov. xxi. 8). But it is very doubtful whether the word rendered 'man,' and equivalent to the Latin *vir*, can rightly be contrasted with 'the pure.' Some therefore have had recourse to the Arabic, and have rendered the first clause: tortuosa est via viri criminibus onusti[1]—a rendering at which the Rabbinic instinct revolts, 'since Hebrew *usus loquendi* and the absence of all reason for applying such an unhebrew word are repugnant[2].' The explanation about to be proposed is based upon a peculiar idiom of the Hebrew

---

[1] Gesen. *Thesaur.* 399 b.   [2] Fürst. *Lex. s. v.* וזר.

language, exemplified below. 'Thou shalt not have in thy bag *divers weights* [lit. *weight and weight*], a great and a small. Thou shalt not have in thine house *divers measures* [lit. *measure and measure*], a great and a small' (Deut. xxv. 13, 14). 'They were not of *double heart* [lit. *heart and heart*]... All these men of war, that could keep rank, came with a perfect heart to Hebron, to make David king over Israel' (1 Chron. xii. 33, 38). 'With flattering lips and with *a double heart* [lit. *heart and heart*] do they speak' (Ps. xii. 3). Double-dealing is thus expressed in the Hebrew idiom by a simple repetition; and according to this usage *homo duplex* would assume the form '*man and man*.' This formula indeed occurs in another sense in Esther i. 8; but may not the idiom in question be capable of a modified expression, by means of two words of opposite meaning, instead of one and the same word repeated, with an *implied* contradiction and antagonism? If so, then an insincere and self-contradictory character might be expressed as well by the formula *one and another*, as by the more usual collocation *one and one;* and it is on this assumption that Prov. xxi. 8, is explained in the *Qab w' Naqi*.

2. The first word in the Hebrew of Prov. xxi. 8[1], is reduplicated from one which means *to turn*, and it may be represented by our vernacular *zigzag*, if taken as an epithet of the following 'way.' But in the Rabbinic commentary referred to it is taken somewhat differently, as descriptive of a person or character; and the verse is said to define such a person, as *one whose way is sometimes that of one man and sometimes that of another*[2]. The general meaning is thus the same as with the former construction, but it is perhaps better to make 'zigzag' a predicate and render the verse as follows:

The way of a double-minded man is zigzag:
But as for the pure, his work is right.

[1] הפכפך דרך איש וזר וזך ישר פעלו:
[2] נתן גדר לאיש הפכפך והוא שים לו לפעמים דרך איש ולפעמים דרך זר:

Thus the proverb is strikingly similar to that in James i. 8:
A double-minded man is unstable in all his ways.

The Hebrew words here rendered *double-minded* are literally 'man and stranger,' or 'one and *another*[1],' and the phrase is taken to imply duplicity, *i.e.* the coexistence, so to say, of two distinct individualities in the same person. This expression is the natural antithesis of '*the pure*, or *sincere*,'which[2] conveys the idea of ἁπλότης or freedom from admixture. The *LXX.* have ἁγνά in the second hemistich, and St James elsewhere contrasts this double-mindedness with purity, using a derivative of ἁγνός in the second clause of the antithesis, thus: 'Cleanse your hands, ye sinners; and *purify* your hearts, ye *double-minded*' (James iv. 8).

3. The LXX. rendering of the proverb occasions some difficulty, but it is not quite clear that they do not intend to imply a *duplicity* of way by σκολιὰς ὁδούς[3], the epithet used likewise in Prov. xxviii. 18, where the literal rendering is, 'perversus *duarum viarum &c.*' This is made to appear still less unlikely by their freedom in rendering the similar expression in Prov. xxviii. 6, where they make no attempt to preserve the Hebrew idiom, but replace by πλουσίου ψεύδους the whole clause: 'than he that is perverse in *his ways* [lit. *two ways*], though he be rich.' The figure of *going two ways* is reproduced in Ecclus. ii. 12: 'Woe be to fearful hearts, and faint hands, and the sinner that goeth two ways.' And it is worthy of remark that Junius[4], commenting upon the passage, uses instinctively the language of St James, and describes the character in question, *viz.* the man of *two* ways, as, 'The man

---

[1] This is the first meaning of זָר. See Job xix. 27, where the LXX. have οὐκ ἄλλος for וְלֹא זָר.

[2] See Ex. xxvii. 20.

[3] Schleusner, *Lex. Vet. Test. s.v.* σκολιὸς σκολιός, seems to consider that the LXX. repeated σκολιός to express the reduplication in הַכְּכָפֵם. But they may have intended to express freely that the way of the double-minded man is crooked. Their words are: πρὸς τοὺς σκολιοὺς σκολιὰς ὁδοὺς ἀποστέλλει ὁ Θεός, ἁγνὰ γὰρ καὶ ὀρθὰ τὰ ἔργα αὐτοῦ. Here Θεός is explanatory, the literal rendering being taken to be: 'The way of the perverse is [by God's ordering] crooked, seeing that pure and right is His doing.'

[4] Quoted by D'Oyly and Mant.

who is *unstable in his ways,* impelled here and there by doubt and distrust.'

4. The contrast between *purity* and *duplicity* (Prov. xxi. 8; James iv. 8) is illustrated by language used in the *Testaments of the xii Patriarchs*[1], where the ἀγαθὴ διάνοια is described as having, not *two tongues,* of cursing and blessing, &c. but μίαν περὶ πάντας εἰλικρινῆ καθαρὰν διάθεσιν. And a further illustration—none the less trustworthy for its indirectness—is afforded by Mic. vi. 11 : '*Shall I count them pure with the wicked balances*[2], and with the bag *of deceitful weights?*' i.e. containing *two* kinds of weights, great and small, as the Targum well expresses it.

We may reiterate in conclusion that, if the first clause of Prov. xxi. 8 be rendered as proposed, *viz.:*

The way of a double-minded man is zigzag;

or, with slight variation :

A double-minded man is changeful in his way;

there results a perfect parallelism between the first hemistich and the second, wherein *pure* or *sincere* contrasts with *double-minded,* and *right* or *straight* with *zigzag.* St James (i. 8), introduces a proverb so strikingly similar to the foregoing that he would seem almost to be citing it; and this conjecture is confirmed by the circumstance, that elsewhere (iv. 8) he uses the same word *double-minded* in direct contrast with the idea of *purity.* This gives much plausibility to the hypothesis of citation : but whether we are dealing with a citation or no, it is more than probable that citations still lie concealed by our imperfect understanding of the passages cited, or, on the other hand, of those into which they are incorporated.

With this remark we leave the great subject of Citation from the Old Testament in the New ; not as one which has been dealt with fully and exhaustively, but with a sense of its

---

[1] *Test.* Benj. 6. On the word εἰλικρινής, see Isocrat. *ad Demon.* § 47, ed. Sandys. With the δίψυχος of St James, compare δίγλωσσος (Prov. xxiv. 22), δίλογος (1 Tim. iii. 8), διπρόσωπος (*Test.* Dan 4, Asher 2—4). Cp. μονοπρόσωπος.

[2] האזכה במאזני רשע:

vastness and complexity which has grown keener and yet keener with the progress of research. It was patent at the outset, that a plan would be indeed pretentious, which should propose to treat of all the main principles—to say naught of details not unimportant—which invite examination ; but the end has seemed even to recede and grow yet more distant, as each upward step has widened the horizon of enquiry. And when now at length we pause, it is not as upon a summit gained, or with an ocean fathomed ; but rather, as with a quickened appreciation of heights yet unscaled, and of depths which rest yet unexplored.

APPENDIX.

On the words עלמה and בתולה.

The renderings of הָעַלְמָה, Is. vii. 14, may be classed under three heads.

1. The word being regarded as a derivative of עָלַם *to hide*, it is taken to mean 'a virgin,' on etymological grounds. The case is thus stated by Rosenmüller, who adopts the rendering παρθένος, though *not* for etymological reasons:—'Nolumus cum pluribus superioris ætatis interpretibus *virginis* notionem voci עַלְמָה vindicare ex ejus etymo, etsi speciosum sit. Observant עַלְמָה esse ab עָלַם, cujus forma niphal *absconditum, occultum esse, ignorari*, designat... Eam vero etymologiam *soli* convenire *virgini*, quæ sic appellata sit, vel, quod nescia consuetudinis viriliis *occulta* hactenus et *tecta* habeat, quæ honestas, alii quam marito, revelari vetat; vel quod, pro more veterum, *domi lateat* et occultetur, non versata in publico, sed sub oculis matris aut custodis clam aliis servetur, cujusmodi virgines appellarunt κατακλείστους, *conclusas* (2 Macc. iii. 19; 3 Macc. i. 18), ut contra *meretricem* Chaldæi נפקת ברא, *prodeuntem foras*, in publico versatam, vocant.'

2. The Jewish interpreters deny that עַלְמָה means *a virgin*. In Is. vii. 14, Aquila, Symmachus and Theodotion render it by νεᾶνις. Gesenius, referring to the Arabic, makes the root mean 'pubes et coeundi cupidus fuit;' and remarks that, 'Etymon a עָלַם i. q. غَلِمَ indubitatum est, neque audiendi qui *puellam* pr. *absconditam* dictam volunt...vel *signatam, obsignatam* (ab Arab. عَلَمَ) i. e. intactam (Schult.).' But a later lexicographer, Fürst, no less strongly opposed to the rendering παρθένος, directly contradicts Gesenius as regards the first meaning of the root, and affirms the *coeundi cupidus fuit* to be only secondary.

3. A third class of interpreters agree that עַלְמָה does not mean etymologically *a virgin*, but think this meaning required by usage, and in Is. vii. 14 by the context. In this class may be numbered Hengstenberg, who thus writes in his *Christology*: 'All parties now rightly agree that the word עַלְמָה is to be derived from עָלַם, in the signification *to grow up*. To offer here any arguments in proof would be a work of supererogation, as they are offered by all dictionaries... Being derived from עָלַם, *to grow up, to become marriageable*, עַלְמָה can only mean *puella nubilis*.'

We proceed to consider the meanings of I. בְּתוּלָה; II. עַלְמָה; III. בְּתוּלִים and עֲלוּמִים.

I. 'Für die *virgo illibata* hatten aber die Hebräer und übrigen Semiten einen ganz andern Ausdruck, namlich בְּתוּלָה, und die dem entsprechenden Wörter (1 Mos. xxiv. 16).' So Gesenius, who adds, not without plausibility: 'Höchst unwahrscheinlich ist es nun, dass die Hebräer für dieselbe Sache zwey ganz synonyme Ausdrücke gehabt.' But it may be questioned whether בְּתוּלָה means παρθένος strictly and etymologically, as is frequently supposed. On the contrary, the derivation from בָּשַׁל, *maturescere*, would seem to satisfy the requirements of the case more completely than those which make בְּתוּלָה etymologically παρθένος. On the affinity of שׁ and ת, see Fürst *Lex. s. l.* שׁ. [חרת, Ex. xxxii. 16, = חרשׁ.] Fürst, in his *Concordance*, but not in his *Lexicon*, gives the derivation proposed, which makes בְּתוּלָה primarily equivalent to 'matura viro,' and only secondarily to 'nondum corrupta aut viro nupta;' nor that, without qualifying additions, and 'wo es ohne Nachdruck steht.' We proceed to notice some of the usages of the word.

a. The corresponding masculine word is בָּחוּר, lit. *choice*, i. e. one in the prime of life. The two occur together in such passages as: 'With thee also will I break in pieces man and woman; and with thee will I break in pieces old and young; and with thee will I break in pieces the *young man* and the *maid*' (Jer. li. 22). Here the contrasts are those of age and sex. Comp. Deut. xxxii. 25; 2 Chron. xxxvi. 17; Is. lxii. 5; Ezek. ix. 6.

b. 'I made a covenant with mine eyes, why then should I think upon a *maid?*' Here (Job xxxi. 1) it seems unnecessary, as Bernard remarks, to superadd the notion of virginity to that of maturity.

Appendix. 343

Comp. 2 Sam. xiii. 2 (where בְּתוּלָה is again used): 'Amnon was so vexed that he fell sick for his sister Tamar; for she was a *virgin.*' In ver. 18, the meaning *matura* seems more appropriate. It is there said that 'the king's daughters that were בְּתוּלֹת' wore a certain kind of robe, which was perhaps 'longior et amplior' (Gesen. *s. v.* מְעִיל). But all the daughters in question would probably be virgins; those that were married and living elsewhere being excluded. If so, then בְּתוּלֹת must have some other meaning than *virgin*, for this would imply no distinction, but be applicable to all alike. It would be however quite natural that the *grown-up* daughters should wear a dress implying a certain dignity; and accordingly it is not improbable that *grown-up* is the true meaning of בְּתוּלָה in this place. Nor does Joel i. 8 (*infra*) favour the opinion that בְּתוּלָה means strictly παρθένος. 'Lament like a בְּתוּלָה girded with sackcloth for the husband (בַּעַל) of her youth.'

c. In Gen. xxiv. 16 it is said of Rebecca, that she was 'a *virgin*, neither had any man known her;' where the last words seem to supplement the foregoing, and to express what they alone could at the most have implied. The full phrase rendered 'virgin' is, נַעֲרָה בְּתוּלָה, i. e. a girl *of full age*, not a *child*, as is shewn by the epithet בְּתוּלָה, but which would have been left doubtful if נַעֲרָה had stood alone. A like form of expression is used in Jud. xxi. 12; and even in Lev. xxi. 14 it is not certain that בְּתוּלָה *of itself* means strictly παρθένος. The high-priest is to take a wife in her virginity (ver. 13): not a widow, or a divorced woman, or profane, or an harlot: 'but he shall take a בְּתוּלָה *of his own people* to wife.' The force of the words italicized must not be overlooked. The harlot is 'the *strange* woman:' אַחֶרֶת (Jud. xi. 2) corresponds to זוֹנָה: and in Deut. xxiii. 17 it is expressly laid down, that 'there shall be no whore of the daughters of ISRAEL, nor a sodomite of the sons of ISRAEL.' The first meaning of בְּתוּלָה might well be *matura*, one in the prime of early womanhood; and the meaning παρθένος might naturally arise therefrom as secondary.

d. Some have assumed, and that, as it would seem, arbitrarily, that the word בְּתוּלָה when applied to cities implies (1) the state of not being conquered; or (2) religious purity, and faithfulness to the

God of Israel. But Rosenmüller, following the Chaldee, remarks on Amos v. 2, that '*virgo* pro cœtu hominum, quacunque se ratione habet, per prosopopœiam accipienda erit.' Jerome indeed defends the hypothesis (2), remarking: '*Virgo* autem appellatur populus Israel, non quia in virginitatis permanserit puritate, sed quia quondam instar virginis Deo sit copulata.' But the name *virgo* is as applicable to the heathen cities Egypt, Babylon, &c. as to the Holy City. Moreover, it is not required by the Hebrew idiom that a city should be represented as a *virgin* proper; but, as in other languages a city may be a *metropolis*, so in Hebrew the suburbs of a city are called its *daughters* (Josh. xv. 45). Again, בְּתוּלָה is applied by Isaiah not only to a *heathen* city, but to one in the prophet's view, already *conquered*, which seems opposed to the theory (1). Thus: 'Come down, and sit in the dust, O *virgin*, daughter of Babylon, sit on the ground: there is no throne, O daughter of the Chaldeans' (Is. xlvii. 1).

In ver. 9 we read: 'These two things shall come to thee in a moment in one day, *the loss of children, and widowhood:*' while St John styles Babylon the 'mother of harlots' (Rev. xvii. 5), and thus writes, with plain reference to Is. xlvii : 'For all nations have drunk of the wine of the wrath of her fornication, and the kings of the earth have committed fornication with her... How much she hath glorified herself, and lived deliciously, so much torment and sorrow give her: for she saith in her heart, I sit a queen, and am no widow, and shall see no sorrow. Therefore shall her plagues come in one day, death, and mourning, and famine' (Rev. xviii. 3, 7, 8).

We shall now proceed to consider the meaning of עַלְמָה.

II. The verb עָלַם is common in Hebrew, and has one well-defined sense, viz. *to conceal* [opp. to יָדַע]: it is natural therefore to attempt an explanation of עַלְמָה as a derivative of this root, before having recourse to comparatively modern dialects. If the primary meaning *to seal* (for which Albert Schultens refers to the Arabic) be assumed, we may explain all the usages of עָלַם in a way which is at least plausible.

(i.) The meanings *seal* and *conceal* are intimately connected; the latter being immediately deducible from the former. Hence the prevalent usages of the *verb* in question may be accounted for.

(ii.) עֹלָם signifies *eternity* (past or future), which is like a *sealed* book (Rev. v. 1).

(iii.) In deriving עַלְמָה we must take into account its masculine correlative עֶלֶם ; and this may be done by a physiological application of the root-meaning *seal*. The words would thus carry with them primarily the negation of development, and would be applicable from the time of infancy to the age of the בחור and בתולה, as their upper limits. For this application of the meaning *seal*, we may compare, החתים (Lev. xv. 3); and Cant. iv. 12, where the beloved is described as מעין חתום, 'fons *obsignata*, de puella casta et intemerata' (Gesen. *Thesaur.* 587 *b*).

(iv.) The *usages* of עֶלֶם and עַלְמָה have yet to be considered. The former occurs in 1 Sam. xvii. 56: 'Enquire thou whose son the *stripling* is.' And in 1 Sam. xx. 22, where it is applied to the נער קטן of ch. xx. 35.

The word עלמה is allowed, if not to mean etymologically παρθένος, at least to be used of παρθένοι, in all cases except two, viz. Cant. vi. 8 and Prov. xxx. 18—20. But in the former passage עלמות is contrasted with *queens* and *concubines*, and would thus seem to designate such as are in fact παρθένοι. The latter passage, which is much disputed, runs as follows: 'There be three things which are too wonderful for me; yea, four which I know not: The way of an eagle in the air; the way of a serpent upon a rock; the way of a ship in the midst of the sea; and the way of a man with a *maid* (דרך גבר בעלמה). Such is the way of an adulterous woman; she eateth, and wipeth her mouth, and saith, I have done no wickedness.' Like phraseology is used in Sap. Sol. v. 10, 11, for the purpose of illustration, but the mention of the *serpent* is omitted, as though unsuited for the application which is made of the passage: nor again are the things in question there described as wonderful and mysterious. But, to return to the passage, the marvel is said to consist in the *invisibility* of the eagle's track, &c. Why then should the eagle be chosen, rather than any other bird? The question is answered by Rosenmüller, who in his answer confounds the want of any mark upon the air with the invisibility of the bird itself. But a ship cannot be said to leave no track; and that especially בלב הים.

All trace no doubt soon vanishes, but less soon in salt-water than in fresh; and thus בְּלֵב הַיָּם[1] instead of being emphatic is made meaningless, not to say inaccurate. Nor, supposing these preliminary difficulties surmounted, is it easy to apply them to the final clause, *via viri in virgine*. The result would be at least disappointing, if the great marvel to which all converges were that the עַלְמָה 'quid vitii sibi hæreat ita dissimulat, ut ab aliis id frustra pervestigatur.' But it is altogether unnatural that the *invisibility* of a bird's track in the air should be described as an impenetrable mystery; and so with the serpent, and the ship.

The word דֶּרֶךְ does not mean ἴχνη or *vestigium*, but *modus agendi*. The flight of the eagle challenges especial admiration (Job ix. 26); the ship[2] at sea, and the strange convolutions of the footless serpent are likewise chosen as fit types of the marvellous. One and all lead up to that crowning mystery, the infatuation of youthful love, which has arrested the attention of parœmiasts, poets and philosophers in all time. After the mention of the 'four things' comes, in ver. 20, an allusion, suggested by the contrast, to the infatuation of an adulterous woman, who 'saith (*sc.* in her heart), I have done no wickedness.'

To recapitulate—we have concluded that עַלְמָה (from the root *obsignavit*) implies a negation of development, and is applicable up to the age at which the term בְּתוּלָה or *matura* becomes applicable. The former word is not used in the Bible of any but παρθένοι, while the latter may imply, but does not expressly predicate, παρθενία. We proceed to notice

(i.) עֲלוּמִים ; (ii.) בְּתוּלִים.

III. These last forms, after the analogy of זְקוּנִים, נְעוּרִים, denote (*a*) the *age* or *time of life* of the עֶלֶם or the עַלְמָה and the בְּתוּלָה ; and (*b*) the *conditions* and *natural concomitants* of those ages. In Jud. xi. 37, the daughter of Jephthah is spared for awhile to bewail the devoted capacities of her early womanhood: אֶבְכֶּה עַל בְּתוּלַי, 'deplorabo ætatem meam virgineam' (Gesen. *Thesaur.*

---

[1] יָם seems here to mean strictly *sea*, though it does not necessarily in all contexts. For the whole phrase, cp. Prov. xxiii. 34.

[2] French and Skinner understand *nautilus*, by 'ship,' in Ps. civ. 26.

205, *b*). In Ezek. xxiii. 3, בְּתוּלֵיהֶן, standing in parallelism with נְעוּרֵיהֶן, denotes the time of incepting maturity. Again, עֲלוּמִים denotes the condition of the עֶלֶם in Job xx. 11, where it stands for the freshness as of extreme youth, in contrast with decay and death; while the בְּתוּלִים are the natural concomitants of the age of the בְּתוּלָה, and their absence therefore implies some defect. Hence בְּתוּלִים means primarily *signa pubertatis*, and then by implication *signa virginitatis* (Deut. xxii. 14). We may compare further Is. liv. 4, where, in a description of the barren that did not bear, בֹּשֶׁת עֲלוּמַיִךְ, 'the shame of thy youth,' stands in parallelism with חֶרְפַּת אַלְמְנוּתַיִךְ, 'the reproach of thy widowhood.'

It has been noticed above that there is *one* Biblical meaning of עלם undisputed, viz. *occultavit, abscondit.* Gesenius adds, that 'in reliquis linguis cognatis hæc radix non reperitur' (*Thesaur.* 1035, *a*). It is noteworthy that the Arabic غلم, to which Gesenius refers עַלְמָה, nearly coincides with a meaning of יָדַע, *to know,* while the Hebrew root עלם has a directly opposite meaning. In Job xx. 11 עֲלוּמִים is said by some to mean radically *strength;* and hence it may be seen how easily that meaning might have come to be thought inherent though not really so. Thus, supposing עָלַם to have meant originally *obsignavit,* the meanings *youth, youthfulness* and *strength* might have been successively derived, and the last may then have been taken as primary in the cognate dialects. But inferences from those dialects are precarious unless corroborated by internal evidence from the more ancient Hebrew.

INDEX OF TEXTS AND PASSAGES.

Genesis.

	Page
ii. 4	xxiii
iii. 5	102
iv. 25	219
ix. 20	317
x. 23	67
xi. 1	xxv
xiv. 17—20	25
xv. 5	219, 298
xv. 7, 8	288, 292
xv. 9—18	292, 297, 299
xviii. 10	195, 325
xxi. 12	195, 219
xxii. 1—14	294
xxiii. 16, 17	298
xxiv. 16	343
xxv. 21	xxv
xxv. 23	195
xxxi. 36	317
xxxv. 19	55
xxxvii. 10	55
xlv. 27	325
xlvii. 31	335
xlviii. 7	55
xlix. 6	146
xlix. 9	52
xlix. 10	xxv, 51, 72

Exodus.

	Page
i. 12	30
ii. 14	215
iv. 19, 20	61
iv. 22	63, 64
vi. 3	xxvi
xii. 7	299
xii. 46	107, 322
xv. 14	335
xv. 17	171
xx. 1	61
xxi. 24	274
xxiv. 6, 8	283, 297, 299
xxv. 8	171

	Page
xxxiii. 19	195
xxxiv. 33	332

Leviticus.

	Page
xi. 42	xxii
xvi. 15	299
xix. 17, 18	260, 262
xxi. 13, 14	343

Numbers.

	Page
ix. 12	107, 322
x. 35	172
xxi. 5—9	119
xxii. 3	30
xxiv. 8	73

Deuteronomy.

	Page
vi. 5	260
vi. 13	xxxi
vi. 16	xxx
viii. 3	xxx
xviii. 15—19	157
xxi. 17	287
xxii. 14	347
xxiii. 17	343
xxv. 4	xxxi, xxxii
xxv. 13, 14	337
xxxii. 18	xxiii
xxxii. 35	262, 312
xxxii. 40	317
xxxii. 43	164, 327

Joshua.

	Page
xv. 45	344

Judges.

	Page
xi. 2	343
xi. 37	347

Ruth.

	Page
ii. 14	235

1 Samuel.

	Page
x. 2	55
xv. 22	178
xvii. 53	317
xviii. 21	232
xxv. 1	133

2 Samuel.

	Page
vii. 12—16	144, 164
vii. 29	20
xiii. 2, 18	343
xxiii. 1—7	20

1 Kings.

	Page
i. 47	335

2 Kings.

	Page
i. 7	96
xv. 37	28
xvi.	28
xxii. 13	181

1 Chronicles.

	Page
v. 2	51
xii. 33, 38	337
xiv. 17	172
xvii. 1, 2	172
xvii. 11—14	144
xxviii. 4	51

2 Chronicles.

	Page
v. 5	171

Index of Texts and Passages. 349

	Page
vi. 41, 42	144
xxiv. 18—22	11, 15
xxviii	28
xxxv. 25	140

Esther.
i. 8	337

Job.
ix. 26	346
xv. 16	252
xix. 27	338
xx. 11	347
xxxi. 1	342
xxxi. 29, 30	262
xxxiv. 7	252

Psalms.
ii.	154
ii. 2, 3	228
ii. 7	27, 157, 229
ii. 8	77
iv. 4	334
v. 10	316
vii. 14	317
viii. 6	24
x. 4	228
x. 7	316
xii. 3	337
xiv. 1—7*	314
xvi.	141, 147
xvi. 3	142
xvi. 8—11	128, 144
xviii. 49	327
xix. 4	92
xxii.	110, 114
xxii. 1	115
xxii. 7, 8	115, 248
xxii. 15	242
xxii. 18	115
xxii. 31	237, 242
xxviii. 4	262
xxxi. 5	115
xxxiv. 10	273
xxxiv. 20	107, 322
xxxv. 4—8	243, 261
xxxv. 19	241
xxxvi. 1—4	316
xxxvii. 25	273
xxxvii. 37, 38	236
xl.	178
xl. 6—8	176, 181, 185
xli. 9	255, 257
xlv.	154

	Page
xlv. 6—8	162, 166
l. 5	295
li.	184
li. 4	324
lii. 3, 4	316
lv. 20	236
lvi.	141
lvii.	141
lviii.	141
lviii. 1	142
lix.	141
lix. 11	142
lx.	141
lxii. 9	324
lxviii.	171
lxviii. 18	167, 170
lxviii. 27	52
lxix.	111, 230
lxix. 4, 9	241
lxix. 19	232
lxix. 21	114, 116, 241
lxix. 22—24	236, 239
lxix. 26	229
lxix. 27, 28	237, 243
lxxi. 16	185
lxxiii. 2	273
lxxviii. 67—69	170
lxxx. 14	xxii
lxxxix. 3—35	144
xci. 5, 6	331
xci. 11, 12	xxx
xcv. 7, 8	135
xcvi. 6—8	329
xcvii. 7	164
cii.	111
cii. 26—28	164
civ. 4	164
civ. 26	346
cix.	226, 245, 258
cix. 20	250, 259, 269
cx.	18
cx. 1	16, 164
cx. 3	17
cxvi. 10	334
cxvi. 11	324
cxvii 1	327
cxxvii. 3	250
cxxxii. 10—14	143
cxxxvii. 8, 9	268
cxxxiv. 14	263
cxl. 3	316
cxlvi. 3	324

Proverbs.
i. 16	316

	Page
vi. 6	xxxiii
x. 24	xiv
xii. 10	xxxii
xx. 17, 18	262
xxi. 8	336, 337, 339
xxv. 21, 22	263
xxviii. 6, 18	338
xxx. 18—20	345

Ecclesiastes.
vii. 20	315

Song of Solomon.
iv. 12	345
v. 10	137
vi. 8	345

Isaiah.
iv. 2	70
vi. 10	92
vii. 4—12	32, 46, 47
vii. 6	xxv
vii. 13—16	30, 33, 41
vii. 17—25	31, 34, 35
viii. 1—4	31
viii. 8	41
viii. 14—19	42, 44
ix. 1	36, 48, 56
ix. 2—7	36, 41, 48
ix. 13	29
x. 15	48, 103
x. 20	29
x. 21	37, 45
xi. 1	68, 71, 75
xi. 10	122, 327
xiv. 19	67
xvii. 9	46
xxi. 10	91
xxii. 13	227
xxv. 7, 8	329
xxvi. 2	xxvi
xxvi. 14	326
xxviii. 16	42
xxix. 9, 10	240
xxxviii. 9—22	31, 140
xl. 10	250, 258
xlvi. 1—7	211
xlvii. 1, 9	269, 344
li. 17, 18	85
lii. 2—12	82
lii. 13—15	74†, 88, 102
liii.	75†, 88

* Prayer-Book Version. † New Translation.

Index of Texts and Passages.

	Page
liii. 1, 2	69, 70
liii. 3	79
liii. 8	85, 126
liii. 9	122
liii. 11, 12	79, 102, 104
liv. 1	197
liv. 2—5	82, 347
lv. 3, 4	128, 142, 144
lvi. 10	75, 126
lix. 7, 8	316
lxi. 10	124
lxii. 11	250
lxiv. 3	75

Jeremiah.

ii. 22	136
vii. 22, 23	214
xx. 17	33
xxiii. 5, 6	237
xxv. 26	xxv
xxx. 9	143
xxxi. 15	xiii, 53
xxxi. 31—34	285
xxxiv. 18—20	292, 298
l. 28	231, 241
li. 11	231, 241
li. 41	xxv

Lamentations.

i. 12	86
ii. 15, 16	86
iii. 12	86
iii. 42—48	85
iv. 12	75

Ezekiel.

xvi. 4	307
xviii. 4	301
xviii. 20—23	303
xix. 10—14	17
xx. 6	34
xxiii. 3	347
xxiii. 8	73
xxxiv. 11	93
xxxiv. 22—24	142
xxxvii. 24—26	143

Hosea.

i. 10	326
ii. 15	62, 213
ii. 19, 20	12
ii. 23	326
iii. 4, 5	143

	Page
v. 14, 15	8
vi. 1—6	1, 9
xi. 1	59, 73, 313
xiii. 9—14	329, 330

Joel.

i. 8	343

Amos.

v. 2	344
v. 18—27	207, 211, 222
vii. 2, 5	75

Obadiah.

ver. 18	xxv

Jonah.

ii. 2, 6	166
ii. 9	10

Micah.

iii. 11	50
v. 2	49
v. 5	50
vi. 11	339
vii. 18	10

Nahum.

i. 14	126

Habakkuk.

i. 5	75

Zechariah.

i. 1	15
iii. 1	246
iii. 8	80
ix. 11	283, 287
xii. 10	313, 322

Malachi.

i. 2, 3	195

Tobit.

iv. 15	278

Wisdom of Solomon.

	Page
v. 10, 11	345
xvi. 5—7	119

Ecclesiasticus.

ii. 12	338

2 Maccabees.

iii. 19	341

3 Maccabees.

i. 18	341

St Matthew.

i. 21	84
i. 22, 23	xiii, 28, 41
ii. 1—6	49, 52
ii. 14	64, 72
ii. 15	59, 64, 73
ii. 16	56
ii. 17, 18	xiii, 49, 54
ii. 23	49, 66
iii. 7	123
iii. 16	118
iv. 3—11	xxx
iv. 12—16	49, 56, 72
v. 17	276
v. 18	xxvii
v. 38, 39	274
vi. 13	124
vii. 12	276, 277
viii. 17	88, 92
ix. 10—13	1
ix. 14	3
x. 31	xxxii
xi. 21—24	58
xii. 5—8	1, 4, 6
xiii. 17	41
xiii. 52	ix
xx. 28	105
xxi. 24—27	22
xxi. 44	42
xxii. 37—40	260, 276
xxii. 42—45	16, 21
xxiv. 3	40
xxiv. 34—37	12, 40, 123
xxvi. 26—28	281, 283, 300
xxvi. 54	257
xxvii. 27—30	241
xxvii. 33—49	115, 242
xxvii. 50	323

Index of Texts and Passages.

St Mark.

	Page
i. 10	118
ii. 10, 11	47
ii. 17	4
ii. 25	5
ii. 27	6
ix. 12	79
x. 45	105
x. 46—48	72
xii. 32	276
xii. 36, 37	16, 21
xv. 28	89
xv. 34	193
xv. 37	323

St Luke.

i. 32, 33	41
i. 46, 47	124
i. 79	41
iii. 21	118
iv. 3—13	xxx
iv. 17	327
v. 31, 32	4
v. 33	3
vi. 9	8
vi. 31	278
ix. 55	271
x. 26, 27	277
xi. 49—51	15
xii. 7	xxxii
xv. 12	287
xvi. 8	123
xvi. 17	xxvii
xviii. 35—39	72
xx. 18	42
xx. 41—44	16, 21
xxii. 20	300
xxii. 28—30	290
xxii. 37	79, 89, 100
xxiii. 35, 46	115, 323
xxiv. 5	42
xxiv. 44	133

St John.

i. 29, 36	89, 105
i. 47	66, 69
ii. 17	241
iii. 14, 15	119, 121
iv. 21, 23	217
v. 7	8
vii. 24	97
vii. 27	23, 97
vii. 42	53
ix. 4	8
x. 11—19	107, 184

	Page
x. 33—36	162
xi. 49—52	110, 149
xii. 38	88, 90, 92
xii. 41	92
xiii. 34	277
xiii. 37, 38	108
xv. 25	241
xvii. 3	12
xviii. 20, 21	99
xix. 19	69
xix. 28	242
xix. 30	116
xix. 33—36	107, 323
xix. 37	312

Acts.

i. 7	40
i. 16—20	134, 242, 254
ii. 23	108
ii. 24	147
ii. 25—28	128, 136
ii. 29—31	136, 147
ii. 34, 35	24
iii. 22, 23	157
iv. 27, 28	108
vii.	207
vii. 37	157
vii. 38—41	223
vii. 41—43	208, 311
viii. 32, 33	89, 96, 123
xiii. 15—28	159
xiii. 32	158
xiii. 33	157
xiii. 34	128, 147, 158
xiii. 35	128
xiii. 36, 37	136, 147
xiii. 41	75
xv. 18	xv
xxiv. 5	67, 69
xxvi. 4, 5	99

Romans.

iii. 4	324
iii. 10—18	314
iii. 26	77
iv. 25	89
v. 18, 19	77
vi. 2—7	302
vi. 23	250
ix. 6—16	147, 195, 325
ix. 25, 26	196, 326
ix. 32, 33	42
x. 14—17	88, 90, 295
xi. 2—11	135, 239, 240
xi. 30, 31	11

	Page
xii. 19—21	263, 276
xiii. 10	277
xv. 1—3	93, 241
xv. 10	327
xv. 21	88

1 Corinthians.

i. 21	91
ii. 9	75
v. 7	106
x. 1—4	221
x. 4—9	60
x. 7—11	xxxi, xxxii
xi. 24	281
xi. 25	287, 300
xiii. 5, 7	275
xv. 21, 22	304
xv. 25	24
xv. 32	227
xv. 50	147
xv. 54, 55	329

2 Corinthians.

iii. 11—13	332, 334
iv. 13	334
iv. 17	36
v. 15, 18	302, 304
v. 21	121

Galatians.

ii. 20	302
iii. 8	220
iii. 13	121
iii. 15—18	218
iii. 27—29	219
iv. 21—23	189
iv. 24—31	190, 193, 206

Ephesians.

ii. 13—16	50, 298, 301
iv. 4—12	168, 173, 175
iv. 26	334

Philippians.

ii. 5—11	88, 101, 184
iv. 11, 13	279

Colossians.

ii. 20	302
ii. 23—25	204
iv. 16	45

Index of Texts and Passages.

2 Thessalonians.

	Page
ii. 6	45

1 Timothy.

ii. 5, 6	299
v. 17, 18	xxxi

2 Timothy.

iv. 14	261

Hebrews.

i. 5—14	24, 164, 329
ii. 11, 12	124
iv. 7	134
iv. 8, 9	135
v. 5, 6	25, 27, 159
vi. 13—18	297
vii. 1—3	25, 98
vii. 21—28	25, 77
viii. 6—13	285
ix. 11—14	285
ix. 15—23	286, 295
ix. 28	100

	Page
x. 1—7	176, 182, 311
x. 10	182
x. 12, 13	24
x. 19—22	301
x. 30	262
xi. 19	293, 295
xi. 21	335
xii. 10—14	124
xii. 18, 22	202
xiii. 8	124

James.

i. 8	338, 339
i. 17	xxxi
iv. 8	338, 339

1 Peter.

i. 10—12	45
ii. 3	124
ii. 8	42
ii. 10	326
ii. 18, 19	105
ii. 22	89
ii. 24, 25	88, 89
iii. 10—12	124

2 Peter.

	Page
i. 19	25
i. 20, 21	149
ii. 22	xxxiii

1 John.

iii. 5	89
iii. 16	108

Revelation.

i. 7	312, 322
ii. 20	270
v. 1	345
v. 5	52, 75
v. 6	106, 322
v. 8, 9	105
xi. 8	66
xiii. 18	xxv
xiv. 5	89
xvii. 5	344
xviii. 3—8	268, 344
xxi. 3	41
xxii. 12	250

INDEX OF SUBJECTS.

Abraham, his meeting with Melchizedek, 25; his two wives, 193, 203; catholicity of the promise to, 220; its twofold confirmation, 291, 297; Christ the SEED of, 218.

Agast, usages of the word, 75, 125.

Albam, xxv.

Allegory, xv, xvii. See *Hagar, Philo.*

Annunciation, the, 41.

Ark of the Covenant, its procession from the house of Obed-Edom to Mount Zion, 20, 171, 172.

Ascension, the, 174.

Assyrian invasion, predicted by Isaiah, 33, 35; by Micah, 50.

Athbash, xxv.

Atonement, and Satisfaction (Jowett), 280; day of, 294.

Babylon, called *Sheshach*, xxv; substituted for Damascus by St Stephen, 223; the curse of, 268; called *virgin*, 344; the fall of, 344.

Baptism, of John, 22; varying accounts of the, 118; symbolism of, 302.

Bethlehem Ephratah, 49; Rachel buried near, 50.

Blood, of a Testament, meaningless, 283; of sprinkling, 299, 304; its purifying effect not primary, 301; the efflux of 'blood and water,' 323.

Cabbalistic speculations, xxiv, 129; their origin, 202.

Captivity, Psalms of the, 113, 184, 234; the spirituality of religion taught by, 177; predicted by Amos, 209; its typology, 239.

Charity, a condition of imperfection, 266; its power, 271; the growth of, 272; its relation to knowledge, 272, 275.

Chiun, a noun substantive, 210; how changed to Remphan?, 222.

Christ, the Physician, 2; greater than the Temple, 6; His lament over

Index of Subjects. 353

Jerusalem, 11; His origin mysterious, 23, 26, 97; His sacrifice final, 24, 182; His priesthood, 25, 305; His settlement in Capernaum, 56; called from Egypt, 59; a Nazarene, 66; His Divinity, 100, 165; the second Adam, 102, 303; the Redeemer, 104, 109; the Lamb of God, 105; the good Shepherd, 107; His throne for ever, 165; like Moses, 215; the Mediator, 295.

Citations, inexactness of, xxi; their contexts disregarded, xxviii; authorship of, 129, 135; abruptly introduced in Hebrew, 75, 227; latent, 88, 336; arguments from styles of citation, 322. See *Formulæ*.

Covenant, of God with Abraham, 291; symbolism of, 292; various forms of, harmonized, 300, 304; the old, done away in Christ, 333.

Crucifixion, narrative of the, 114, 323.

David, last words of, 20; his relation to the Messiah, 21; a name of the Messiah, 52, 153; the sure mercies of, 128; the Prophet, 142; Psalms of, 18, 133, 184.

Egypt, the flight into, 59; the idols fall before Christ, 65; Israel's election in, 64.

Enemies, destroyed by charity, 265; why to be forgiven? 266.

Ethics, Christian and Jewish, 260; practical and ideal, 267; originality of Christian, 276.

Formulæ of citation, xi; indefinite?, xiii; Rabbinic, xiv; classical, 72; remarks on special, 134. See 57, 70, 116.

Future state, its relation to ethics, 272.

Good Shepherd, the, 107.

Gospel, before the Law, 218; one in principle therewith, 262; genuineness of St John's, 323; Apocryphal Gospels quoted, 64.

Hagar, St Paul's allegory of, 193; Philo's, 203; interpretations of the word, 199; to be omitted in Gal. iv. 25?, 198, 205.

Hebrew text, preservation of, xxii; its letters counted, xxii; wilfully corrupted?, xxiv, 327; Masoretic, xxiii; ante-Masoretic, xxvii.

Hellenistic dialect as vernacular, 318.

Hezekiah, not Immanuel, 37; thought to be the Messiah, 39; not the subject of Ps. xxii., 110; his hymn, 140.

Hillel, on the Messiah, 39; anecdote of, 277.

Immanuel, prophecy of, 28, 50; land of, 34; titles of, 36.

Imprecations, in the Psalms, 224; in the New Testament, 261, 271.

Incarnation, indistinctly foreseen, 45; symbolized by the covenantal sacrifice, 293.

Infancy, formulæ describing, 33; Gospel of the, 64.

Innocents, murder of the, 56.

Isaac, the child of promise, 193. See *Resurrection*.

Jonah. See *Resurrection*.

Josiah, public lamentations for, 140.

Judas, the guide to them that took Jesus, 242; the Scripture how applicable to?, 256.

Knowledge, of God, 12. See *Charity*.

Lamb, of God, 105; the Paschal, 107, 294; different words for, 322.

Maher-shalal-hash-baz, not Immanuel, 30.

Matthias, ordination of St, 257.

Mediation, its primary meaning, 296; implies *inclusion* not *intervention*, 299; of Moses, 299, 304; of Christ, 280, 301.

Melchizedek, a type of Christ, 26.

Messiah, birthplace of, 52; his relation to David, 21; the Branch, 35, 70; the suffering, 74; the servant of the Lord, 82, 102; popular conception of, 71, 86; expected prematurely, 39. See *Shiloh*.

Messianic, interpretations of the Old Testament, xvii; ideal, xxxiv; hope of David, 19; interpretation of Is. vii., 35; of Is. liii., 78; Psalms, 22, 113, 154. See *Rashi*.

Michtam, the meaning of, 136; compared with Michtab, 140; Psalms designated, 141.

Moloch, an incorrect rendering, 210; worshipped in the wilderness?, 212.

Nazarene, derived from Netser, 67; meaning of, 69.

Old Testament, nomenclature of its

23

books, 133; imprecatory language of, 260.

Parable, definition of a, xxxiv; of the Tares, 272; of the Prodigal Son, 287.
Philo, as an allegorist (Jowett), 187; on the brazen serpent, 121; his allegory of Hagar, 203.
Predestination, 243.
Prophecy, its relation to history, xxxi; of Immanuel, 28, 50; its Messianic interpretation, 35; of Shiloh, 40, 51; lost, 45; unwritten, 70; unconscious, 23, 149; double sense of, xxxiv, 149.
Proverbs, teaching by, xxxii.
Psalms, titles of, 177; non-natural interpretation of, 113, 269, 273; written for congregational use, 116; coextensive with Hagiographa, 133; the monumental, 136. See *Captivity, David, Imprecations, Messianic, Type.*

Qab w'Naqî quoted, 129, 337.

Rachel, weeping for her children, 53; her sepulchre, 55.
Ramah, 55.
Rashi, on the Messianic interpretation of the second Psalm, xvii.
Remphan, not mentioned in the Hebrew, 311. See *Chiun.*
Resurrection, Christ's, predicted by David, 147; Ps. ii. 7 applied to?, 157; typified by Jonah, 165; (symbolical) of Isaac, 293; the general, 329.
Righteousness, manifestation of God's, 237.

Sabbath, 4, 6.
Sacraments, symbolism of, 300, 301.
Sacrifice, contrasted with mercy, 1; with obedience, 181; teaching of captivity with respect to, 177; spiritual meaning of, 106; the symbolism of, 280; its representative nature, 122, 294, 302. See *Wilderness.*
Sanctuary, a type of heaven, 170, 284; saying of Rashi upon, 170; God dwells in, figuratively, 171, 217; Ark removed to, 20, 172.
Scripture and Science, 131.
Septuagint, as a medium of citation, xix, 306; wilful corruption of, 307, 313; inspiration of, 308; why generally adopted in citation, 309; non-Septuagintal citations, 312, 332; assimilated to the New Testament, 314; to the Hebrew, 317; its double renderings, 317, 328; its theological importance, 319.
Serpent of brass, 119.
Shiloh, prophecy of, 37, 40; Messianic, xxv.
Signs, four kinds of, 44.
Spiritual language at first typical and pleonastic, 154; spiritual interpretations, xxxii, 98, 150.
Stephen, apology of St, 215; its effect on St Paul, 222.

Temple, not built till Solomon's time, 217; cleansing of the, 241.
Testament. See *Will.*
Traditional exegesis, value of, xv, xvii.
Type, the word, xxix; spiritual ideas expressed by types, xxxiv; typical characters in the Psalms, 113, 270.

Vail, of Christ's flesh, 301; on Moses' face, 333.
Virgin, the, 45; meanings of the two words translated, 341.

Wilderness, the forty years in, 214; sacrifice not offered in, 212; but in what sense?, 213.
Will, the idea classical and non-Biblical, 287, 289; inappropriate in Heb. ix., 285; and subversive of the argument, 289.

INDEX OF GREEK WORDS AND PHRASES.

	Page
ἀκοή	91
ἀλληγορούμενα	191, 206
ἀμνός	322
ἄνθρακας πυρός	263
ἀνθ' ὧν κατωρχήσαντο	313, 322
ἀνίστημι	158
ἁρπαγμός	101
αὐτάρκεια	279
γενεά	98, 123
γεννῶσα	206
διαθήκη	283, 289
διὰ στόματος	134
διαφθορά	145
δίψυχος	339
ἑαυτὸν ἐκένωσεν	103
ἐγκαταλείψεις εἰς	146
ἔδει πληρωθῆναι	256
ἔδωκεν δόματα τοῖς ἀνθρώποις	167
εἶδε διαφθοράν	147
εἰλικρινής	339
εἰσερχόμενος εἰς τὸν κόσμον	186
εἰς νῖκος	330
ἐκκλίνοντες ὀπίσω	317
ἐμεσίτευσεν ὅρκῳ	297
ἐν τῷ αἵματι	300
ἐν τῷ τόπῳ οὗ ἐρρέθη	326
ἐν Χριστῷ	279, 301
ἐξ Αἰγύπτου	64, 73, 313
ἐξουδενωθῇ	79
ἐπὶ νεκροῖς	295
ἐστιν ἔχοντα	204
Ζωφασημίν	67
ἡγεμόσιν	53
ἡ παρθένος	45, 341
ἵνα πληρωθῇ	xiii, 58, 73
κάλαμος	118

	Page
κατάνυξις	240
κεραία	xxvii
κληρονομήσει πολλούς	77, 104
κληρονομία	288
κρίσις ἤρθη	96
μεσίτης	296
Ναζωραῖος	66
ὁδὸν θαλάσσης	57, 72
ὄξος	117, 234
ὀργίζεσθε	334
ὅτι ἐν Χριστῷ καταργεῖται	333
ὅτι κατηριθμημένος ἦν	148, 255
Οὕξ	67
περιθεὶς ὑσσώπῳ	118
πίστις	321
Ῥαιφάν	222
σκολιός	338
σπέρμα	218
στηλογραφία	136, 140
σῶμα	176, 311
τὰ ὅσια Δαβίδ	129
τὸ γὰρ Ἄγαρ	175, 198, 205
τὸ δὲ ἀνέβη	175
τὸν ὅσιόν σου	129
τόπος	327
τὸ ῥηθὲν διὰ τῶν προφητῶν	70
τότε ἐπληρώθη	xii, xiii, 72
χολή	117
χρόνῳ τῷ ζῶντι	325
ψεύστης	324
ψυχὴν τίθημι	109
ὠργίσθησαν	335
ὡσεὶ περιστεράν	118
ὦτια	176

INDEX OF HEBREW WORDS AND PHRASES.

Page		Page	
331	אחי	163	כסאך אלהים
179, 183	אזנים כרית לי	325	כעת חיה
77, 104	אחלק לו ברבים	48	לא הגדלת
337	איש ואיש	48, 103	לא עץ
337	איש וזר	47	לדעתו
162	אלהים	134	לפיכך
166	אלהים אלהיך	169	לקחת מתנות באדם
32, 47	אם לא תאמנו	236	לשלומים
129, 170	אמת	232	מוקש
232	אנושה	72	מחקק
346	אניח	17	מטה עזך
141	בני אדם	252	מים
53	באלפי יהודה	136	מכתם
117	בברותי	145	נפש
342	בתולה	67, 75	נצר
331	דבר	345	עלמה
346	דרך	134	על פי
334	האמנתי כי אדבר	17, 335	על ראש המטה
180, 185	הנה באתי	247	צום
211	ונשאתם	51	צעיר להיות
218	זרעים	17, 117, 235	ראש
144	חסידך	xxvi	שדי
10	הפץ חסד	145	שחת
13	חצבתי בנביאים	252	שמן
75, 125	יזה	129	שקר
229, 242	יספרו אל	146	תעזב לי
146	כבודי	30, 46	תעזב מפני
210	כוכב אלהיכם		

CAMBRIDGE: PRINTED BY C. J. CLAY, M.A. AT THE UNIVERSITY PRESS.

CAMBRIDGE,
March, 1869.

LIST OF WORKS

PUBLISHED BY

MESSRS. DEIGHTON, BELL, & CO.

Agents to the University.

ALFORD (DEAN) The Greek Testament: with a critically revised Text; a Digest of Various Readings; Marginal References to Verbal and Idiomatic Usage; Prolegomena; and a Critical and Exegetical Commentary. For the use of Theological Students and Ministers. By HENRY ALFORD, D.D., Dean of Canterbury.

    Vol. I. *Sixth Edition*, containing the Four Gospels. 1*l*. 8*s*.

    Vol. II. *Fifth Edition*, containing the Acts of the Apostles, the Epistles to the Romans and Corinthians. 1*l*. 4*s*.

    Vol. III. *Fourth Edition*, containing the Epistle to the Galatians, Ephesians, Philippians, Colossians, Thessalonians,—to Timotheus, Titus, and Philemon. 18*s*.

    Vol. IV. Part I. *Third Edition*, containing the Epistle to the Hebrews, and the Catholic Epistles of St. James and St. Peter. 18*s*.

    Vol. IV. Part II. *Third Edition*, containing the Epistles of St. John and St. Jude, and the Revelation. 14*s*.

———— The Greek Testament. With English Notes, intended for the Upper Forms of Schools and Pass-men at the Universities. By HENRY ALFORD, D.D. Abridged by BRADLEY H. ALFORD, M.A., late Scholar of Trinity College, Cambridge. One vol., crown 8vo. 10*s*. 6*d*.

———— The New Testament for English Readers. Containing the Authorised Version, with additional corrections of Readings and Renderings; Marginal References; and a Critical and Explanatory Commentary. By HENRY ALFORD, D.D. In two volumes.

    Vol. I. Part I.   Containing the First Three Gospels. *Second Edition*. 12*s*.

    Vol. I. Part II.   Containing St. John and the Acts. 10*s*. 6*d*.

    Vol. II. Part I.   Containing the Epistles of St. Paul. 16*s*.

    Vol. II. Part II.   Containing the Epistle to the Hebrews, the Catholic Epistles, and the Revelation. 16*s*.

———— Eastertide Sermons, preached before the University of Cambridge, on Four Sundays after Easter, 1866. By HENRY ALFORD, D.D. Small 8vo. 3*s*. 6*d*.

———— A Plea for the Queen's English; Stray Notes on Speaking and Spelling. By HENRY ALFORD, D.D. Small 8vo. 5*s*.

———— Letters from Abroad. By HENRY ALFORD, D.D. Small 8vo. 7*s*. 6*d*.

APOSTOLIC EPISTLES, A General Introduction to the, with a Table of St. Paul's Travels, and an Essay on the State after Death. *Second Edition, enlarged.* To which are added, A Few Words on the Athanasian Creed, on Justification by Faith. and on the Ninth and Seventeenth Articles of the Church of England. By a BISHOP'S CHAPLAIN. 8vo. 8s. 6d.

BABINGTON (CHURCHILL, B.D., F.L.S.) An Introductory Lecture on Archæology, delivered before the University of Cambridge. By CHURCHILL BABINGTON, B.D., F.L.S. 8vo. price 3s.

BARRETT (A. C.) Companion to the Greek Testament. For the use of Theological Students and the Upper Forms in Schools. By A. C. BARRETT, M.A., Caius College; Author of "A Treatise on Mechanics and Hydrostatics." *New Edition, enlarged and improved.* Fcap. 8vo. 5s.

> This volume will be found useful for all classes of Students who require a clear epitome of Biblical knowledge. It gives in a condensed form a large amount of information on the Text, Language, Geography, and Archæology; it discusses the alleged contradictions of the New Testament and the disputed quotations from the Old, and contains introductions to the separate books. It may be used by all intelligent students of the sacred volume; and has been found of great value to the students of Training Colleges in preparing for their examinations.

BARRY (A., D.D.) The Doctrine of the Spirit: Three Sermons preached before the University of Cambridge in February and March, 1867. By ALFRED BARRY, D.D., Principal of Cheltenham College, formerly Fellow of Trinity College, Cambridge. Cr. 8vo. 2s. 6d.

BEAMONT (W. J.) Cairo to Sinai and Sinai to Cairo. Being an Account of a Journey in the Desert of Arabia, November and December, 1860. By W. J. BEAMONT, M.A., formerly Fellow of Trinity College, Cambridge. With Maps and Illustrations. Fcap. 8vo. 5s.

———— A Concise Grammar of the Arabic Language. Revised by SHEIKH ALI NADY EL BARRANY. By W. J. BEAMONT, M.A. Price 7s.

BENSLY (R. L.) The Syriac Version of the Fourth Book of Maccabees. Edited from Seven MSS., by ROBERT L. BENSLY, M.A., Reader in Hebrew, Caius College, and Sub-Librarian of the University Library. [*Preparing.*

BLUNT (J. J.) Five Sermons preached before the University of Cambridge. The first Four in November, 1851, the Fifth on Thursday, March 8th, 1849, being the Hundred and Fiftieth Anniversary of the Society for Promoting Christian Knowledge. By J. J. BLUNT, B.D., formerly Lady Margaret Professor of Divinity, Cambridge. 8vo. 5s. 6d.
CONTENTS: 1. Tests of the Truth of Revelation.—2. On Unfaithfulness to the Reformation.—3. On the Union of Church and State.—4. An Apology for the Prayer-Book.—5. Means and Method of National Reform.

BONNEY (T. G.) The Alpine Regions of Switzerland and the Neighbouring Countries. A Pedestrian's Notes on their Physical Features, Scenery, and Natural History. By T. G. BONNEY, B.D., F.G.S., &c., Fellow of St. John's College, Cambridge; Member of the Alpine Club. With Illustration by E. WHYMPER. 8vo., 12s. 6d.

———— Death and Life in Nations and Men. Four Sermons preached before the University of Cambridge, in April, 1868. By T. G. BONNEY, B.D., Fellow of St. John's College. 8vo., price 3s. 6d.

BROWNE (BP.) Messiah as Foretold and Expected. A Course of Sermons relating to the Messiah, as interpreted before the Coming of Christ. Preached before the University of Cambridge in the months of February and March, 1862. By the Right Reverend E. HAROLD BROWNE, D.D., Lord Bishop of Ely. 8vo. 4s.

BULSTRODE (G.) Fifteen Sermons preached at the Evening Service in Ely Cathedral. By GEORGE BULSTRODE, M.A., of Emmanuel College, Cambridge, Vicar of Holy Trinity, Ely. 5s.

BURN (R.) Rome and the Campagna. An Historical and Topographical Description of the Site, Buildings and Neighbourhood of Ancient Rome. With Engravings, Maps, and Plans. By R. BURN, M.A., Fellow and Tutor of Trinity College, Cambridge.
[*Preparing.*

CAMBRIDGE University Calendar, 1869. 6s. 6d.

CAMPION (W. M.) Nature and Grace. Sermons preached in the Chapel Royal, Whitehall, in the year 1862-3-4. By WILLIAM MAGAN CAMPION, B.D., Fellow and Tutor of Queens' College, Cambridge, Rector of St. Botolph's, Cambridge, and one of her Majesty's Preachers at Whitehall. Small 8vo. 6s. 6d.

CHEVALLIER (T.) Translation of the Epistles of Clement of Rome, Polycarp and Ignatius; and of the Apologies of Justin Martyr and Tertullian; with an Introduction and Brief Notes Illustrative of the Ecclesiastical History of the First Two Centuries. By T. CHEVALLIER, B.D. *Second Edition.* 8vo. 12s.

COOPER (C. H. and THOMPSON). Athenae Cantabrigienses. By C. H. COOPER, F.S.A., and THOMPSON COOPER, F.S.A.

This work, in illustration of the biography of notable and eminent men who have been members of the University of Cambridge, comprehends, notices of: 1. Authors. 2. Cardinals, archbishops, bishops, abbats, heads of religious houses and other Church dignitaries. 3. Statesmen, diplomatists, military and naval commanders. 4. Judges and eminent practitioners of the civil or common law. 5. Sufferers for religious and political opinions. 6. Persons distinguished for success in tuition. 7. Eminent physicians and medical practitioners. 8. Artists, musicians, and heralds. 9. Heads of colleges, professors, and principal officers of the university. 10. Benefactors to the university and colleges or to the public at large.

Volume I. 1500—1585. 8vo. *cloth.* 18s.   Volume II. 1586—1609. 18s.

DINGLE (J.) Harmony of Revelation and Science. A Series of Essays on Theological Questions of the Day. By J. DINGLE, M.A., F.A.S.L., Incumbent of Lanchester, Durham. Crown 8vo. 6s.

DONALDSON (J. W.) The Theatre of the Greeks. A Treatise on the History and Exhibition of the Greek Drama: with various Supplements. By J. W. DONALDSON, D.D., formerly Fellow of Trinity College, Cambridge. *Seventh Edition,* revised, enlarged, and in part remodelled; with numerous illustrations from the best ancient authorities. 8vo. 14s.

—————— **Classical Scholarship and Classical Learning** considered with especial reference to Competitive Tests and University Teaching. A Practical Essay on Liberal Education. By J. W. DONALDSON, D.D. Crown 8vo. 5s.

LIST OF WORKS PUBLISHED BY

ELLIS (ROBERT.) Enquiry into the Ancient Routes between Italy and Gaul; with an Examination of the Theory of Hannibal's Passage of the Alps by the Little St. Bernard. By ROBERT ELLIS, B.D., Fellow of St. John's College, Cambridge. 8vo. 6s.

ELLIS (A. A.) Bentleii Critica Sacra. Notes on the Greek and Latin Text of the New Testament, extracted from the Bentley MSS. in Trinity College Library. With the Abbé Rulotta's Collation of the Vatican MS., a specimen of Bentley's intended Edition, and an account of all his Collations. Edited, with the permission of the Masters and Seniors, by A. A. ELLIS, M.A., late Fellow of Trinity College, Cambridge. 8vo. 8s. 6d.

ELLIS (ROBERT LESLIE). The Mathematical and other Writings of ROBERT LESLIE ELLIS, M.A., formerly Fellow of Trinity College, Cambridge. Edited by WILLIAM WALTON, M.A., Trinity College, with a Biographical Memoir by the Very Reverend HARVEY GOODWIN, D.D., Dean of Ely. Portrait. 8vo. 16s.

EWALD (H.) Life of Jesus Christ. By H. EWALD. Edited by OCTAVIUS GLOVER, B.D., Emmanuel College, Cambridge. Crown 8vo. 9s.

——— The Prophet Isaiah. Chapters I—XXXIII. From the German of H. EWALD. By OCTAVIUS GLOVER, B.D. Crown 8vo. 6s.

FAMILY PRAYERS from or in the Style of the Liturgy; with Occasional Prayers and Thanksgiving. By Dr. HAMMOND, Bishop ANDREWS, and others. Crown 8vo. 3s.

FORSTER (CHARLES, B.D.) A New Plea for the Authenticity of the Text of the Three Heavenly Witnesses; or, Porson's Letters to Travis Eclectically Examined, and the External and Internal Evidences for 1 John v. 7 Eclectically Re-surveyed. By CHARLES FORSTER, B.D., Six-Preacher of Canterbury Cathedral, and Rector of Stisted, Essex; Author of "The Apostolic Authority of the Epistle to the Hebrews." 8vo. 10s. 6d.

FRANCIS (JOHN). "The Exercise of the Active Virtues, such as Courage and Patriotism, is entirely consistent with the Spirit of the Gospel:" being the Burney Prize Essay for 1863. By JOHN FRANCIS, B.A., Vice-Principal of Bishop Otter's Training College, Chichester. 8vo. 2s.

FULLER (J. M.) Essay on the Authenticity of the Book of Daniel. By the Rev. J. M. FULLER, M.A., Fellow of St. John's College, Cambridge. 8vo. 6s.

FURIOSO, or, Passages from the Life of LUDWIG VON BEETHOVEN. From the German. Crown 8vo. 6s.

GLOVER (O.) A Short Treatise on Sin, based on the Work of Julius Müller. By O. GLOVER, B.D., Fellow of Emmanuel College, Cambridge. Crown 8vo. 3s. 6d.

——— Doctrine of the Person of Christ, an Historical Sketch. By OCTAVIUS GLOVER, B.D., Fellow of Emmanuel College, Cambridge. Crown 8vo. 3s.

"It is pleasant to welcome such a well-reasoned, thoughtful treatise as Mr. Glover's on the Doctrine of the Person of Christ. . . . The whole book will be found most useful to students of Theology, especially when preparing for examination, the ten chapters being compact and well arranged."—*Church and State Review*

GOODWIN (DEAN). Doctrines and Difficulties of the Christian Religion contemplated from the Standing-point afforded by the Catholic Doctrine of the Being of our Lord Jesus Christ. Being the Hulsean Lectures for the year 1855. By H. GOODWIN, D.D. 8vo. 9s.

——— 'The Glory of the Only Begotten of the Father seen in the Manhood of Christ.' Being the Hulsean Lectures for the year 1856. By H. GOODWIN, D.D. 8vo. 7s. 6d.

——— Essays on the Pentateuch. By H. GOODWIN, D.D. Fcap. 8vo. 5s.

——— Parish Sermons. By H. GOODWIN, D.D. 1st Series. *Third Edition.* 12mo. 6s.

——— 2nd Series. *Third Edition.* 12mo. 6s.

——— 3rd Series. *Third Edition.* 12mo. 7s.

——— 4th Series, 12mo. 7s.

——— 5th Series. With Preface on Sermons and Sermon Writing. 7s.

——— Four Sermons preached before the University of Cambridge, in the Season of Advent, 1858. By H. GOODWIN, D.D. 12mo. 3s. 6d.

——— Christ in the Wilderness. Four Sermons preached before the University of Cambridge in the month of February, 1855. By H. GOODWIN, D.D. 12mo. 4s.

——— Short Sermons at the Celebration of the Lord's Supper. By H. GOODWIN, D.D. *New Edition.* 12mo. 4s.

——— Lectures upon the Church Catechism. By H. GOODWIN, D.D. 12mo. 4s.

——— A Guide to the Parish Church. By HARVEY GOODWIN, D.D. Price 1s. *sewed*; 1s. 6d. *cloth.*

——— Confirmation Day. Being a Book of Instruction for Young Persons how they ought to spend that solemn day, on which they renew the Vows of their Baptism, and are confirmed by the Bishop with prayer and the laying on of hands. By H. GOODWIN, D.D. *Eighth Thousand.* 2d., or 25 for 3s. 6d.

——— Plain Thoughts concerning the meaning of Holy Baptism. By H. GOODWIN, D.D. *Second Edition.* 2d., or 25 for 3s. 6d.

——— The Worthy Communicant; or, 'Who may come to the Supper of the Lord?' By H. GOODWIN, D.D. *Second Edition.* 2d., or 25 for 3s. 6d.

LIST OF WORKS PUBLISHED BY

GOODWIN (DEAN). The Doom of Sin, and the Inspiration of the Bible. Two Sermons preached in Ely Cathedral: with some Prefatory Remarks upon the Oxford Declaration. By HARVEY GOODWIN, D.D. Fcap. 8vo. 1s. 6d.

———— Hands, Head, and Heart; or the Christian Religion regarded Practically, Intellectually, and Devotionally. In Three Sermons preached before the University of Cambridge. By HARVEY GOODWIN, D.D. Fcap. 8vo. 2s. 6d.

———— The Ministry of Christ in the Church of England. Four Sermons Preached before the University of Cambridge. I.—The Minister called. II.—The Minister as Prophet. III.—The Minister as Priest. IV.—The Minister Tried and Comforted. By H. GOODWIN, D.D., Dean of Ely. Fcap. 8vo. 2s. 6d.

———— The Appearing of Jesus Christ. A short Treatise by SYMON PATRICK, D.D., formerly Lord Bishop of Ely, now published for the first time from the Original MS. Edited by the DEAN OF ELY. 18mo. 3s.

———— Commentaries on the Gospels, intended for the English Reader, and adapted either for Domestic or Private Use. By HARVEY GOODWIN, D.D. Crown 8vo.
S. MATTHEW, 12s.   S. MARK, 7s. 6d.   S. LUKE, 9s.

———— On the Imitation of Christ. A New Translation. By the DEAN OF ELY. With fine Steel Engraving after GUIDO. *Third Edition.* Fcap. 8vo. 5s.

GREGORY (DUNCAN FARQUHARSON). The Mathematical Writings of DUNCAN FARQUHARSON GREGORY, M.A., late Fellow of Trinity College, Cambridge. Edited by WILLIAM WALTON, M.A., Trinity College, Cambridge. With a Biographical Memoir by ROBERT LESLIE ELLIS, M.A., late Fellow of Trinity College. 1 vol. 8vo. 12s.

GROTE (J.) Exploratio Philosophica. Rough Notes on Modern Intellectual Science. Part I. By J. GROTE, B.D., formerly Professor of Moral Philosophy at Cambridge. 8vo. 9s.

HARDWICK (ARCHDEACON). History of the Articles of Religion. To which is added a series of Documents from A.D. 1536 to A.D. 1615. Together with illustrations from contemporary sources. By CHARLES HARDWICK, B.D., late Archdeacon of Ely. *Second Edition, corrected and enlarged.* 8vo. 12s.

HUMPHRY (W. G.) An Historical and Explanatory Treatise on the Book of Common Prayer. By W. G. HUMPHRY, B.D., late Fellow of Trinity College, Cambridge. *Third Edition, revised and enlarged.* Small post 8vo. 4s. 6d.

KENT's Commentary on International Law. Revised, with notes and Cases brought down to the present year. Edited by J. T. ABDY, LL.D., Regius Professor of Laws in the University of Cambridge, 8vo. 16s.

LAMB (J.) The Seven Words Spoken Against the Lord
Jesus: or, an Investigation of the Motives which led His Contemporaries to reject Him. Being the Hulsean Lectures for the year 1860. By JOHN LAMB, M.A., Senior Fellow of Gonville and Caius College, and Minister of S. Edward's, Cambridge. 8vo. 5s. 6d.

LEAKE (COLONEL). The Topography of Athens, with some
remarks on its Antiquity. *Second Edition.* Two vols. 8vo., with Eleven Plates and Maps. By COLONEL LEAKE, Vice-President of the Royal Society of Literature, of the Royal Geographical Society, &c. (Pub. at 30s.) 15s.

———— Travels in Northern Greece. Four vols., 8vo. with Ten Maps and Forty-four Plates of Inscriptions. By COLONEL LEAKE. (Pub. at 60s.) 30s.

———— Peloponnesiaca, a Supplement to Travels in the Morea. Five Maps. By COLONEL LEAKE. (Pub. at 15s.) 7s. 6d.

———— On Some Disputed Questions in Geography, with a Map of Africa. By COLONEL LEAKE. (Pub. at 6s. 6d.) 4s. 6d.

———— Numismata Hellenica, with Supplement and Appendix, completing a Descriptive Catalogue of Twelve Thousand Greek Coins, with Notes Geographical and Historical, Map, and Index. By COLONEL LEAKE. 4to. (Pub. at 63s.) 42s.

LEAPINGWELL (G.) Manual of the Roman Civil Law,
arranged according to the Syllabus of Dr. HALLIFAX. By G. LEAPINGWELL, LL.D. Designed for the use of Students in the Universities and Inns of Court. 8vo. 12s.

LEATHES (STANLEY). The Birthday of Christ, its Preparation,
Message, and Witness. Three Sermons preached before the University of Cambridge, in December, 1865. By STANLEY LEATHES, M.A., Preacher and Assistant Minister, St. James's, Piccadilly, Professor of Hebrew, King's College, London. Fcap. 8vo. 2s.

MACKENZIE (BISHOP), Memoir of the late. By the DEAN
OF ELY. With Maps, Illustrations, and an Engraved Portrait from a painting by G. RICHMOND. Dedicated by permission to the Lord Bishop of Oxford. *Second Edition.* Small 8vo. 6s.

The Large Paper Edition may still be had, price 10s. 6d.

MAIN (R.) Twelve Sermons preached on Various Occasions
at the Church of St. Mary, Greenwich. By R. MAIN, M.A., Radcliffe Observer at Oxford. 12mo. 5s.

MASKEW (T. R.) Annotations on the Acts of the Apostles.
Original and selected. Designed principally for the use of Candidates for the Ordinary B.A. Degree, Students for Holy Orders, &c., with College and Senate-House Examination Papers. By T. R. MASKEW, M.A. *Second Edition, enlarged.* 12mo. 5s.

LIST OF WORKS PUBLISHED BY

MILL (W. H.) Observations on the attempted Application of Pantheistic Principles to the Theory and Historic Criticism of the Gospels. By W. H. MILL, D.D., formerly Regius Professor of Hebrew in the University of Cambridge. *Second Edition, with the Author's latest notes and additions.* Edited by his Son-in-Law, the Rev. B. WEBB, M.A. 8vo. 14s.

——— Lectures on the Catechism. Delivered in the Parish Church of Brasted, in the Diocese of Canterbury. By W. H. MILL, D.D. Edited by the Rev. B. WEBB, M.A. Fcap. 8vo. 6s. 6d.

——— Sermons preached in Lent 1845, and on several former occasions, before the University of Cambridge. By W. H. MILL, D.D. 8vo. 12s.

——— Four Sermons preached before the University on the Fifth of November and the three Sundays preceding Advent, in the year 1848. By W. H. MILL, D.D. 8vo. 5s. 6d.

——— An Analysis of the Exposition of the Creed, written by the Right Reverend Father in God, J. PEARSON, D.D., late Lord Bishop of Chester. Compiled, with some additional matter occasionally interspersed, for the use of Students of Bishop's College, Calcutta. By W. H. MILL, D.D. *Third Edition, revised and corrected.* 8vo. 5s.

MISSION LIFE among the Zulu-Kafirs. Memorials of HENRIETTA, Wife of the Rev. R. Robertson. Compiled chiefly from Letters and Journals written to the late Bishop Mackenzie and his Sisters. Edited by ANNE MACKENZIE. Small 8vo. 7s. 6d.

NEALE (JOHN MASON.) Seatonian Poems. By J. M. NEALE, M.A., formerly Scholar of Trinity College. Fcap. 8vo. 6s.

NEWTON (SIR ISAAC) and Professor Cotes, Correspondence of, including Letters of other Eminent Men, now first published from the originals in the Library of Trinity College, Cambridge; together with an Appendix containing other unpublished Letters and Papers by Newton; with Notes, Synoptical View of the Philosopher's Life, and a variety of details illustrative of his history. Edited by the Rev. J. EDLESTON, M.A., Fellow of Trinity College, Cambridge. 8vo. 10s.

PALMER (E. H.) Oriental Mysticism. A Treatise on the Sufiistic and Unitarian Theosophy of the Persians. Compiled from Native Sources by E. H. PALMER, Fellow of St. John's College, Cambridge, Member of the Asiatic Society, and of the Société De Paris. Crown 8vo. 3s. 6d.

PEARSON (J. B.) The Divine Personality, being a Consideration of the Arguments to prove that the Author of Nature is a Being endued with liberty and choice. The Burney Prize Essay for 1864. By J. B. PEARSON, B.A., Fellow of St. John's College. 8vo. 1s. 6d.

PEROWNE (J. J. S.) Immortality. Four Sermons preached before the University of Cambridge. Being the Hulsean Lectures for 1868. By J. J. S. PEROWNE, B.D., Vice-Principal and Professor of Hebrew in St. David's College, Lampeter. 8vo.

PEROWNE (E. H.) The Godhead of Jesus; being the Hulsean Lectures for 1866; to which are added Two Sermons preached before the University of Cambridge on Good Friday and Easter Day, 1866. By E. H. PEROWNE, B.D., Fellow and Tutor of Corpus Christi College, Hulsean Lecturer, formerly one of her Majesty's Preachers at the Chapel Royal, Whitehall. 8vo. 5s.

PIEROTTI (ERMETE). Jerusalem Explored: being a Description of the Ancient and Modern City, with upwards of One Hundred Illustrations, consisting of Views, Ground-plans, and Sections. By ERMETE PIEROTTI, Doctor of Mathematics, Captain of the Corps of Engineers in the army of Sardinia, Architect-Engineer to his Excellency Sooraya Pasha of Jerusalem, and Architect of the Holy Land. Translated and edited by T. G. BONNEY, B.D., St. John's College. 2 vols. imperial 4to. 5l. 5s.

—————— The Customs and Traditions of Palestine Compared with the Bible, from Observations made during a Residence of Eight Years. By Dr. ERMETE PIEROTTI, Author of "Jerusalem Explored." Translated and edited by T. G. BONNEY, B.D., St. John's College. 8vo. 9s.

PHILLIPS (GEO.) Short Sermons on Old Testament Messianic Texts, preached in the Chapel of Queens' College, Cambridge. By GEO. PHILLIPS, D.D., President of the College. 8vo. 5s.

—————— A Syriac Grammar. By the Rev. G. PHILLIPS, D.D., President of Queens' College. *Third Edition, revised and enlarged.* 8vo. 7s. 6d.

PRITCHARD (C.) Analogies in the Progress of Nature and Grace. Four Sermons preached before the University of Cambridge, being the Hulsean Lectures for 1867; to which are added Two Sermons preached before the British Association. By C. PRITCHARD, M.A., President of the Royal Astronomical Society, late Fellow of S. John's College. 8vo. 7s. 6d.

PSALTER (The) or Psalms of David in English Verse. With Preface and Notes. By a Member of the University of Cambridge. Dedicated by permission to the Lord Bishop of Ely, and the Reverend the Professors of Divinity in that University. 5s.

ROMILLY (J.) Graduati Cantabrigienses: sive Catalogus exhibens nomina eorum quos ab anno academico admissionum 1760 usque ad decimum diem Octr. 1856. Gradu quocunque ornavit Academia Cantabrigiensis, e libris subscriptionum desumptus. Cura J. ROMILLY, A.M., Coll. 88. Trin. Socii atque Academica Registrarii. 8vo. 10s.

SCHOLEFIELD (PROF.) Hints for some Improvements in the Authorised Version of the New Testament. By J. SCHOLEFIELD, M.A., formerly Professor of Greek in the University of Cambridge. *Fourth Edition.* Fcap. 8vo. 4s.

SCRIVENER (F. H.) Plain Introduction to the Criticism of the New Testament. With 40 Facsimiles from Ancient Manuscripts. For the Use of Biblical Students. By F. H. SCRIVENER, M.A., Trinity College, Cambridge. 8vo. 15s.

——————— **Codex Bezæ Cantabrigiensis.** Edited, with Prolegomena, Notes, and Facsimiles. By F. H. SCRIVENER, M.A. 4to. 26s.

——————— **A Full Collation of the Codex Sinaiticus** with the Received Text of the New Testament; to which is prefixed a Critical Introduction. By F. H. SCRIVENER, M.A. *Second Edition, revised.* Fcap. 8vo. 5s.

"Mr. Scrivener has now placed the results of Tischendorf's discovery within the reach of all in a charming little volume, which ought to form a companion to the Greek Testament in the Library of every Biblical student."—*Reader.*

——————— **An Exact Transcript of the CODEX AUGIENSIS,** Græco-Latina Manuscript in Uncial Letters of S. Paul's Epistles, preserved in the Library of Trinity College, Cambridge. To which is added a Full Collation of Fifty Manuscripts containing various portions of the Greek New Testament deposited in English Libraries: with a full Critical Introduction. By F. H. SCRIVENER, M.A. Royal 8vo. 26s.

The CRITICAL INTRODUCTION *is issued separately, price 5s.*

——————— **Novum Testamentum Græcum, Textus Stephanici,** 1550. Accedunt variæ lectiones editionem Bezæ, Elzeviri, Lachmanni, Tischendorfii, et Tregellesii. Curante F. H. SCRIVENER, M.A. 16mo. 4s. 6d.

An Edition on Writing-paper for Notes. 4to. half-bound. 12s.

SELWYN (PROFESSOR). Excerpta ex reliquiis Versionum, Aquilæ, Symmachi, Theodotionis, a Montefalconio aliisque collecta. GENESIS. Edidit GUL. SELWYN, S.T.B. 8vo. 1s.

——————— **Notæ Criticæ in Versionem Septuagintaviralem.** EXODUS, Cap. I.—XXIV. Curante GUL. SELWYN, S.T.B. 8vo. 3s. 6d.

——————— **Notæ Criticæ in Versionem Septuagintaviralem.** Liber NUMERORUM. Curante GUL. SELWYN, S.T.B.. 8vo. 4s. 6d.

——————— **Notæ Criticæ in Versionem Septuagintaviralem.** Liber DEUTERONOMII. Curante GUL. SELWYN, S.T.B. 8vo. 4s. 6d.

——————— **Origenis Contra Celsum.** Liber I. Curante GUL. SELWYN, S.T.B. 8vo. 3s. 6d.

——————— **Testimonia Patrum in Veteres Interpretes,** Septuaginta, Aquilam, Symmachum, Theodotionem, a Montefalconio aliisque collecta paucis Additis. Edidit GUL. SELWYN, S.T.B. 8vo. 6d.

——————— **Horæ Hebraicæ. Critical and Expository Observations** on the Prophecy of Messiah in Isaiah, Chapter IX., and on other Passages of Holy Scripture. By W. SELWYN, D.D, Lady Margaret's Reader in Theology. *Revised Edition, with Continuation.* 8s.

SELWYN (PROFESSOR). Waterloo. A Lay of Jubilee for June 18, A.D. 1815. *Second Edition.* 3s.

————— Winfrid, afterwards called Boniface. A.D. 680—755. Fcp. 4to. 2s.

SINKER (R.) The Characteristic Differences between the Books of the New Testament and the immediately preceding Jewish, and the immediately succeeding Christian Literature, considered as an evidence of the Divine Authority of the New Testament. By R. SINKER, M.A., Chaplain of Trinity College, and late Crosse and Tyrwhitt University Scholar. Small 8vo. 3s. 6d.

————— Testamenta XII Patriarcharum; ad fidem Codicis Cantabrigiensis edita: accedunt Lectiones Cod. Oxoniensis. The Testaments of the XII Patriarchs: an attempt to estimate their Historic and Dogmatic Worth. By R. SINKER, M.A. Small 8vo. 7s. 6d.

STUDENT'S GUIDE (The) to the University of Cambridge. *Second Edition, revised and corrected in accordance with the recent regulations.* Fcap. 8vo. 5s.

CONTENTS: Introduction, by J. R. SEELEY, M.A.—On University Expenses, by the Rev. H. LATHAM, M.A.—On the Choice of a College, by J. R. SEELEY, M.A.—On the Course of Reading for the Classical Tripos, by the Rev. R. BURN, M.A.—On the Course of Reading for the Mathematical Tripos, by the Rev. W. M. CAMPION, B.D.—On the Course of Reading for the Moral Sciences Tripos, by the Rev. J. B. MAYOR, M.A.—On the Course of Reading for the Natural Sciences Tripos, by Professor LIVEING, M.A.—On Law Studies and Law Degrees, by Professor J. T. ABDY, LL.D.—On the Ordinary B.A. Degree, by the Rev. J. R. LUMBY, M.A.—Medical Study and Degrees, by G. M. HUMPHRY, M.D.—On Theological Examinations, by Professor E. HAROLD BROWNE, B.D.—Examinations for the Civil Service of India, by the Rev. H. LATHAM, M.A.—Local Examinations of the University, by H. J. ROBY, M.A.—Diplomatic Service.—Detailed Account of the several Colleges.

TERTULLIANI Liber Apologeticus. The Apology of Tertullian. With English Notes and a Preface, intended as an Introduction to the Study of Patristical and Ecclesiastical Latinity. By H. A. WOODHAM, LL.D. *Second Edition.* 8vo. 8s. 6d.

TODD (J. F.) The Apostle Paul and the Christian Church of Philippi. An Exposition Critical and Practical of the Sixteenth Chapter of the Acts of the Apostles and of the Epistles to the Philippians. By the late J. F. TODD, M.A., Trinity College, Cambridge. 8vo. 9s.

TURTON (BISHOP). The Holy Catholic Doctrine of the Eucharist, considered in reply to Dr. Wiseman's Argument from Scripture. By T. TURTON, D.D., late Lord Bishop of Ely. 8vo. 8s. 6d.

VERSES and Translations. By C. S. C. *Third Edition.* Fcap. 8vo. 5s.

WIESELER's Chronological Synopsis of the Four Gospels. Translated by E. VENABLES, M.A., Canon of Lincoln, Examining Chaplain to the Bishop of London. 8vo. 13s.

12 WORKS PUBLISHED BY DEIGHTON, BELL, & CO.

WHEWELL (Dr.) Elements of Morality, including Polity. By W. WHEWELL, D.D., formerly Master of Trinity College, Cambridge. *Fourth Edition*, in 1 vol. 8vo. 15s.

——————— Lectures on the History of Moral Philosophy in England. By the Rev. W. WHEWELL, D.D. *New and Improved Edition, with additional Lectures.* Crown 8vo. 8s.

The Additional Lectures are printed separately in Octavo for the convenience of those who have purchased the former Edition. 3s. 6d.

——————— Astronomy and General Physics considered with reference to Natural Theology (Bridgewater Treatise). By W. WHEWELL, D.D. *New Edition*, small 8vo. (Uniform with the Aldine.) 5s.

——————— Sermons preached in the Chapel of Trinity College, Cambridge. By W. WHEWELL, D.D. 8vo. 10s. 6d.

——————— Butler's Three Sermons on Human Nature, and Dissertation on Virtue. Edited by W. WHEWELL, D.D. With a Preface and a Syllabus of the Work. *Fourth and Cheaper Edition.* Fcap. 8vo. 2s. 6d.

WILLIS (R.) The Architectural History of Glastonbury Abbey. By R. WILLIS, M.A., F.R.S., Jacksonian Professor. With Illustrations. 8vo. 7s. 6d.

WILLIAMS (ROWLAND). Rational Godliness. After the Mind of Christ and the Written Voices of the Church. By ROWLAND WILLIAMS, D.D., Professor of Hebrew at Lampeter. Crn. 8vo. 10s. 6d.

——————— Paraméswara-jnyána-goshthi. A Dialogue of the Knowledge of the Supreme Lord, in which are compared the claims of Christianity and Hinduism, and various questions of Indian Religion and Literature fairly discussed. By ROWLAND WILLIAMS, D.D. 8vo. 12s.

WOLFE (A.) Family Prayers and Scripture Calendar. By A. WOLFE, M.A., late Fellow and Tutor of Clare College, Cambridge, Rector of Fornham All Saints, Bury St. Edmund's. Fcp. 2s.

WRATISLAW (A. H.) Notes and Dissertations, principally on Difficulties in the Scriptures of the New Covenant. By A. H. WRATISLAW, M.A., Head Master of Bury St. Edmund's School, late Fellow of Christ's College, Cambridge. 8vo. 7s. 6d.

CAMBRIDGE:—PRINTED BY JONATHAN PALMER.

CPSIA information can be obtained
at www.ICGtesting.com
Printed in the USA
LVHW101134130120
643336LV00008B/99/P